M000159641

QUANTITATIVE TRADING STRATEGIES

Harnessing the Power
of Quantitative Techniques to
Create a Winning Trading Program

Other books in The Irwin Trader's Edge Series

QUANTITATIVE TRADING STRATEGIES

Harnessing the Power
of Quantitative Techniques to
Create a Winning Trading Program

LARS N. KESTNER

McGraw-Hill

New York Chicago San Francisco Lisbon London Madrid
Mexico City Milan New Delhi San Juan Seoul
Singapore Sydney Toronto

The McGraw·Hill Companies

Library of Congress Cataloging-in-Publication Data

Kestner, Lars N.
    Quantitative trading strategies : harnessing the power of quantitative techniques to create a
    winning trading program / by Lars Kestner.
        p.   cm.
    Includes index.
    ISBN 0-07-141239-5   (hardcover : alk. paper)
    Stocks—Mathematical models.   2. Portfolio management—Mathematical
models.   I. Title.
HG4661.K37 2003
332.64—dc21

Copyright © 2003 by Lars Kestner. All rights reserved. Printed in the United States of America. Except as permitted under the United States Copyright Act of 1976, no part of this publication may be reproduced or distributed in any form or by any means, or stored in a data base or retrieval system, without prior written permission of the publisher.

1 2 3 4 5 6 7 8 9 0 AGM/AGM 0 9 8 7 6 5 4 3

ISBN 0-07-141239-5

McGraw-Hill books are available at special discounts to use as premiums and sales promotions, or for use in corporate training programs. For more information, please write to the Director of Special Sales, Professional Publishing, McGraw-Hill, Two Penn Plaza, New York, NY 10121-2298. Or contact your local bookstore.

Disclaimer

The information contained within this text is presented for educational use only. No solicitation has been or will be made by the author or publisher that anyone should make a financial decision based on the contents of this text. Although great care has been taken to maintain the correctness of the information contained, its accuracy cannot be guaranteed.

Commodity and stock trading has the potential for substantial loss. Hypothetical or simulated performance results have certain limitations. Unlike an actual performance record, simulated results do not represent actual trading. Also, since the trades have not actually been executed, the results may have under- or overcompensated for the impact, if any, or certain market factors, such as lack of liquidity. Simulated trading programs in general are also subject to the fact that they are designed with the benefit of hindsight. No representation is being made that any account will or is likely to achieve profits or losses similar to those shown.

 This book is printed on recycled, acid-free paper containing a minimum of 50% recycled de-inked paper.

To my parents, Neil and Arlene Kestner:
All your support has made me the person I am today

All of the author's proceeds from this book will be
donated to the Windows of Hope Family Relief Fund.
The Windows of Hope Family Relief Fund provides
aid, future scholarships, and funds to the families
of victims who worked in the food, beverage, and
hospitality professions at the World Trade Center.

ACKNOWLEDGMENTS

I wish to thank many individuals who both directly and indirectly led to the creation of this book:

My parents, Neil and Arlene, have always challenged me to pursue my dreams—however lofty those dreams might be.

I am grateful to Kristen, who put up with a lot of late stressful nights while I was writing this book.

Many thanks to my friends who, over the years, have helped shape both my career and my thoughts on the markets: Andy Constan, Scott Draper, Leon Gross, Ken Mackenzie, Bryan Mazlish, and Josh Penner. A debt of gratitude also goes to Thom Hartle, former editor of *Stocks and Commodities* magazine, for publishing some early work from an over-achieving 19-year-old. That publication gave me confidence to take my ideas and research much further. In addition, I must thank Scott Bieber and Nick Cicero for editing early versions of this manuscript and adding constructive criticism. Also invaluable were Stephen Issacs and Scott Kurtz of McGraw-Hill for taking a very rough set of ideas and turning them into a wonderfully crafted text. Final gratitude goes to my cats Thomas and Grey, who, with all their steps on my laptop's keyboard late at night, are probably owed some portion of the copyright as coauthors.

C O N T E N T S

Chapter 5

Performance of Portfolios: *Maintaining Returns While Decreasing Risk*   99

Chapter 6

Optimizing Parameters and Filtering Entry Signals: *Improving the Basic Strategy*   109

O fortune,
Variable as the moon,
You ever wax and wane;
This detestable life now maltreats us,
Then grants us our wildest desires;
It melts both poverty and power
Like ice.
—from the scenic cantata *Carmina Burana*
by Carl Orff (1895-1982), translated by
Lucy E. Cross

My Reasons for Writing This Book

Like the quote above, this book is about risk. The focus of this book is to develop trading strategies that buy and sell financial assets while managing the risk associated with these positions. While we have no idea if our next trade will be a winner or loser, by using quantitative tools to identify reward and risk, we can diminish risk while maintaining expected gains. This is the key to long-term trading success. Most of the tools in this book have been studied over the past 50 years by academics and have been employed by Wall Street professionals over the past 20 years. Unfortunately there has been a gap when it comes to explaining and teaching these techniques to the investing public. This book attempts to fill that void by presenting the advanced concepts in systematic trading, risk management, and money management that have long been missing.

First and foremost, this book explores the ability of quantitative trading strategies to time the markets. Quantitative trading strategies are a combination of technical and statistical analysis which, when applied, generate buy and sell signals.

These signals may be triggered either through price patterns or values of complex indicators calculated from market prices. Once these trading strategies are formed, their performance is tested historically to validate the trading ideas. Essentially, we determine if a strategy has worked in the past. If a strategy has generated profits historically, this gives credence to future performance. After the performance is tested, we select the markets to be traded. By trading a widely diversified port-folio, we are able to minimize our risk while maintaining expected reward. Developing the idea, testing historical performance, and picking markets to trade are a few of the many techniques required for efficient and profitable trading strategies. While a few books have touched on various areas of the development process, I believe this book is the first to fully capture all the nuances of the trad-ing process. While some books provide anecdotal evidence based on one or two of the author's experiences, this book backs up concepts with theoretical explanation, real life results, and references to academic research. My goal in writing this book is to set the record straight with time-tested statistics—not with untested theories and market lore passed down through the ages.

A New Approach for Analyzing Markets

There are numerous methods being used to analyze the markets. Most investors and traders will look at fundamental data to assess whether they believe the market is going to move higher or lower. In the equity markets, investors will look at earnings, product sales, and debt loads to determine a company's fair valuation. A comparison of this valuation to business prospects then determines a fair valuation for the company. In commodities, investors will look at trends in supply and demand. Poor weather conditions can hurt a crop outlook and raise prices. Lack of end demand during a recession can cause prices to fall. Studying these fundamen-tal factors is the most common method of analyzing markets.

Another growing method of analysis is technical analysis. Technical analysis does not attempt to predict market movements based on fundamentals. Instead, technical analysts believe that one market participant, however well informed, is unlikely to have better information than the combination of all other market par-ticipants. As a result, technical analysts believe that price action is the best source of information. Market forecasts are made using chart patterns, most of which have been studied over decades. Catchy names such as "head and shoulders top," "symmetrical triangle," and "trendline" are a large part of the technical analyst's toolbox. Typically, the technical analyst relies on a good bit of discretion for his or her trading ideas. While a pattern may look like a buy signal to one technical ana-lyst, another may see a different pattern emerging and actually be preparing to sell the market.

This book takes a somewhat different approach than relying solely on funda-mental or technical analysis. While most of the strategies studied in this book use past prices to predict future prices (as would a technical analyst), every strategy is specifically defined using rigid rules. This quantitative process removes the subjectivity from which both fundamental and technical analysts suffer. Once strategies are defined using sound statistical properties, they are thoroughly tested on historical prices to determine profitability over past years. Only ideas that have stood the test of time will be considered for real-time trading. One benefit of historical performance testing is that traders are more likely to have confidence during poor trading performance when years of theoretical backtesting have shown that the strategy being traded is viable and profitable.

Creating, Testing, and Implementing a Quantitative Trading Strategy

One recurrent theme in this book is the absolute need to test theories. Hours of debate may not be able to settle differences of opinion over literature or politics. In these very imprecise subjects, there are no constant truths. There are no definite answers. Should we increase government spending to restart the economy or should we pay down debt to lower interest rates? Was John Steinbeck or William Faulkner or someone else the best American-born author? No amount of study will lead us to definitive answers.

The subject matter of this book, which I call quantitative trading, does not suffer from this same fate. Whenever we make statements about the market, we can perform mathematical and statistical tests to determine if we are correct in our beliefs. Do changes in interest rates affect returns on the stock market? If corn prices have been rising, is it likely that they will continue to do so in the near future? Considering that historical data for market prices is available back to the turn of the twentieth century in many cases, we can study historical market prices and usually find answers to these questions once we quantify each of these questions. Answering questions usually comes down to creating a mathematical or statistical test and then analyzing the results. The remainder of this book will attempt to answer questions aimed at understanding exactly how markets behave and how investors and traders can profit from this information.

Most of our study involves creating, testing, and applying trading strategies. A trading strategy (also called a trading system or trading methodology) is a set of rules that signal the trader when to buy, when to sell, and when to sell short a market. The buy and sell decisions are typically generated by price patterns and indicators. These strategies can be very simple such as buy on Wednesday and sell on Friday. The signals can also be very complex and include statistical regression and relationships between many related markets. One positive is that many of the most profitable trading systems over the past twenty years are actually very simple in nature. Most of the concepts in this book are simplistic and require no more than a high school math background to understand.

Another important component of the trading system development process is the ability to change the values we input into our rules. For example, we might buy if today's close is greater than the close 10 days ago. We can vary the 10-day lookback period in an attempt to improve performance. The procedure of changing parameter values to improve performance is called optimization.

The most vital part of trading system development is performance testing. When we test historical performance, we first want to see if our strategies have been profitable in the past. Because many strategies will be profitable historically, we need a methodology to compare the profitability among trading strategies. Very often the most profitable system is not the best system for our trading. In fact, I believe most traders use outdated and inconsistent performance measures to evaluate historical performance. For this reason we will use superior measures such as the Sharpe Ratio and K-Ratio for our performance evaluation.

Finally, we need to develop a money management plan for trading our strategies. With leverage so readily available through the futures markets and margin stock accounts, we need to quantify exactly how much leverage is ideal, making sure not to cross over this threshold into trading too aggressively. While this topic sounds very basic, some of the brightest and largest money managers in the world have suffered tremendously by not adhering to money management rules.

The Wide Spectrum of Markets Available for Trading

Once we have designed and tested our trading strategy, the next choice is to decide which markets to trade. The choices these days are enormous and include stocks, exchange-traded funds, futures, and other markets. Our quantitative trading strategies are applicable to each. The beauty of quantitative trading is the ease of applying a predefined set of rules to multiple markets. The incremental effort of applying a strategy to one additional market is negligible. Just turn on the computer and in seconds the strategy spits out buy, sell, or flat. With technology these days, it would be entirely possible for one person alone to trade hundreds, if not thousands, of markets.

This book will focus on three distinct markets: stocks, futures, and relative value markets. Stocks represent a claim on the assets of a company after all creditors such as banks and bondholders are paid in full. Shares of companies trade on three major markets in the United States: the New York Stock Exchange (NYSE), the American Stock Exchange (AMEX), and the NASDAQ. While the NYSE and AMEX are physical trading floors where buyers and sellers meet to trade shares, the NASDAQ is a linkage of market makers negotiating prices with customers and with each other. Stocks can be bought, sold, and sold short. If we think a stock is going to gain, we buy shares in anticipation of selling them at a higher price in the future. If we think a stock is going to decline, we sell a stock short. To sell a stock short, your broker borrows shares from another client and sells them on your behalf, and you hope to buy the shorted shares back at a lower price.

Futures contracts are traded on financial, agricultural, petroleum, and other products. The futures markets were originally devised as a means for suppliers and end users to hedge risks associated with their business. For example, a farmer planting corn cannot sell this corn on the market. The corn must grow, be harvested, and then processed before being sold. Prices might change dramatically between the time of the corn being planted and when it is sold at the market. This represents a large risk to the farmer whose revenue depends on the price of corn at the time of final sale. Similarly, a food company who needs corn to produce its breakfast cereal is also exposed to changes in corn prices. Futures markets are intended to allow both the producers and users of a product a means to hedge. A corn contract is an obligation to buy or sell a set amount and grade of corn at some point in the future. In June, the farmer we spoke of might sell 10,000 bushels of corn deliverable in September to lock in his selling price at harvest time. The cereal company, knowing that they will be buying corn in the future for their products, might buy 100,000 bushels of September corn in order to lock in their costs. Due to the high leverage and low transaction costs associated with the futures market, these markets have long been a popular trading vehicle for quantitative traders. Much like stocks, futures can be bought, sold, and sold short.

In most books on trading, the variety of markets usually ends at stocks and futures. In this book we will take quantitative trading one step further by applying our strategies to some newer markets that are actively traded by hedge funds and Wall Street trading desks. While markets such as yield curve spreads, credit spreads, volatility, stock pairs, and commodity substitutes may seem esoteric to most individual investors, billions of dollars are traded everyday in these products. Most of these markets are actually combinations of other markets where one asset is bought and the other asset is sold short. For example, a popular trade is to buy the 30-year Treasury Bond and sell the 5-year Treasury Note when the yield curve is steeply upward sloping. By combining two or more assets, we can create price data for these "relative value" markets. Once we design and test our quantitative trading strategies, we can implement them on these new markets to gain access to products outside the typical stock and futures markets. There is truly no limit to quantitative trading. Give a quantitative trader some price data and he can develop a trading strategy. Whenever new markets are created in the future, quantitative traders will be there to profit.

Exploring the Possibilities and Limitations of Quantitative Trading

The Efficient Markets Hypothesis (EMH) is an academic theory which states that, on some level, it is impossible to successfully time the market consistently. Three forms of the EMH exist: strong form EMH, semi-strong form EMH, and weak form EMH. The strong form of EMH suggests that all information, both public and private, is always incorporated into current prices. The last price reflects all information including unannounced crop reports, yet-to-be-released company earnings, and even the merger that is currently being negotiated between Company ABC and Company XYZ. The semi-strong form of the EMH states that current prices reflect all information in the public domain, including annual company reports, USDA crop estimates, Wall Street research reports, and quality of corporate management. The weak form EMH suggests that prices already reflect all information that can be derived from analyzing historical market data, such as closing prices, volume, and short interest.

All three forms of the EMH (strong, semi-strong, and weak form) suggest that our attempts to make money by buying and selling based on prior price patterns are hopeless. While the EMH was widely accepted in the 1970s and 1980s, recent research has found cracks in its premise. Both academic and industry research have detected that some inefficiencies continue to persist over time. For example, buying stocks that have underperformed over the past three years tend to outperform for the three years following. Some price patterns can significantly predict future returns. Certain strategies which follow trends produce consistent results when traded on a basket of futures markets. These cracks in the EMH hint that markets may not be as efficient as was once thought. Perhaps our quantitative trading strategies can accurately detect and exploit certain patterns that are consistently profitable.

The idea of using quantitative trading strategies is not new. Large institutional money managers such as John W. Henry & Company, Trout Trading and Management Company, Citadel Investment Group, and Renaissance Technologies have been using these strategies for years with great success. Their funds are widely considered the best of the best. The rest of this book will attempt to create a trading program that comes close to attaining the astonishing results of these large money managers.

Lars Kestner
May 2003

QUANTITATIVE TRADING STRATEGIES

Harnessing the Power
of Quantitative Techniques to
Create a Winning Trading Program

PART ONE

Structural Foundations for Improving Technical Trading

In the first half of *Quantitative Trading Strategies* we'll be taking a close look at current techniques used in quantitative and technical trading. This half will introduce basic concepts as well as some of the more advanced techniques that systematic traders use in day-to-day operations. In the second half of the book, using this foundation, we'll go on to study more complex and cutting edge trading methods.

We'll begin with a discussion on the origins of quantitative trading and its evolution to modern day application. To trade effectively, it's necessary to understand how markets react on a daily basis, and to be able to isolate tendencies such as average price, volatility, and relationships to other markets. To this end, we will also study the statistics and basic properties of market behavior.

From there, we'll move on to the building blocks of systems—entries, exits, and filters—and present specific examples of each, to better prepare the reader for the more advanced concepts to be discussed later. Then we'll cover trading strategy performance, paying particular attention to certain problems associated with popular performance measures such as percent return, profit factor, and profit to drawdown. Specifically, we will illustrate how the same profit-to-drawdown statistic may be good for one system and bad for another.

Following our look at performance evaluation, we will explore the topic of diversification and explain why trading a portfolio of markets enhances the overall performance of technical trading strategies. In most circumstances, trading a portfolio of markets produces better reward-to-risk characteristics than trading any single market on its own. We examine the benefits of trading a diversified portfolio of markets, strategies, and parameters in our trading accounts.

We'll close out the first part of the book with a discussion of the positives and negatives of filtering entries and optimizing parameters. Optimization is an often hotly contested concept. Using real world results, we will attempt to quantify its benefits.

CHAPTER 1

Introduction to Quantitative Trading

How Statistics Can Help Achieve Trading Success

TRADING STRATEGIES AND THE SCIENTIFIC METHOD

Trading is an unbelievably competitive business. Unlike other industries, there are no barriers to entry and the capital requirements are very low. These days, anyone in America can open an online trading account in minutes. Concurrently, given the competition in the brokerage industry, trading costs such as commissions have declined. With the market open to so many participants, different styles of trading and investing have emerged. Speak with 100 traders and it's likely that you'll hear 100 different trading philosophies. Momentum, value, trend following, and pairs trading are a few of the trading methodologies used today. Instead of declaring one strategy superior to any other, my personal approach as a trader is to test as many strategies on as much historical data as possible in order to scientifically study the merits of each methodology. Assessing historical performance means:

1. Following the scientific method by creating a hypothesis (our trading method)
2. Testing the hypothesis (back-test on historical data)
3. Drawing conclusions based on our data (evaluating results and implementing a trading program)

When we analyze the markets within the context of the scientific method, we become quantitative traders.

The life of a quantitative trader is unique. While the trading process itself is similar from day to day, the results and outcomes are always unknown. Intrigued by the possibility of new trading theories, quantitative traders research ideas every day that have never been explored before. Today may very well be the day a trader discovers a new strategy that puts his or her trading over the top.

So much about trading has changed in such a short time. With the advances in technology and the advent of the home computer, there's been an increase in the number of quantitative traders using statistical and numerical methods to determine when to buy and when to sell. While these methods are sometimes complex computer programs whose calculations require hours to perform, more often the strategies are simple rules that can be described on the back of an envelope.

New software has allowed traders to test ideas without having to risk a dime of capital. Before, traders could only speculate if their methods had any historic precedent of profitability. These days, using the new software, strategies can be tested over thousands of markets spanning the globe, giving traders the confidence that their methods have stood the test of time. The entire process can now be accomplished in a couple of minutes.

Of course, before all this wonderful technology became so readily available, most trading decisions were made by analyzing news and price charts, and being in touch with gut feelings. Some of these so called "discretionary traders" naturally possess this gut feel of market direction and can trade profitably without the need for systematic rules, but it's rare. It requires getting a handle on one's emotions and being able to process information in an unbiased manner, and only a handful of very talented discretionary traders have achieved this and been successful.

One question that's long been argued is whether discretionary traders are on the whole better than their quantitative trading counterparts. The Barclay Group, a research group dedicated to the field of hedge funds and managed futures, has maintained performance records of various Commodity Trading Advisers based on their trading style. CTAs are individuals or firms that advise others about buying or selling futures and futures options, with some of the largest CTAs managing over $2 billion. Any CTA whose trading is at least 75 percent discretionary or judgment-oriented is categorized as a discretionary trader by Barclays, while any CTA whose trading is at least 95 percent systematic is classified as systematic. From these two categories, Barclays maintains the Barclays Systematic Traders Index and the Barclays Discretionary Traders Index. Both indices are compiled based on the monthly profit and loss of the underlying money managers.

At any rate, concerning our question about discretionary versus quantitative traders: Between 1996 and the end of 2001, the average annual return on the systematic (or quantitative) group was 7.12 percent, versus only 0.58 percent for the discretionary group. What's more, the systematic index outperformed the discretionary index in five out of the six years in the test period. These statistics suggest that we may want to focus our trading on the systematic side. Figure 1.1 details the performance of the systematic traders in relation to discretionary traders from 1996 through 2001.

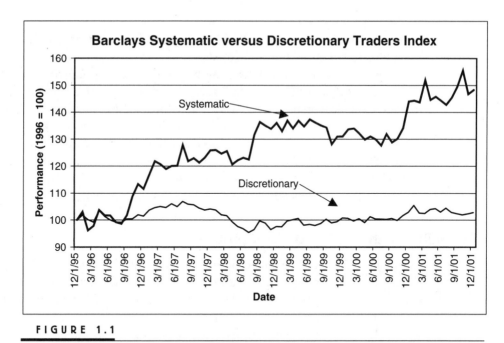

FIGURE 1.1

Barclays Systematic versus Discretionary Traders Index. As seen above, the Systematic Traders Index has consistently outperformed the Discretionary Traders Index.

THE ORIGINS OF THIS BOOK

At age 12, my father, a theoretical chemist, brought home a couple of books about the stock market from his office during his annual cleaning. Knowing that I was interested in business (even at that age), my father casually presented me with the books. That day forever changed my life.

I forget the title of the first book, but the second was the investment classic *Technical Analysis of Stock Trends.* First published in 1948, the Robert Edwards and John Magee book is widely considered the classic text on technical analysis and the original reference for many of today's trading patterns, such as triangles, wedges, head and shoulders, and rectangles. At that first reading, I was enthralled. Before I knew it, I was reading everything I could find related to technical analysis.

When I was 15 years old, I received an advertisement in the mail for a trading strategy designed to trade the overnight moves in the 30-year Treasury bond futures market. The thought of creating a fixed rule strategy to take human discretion out of the trading process fascinated me, and I set out to develop trading systems for trading the futures markets. Since that time, I have created and tested thousands of ideas. My first published work, when I was 19, was featured in *Technical Analysis of Stock and Commodities.* Later, I published further research in *Futures* magazine as well. In 1996, I published a 250-page trading manual entitled *A Comparison of*

Popular Trading Systems. It detailed 10 years of performance data of 30 popular systems tested on 29 futures markets.

For years, I was puzzled why books introducing unique ideas and trading strategies never confirmed their past performance by presenting a simulation of results. I endeavored in my trading manual to shed light on that question. Over 50 percent of the strategies I tested lost money—even before taking into account transaction costs such as commission and slippage. In addition, the best performing strategies were those most simplistic in nature—neither complex nor esoteric. Although I set out to prove the value of these new strategies, I quickly learned the importance of independently verifying trading performance.

NEW MARKETS AND METHODS OF TRADING

The introduction of financial futures in the early 1980s, the proliferation of equities in the American household portfolio, and the deregulation of various industries such as energy marketing has spawned many new products and markets. With these new markets have come opportunities.

Using quantitative analysis as a way to spot trading opportunities has become popular. Such analyses study markets based on historical information like prices, volume, and open interest.

System trading is one example of quantitative analysis. It involves traders automating buy and sell decisions by building mathematical formulae to model market movement. Among this method's advantages is that the human element is removed from trading positions, as discussed above. Even successful traders tend to take profits too early in the trade, giving up a larger profit down the line. Or even worse, traders hold on to losses that eventually cause their demise. The beauty of a mechanical trading system is that no trades are executed unless the trading system deems it necessary. This is the key to the success of mechanical trading systems: removing the irrational emotional element.

Perhaps we've gotten ahead of ourselves. Let's ask first: What are trading systems?

A trading system is a set of fixed rules that provide buy and sell signals. A simplistic example would be to buy a market if its price rose above the average of the past 20 closes and sell if prices fell below its average of the past 20 closes. If the market continually rises, you will be long in that market. The longer the market rises, the more money you make. Very simply, you're following the trend of the market. Typically, returns using a trend-following approach applied to a diverse set of markets are higher than returns of the S&P 500, with similar or even smaller risk.

THE SCIENTIFIC BENT AND QUANTITATIVE TRADING

You might ask: With numerous books written about trading systems and methods available and more coming out each month, why read this particular book? I'd answer that *Quantitative Trading Strategies* is unique because I bring quantitative analysis into the mainstream by presenting concepts in a realistic and logical manner.

While most books promote a specific trading method, they often fail to produce historical track records of their ideas or a background of other trading methods. In this book, I will take old and new trading ideas and test them on a wide portfolio of markets. While other books specifically focus on stocks or futures, this book will apply quantitative trading strategies to all markets.

We will apply techniques to futures, stocks, and some new markets that readers may not be familiar with. In addition, we'll test the historical performance of both current popular systems and some new ideas I have formulated over the past 15 years of trading. These tests will be run on 29 commodities, 34 stocks and stock indices, and 30 relative value markets on the past 12 years of daily price data. Historical performance will be examined from multiple angles.

Further, I will illustrate how readers can recreate my results and create, test, and evaluate trading systems on their own. In addition, I will outline both the benefits and the limitations of quantitative analysis by analyzing many of the tools I use as a trader. And, drawing on personal experience, I'll also illustrate certain points by drawing on anecdotes from my trading career.

While it's important to illustrate the profitability of quantitative trading methods, it's equally important to discuss the method's limitations. No traders make money every day. Very few make money every month. Some strategies that performed profitably in the past will break down and become unprofitable in the future. Trading with quantitative strategies involves much risk—risk that we hope to limit by using state of the art techniques to design, test, and trade our trading methods.

Readers will notice that I continually refer to the process of using fixed rules to trade markets based on previous price history as *quantitative trading,* rather than the popular term, "technical analysis," typically used in the industry. The reason for this distinction has to do with the quality of analysis. I admit to having disdain for technical analysts who use charts to explain past price action. An example is to draw trendlines, or lines that connect market tops or bottoms (see Figure 1.2). The theory is that the extension of these lines will act as support or as a resistant in the market's future moves. You will often hear statements such as the following from more traditional technical analysts:

Statement 1: "The S&P 500 has been selling off due to a break of the six month trendline at 1100."

The preceding statement provides very little predictive value in the trading process. Attempting to reconcile past market action using technical analysis is nonsensical. Markets decline due to news and information. Poor corporate earnings, worries over corporate accounting practices, excess crop supply, and lack of end-user demand for products are just a few of the many possible reasons for a market to decline. When explaining history, we can usually create a clear picture

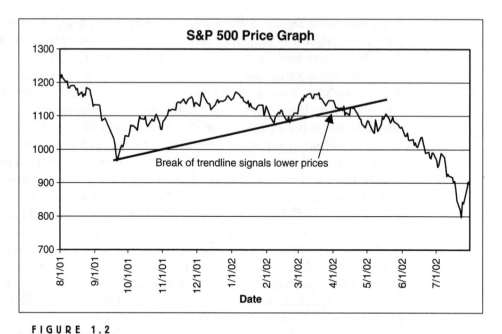

FIGURE 1.2

S&P 500 Price Graph. Once prices broke a trendline connecting September and February lows, prices headed much lower.

of the market factors that caused rallies and declines. History and hindsight are always 20/20.

While I believe using technical analysis and chart reading to explain past market behavior is foolish, technical analysis can help in predicting future market moves. Consider the usefulness of the following statement:

> *Statement 2:* "A break of the six month trendline may bring about extra sellers into the market and drive prices lower."

This statement has merit and can be used by traders. Because the market is breaking below previous support, we are likely to see lower prices in the near term. Therefore, we should sell long positions and establish short positions. Skillful technical analysts will make accurate market calls based predominately on price action and leave the explanation of historical market moves to the fundamental analysts dissecting news and new information.

While the second statement above may be useful to traders, we can take the process one step further by incorporating historical performance. After all, are we sure that breaks of trendlines are a precursor to lower prices? How often in the past has this strategy worked? Consider the following statement, which suggests that we take action based on a particular price formation—the crossing of a moving average:

> *Statement 3:* "Because the market crossed below its 200-day moving average, we expect prices will continue their decline."

In this case, the technical analyst is predicting lower prices due to price closing below its average of the past 200 days. The 200-day moving average is frequently used in market timing, and the above example is commonly used in practice. While Statement 3 does involve a forward-looking prediction, we can add more value to the trading forecast. For example, if we followed the fixed-rule-trading strategy of buying when a market rose above its 200-day moving average and selling when the market fell below its 200-day moving average, would we beat a buy-and-hold strategy? How much incremental return did an investor make by following the 200-day moving average rule over the past 5 or 10 years? The crossing of the 200-day moving average is a market prophecy that has existed for years. But does it stand up to statistics and historical testing?

In this book, we will attempt to solve the two problems cited above. First, unlike Statement 1, all of our trading analysis will be geared for future trades—not to explain previous price action. Second, unlike Statement 3, when we suggest using a trading strategy that generates buy and sell signals, we'll test that strategy over many differing markets, each comprising multiple years of data. These results will be scrutinized to separate promising ideas from those fated to be unprofitable. After all, if an idea has not been profitable in the past, why should we use it in the future?

THE PIONEERS OF QUANTITATIVE TRADING

Quantitative trading dates back to the turn of the 20th century. W. D. Gann, Richard Donchian, Welles Wilder, and Thomas DeMark are among its well-known pioneers.

William D. Gann

In the early 1900s, Gann made his name as a young stock and commodity broker. A legendary trader, Gann put his ideas and his credibility on the line in an interview with the *Ticker and Investment Digest* magazine in 1909 (Kahn, 1980). The magazine published a four page interview in which Gann recounted his trading record. His forecasts were incredibly accurate. During October 1909, according to the interview, Gann made 286 trades in various stocks, 264 of which were profitable and only 22 resulting in losses.

Although Gann subsequently wrote a number of books, none truly describe his methods. From what has been published, it appears that his techniques ran the gamut from creating new price charts based on movement independent of time to more complex numerology methods, including squares of price and time. Gann's *How to Trade in Commodities* is one of my all-time favorite classics.

Richard Donchian

Born in 1905, Robert Donchian established the first futures fund in 1949 (Jobman, 1980). The fund struggled for the first 20 years, as Donchian traded commodity markets with a discretionary technical trading strategy. Having started in the trading business during the deflationary 1930s, his outlook was continually biased toward the bearish side. This bias hurt the fund's performance during many of the commodity rallies of the 1950s and 1960s. It was not until Donchian quantified his trading approach in the 1970s that steady profits resulted.

Despite never writing books on the subject of trading, Donchian utilized techniques that are extremely popular and the basis of many of today's strategies. Among his contributions to the industry are the dual moving average crossover strategy, as well as the channel breakout strategy. I included these two strategies to contrast more recent systems in my *Comparison of Popular Trading Systems.* Much to my surprise, these two systems were among the best-performing systems tested. We will explore Donchian's work in more detail later in the book.

Welles Wilder

New Concepts in Technical Trading by Welles Wilder, published in 1978, was one of the first books that attempted to take discretion out of the trader's hands and replace trading decisions with mathematical trading methodologies. Wilder introduced the Relative Strength Index, an oscillator that is standard in nearly every software package today, the Parabolic Stop and Reverse system, and seven other methods. His strictly quantitative methods make him a pioneer in the field of quantitative trading.

Thomas DeMark

After writing a trading advisory service in the early 1980s, Thomas DeMark went to work for Tudor Investment Corporation, one of the most prestigious Commodity Trading Advisers in the world. Paul Tudor Jones was so impressed with DeMark that the two opened a subsidiary, Tudor Systems Corporation, for the sole purpose of developing and trading DeMark's ideas.

Keeping the bulk of his trading techniques to himself throughout his trading career, DeMark, who has been called the "ultimate indicator and systems guy" (Burke, 1993), decided to give the rest of the world a glimpse of his methods when he published *The New Science of Technical Trading* in 1994. A sequel, *New Market Timing Techniques,* followed in 1997. If any readers have not read these two books, I strongly suggest you do so. Testing and evaluating the ideas in these two books alone might take years for any one person. Among DeMark's contributions are his Sequential indicator (a countertrend exhaustion technique), DeMarker and REI (new takes on oscillators), as well as numerous other systematic trading strategies.

THE RECENT EXPLOSION OF QUANTITATIVE TRADING

The proliferation of modern quantitative trading began with a handful of futures traders in the 1970s. Armed with IBM mainframes and punch cards, these traders began to test simplistic strategies on historical market data. The high leverage and low transaction costs made futures markets a perfect match for this new breed of trader.

Nowadays, quantitative trading is completely accepted and practiced by many large professional commodity money managers. CTAs such as John Henry and Jerry Parker of Chesapeake Capital manage over a billion dollars each using trading systems to place bets on markets spanning the globe. A recent survey found that over 75 percent of CTAs use trading systems. In fact, Jack Schwager, author of the critically praised books *Market Wizards* and *New Market Wizards*, has managed institutions' funds using trading systems applied to commodity markets.

It was not until the mid-1970s that two changes in the market made quantitative trading feasible for equities: the end of regulated commissions, and the introduction of the Designated Order Turnaround system (DOT).

Until 1975, the New York Stock Exchange fixed the minimum commission of stock trading. According to Robert Schwartz, a finance professor at the Zicklin School of Business, rates for typical large institutional orders during the era of fixed commissions was about 0.57 percent of principal. If I traded 50,000 shares of a $50 stock, this would amount to $0.29 per share in commission costs. These extraodinarily high costs hindered quantitative traders from entering the equity markets.

Although lower transaction costs after the elimination of the fixed commission structure pushed stocks closer to the realm of quantitative traders, it was the creation of the DOT in 1976 that truly opened the equity markets. Prior to the DOT, all orders were required to be delivered to the specialist on the NYSE via a floor broker—both a timely and costly procedure. With the introduction of the DOT—and subsequent upgrades such as the SuperDOT—orders of virtually any size may now be delivered electronically and virtually instantaneously to the floor of the NYSE.

TODAY'S QUANTITATIVE TRADERS

There are a number of modern quantitative traders with very successful long-term track records. Some managers trade only futures, while others trade a multitude of investment products, including foreign and domestic stocks, convertible bonds, warrants, foreign exchange, and fixed income instruments. Monroe Trout, John Henry, Ken Griffin, and Jim Simons are among the best money managers in the world. Their focus is almost entirely quantitative in nature.

Monroe Trout

A legend in the quantitative trading arena, Trout began conducting research for a noted futures trader at the age of 17. After graduating from Harvard, he went to work for another well-known trader, Victor Neiderhoffer (Schwager, 1992).

Working on the floor of the New York Futures Exchange, Trout mostly scalped markets to make a living. In 1986 he moved upstairs and started a Commodity Trading Adviser in an effort to concentrate on position trading. Until he retired in 2002, his Trout Trading Management Company produced some of the highest risk-adjusted returns in the industry.

Over the years, Trout and his staff have tested and implemented thousands of models for actual trading. According to *New Market Wizards* by Jack Schwager, Trout's trading is approximately half systematic and half discretionary, with an emphasis on minimizing transaction costs.

John Henry

Popularly recognized as the man who bought the Boston Red Sox in 2002, in the trading arena John Henry is known as the founder of John W. Henry & Company (JWH) in 1982. An owner of farmland, Henry began trading agricultural markets in the 1970s as a means to hedge the prices of his crops. During a summer trip to Norway in 1980, his trading methodology was shaped while reading the works of W. D. Gann and other trend followers. Shortly afterward, he developed a quantitatively based system to trade futures, the bulk of which remains largely unchanged today.

After wildly successful periods in the late 1980s and early 1990s, JWH underwent an overhaul of their trading methodology. While the signals generated from the system were largely kept intact, new risk management policies were instituted to improve risk-adjusted returns. Since the overhaul, JWH has continued its run of success. John Henry summarizes his trading philosophy in four points: long-term trend identification, disciplined investment process, risk management, and global diversification.

> We do not try to predict trends. Instead we participate in trends that we have identified. While confirmation of a trend's existence is sought through a variety of statistical measures, no one can know a trend's beginning or end until it becomes a matter of record.
> —*John W. Henry & Company marketing brochure*

JWH's flagship Financial and Metal's fund has annualized average returns of 30 percent since its inception in October 1984. The firm currently manages over $1 billion, much of which has been placed from retail customers through public futures pools.

Ken Griffin

Not your typical Ivy League student, as a sophomore at Harvard University in 1987, Ken Griffin petitioned for permission to install a satellite to receive real-time stock prices in his dorm room. Equity markets were becoming volatile, and Griffin was managing over $250,000 of Florida domiciled partnerships.

Prior to the Crash of 1987, Griffin, whose trading focused on quantitative methods, was short the market. He'd read a negative article in *Forbes* magazine on the business prospects of Home Shopping Network and shorted the stock by purchasing put options. As the stock slid, Griffin was surprised when the options sold at a price less than their apparent value. After learning that the difference was due to the market maker's "take," he attempted to gain a better understanding of derivative instruments. He spent hours at the Harvard Business School Library, researching the popular Black-Scholes option pricing model, and stumbled on what would become his bread and butter: trading and arbitraging convertible bonds.

After graduating, Griffin opened Wellington Partners with $18 million in capital. The fund, still open today, initially traded convertible bonds and warrants from the United States and Japan. Over the past decade, Citadel Investment Group (Griffin's umbrella organization) has entered virtually every business associated with finance, including risk arbitrage, distressed high yield bonds, government bond arbitrage, statistical arbitrage of equities, and private placements. In each case, Citadel is supporting its trading in these new markets with advanced technology and analytical methods usually seen in only the most quantitative of products. Their goal is to quantify all trading decisions by replacing the human element of decision making with proven statistical techniques. Citadel currently manages over $6 billion.

Jim Simons

If I mentioned the name Renaissance Technology Corporation on Wall Street, the typical reply might be, "No thanks. I got creamed in technology stocks." Renaissance Technology, run by prize-winning mathematician Jim Simons, has everything to do with technology but nothing to do with losses. If you have not heard of Simons or his firm, you are not alone. Keeping a low profile, Renaissance has posted some of the best returns in the industry since its flagship Medallion fund was introduced in 1988.

After receiving his undergraduate degree from the Massachusetts Institute of Technology and a Ph.D. from the University of California at Berkeley, Jim Simons taught mathematics at MIT and Harvard. Successfully investing in companies run by his friends, Simons left academia and created Renaissance Capital in 1978. In the ensuing 24 years the firm has aimed to find small market anomalies and inefficiencies that can be exploited using technical trading methods. Surrounding himself with over 50 Ph.D.'s, and resembling an academic think tank more than a cutting edge trading firm, Simons's operation manages over $4 billion.

> The advantage scientists bring into the game is not their mathematical or computational skills than their ability to think scientifically. They are less likely to accept an apparent winning strategy that might be a mere statistical fluke.
>
> —*Jim Simons, founder of Renaissance Technology*

WHY QUANTITATIVE TRADING IS SUCCESSFUL

Though quantitative traders are certainly curious about how they will make money applying quantitative analysis to the markets, the more encompassing question is *why* they can make money in the markets. After all, why should there be any profits to trading?

Most traders have studied the efficient markets hypothesis, or EMH, which states that current prices reflect not only information contained in past prices, but also all information available publicly. In such efficient markets, some investors and traders will outperform and some will underperform, but all resulting performance will be due to luck rather than skill.

The roots of the efficient markets hypothesis date back to the year 1900, when French doctoral student Louis Bachelier suggested that the market's movements follow Brownian motion. (The term is attributed to Robert Brown, an English botanist who in 1827 discovered that pollen grains dispersed in water were continually in motion but in a random, nonpredictable manner.) Brownian motion is essentially another term for random motion, synonymous with the popular drunkard's walk example. If a drunk man begins walking down the middle of a road, his lack of balance will cause him to veer either left or right. The direction of each step is random—almost like flipping a coin. At the end of our friendly drunkard's walk, he could be anywhere—from far left to far right. Perhaps he even wandered both ways but ended in the middle of the road. The point is, the motion of the walk is completely unpredictable. The random motion of the drunk man is often used to explain the rise and fall of market prices: completely random and unpredictable (alcohol not necessary).

The term Brownian motion was largely unused until 1905, when a young scientist named Albert Einstein succeeded in analyzing the quantitative significance of Brownian motion. Despite the connection to Einstein's and others' work in the natural sciences, Bachelier's paper, "Theorie de la Speculation," went largely unnoticed for half a century. In the 1950s the study of finance began to rise in popularity as equities became a larger part of Americans' investing behavior and academic research was performed in an attempt to detect the possible cyclical nature in stock prices.

As the number of unsuccessful studies increased, the theory that markets were efficient became widely accepted and the EMH gained significant credibility. The efficient markets hypothesis remained popular during the 1960s and 1970s, as a number of simplistic studies added credence to the theory that no effort of quantitative trading could succeed over the long run. But as computing power increased and allowed for more detailed analysis in the 1980s, some holes in the theory of perfect market efficiency were uncovered. Indeed, the idea of perfectly efficient markets has now been questioned.

In the Spring 1985 edition of the *Journal of Portfolio Management*, Barr Rosenberg, Kenneth Reid, and Ronald Lanstein produced a study that shed doubt on the value of the EMH. The three studied monthly returns of the 1400 largest stocks from 1973 to 1984. Each month, long and short portfolios were created using the 1400 stocks available. Employing advanced regression techniques, a long portfolio was created using stocks that had underperformed the previous month, and a short portfolio was created using stocks that outperformed the previous month. The long and short portfolios were optimized so that both had equal exposure to quantifiable factors such as riskiness, average market capitalization, growth versus value tilts, and industry exposure. Thus, returns of one portfolio versus another could not be explained due to factors such as industry concentration, or concentration of small cap or large cap stocks. The portfolio was reselected each month and new stocks were chosen for both long and short portfolios.

The results: The average outperformance by buying losers and shorting winners was 1.09 percent per month, a strategy that produced profits in 43 out of 46 months. These results suggested that the market is not efficient and that active investors could indeed outperform the market.

In another study, Louis Lukac, Wade Brorsen, and Scott Irwin (1990) studied the performance of 12 technical trading systems on 12 commodity futures between 1975 and 1984. The trading rules were taken straight from popular trading literature, with all but a handful of methods best described as "trend-following" in nature. The nine methods of examination included the channel breakout, parabolic stop and reverse, directional indicator system, range quotient system, long/short/out channel breakout, MII price channel, directional movement system, reference deviation system, simple moving average, dual moving average crossover, directional parabolic system, and Alexander's filter rule.

The results: 7 of the 12 strategies generated positive returns, with four generating profits significantly greater than zero using very strict statistical tests. Usually, data from non-natural sciences does not pass statistical tests of significance. The fact that Lukac, Brorsen, and Irwin were able to find trading results that pass these stringent tests is remarkable. Of these four strategies, average monthly returns ran from +1.89 to +2.78 percent, with monthly standard deviations of 12.62 to 16.04 percent. Two of the profitable systems were the channel breakout and dual moving average crossover. They will be the base of comparison for new trading models we develop later in the book.

And in still another study, Andrew Lo, Harry Mamaysky, and Jiang Wang (2000) attempted to quantify several popular trading patterns and their predictive power on stock prices. After smoothing prices, the three quantified 10 price patterns based on quantified rules. These patterns, shown in Figures 1.3 through 1.12, have long been a fixture in technical trading since they were first introduced by Edwards and Magee in 1948. The names correspond to the similarity of the patterns to various geometric shapes and their resemblance to real life objects.

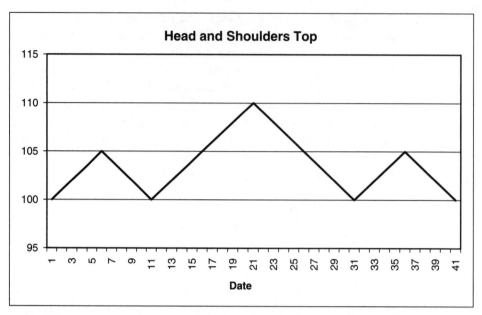

FIGURE 1.3

Head and Shoulders Top.

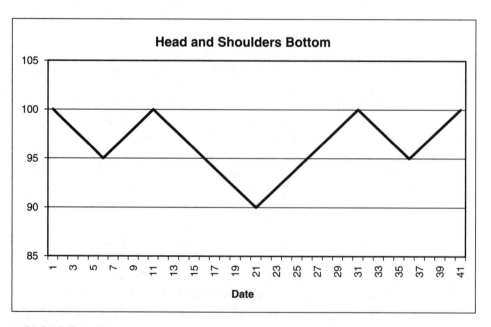

FIGURE 1.4

Head and Shoulders Bottom.

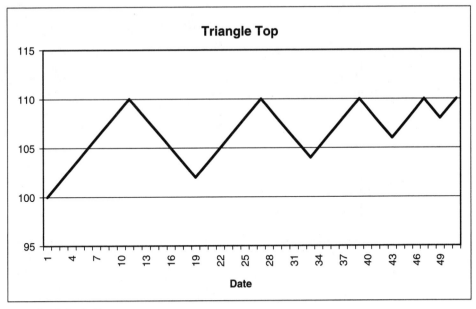

FIGURE 1.5

Triangle Top.

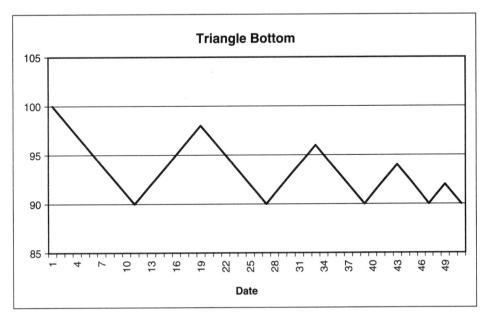

FIGURE 1.6

Triangle Bottom.

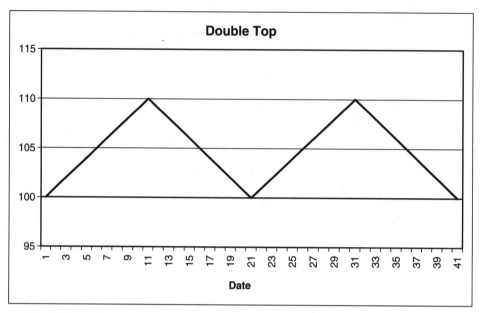

FIGURE 1.7

Double Top.

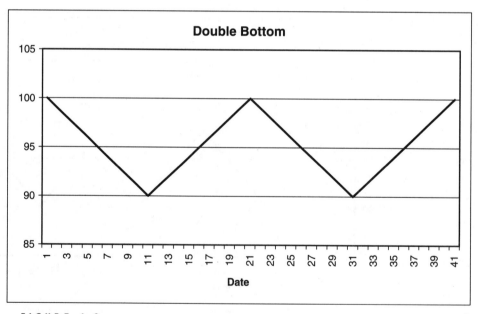

FIGURE 1.8

Double Bottom.

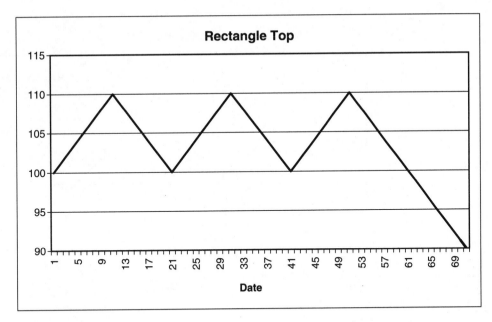

FIGURE 1.9

Rectangle Top.

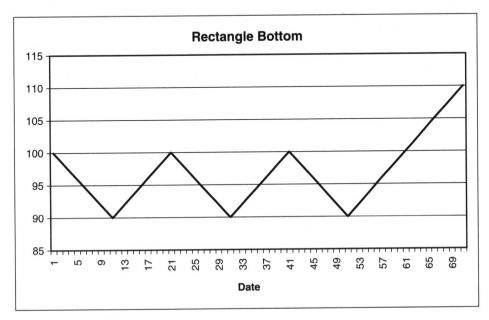

FIGURE 1.10

Rectangle Bottom.

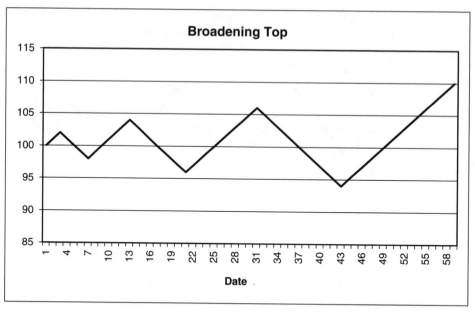

FIGURE 1.11

Broadening Top.

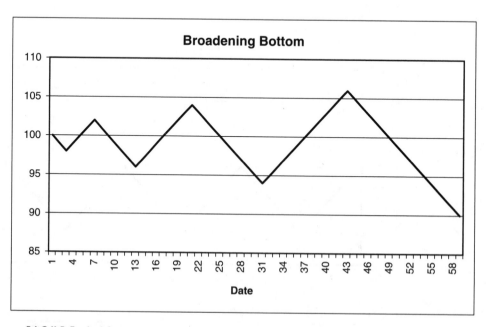

FIGURE 1.12

Broadening Bottom.

While technical traders have relied on these patterns for years, only recently have academics attempted to quantify the attributes of these formations. Once we systematically identify the appearance of these patterns, we can explore the profitability of trading signals that these patterns generate. Curtis Arnold and Thomas Bulowski have done excellent work in this field over the past decade. *Curtis Arnold's PPS Trading System* was one of the first works to systematically define trading patterns and test trading rule validity when these patterns occurred. Whereas interpreting charts was very much an art, Arnold defined each pattern and systematically tested trading rules to buy and sell based on when these patterns occurred. Thomas Bulowski has taken this research even further with his books *Encyclopedia of Chart Patterns* and *Trading Classic Chart Patterns*.

At any rate, Lo, Mamaysky, and Wang tested the 10 patterns mentioned above on NYSE, Amex, and Nasdaq stocks between 1962 and 1996. In addition, the researchers generated numerous paths of random price movement akin to the Brownian motion discussed earlier. The same rules were used to detect patterns on the random data. If market prices are truly random and follow Brownian motion (or drunkard's walk, if you prefer), then two similarities in the data should emerge:

1. The occurrence of each of the 10 patterns on actual stock data should roughly match the occurrence of patterns on the randomly generated data.
2. Returns from trading signals associated with specific patterns on the actual stock data should not be different from zero.

If we can make money trading these patterns, then we have reasons to believe that markets are not efficient. Surprisingly, Lo and company found that several patterns, such as head shoulder tops and bottoms, occurred with much greater frequency in actual price data than did in the randomly generated price series. In addition to the increased frequency of some patterns, returns following certain patterns' presence were also significant—specifically, declines following the head and shoulders top, and rallies that followed the head and shoulders bottom.

BIRTH OF A NEW DISCIPLINE

The results seen in the above-mentioned studies have led to researchers to investigate the reasons why some market inefficiencies can withstand over time. The most popular theories study patterns in human behavior. The tendency of individuals to move as a crowd and create market bubbles led to new thinking about how markets operate. Focus began to turn to the behavior of individuals and whether this behavior, predictable or not, leads to panics and manias in the markets. This new branch of finance studies psychology and sociology as it applies to financial markets and financial decisions.

Behavioral Finance and the Flaw of Human Nature

Behavioral finance, as it is now known, has attracted some of the top minds in academic finance. It is a combination of classical economics and the principles of behavioral psychology. This new science has been used as a vehicle to study potential causes of market anomalies and inefficiencies that inexplicably seem to repeat over time. By studying how investors systematically make errors in their decision-making process, academics can explain and traders can exploit the psychological aspect of investing.

Many ideas of behavioral finance were spawned by the work of Amos Tversky and Daniel Kahneman, psychologists who studied how people made choices regarding economic benefit. Among the most popular of Kahneman and Tversky's discoveries were *prospect theory* and *framing*. Prospect theory, as we will see later in this chapter, deals with the fact that individuals are reluctant to realize losses and quick to realize gains. Framing deals with how answers can be influenced by the manner in which a question is posed. One example of framing from a 1984 study by Kahneman and Tverksy illustrates this point. The pair asked a representative sample of physicians the following two questions:

> Imagine that the United States is preparing for the outbreak of an unusual Asian disease, which is expected to kill 600 people. Two alternative programs to combat the disease have been proposed. Assume that the exact scientific estimates of the consequences of the program are as follows: If program A is adopted, 200 people will be saved. If program B is adopted, there is a one-third probability that 600 will be saved and a two-thirds probability that no people will be saved.
>   *Which of the two programs would you favor?*

> Imagine that the U.S. is preparing for the outbreak of an unusual Asian disease, which is expected to kill 600 people. Two alternative programs to combat the disease have been proposed. Assume that the exact scientific estimates of the consequences of the program are as follows: If program C is adopted, 400 people will die. If program D is adopted, there is a one-third probability that nobody will die and a two-thirds probability that 600 people will die.
>   *Which of the two programs would you favor?*

Both these questions present the exact same scenario. In programs A and C, 200 people would live and 400 people would die. In programs B and D, there is a one-third probability that everyone would live and a two-thirds probability that everyone would die. Programs A and C lead to exactly the same outcome, as do programs B and D. The only difference between the first and second question is in framing. The first question is positively framed, viewing the dilemma in terms of lives saved. The second question is framed negatively, the results measured in lives lost. This framing affects how the question is answered.

Kahneman and Tversky discovered that while 72 percent of the physicians chose the safe and sure strategy A in the first question, 72 percent voted for the risky strategy D in the second question. This is illogical, as anyone who picks strategy A should also pick strategy C, since the stated outcome in both cases are exactly the same. The experiment shows that how we frame questions can influence the responses we receive.

Much of Kahneman and Tversky's work displays a tendency for people to make inconsistent decisions when it comes to economic decisions. Other economists have taken the pair's work and applied its value to the question of market efficiency. This brings up the logical question: If individuals make inconsistent decisions, can this lead to inefficient financial markets due to irrationality?

Irrational Decision Makers

While most people believe that all investors must act "rationally" for a market to be efficient, this is not accurate. Buyers will buy to the point of their perceived fair value, and sellers will sell down to the point of their perceived fair value. The price at which an equal number of buyers and sellers meet is the clearing market price. When positive information is released, investors rationally bid a stock higher on the revised fair value of business prospects. Even if a handful of investors and traders act irrationally by buying and selling based on irrelevant information (such as moon phases or what their pets bark), the market should still be priced efficiently. Chances are that if one irrational investor is buying, then another is selling.

Market efficiency runs into trouble when the actions of irrational investors do not cancel out. Consider the situation where irrational investors all pile on and buy the market at the same time or they all run for the exits at the same time. If all the irrational investors buy or sell together, they can overwhelm the rational investors and cause market inefficiencies.

Let's take, as an example, XYZ Inc., and say it's trading at $100, with 100 investors following it. The 80 rational investors have decided $100 is the fair value of the company based on future business prospects. The other 20 buy and sell based on irrelevant information. As XYZ's revenues increase, rational investors bid the stock up to $120—buyers are willing to pay the higher price based on improved business prospects. Now the 20 irrational investors, all momentum players, begin to buy the stock due to its performance, driving the stock up to $135. They buy from rational people who are willing to sell their stock above their perceived fair value. Ten of the rational investors, who either believe they're misinterpreting the information or who feeling pain because they are not long in XYZ, become irrational and also buy the stock, driving it up to $145. This process can spiral out of control and create a positive feedback loop, causing unbelievable valuations. All this started with 20 irrational investors and a small amount of positive news in XYZ Inc.

When irrational investors move together, market irrationality can exist and take hold for quite some time, eventually leading to bubbles, panics, and crashes. This theory might explain the technology boom and bust of the late 1990s and early 2000s. As public investors and day traders craved technology stock exposure, their thought process shifted from rational methods of valuation to the irrational belief that valuation was not important. Like many, I saw my peers making a lot of money in the market and felt compelled to get on board and not be left behind. My buying the market had nothing to do with fair valuation or expected business prospects of the companies I bought. Instead, it was motivated by fear of being the only one not getting rich in the market. Similar herd mentality was also present during panics in 1987, 1989, and 1997. Afraid that they would be left holding the bag when the market made a low, otherwise rational investors can become irrational. As a result, they sell investments to raise cash, either hoping to miss some of the decline or, at the very least, to outperform their peers.

An article originally published in the *Journal of Finance* is credited with beginning the behavioral finance revolution. In 1986, Werner DeBondt and Richard Thaler studied the return differences of the best and worst performing stocks from 1926 through 1982. Stocks with the best three year returns were assembled into a portfolio of winners, and those with the worst three year returns were gathered into a portfolio of losers. DeBondt and Thaler noticed that over one to five years after the portfolios were created, those that contained previously underperforming stocks significantly outperformed portfolios of previously outperforming stocks by between 4 and 6 percent per year. This outperformance occurred whether a narrow (35) or a broader number of stocks (80+) were chosen for each portfolio. They concluded that investors overreact to unexpected news events, placing too much emphasis on recent news and earnings.

Investors begin to expect companies that have consistently beat earnings estimates to continue to do so in the future. Then, at some point business prospects slow, the company only meets or even misses estimates, and investors run for the exit in the stock. Similarly, companies that continually perform worse than expected are labeled as "terrible" and with no turnaround potential. Eventually, their business prospects also recover, and investors run to buy the stock. This short-term thinking among investors can create market inefficiencies.

Robert Shiller of Yale University might be the most widely known behavioral economist. Shiller's ground-breaking work on market volatility in the 1980s redefined how economists look at the stock market. In 1981 he suggested that market prices were as much as 5 to 13 times too volatile based on their drivers of value: cashflow. While stock prices should move proportionally to changes in a company's expected cashflow (cashflows will eventually be passed on to investors via dividends), Shiller found that stock prices were more volatile than what would be predicted by the volatility in underlying dividends. He hypothesized that the excess volatility could be attributed to investors' psychological behavior and the fact that investors overreact to both positive and negative news. Although some have criticized Shiller's methods (Schwert, 1991), his arguments have set off a new wave of thinking about the effect of investor psychology on the movement of prices.

Despite the academic research suggesting that inefficiencies do exist in financial markets, many people question the profitability of quantitative trading. You might ask: Why should fixed rules generating buy and sell signals ever be superior to human discretion and the ability to evaluate problems on a situation-by-situation basis? (Indeed, they appear to, as seen in the results cited earlier in the chapter showing that systematic money managers have outperformed their discretionary counterparts.) The answer is: Human discretion has a habit of sabotaging performance. Over the past decade, psychological and financial research have come together to explain the nature of such emotional tendencies and to shed light on why some market patterns continue to exist over the years.

Selling Winners and Holding Losers

Studies of human bias in economic situations shed light on how the mind affects trading decisions. In one such study conducted in 1998, Terrance Odean, professor of finance at the University of California, examined 10,000 accounts at a large discount brokerage firm to determine if individuals' trading styles differed between winning trades and losing trades made from 1987 and 1993. He found a significant tendency for investors to sell winning stocks too early and hold losing stocks too long. Over his test period, investors sold approximately 50 percent more of paper profits on winning trades than they sold of paper losses in losing trades.

Based on the data, Odean concluded that winning stocks were sold quicker and more frequently than losing stocks. Although the results were a bit surprising, this behavior by investors could make sense. When we buy stocks, we're placing a bet that a company is undervalued. Stocks that increase in value are logically becoming less undervalued as they rise, while stocks that decrease in value are logically becoming more undervalued. Winning stocks that have increased in value could be considered not as cheap as when they were purchased. Losing stocks that have declined in value could be considered cheaper than when purchased. In this case, it makes sense to sell the winning stocks that have become less cheap and hold losing stocks that have become cheaper.

Although the logic is sound, Odean's results show that the opposite actually occurs. Winning stocks that were sold continued to rise, while losing stocks that were held continued to fall in value. In the year following sales, stocks sold with gains by individual investors outperformed the market by an average 2.35 percent. At the same time, losing stocks that were held underperformed the market by an average of 1.06 percent. Odean discovered, on average, that investors underperform the market by selling their winners too early and holding on to their losers too long. Based on purely economic terms, it's unclear why they behaved in this manner; psychology may provide the missing link. Clearly, the more profitable course of action suggested by the study is to buy winning stocks and sell losing ones.

Two theoretical underpinnings dominate the tendency to sell winners and ride losers: *prospect theory* and *mean reversion theory*.

Prospect Theory.   Prospect theory adapts psychologists' Daniel Kahneman and Amos Tversky's theories to financial markets. It suggests that investors are more risk averse when dealing with profitable investments and more risk seeking in investments with losses. We all enjoy winning and take pain in losing. As a result, investors and traders take winners very quickly (to placate our psyche) and hold on to losers (to hold on to hope that the losers may eventually become winners).

To demonstrate, give people the following choice:

Game 1
75 percent chance of making $1000
25 percent chance of making $0
or
100 percent chance of making $750

We can calculate the expected value of each game by summing the product of each outcome's probability by its payout:

Expected payout of risky choice = 75% · $1000 + 25% · $0 = $750

While the expected value of both options is the same in Game 1, individuals tend to be very risk averse with gains. Most people will take the certain $750 rather than take the risk for a higher payout. Now consider Game 2, which presents the exact same choice, only among losses:

Game 2
75 percent chance of losing $1000
25 percent chance of losing $0
or
100 percent chance of losing $750
Expected payout of risky choice = 75% · –$1000 + 25% · $0 = –$750

In Game 2, most people will choose to risk the chance to come out even and take the first option. While both options have the same expected value, the possibility of coming out without a loss is often too much to pass up. Basically, the tendencies revealed in both games show that individuals are risk averse with their winnings and risk seeking with their losses.

This, of course, jibes with Terrence Odean's research. From practical experience, I can add that I've often caught myself holding on to losing trades while thinking, "If I can only get out even on this trade," or taking it so far as to calculate breakeven points in hopes of avoiding the disappointment of closing out a losing trade. If prospect theory is alive and well in the financial markets, we may be able to take advantage of human nature by designing trading strategies that are not susceptible to the inconsistent thinking embedded in human nature.

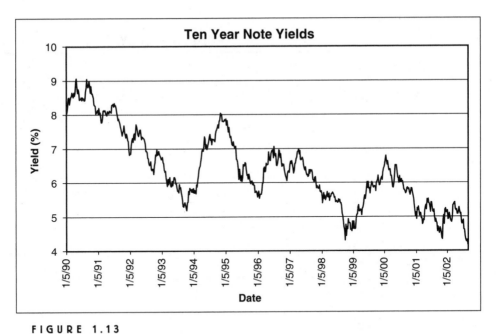

FIGURE 1.13

Ten Year Note Yields. Yields tend to mean revert between 5% and 8% during the 1990s.

Mean Reversion Theory.   The second theory explaining why investors sell winners and hold losers is that investors buy and sell stocks as if they expect mean
reversion in prices. Mean reversion occurs when a series of numbers eventually
reverts back to a long-term average. A good example is interest rates. As measured
by the yield on the 10-year Treasury bond, interest rates have traded in a range
mostly between 5 and 8 percent over the past 10 years (see Figure 1.13).

More often than not, when interest rates are low, they are met by supply from
issuers looking to borrow money. This leads to an increase in rates. Conversely,
when rates are high, they are met by demand from investors looking to lock in the
abnormally high interest rates. This causes interest rates to decline to more normal
levels. If investors believe that stock prices move in a similar path, they will be
willing to sell stocks that rally and hold stocks that decline—believing that each
will eventually return to its more normal level.

For example, consider stock XYZ, as seen in Figure 1.14. It trades between $50
and $55 for many months before breaking below this range to $45. When looking at
the graph of the stock, the mean reversion associated with human nature would lead
us to believe that the move was abnormal and that it should be bought. A similar
example is stock ABC in Figure 1.15. When ABC breaks above $50 per share after
also trading between $45 and $50, we might believe that the stock should be sold on
the basis that it too will reenter its previously established $45 to $50 range again.

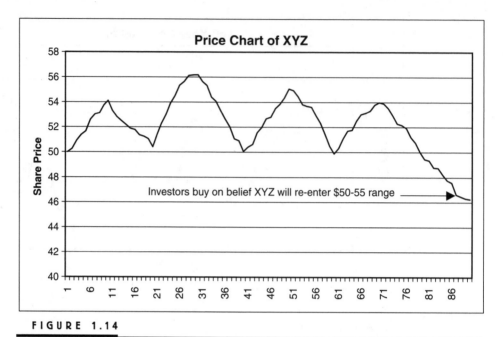

FIGURE 1.14

Price Chart of XYZ. Investors will buy XYZ on a break below $50, expecting a return to the $50-$55 range.

Paul Andreassen, a Harvard psychologist, conducted two experiments in the mid-1980s to determine if people traded based on mean reversion (1988). Andreassen gave test subjects an arbitrary amount of money in a fictitious brokerage account. Randomly generated stock prices were shown to the subjects every 30 seconds over 120 total trials. At the end of each trial, subjects were allowed to buy or sell stock, subject to the amount of money in their experimental account. Each subject's compensation for their role in the experiment was determined by how well they traded, so each had economic incentive to perform optimally.

Andreassen found evidence that the test subjects more often bought stocks on declining days and sold stocks on days in which prices rose. One strong explanation of this behavior is that human nature assumes that prices will mean revert. When presented with a series of stock prices, it is human nature to expect that prices will return to their most recent equilibrium level. This belief contrasts with the more traditional theory that market prices are independent and follow a random walk where prices may move up or down with equal likelihood.

There are a number of quantitative techniques we can utilize to take advantage of investors' tendencies to sell winners too early and hold losers too long. Most of these models fall under the class of trend-following systems. Trend fol-

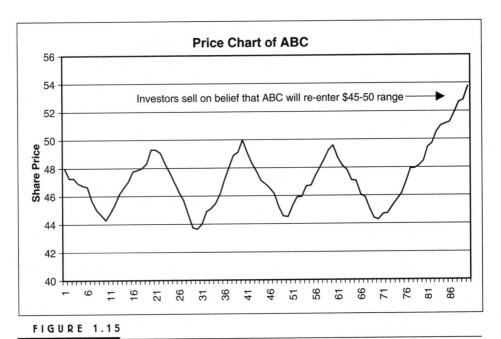

FIGURE 1.15

Price Chart of ABC. Investors will sell ABC on a rise above $50, expecting a return to the $45-$50 range.

lowing strategies buy strong markets and sell weak markets. We may be able to explain the success of these trend-following strategies using a combination of prospect theory and mean reversion theory.

Trend-Following Systems.   When prices rise above recent ranges, prospect theory dictates that traders with long positions will exit trades while traders losing money on short positions will hold their trades. Traders who are long will be risk averse with their gains and will sell long positions in order to lock in gains and feel mentally rewarded. At the same time, traders who are short will be reluctant to close their short positions with losses. They hope the market will turn so they might exit without loss.

In addition, as the market rises above the old trading range, mean reversion thinking will suggest that the market has overextended itself on the rally and will eventually return to its previous trading range. Traders whose minds detect the mean reverting process will establish short positions due to a belief that prices will return to their norm. Of course, traders selling the breakout are eventually doomed. New information has hit the market and prices are destined to head higher. Those who fight the trend will lose, while traders who trade with the breakout will feast on the natural human tendencies of those market participants unable to take trading losses.

Traders whose minds are distracted by prospect theory or mean reversion tendencies will likely lose over time. Whether due to a change in underlying fundamentals or a shift in sentiment, market prices are moving for a good reason. Smart traders ignore the human bias of both prospect theory and mean reversion and establish positions in the direction of the breakout, while other traders with losing positions hold on. The pain of these losing trades is eventually realized, and losses are very often closed near a market extreme. As we will see, using quantitative trading strategies will mitigate these human tendencies and generate trading strategies based on optimal historical performance—not psychological tendencies.

The tendencies in human nature that result in prospect theory and mean reversion can generate great losses for pure discretionary traders. As research cited in later chapters will show, the preferred strategy in many markets is to sell new lows and buy new highs. Readers should keep in mind that this is merely only one example of utilizing systematic methods to take advantage of market inefficiencies. We will also explore methods to buy when everyone is selling, to trade off very short-term strength and weakness, as well as trade the difference among similar or substitutable markets that may reach extremes.

In each case, the very reasons that human nature influences our thinking may allow quantitative trading systems to profit. After all, quantitative systems follow models with specific rules based on historical performance and use the scientific process, instead of human intuition, to drive their strategies.

In some ways, I find it ironic that trading can be so difficult and such a mental struggle. After all, this is the only profession where every decision is a binary choice. There are only two actions a trader can make: buy or sell. But as can be seen by the above discussion on irrational buying and selling, there are obstacles that can make that binary choice difficult.

TECHNOLOGY AND INEFFICIENCIES IN FINANCIAL MARKETS

Inefficiencies do exist in financial markets, albeit not forever. Financial history tells wonderful stories about traders exploiting inefficiencies over the past 30 years.

Zero Coupon Bonds

In the 1970s the U.S. Treasury first allowed its coupon debt to be stripped into zero coupon instruments. A 10-year bond that paid 20 coupons and a repayment of principal could be stripped into 20 zero coupon bonds. These zero coupon bonds, unlike a traditional bond that pays a coupon semiannually, are debt obligations that pay no coupons. Instead, zero coupon bonds trade at a discount to face value. Over time, the bonds accrete to par value, with investors receiving their principal (and effectively their interest payments) at maturity. Investment banks found that many institutions such as insurance companies preferred these zero coupon instruments, and so they began to offer them as products. Of course, if we sum the value of these stripped coupon bonds, it must equal the value of the nonstripped bond. The parts must sum to the whole. Smart bond traders were often able to sell the coupon strips at a price higher than the original bond, profiting the difference in buy and sell values without any risk. Such true arbitrage did not last long, as technology became widespread to determine the fair values of these strip instruments.

Call and Put Contracts

As stock option contracts became popular in the early 1980s, there were dramatic differences in listed call and put contracts of the same security. Options are derivative instruments that provide the buyer with the right, but not the obligation, to buy or sell a stock at a specified price within a specified time frame. For example, with XYZ trading at $100, I might pay $2 for the right to buy the stock at $100 within the next month. If the stock is above $100, I will exercise my right and buy the stock. If the stock finishes below $100 (whether $98 or $50), I simply walk away and allow my option to expire.

Options are popular with retail investors and hedge funds as a means to change their profit and loss profile. Some use options for leverage, while others use them as a means to hedge financial risk. Options come in two forms: calls and puts. A call option is the right—but again, not the obligation—to buy a stock at a specific price with a specific expiration. A put option is the right, but not the obligation, to sell a stock at a specific price with a specific expiration. The cost for this right is paid up front and is often referred to as the *option premium.*

A paper written in 1974 by Fisher Black and Myron Scholes detailed the relative equivalence of a call and put contract and hence the relationship between call premiums and put premiums. Using the Black-Scholes equation this paper made famous, traders were able to buy one instrument, sell the other, and hedge the resulting risk with underlying stock. Traders could make $0.25 to $1.00 per share in the process—without any risk! In fact, in the early days, the equivalence of calls and puts was so misunderstood that call and put options even traded in separate parts of the option exchange floors, with separate brokers and market makers for each instrument. But again, technology caught up and this arbitrage opportunity eventually disappeared from the market.

Futures Contracts

In the mid 1980s, Salomon Brothers' Bond Arbitrage Group (members of which later became the core of Long Term Capital Management) bought government bonds in the cash market while shorting the 30-year bond future. Futures contracts have a definitive life. At expiration, buyers will receive physical delivery and sellers are required to physically deliver assets subject to the terms of the contract. In agricultural products, the delivery is subject to a certain quality grain. In financial products, delivery is either cash or a specific pool of bonds. The 30-year Treasury bond future, traded on the Chicago Board of Trade, calls for delivery of U.S. Treasury bonds that are not callable for at least 15 years. With over 30 bonds that meet these specifications, the CBOT publishes a conversion factor table detailing how much of each bond would be needed to fulfill delivery requirements. The daily mismatch between bond prices and the conversion factors leads to one bond becoming cheaper to deliver than any other bonds.

In the early 1980s, bond futures would sometimes trade expensive compared to the underlying cheapest-to-deliver bond. Salomon Brothers sold bond futures and simultaneously purchased the cheapest bonds deliverable into the corresponding futures contract, profiting from the relative mispricing of the futures contract. At maturity, they would deliver the cheapest bonds held in inventory against their short futures positions. This left the firm with no position and a bankload of profits. But like all other examples, the technology and the models for these cheapest-to-deliver bonds became widespread and the inefficiency disappeared from the marketplace.

Options Pricing

Even more recently, sophisticated stock option traders could buy options on individual stocks and sell stock index options to create a profitable risk-free payoff based on the diffusion of individual stock returns. The primary driver in options pricing is volatility. Unlike stock price, interest rates, and dividends, volatility is the only variable either unknown or unhedgeable in the Black-Scholes option pricing formula. There exists a specific relationship between the volatilities of stocks that comprise an index (such as the components of the S&P 500) and the volatility of that index (such as options on the S&P 500).

For example, if the volatility of Intel, General Electric, and Exxon rise, chances are that volatility on the S&P 500 will also rise. Sophisticated options traders often trade the difference in volatility between individual stock options (such as INTC, GE, and XOM) and index options (such as the S&P 500). Fair pricing between the stock and index options is based on the correlation of stocks to other stocks in the index. At times during the late 1990s, this correlation was priced in the options markets above +1.0, a theoretical impossibility. Quantitative traders were able to exploit profits. But as pricing systems improved and other traders noticed the inefficiency, these profit opportunities also disappeared.

The constant theme throughout these stories is that traders with the best quantitative analysis are able to capitalize on market inefficiencies when they appear. Because these money-making opportunities do not last forever, traders must always continue research efforts to discover new techniques. Inefficiencies similar to those mentioned above do exist in the markets today, and we will attempt to identify these opportunities elsewhere in the book.

Are there inefficiencies in the stock and futures markets? Yes. I believe that inefficiencies are always present and that the notion of truly efficient markets is an impossibility. If markets were perfectly efficient, traders would stop research and no longer continue to look for profitable trading strategies or undervalued companies. As soon as this research stopped, inefficiencies would reappear as traders disappeared from the market place. With the reappearance of these inefficiencies, traders would slowly begin to exploit them again, bringing the market back to efficiency.

Think of market efficiency as a rubber band. If it stretches too far away from efficiency, then forces (traders entering the market) will snap the rubber band back toward efficiency. If efficiency is stretched the other way, toward perfect efficiency, forces (traders exiting the market) will push markets away from efficiency. Regardless of how tight or loose the rubber band, traders with the best models based on statistics and mathematics will always be able to make money.

MERITS AND LIMITATIONS OF FUNDAMENTAL ANALYSIS

If there are profits in quantitative trading, should we bother studying fundamental analysis as well?

I believe there is money to be made on the fundamental side. But like the quantitative side, the fundamental side has grown quite efficient. As hedge funds have become more popular and their numbers and assets have grown, better independent fundamental analysis is being performed on companies' balance sheets and earnings streams. A hedge fund might have a single analyst covering each industry or sector. As analysts break these companies apart, they note their customer base, geographic breakdown of revenues, technology on the horizon, and competitive advantages or disadvantages. Their wealth of knowledge and expertise creates their advantage when evaluating a firm's operating performance.

At the same time, fundamental analysis could learn some lessons from the quantitative side. Over the past five years, I have seen numerous methods employed to value technology stocks. I've seen the same analyst value the same company using price-to-earnings, price-to-sales, and price-to–earnings growth all in one five-year period. Because corporate earnings can be very volatile, fundamental analysts have had trouble refining their valuation techniques. Take, for example, the stock price, trailing year earnings, and price-to-earnings ratios for Intel, General Electric, and General Motors

In the case of Intel and General Electric, prices actually topped before earnings per share hit their high. Intel's highest quarterly close was made in July 2000, while its highest trailing 12-month earnings per share topped six months later with the quarter ending December 2000 (Figure 1.16). The same instance occurred with General Electric, whose quarterly high price peaked in April 2000, while 12-month trailing earnings per share was still rising at the end of 2001 (Figure 1.17). General Motors price peaked in April 2000, which followed its earnings peak, occurring in the quarter ending December 1999 (Figure 1.18). Despite the fact that 12-month trailing earnings held in a range of $8 and $10 between December 1999 and December 2000, GM's stock price fell from 93 to 53 over that same time frame.

My point is, while earnings do drive stock performance, they are not the only factor. Even if you knew the next year's exact earnings numbers for these three stocks, it may not have helped your trading performance. Stocks often fall despite increases in earnings. This can happen due to changes in business outlook, valuations that exceed earnings potential, or products that become obsolete or are subject to fierce competition. While there's no substitute for solid fundamental analysis, I believe that using quantitative trading strategies can detect factors that affect stock prices more quickly than waiting for earnings announcements and company conference calls. The old adage, "Prices move first and fundamentals follow" holds true.

While there are good fundamental analysts performing very rigorous work, when analyzing companies' earnings potential, even the best analysts are subject to the market's underreaction and overreaction. One such example is the Nasdaq 100, an index comprised of the 100 largest nonfinancial companies traded on the Nasdaq. This index is very heavily weighted in technology, telecommunications, and biotechnology. Figure 1.19 details its price action during 2000. Markets are not necessarily as efficient or as rational as one might expect. The Nasdaq 100 rallied from 1008 at the start of 1998 to a high of 4708 in early 2000. That corresponds to a return of 367 percent in just over two years.

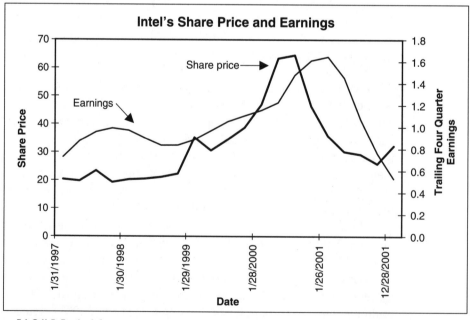

FIGURE 1.16

Intel's Share Price and Earnings. While share prices can be driven by earnings, often a price will lead changes in earnings by a year or more.

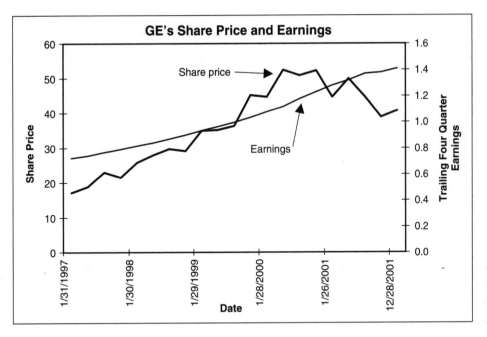

FIGURE 1.17

GE's Share Price and Earnings. While share prices can be driven by earnings, often a price will lead changes in earnings by a year or more.

This irrational exuberance can be hard to exploit using fundamental analysis, since irrationalities have a habit of stretching well beyond reasonable valuations. As ridiculously overvalued as many of the dot-coms were, with no legitimate business plans, let's focus on the survivors with real revenues. Two good examples are Cisco Systems and Amazon.com. For those unfamiliar with each, Cisco sells hardware and software for computer networking, and Amazon.com is a large online retailer of books, electronics, and computer software.

Caught up in the Internet revolution, Amazon and Cisco saw their share prices rise to astronomical heights between 1998 and 2000. Prevailing valuation measures such as price-to-earnings and price-to-sales were thrown out the window. We were entering an entirely new period, where technology would supplant the rest of the economy in terms of growth and future earnings. Prominent stock analysts such as Henry Blodget of Merrill Lynch and Mary Meeker of Morgan Stanley were able to move share prices dramatically by issuing favorable comments in their research reports. In a bold move, Blodget, then at CIBC Oppenheimer, raised his price target on Amazon.com from $150 to $400 per share on December 16, 1998. The stock responded with an 20 percent rise, from $243 to $289.

There is no doubt that the technology stock bubble of 1998 through 2000 led to unbelievable valuations. But even if your analysis concluded in 1999 that these

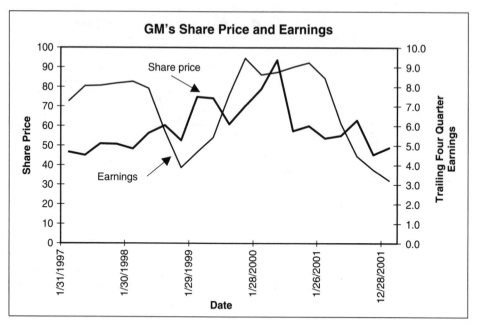

FIGURE 1.18

GM's Share Price and Earnings. While share prices can be driven by earnings, often a price will lead changes in earnings by a year or more.

stocks were overvalued, short positions would have been at best frustrating and at worst dangerous. Markets can become overvalued and remain overvalued for many years. Likewise, periods of relative cheapness can persist until a catalyst sparks investor interest.

Most investors think of the technology bubble as one large rally from 1997 through 2000, followed by a slow, steady decline. In fact, moves in individual stocks saw many up and downs during that time frame. Split adjusted, Amazon began 1998 around $5 per share. From 1998 to 2001, the stock ran up to $92, sold off to $45, rallied back to $105, sold off back down to $43, rallied to $106, and then declined to a low of $6 per share in September 2001 (Figure 1.20). Those are moves of +1700, –52, +135, –59, +150, and –94 percent. Cisco began 1998 at $10 per share. It, too, had very volatile moves. Cisco rallied to $17, declined to $11, skyrocketed to $80, sold off to $51, rallied back to $68, sold off to $11, and then rallied to $22 in December 2001 (Figure 1.21). Those are moves of +78, –36, +630, –37, +35, –84, and +94 percent.

The point is, even in bubbles and bursts, stocks do not move in straight lines. While changes in long-term fundamentals may not occur very often, this does not preclude stocks from making spectacular rises and devastating declines. Amazon and Cisco have produced enough movement up and down over the past five years

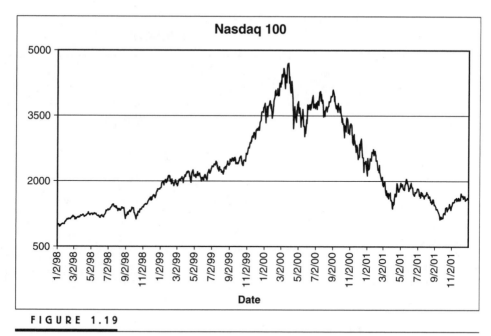

FIGURE 1.19

Nasdaq 100. The Nasdaq 100 rose extraordinarily between 1998 and 2000.

FIGURE 1.20

Amazon.com (AMZN). Amazon.com was very volatile between 1998 and 2001.

FIGURE 1.21

Cisco (CSCO). Cisco, a maker of computer networking software and hardware, also saw amazing price gains between 1998 and 2000.

to make any trader excited with opportunity. The beauty of quantitative analysis is that we can capture these moves without a change in underlying fundamentals. Our models should be able to determine changes in price trends and allow us to profit from volatility instead of suffering from it.

The problem with fundamental analysis is that the underlying fundamentals of companies change very slowly, making it difficult to capitalize on volatile price swings in the equity market, which are typically caused by investor sentiment and perception. Employing fundamental analysis successfully requires that markets return to rationality and efficiency sooner rather than later—a property that often does not occur. There are very talented and bright fundamental analysts, but to take advantage of the short-term swings in the markets—whether it be stocks, futures, or other markets—we will focus on the quantitative side and use past market prices to generate trading signals.

CHAPTER 2

An Introduction to Statistics

Using Scientific Methods to Develop Cutting Edge Trading Strategies

MEASURING THE MARKETS USING STATISTICS

While mastery of statistics is not an absolute necessity in becoming a successful trader, knowing the mathematics and principles behind price action will give you an upper hand when it comes to trading. To that end, this section introduces statistical properties that relate to financial markets, such as the concepts of mean, standard deviation, and correlation of returns.

Descriptive statistics are tools that allow traders to better understand and comprehend data in an easy and effective manner. Instead of presenting the height measurements of 100 men, I could instead offer that the average height of these 100 men is 5 feet 8 inches. By providing one descriptive statistic (the mean), I have characterized a quality of the entire sample of height measurements. I can take this process further by revealing that the standard deviation of heights is 3 inches (as we will explore later, standard deviation is a measure of the dispersion of data within a group). Now, with only two pieces of information—the mean and standard deviation—I can make accurate deductions regarding the distribution of the heights among all 100 men, including the shortest and tallest.

Similarly, by calculating descriptive statistics on market prices, market returns, and market volume, we can learn much about the nature of recent price movement. These descriptive statistics will become the building blocks for our quantitative trading systems.

Understanding the statistics behind markets can help when creating new trading ideas. A market's expected movement is very important for the quantitative trader to determine the difference between random and significant price movement. These properties can also aid in developing risk management strategies for a portfolio of trading strategies.

MEAN AND AVERAGE OF RETURNS AND PRICES

The mean of a series, more commonly referred to as the average, is a measure of central location. The mean is the sum of the values in a distribution divided by the number of data points in the distribution. The mean is defined as:

$$\mu = \frac{\sum x}{N}$$

where μ is the formulaic definition of mean, $\sum$ is a mathematical procedure which means to sum over all values, and N is the number of data points in the series

In the sample data in Figure 2.1, the mean is 5.4.

MEASURING THE DISPERSION OF RETURNS

The mean of a series is a very important descriptive statistic because it determines the central tendency of a series. Often, however, we need to understand more about a data set that just the mean. We may wish to measure how widely values spread across a distribution. Do the values clump closely around a central point or are they distributed widely? The most popular methods used to measure the dispersion of values are *variance* and *standard deviation.*

Data point	Data
1	5
2	3
3	7
4	8
5	4
Sum	27
N	5
Mean	5.4

FIGURE 2.1

Calculating the mean. The average of a series is calculated by summing all the data points and dividing by the number of data points.

Variance is defined as the average squared deviation around the mean and is represented by the following formula:

$$\text{Variance} = \sigma^2 = \frac{\Sigma\,(x - \mu)^2}{N}$$

Variance, often represented by σ^2, measures how wide the spread of values span from the mean. Using the same sample data as above, we calculate that the variance of the values is 3.4 (see Figure 2.2).

We will also calculate the variance using the weekly returns for the S&P 500 and Nasdaq 100 during 2001. The mean of the S&P 500 is –0.20 percent, and the mean of the Nasdaq 100 is –0.47 percent. The variance of weekly returns is 0.10 for the S&P 500 and 0.48 for the Nasdaq 100.

Notice that the Nasdaq 100 has a larger variance than the S&P 500. The variance calculation tells us that the returns of the Nasdaq 100 vary more widely and are more volatile than the returns of the S&P 500. We confirm this graphically by plotting a frequency distribution of the returns of the S&P 500 and Nasdaq 100. A frequency distribution of a series graphs the number of occurrences within a range of values, as can be seen in Figure 2.3.

Note that the returns of the Nasdaq 100 vary more widely than that of the S&P 500. This is because it's comprised of riskier companies, those that focus on technology, telecommunications, and health care. Where the S&P 500's largest monthly gain was 7.8 percent and its largest loss was 11.6 percent, the Nasdaq 100 managed to gain 18.4 percent and lose 17.5 percent in its best and worst months.

The variance calculation quantifies the dispersion of values. However, in the practical world, we use standard deviation more often than variance. We take the square root of variance to arrive at standard deviation. The standard deviation has some wonderful properties that we can apply toward our data for further analysis. We will investigate these properties later in this chapter.

Data point	Data	Difference from mean	Difference squared
1	5	−0.4	0.16
2	3	−2.4	5.76
3	7	1.6	2.56
4	8	2.6	6.76
5	4	−1.4	1.96
Sum	27	Sum	17.20
N	5	N	5
Mean	5.4	Variance	3.44

FIGURE 2.2

Calculating the variance. Variance is the average squared deviation from the mean.

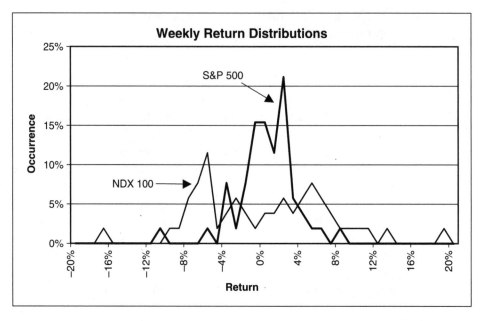

FIGURE 2.3

Weekly Return Distributions. Being less volatile, the S&P 500's returns are more closely spread than the more volatile Nasdaq 100.

$$\text{Standard deviation} = \sigma = \sqrt{Variance}$$

CORRELATION

Correlation is another important descriptive statistic. It measures the strength of a relationship between two series. Correlation can range from −1 to +1, where the extreme values indicate a perfect relationship, while a value of zero indicates no relationship at all. The correlation statistic is calculated by multiplying the difference of one series from its mean by the corresponding difference of another series from its mean, taking the average product, and then dividing by the product of the standard deviation of both series. The equation looks like this:

$$\text{Correlation} = \rho = \frac{\frac{1}{N} \sum (x - \mu_x)(y - \mu_y)}{\sigma_x \sigma_y}$$

The best way to think about correlation is by graphing a scatterplot of two series. A scatterplot graphs values of one series against values of another series, as you can see in the figures below.

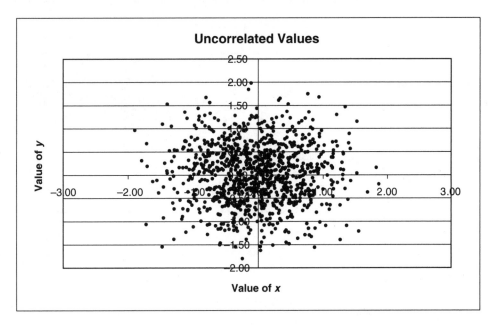

FIGURE 2.4

Uncorrelated Values. When the value of *y* is plotted against the value of *x*, we see that no relationship exists.

These graphs present three general states of correlation. In Figure 2.4, the scatter-plot suggests that the relationship between *x* and *y* is random, and thus no correlation exists. In Figure 2.5, *y* increases as *x* does. This indicates a positive correlation between *x* and *y*. In Figure 2.6, a different relationship exists. As *x* increases, *y* decreases, indicating negative correlation.

Correlation can also be misused. When measuring the correlation of market data, it is important to perform your analysis using returns rather than prices. In most instances, the correlation of prices can trick the trader into believing there is a meaningful relationship between two series, when in reality no such pattern exists.

Consider, for example, the relationship between the S&P 500 and natural gas. When we create a scatterplot of these two data series, a strong positive relationship is observed. The correlation in prices is 0.70, which would indicate a strong relationship between natural gas and the S&P 500 (see Figure 2.7). If two series drift in similar or opposite directions over the life of the data, however, such as they do in this example, the correlation numbers will become "artifacts." Used in the statistical sense, the term artifact refers to a result that is misleading and probably biased. In fact, if in our example we calculate the correlation of weekly *returns* instead of prices (Figure 2.8), we see that the correlation is nearly zero. This correlation number is a more accurate representation of the "true" relationship between natural gas and the S&P 500 than the 0.70 price correlation.

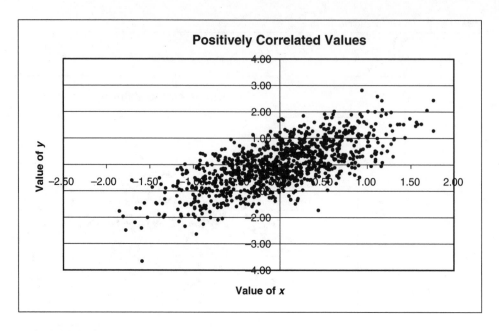

FIGURE 2.5

Positively Correlated Values. When the value of *y* is plotted against the value of *x*, we see that a positive relationship exists.

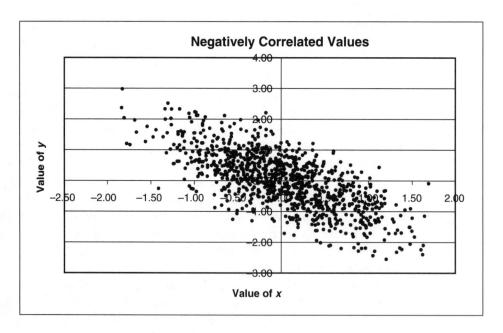

FIGURE 2.6

Negatively Correlated Values. When the value of *y* is plotted against the value of *x*, we see that a negative relationship exists.

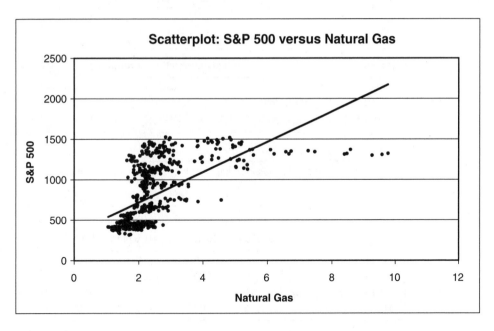

FIGURE 2.7

Scatterplot: S&P 500 versus Natural Gas Prices. While statistical analysis would show a significant relationship between the level of the S&P 500 and natural gas prices, chances are this relationship will not hold true in the future.

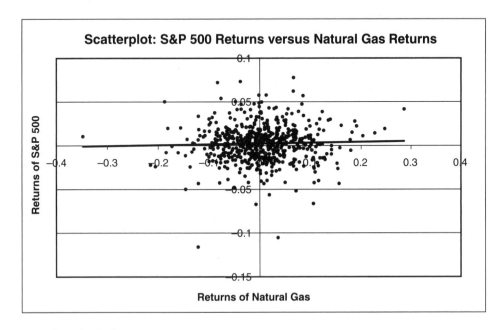

FIGURE 2.8

Scatterplot: S&P 500 Returns versus Natural Gas Returns. When weekly percent price changes are examined, we see that virtually no link exists between the S&P 500 and natural gas prices.

Stocks	Weekly correlation of returns
Ford/General Motors	0.73
Merrill Lynch/Morgan Stanley	0.80
Merck/Pfizer	0.65

FIGURE 2.9

Correlation of Selected Stock Pairs. Companies in the same industry often have large positive correlations.

	S&P 500	Gold	10-year yields	Oil
S&P 500	1.00	0.10	0.17	0.03
Gold	0.10	1.00	−0.17	0.07
10-year Treasury yields	0.17	−0.17	1.00	−0.20
Oil	0.03	0.07	−0.20	1.00

FIGURE 2.10

Correlation of Macroeconomic Variables. Correlation among equities, bonds, and commodities is not as high as correlation among stocks.

Some markets are highly correlated, while others seem to have no effect on one another. Stocks of the same industry typically have very high correlations. The correlation of weekly returns for selected pairs of stocks from 2001 is listed in Figure 2.9.

Interest rates, gold, and the stock market have smaller correlations with each other. For example, as can be seen in Figure 2.10, correlations between these four markets run from a low of −0.20 for oil and 10-year yields, to a high of 0.17 correlation between S&P 500 returns and changes in 10-year yields.

THE USEFULNESS OF THE NORMAL DISTRIBUTION

Standard deviation is a popular method of measuring dispersion, primarily due to its properties under certain circumstances, specifically those associated with a normal distribution. When we say that a distribution is "normal," we're making a statement about the probabilities of values occurring. Normal distributions pile high toward the center of the distribution and fan out toward the edges.

The normal distribution is sometimes referred to as a *bell curve*, due to its shape (as seen in Figure 2.11). Probably the most useful and most studied distribution in statistics, it's also referred to as "Gaussian," in honor of the German mathematician Karl Freidrich Gauss.

The equation for determining normal distribution looks like this:

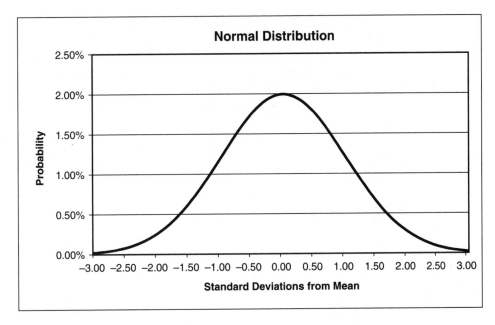

FIGURE 2.11

Normal Distribution. The normal distribution looks like a bell, often leading to its "bell shaped" nickname.

$$p\,(x) = \frac{1}{\sigma\sqrt{2\pi}}\, e^{\frac{-(x-\mu)^2}{\sigma^2}}$$

Once we know that a series follows a normal distribution, we can infer tremendous information about the range of values using only the mean and standard deviation of the series. For example, we know that roughly 68.26 percent of the values in a normal distribution fall between ±1 standard deviation of the mean, 95.44 percent fall between ±2 standard deviations, and 99.74 percent between ±3 standard deviations.

A quick exercise in Microsoft Excel shows the value of the normal distribution. Generate 1000 normally distributed random values by entering *=NORM-SINV(RAND())* into empty cells. Next, calculate the mean and standard deviation. In my run, I find a mean of 0.01 and a standard deviation of 0.99. Using the properties of the normal distribution, I know the following:

68.26 percent of the values should fall between ±1 standard deviation: −0.99 and +1.00
95.44 percent should fall between ±2 standard deviations: −1.98 and +1.99
99.74 percent should fall between ±3 standard deviations: −2.97 and +2.98

When I sort my values in Excel, I find that my distribution closely matches the normal, as in Figure 2.12.

Market returns and prices follow some very specific tendencies associated with the normal distribution. These tendencies are constant regardless of product—stocks, futures, and currencies all have these properties. Over short time periods, percentage market returns (dividing today's price by yesterday's price and subtracting the value of one) are roughly normally distributed, following the popular bell shape normal curve. Figure 2.13, below, depicts the daily return distribution for the S&P 500 over the last five years. The bars represent the actual return distributions, while the smooth line is the expected distribution based on a perfect normal distribution.

Standard deviation range	Expected	Actual
−1 to +1	68.26%	68.80%
−2 to +2	95.44%	95.70%
−3 to +3	99.74%	100%

FIGURE 2.12

Excel Exercise. By pulling random numbers into Excel, we see that their range is almost exactly what we would expect given from the normal distribution.

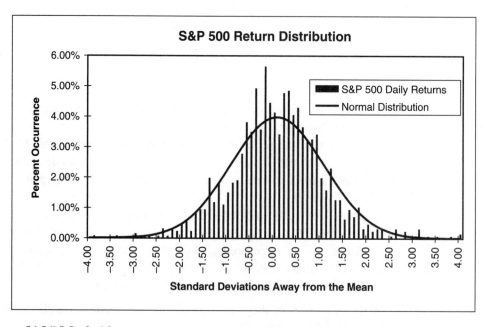

FIGURE 2.13

S&P 500 Return Distribution. Daily returns of the S&P 500 between 1997 and 2001 look similar to a normal distribution, except for more than expected occurrences near the middle and tails of the return distribution.

THE IRREGULARITY OF MARKET VOLATILITY

As seen above, returns follow the normal curve very closely. The small departures include high peaks near the middle of the distribution and fat tails toward each edge. This distribution is referred to as "leptokurtic" from the Greek word *leptos*, meaning small or narrow. The fact that short-term market returns do not follow a typical normal distribution had plagued economists for some time. Recent evidence has shown that the leptokurtic distribution likely results from the fact that the standard deviation of returns varies over time.

Traders may have a better understanding of nonconstant market volatility than economists. When the market is slow, quiet, and no new news is hitting the tape, the market tends to remain in a state of low volatility for days or weeks. On the other hand, when markets are very volatile, they tend to take days or weeks of further above average volatility until news and price changes are digested.

Economists have created a new class of models to explain how volatility varies over time. These models are called GARCH, for Generalized Auto Regressive Conditional Heteroskedasticity. A GARCH process exists when volatility itself changes over time, wandering back and forth around a long-term average. In the Figure 2.14, below, we see the standard deviation of daily returns for the S&P 500 over a one month period. We can measure the volatility over short time frames by calculating a rolling 20-day standard deviation of percent returns.

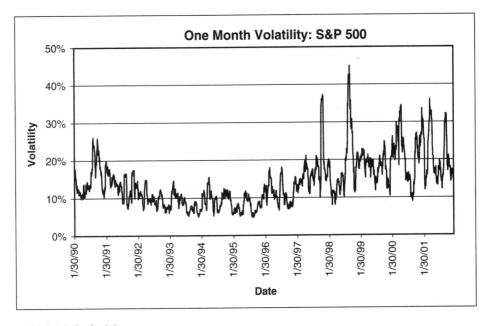

FIGURE 2.14

One Month Volatility: S&P 500. Volatility tends to bounce between 10% and 20%.

We start by calculating the standard deviation of the first 20 returns. On the next day, we drop the first return from our calculation, add the 21st return, and recalculate the standard deviation of returns. The following day we drop the second return and add the 22d return in our calculation of standard deviation. And so on. Each value of the 20-day standard deviation will have 19 common return points as the value before and value after. In this sense, the calculation "rolls" with each day, hence the expression "rolling volatility."

We must make an adjustment to our standard deviation calculation. While the resulting standard deviation is reported in daily units, it is much more common to refer to volatility on an annualized basis. Because volatility scales with the square root of time, we multiply our daily standard deviation by the square root of trading days in a year (typically 252 for equity markets). The result of this adjustment is an annualized standard deviation, or volatility.

Note that in the above graph of the S&P 500, volatility tends to meander back and forth around the mean of 18 percent. While periods of low volatility may exist for short periods of time, volatility eventually returns to the long-term mean. Periods of high volatility can also only last so long before returning to the long-term mean. Such mean reversion of standard deviation is the backbone of GARCH models. This property of volatility is common to almost all markets. Periods of high volatility are often followed by further periods of high volatility, slowly decreasing to more normal levels over time. Similarly, periods of low volatility are often followed by further periods of low volatility, eventually returning to normal levels over time.

Research has shown that these GARCH models explain the volatility of markets with strong statistical significance. In addition, academic studies have found that when returns are adjusted for this varying volatility, the high peaks near the middle of the distribution and fat tails towards the extremes diminish and leave a more normal looking distribution. Although GARCH cannot or does not predict market returns or prices, the concept of nonconstant volatility has important implications for generating trading signals as well as managing the risk of portfolios.

THE RANGE OF VOLATILITIES

It's important to understand the statistics behind market prices so we can accurately analyze market information. One important distinction among markets is their varying degree of volatility. As already noted, markets do not possess constant volatility; rather, their volatilities are constantly changing over time. In the example above, we see that annualized volatility of the S&P 500 is typically between 15 and 25 percent, but also can spend long periods outside these ranges. In fact, the trend in the late 1990s was one of increasing volatility.

Traders should have been aware that trading an equal dollar value of the S&P 500 in the late 1990s was riskier than doing so in the early 1990s. Volatility of the

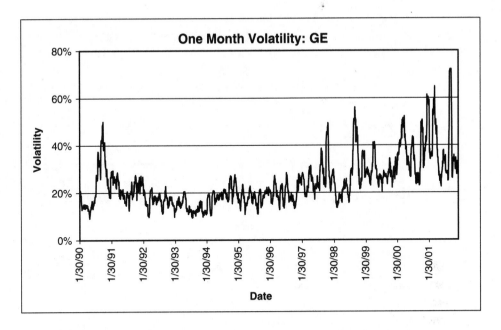

FIGURE 2.15

One Month Volatility: GE. Volatility tends to bounce between 20% and 40%.

S&P 500, when measured by standard deviation of percent returns, increased between 1995 and 2000. General Electric and Intel have similar volatility stories as the S&P 500, as shown in Figures 2.15 and 2.16. Matching the rise in volatility of the S&P 500, the volatility of daily returns from GE and Intel (INTC) expanded between 1998 and 2000.

If we know a market's annualized volatility, we can calculate the daily risk of being long or short. For example, the annualized volatility of the S&P 500 is around 20 percent. The daily standard deviation of being long or short the S&P 500 is equal to the value of the portfolio multiplied by the annualized standard deviation divided by the square root of 252:

$$\text{Daily standard deviation} = \frac{(\text{Notional \$}) \, (\sigma_{Annualized})}{\sqrt{252}}$$

We divided by the square root of 252 (the number of trading days in a year) in the above equation to scale the volatility from annual to daily. Because standard deviation scales proportionately to the square root of time, we must adjust volatility numbers to arrive at apples-to-apples comparisons. Suppose we have $20 million long exposure to the S&P 500. Our daily standard deviation would be:

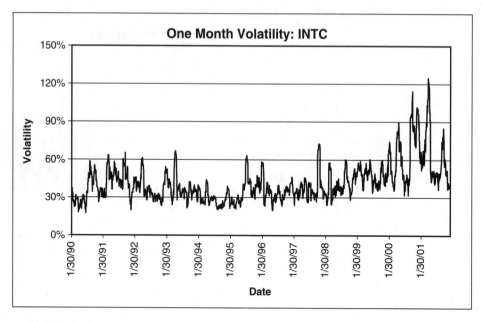

FIGURE 2.16

One Month Volatility: INTC. Volatility tends to bounce between 30% and 60%.

$$\text{Daily standard deviation} = \frac{(\$20,000,000)(20\%)}{\sqrt{252}} = \$252,000$$

In the example above, we can create what statisticians call "confidence intervals" around the daily standard deviation of $252,000. Using the normal distribution, 68 percent of the time we should make or lose between plus and minus one standard deviation ($252,000), and 95 percent of the time we should make or lose between plus and minus two standard deviations ($504,000).

Many traders have the misperceived notion that the S&P 500 is a very volatile market. Compared to most commodities and individual stocks, this is not true. As can be seen in the graph of annualized volatility for various markets from 1997 to 2001 (Figure 2.17), it is the fifth *least* volatile market. When traders say the S&P 500 futures are volatile, what they're really talking about is the notional size of the futures contract compared to other futures contracts. The notional value of the S&P 500 futures contract at the time of this writing is ($250)(800) = $200,000, whereas the notional value of crude oil, a more volatile market—as noted in the graph—is only ($1000)(30) = $30,000.

The difference between price volatility, as measured solely by daily percentage returns, and dollar volatility, measured by daily dollar returns of a futures con-

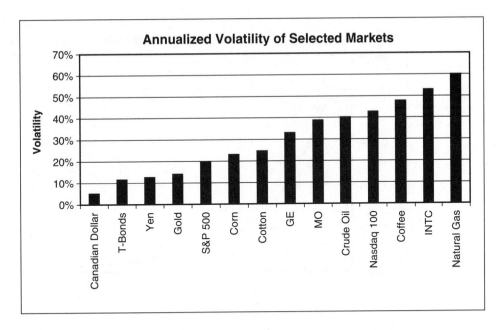

FIGURE 2.17

Annualized Volatility of Selected Markets. Commodities have some of the smallest volatility while individual stocks can be very volatile.

tract, will become important for determining the number of contracts to trade when entering a market.

The annualized volatility during 2001 for the 14 arbitrarily chosen commodities and markets in the graph shows that currencies such as the Canadian dollar and the Japanese yen are among the least volatile markets. Technology stocks such as Intel and the Nasdaq 100 are among the most volatile.

THE LOGNORMALITY OF MARKET PRICES

While short-term market returns can best be described as normally distributed, market prices follow a *lognormal* distribution. This is somewhat similar to the normal distribution in its shape, except the left- and right-hand side of the distribution is not symmetrical, as seen in Figure 2.18. The right-hand tail slowly extends outward, while the left-hand tails toward zero more abruptly. The lognormal distribution of prices is used commonly and is the basis for the Black-Scholes option pricing formula.

Readers might question the link that causes short-term returns to follow a normal distribution but prices to follow a lognormal distribution. The answer lies in compounding of returns. Consider a $100 stock and two scenarios:

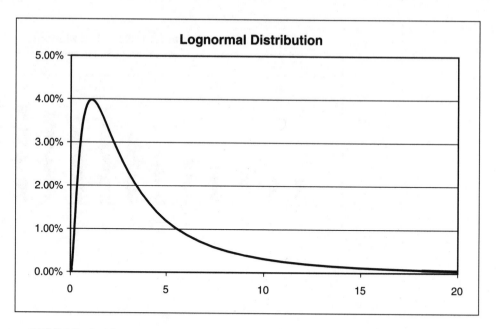

FIGURE 2.18

Lognormal Distribution. The lognormal distribution has a longer right-hand side tail than the normal distribution.

1. A gain of 50 percent on Day 1 and a gain of 50 percent on Day 2
2. A loss of 50 percent on Day 1 and a loss of 50 percent on Day 2

At the end of the two-day period, the stock will finish at $225 = ($100)(1.5)(1.5) in the first example and $25 = ($100)(0.5)(0.5) in the second example. Scenario 1 leads to a dollar return of +$125, while Scenario 2 leads to a dollar return of –$75. Though each scenario has a 25 percent chance of occurring, the former generates a more positive return than the latter does a negative return. As a result, the right tail of a lognormal extends further from the mean than does the left tail.

This characteristic will appear on several occasions throughout this book, and as we'll see later, it has important implications for money management.

CHAPTER 3

Creating Trading Strategies

The Building Blocks That Generate Trades

This chapter will provide an introduction to the concepts behind trading strategies. While the material may be old hack for some, the concepts are nevertheless important for building the better, more reliable systems and strategies we'll examine later.

There are three building blocks for creating any system: *entries*, *exits*, and *filters*. Entries are the signals that generate the opening buy and sell orders for new positions. Exits indicate that the expected value of a trade has diminished to the point that the trade should be closed. Filters persuade the trader to only take the entries with highest expected profits over the life of a system.

THE NEED TO EXPLAIN PRICE CHANGES

My trading experience has uncovered some strange peculiarities on Wall Street. There seems to be a constant need to justify or explain every single movement in the market. What caused the Dow to fall 25 points? Why are bonds up today?

In some instances, such as earnings reports, economic news releases, or crop reports, the answers are in plain sight. But in many, there is no single driver of price movement. Such single pieces of information rarely cause large amounts of capital to be allocated. Instead, it is usually a confluence of days or even weeks of information that change an investment philosophy from bearish to bullish or vice versa.

To highlight the confirmation required in the investment process, consider the following: A strong economic report might cause a mutual fund portfolio manager to consider buying stocks that may benefit from an upturn in the economy. The fund manager notices two companies in a cyclical industry that report better than expected earnings. Not yet convinced, the manager visits the companies' headquarters and also conducts channel checks with suppliers and distributors to see how orders are tracking in the current quarter. Convinced one of the stocks is now poised for higher prices, the fund manager begins to accumulate a large position in the stock. The buying pressure drives the company's stock price up $2 on the day.

Was there any news on this specific trading day to explain the sharp rise in the stock? No. It was a confluence of many pieces of information over several weeks that caused the stock to rise.

It's very hard to explain the day-to-day movements of market prices. Our trading strategies should not try to do so since prices are noisy and probably best explained by the random walk model. Instead, we will focus on predicting the market's daily direction correctly roughly 52 to 55 percent of the time. Even if we are correct only 52 percent of the trading days in the year, we should expect to make money 72 percent of the years when we trade. If we can increase the reliability of our forecasts to 55 percent daily accuracy, we become 94 percent likely to make money in any given year. The point is, a small increase in daily accuracy goes a long way in increasing our chances of being profitable for the year. The entries, exits, and filters below will aid in our trading decisions and increase our daily accuracy when trading.

TRADING STRATEGY ENTRIES

Entry signals are the engines that drive trading systems. Often, the bulk of time spent on creating new systems is consumed while devising entry signals. With so many ideas to choose from, testing can become a 24-hour-a-day job.

A few of the many entry methodologies used today include moving averages, channel breakouts, momentum, volatility breakouts, oscillators, and price patterns. These basic techniques have become the foundation for wonderfully complex new ideas. In order to build better systems later in this book, we must first understand the basics of current entry techniques.

Trend-Following Techniques

Trend-following methods generate buy signals while the market is in a period of strength. In contrast, sell signals are generated during periods of weakness. Although trend followers will never buy market bottoms or sell market tops, the middle of a trend is often enough to produce profitable trading. Typical trend following strategies will employ moving averages, channel breakouts, momentum readings, or volatility breakouts to signal entries.

Moving Averages

For over 50 years, moving averages have been used by traders. Essentially, a moving average is the mean of a time series, but updated and recalculated each trading day. Moving averages come in many different shapes and sizes. The most common are: *simple*, *weighted*, and *exponential*.

The most basic of the above three, the simple moving average, is an average of values recalculated every day. As time passes on, older values are replaced by more current values. The result is that the average "moves" over time. An *n*-day simple moving average is calculated by summing the previous *n* days of values (usually closes) and dividing by the value of *n*. Shorter values of *n* produce tighter moving averages, which hug closing data more closely than moving averages created with larger values of *n*.

$$\text{Simple } n\text{-day moving average} = \frac{1}{N} \Sigma \, Close_X$$

Numerous variations of the moving average have been created and studied over time. Some of the innovations involve the weighting, smoothing formulas, and overall structure of how the average is calculated. Besides the simple moving average, the second most common form is the exponential moving average. It is calculated using today's price value and yesterday's moving average value. The smoothing factor, α, determines how quickly the exponential moving average responds to current market prices. Large values of α will track prices more closely than smaller values of α.

$$\text{Exponential moving average} = x_t = (\alpha)\, close_t + (1 - \alpha)\, x_{t-1}$$

$$\text{where } \alpha \text{ of moving average in days} = \frac{2}{1 + \text{days}}$$

The weighted moving average is the third most common. Unlike simple moving averages that weight each price equally, weighted moving averages typically assign higher weights to more recent data points. An example of a weighted moving average would be:

$$\text{Weighted moving average} =$$

$$\frac{1}{(4 + 3 + 2 + 1)} \, (4 \cdot close_t + 3 \cdot close_{t-1} + 2 \cdot close_{t-2} + 1 \cdot close_{t-3})$$

The basic trading signals for moving averages are triggered when prices cross above or below a moving average. When prices cross above the moving average, higher prices are likely and it signals that it's time to buy. When prices cross below the moving average, a declining market is expected and it's time to sell. Moving averages of 20 to 100 days are commonly used to generate buy and sell signals. Shorter moving averages will respond quicker to recent price movement

and generate more trading signals than will longer moving averages, which produce trading signals infrequently.

Other variations of moving average strategies combine more than one moving
average to generate trading signals when a faster moving average—smaller n in a
simple moving average or larger α in an exponential moving average—crosses
above or below a slower moving average (larger n or smaller α). Moving averages
of 10 and 40 days are commonly used to generate signals in the dual moving average crossover system (Figure 3.1).

Moving Average Rules

Variation 1

- Buy when close crosses above x day moving average
- Sell when close crosses below x day moving average

Variation 2

- Buy when x day moving average crosses above y day moving average
- Sell when x day moving average crosses below y day moving average

Due to the smoothing of prices, moving averages will always lag current
prices. As prices trend higher, the average will always trail current prices. The

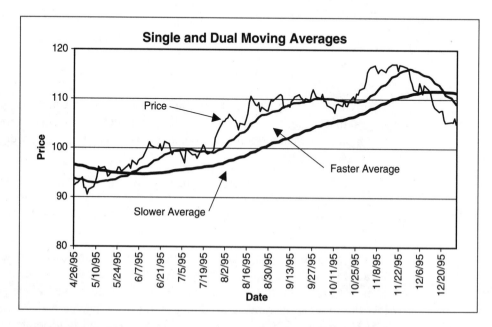

FIGURE 3.1

Single and Dual Moving Averages. Averages are often used to generate trading signals.

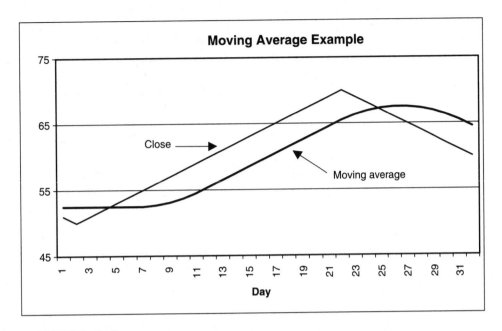

FIGURE 3.2

Moving Average Example. The lag of a moving average allows traders to stay on board of trends.

example above, Figure 3.2, illustrates a 20-day simple moving average of a market that increases one point a day, then declines one point per day. As can be seen, the moving average always trails under prices on the way up and never catches prices on the way down.

While many traders curse this lag, I value it. The lag of moving averages is what enables profits to be made during trending periods. When prices trend away from the moving average, trading signals are generated. As long as prices continue in the direction of the trend, the moving average will always lag current prices. The longer the trend, the more profitable the moving average strategy will be. In a market that oscillates in a cyclical sideways fashion, lag can be a problem. But more frequently than not, no discernible cyclical action can be identified in market prices, and we can use the moving average's lag to climb aboard the predominant trend of the market.

The major drawbacks associated with moving average strategies are the whipsaws associated with choppy market action. If a market shows signs of strength, then prices will cross above the moving average and generate buy signals. When prices quickly reverse and fall below the moving average, longs will be sold with a loss and new short positions established.

Figure 3.3 shows how whipsaws can eat into trading capital. As the market rallies and then declines with no discernible trends, the short-term trades

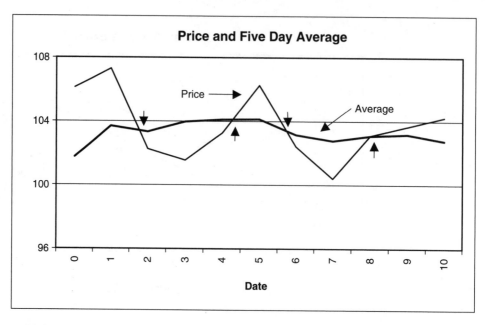

FIGURE 3.3

Price and Five Day Average. Whipsaws are created when prices frequently rise above and fall below moving averages.

lead to losses. We enter short on Day 2 at 103, close our short two days later at 104 for a one point loss and establish a long position. Two days later we close our long as the market declines, leading to another losing trade. Finally, on Day 8, we enter long again. If markets are prone to short and violent moves with many reversals along the way, moving average systems are likely to suffer. Using longer length moving averages can cut down on this whipsaw somewhat, but for the most part, whipsaws are an unfortunate part of moving average trading systems.

Channel Breakouts

Richard Donchian, whom we briefly discussed in Chapter 1, was a pioneer in systematic futures trading. He is credited as the first to use channel breakouts in his trading. Channel breakouts derive their name from channels that are created when plotting a running tally of the highest highs and lowest lows over a fixed interval of days. A 20-day channel involves calculating and plotting the highest and lowest close over the past 20 days. As new price highs or lows are made, the channel moves higher and lower, contracting and expanding with market volatility (see Figure 3.4).

Over the past few years, channel breakouts have overtaken the popularity of moving averages. This popularity is likely due to the wonderful stories of trading legend Richard Dennis and his "turtle" offspring.

In the early 1980s, Richard Dennis and partner William Eckhardt debated if trading could be taught successfully. To settle the argument, they hired a group of novice traders from varying backgrounds. The pair taught the basics of their trading system and sent their pupils into the world to trade. In its simplest form, their system was akin to a channel breakout strategy originally introduced by Richard Donchian. Using this basic strategy, many of the turtles have become wonderfully successful public money managers, managing billions of dollars with lucrative long-term track records.

The channels are incorporated into a trading strategy. Entries are executed when prices penetrate the channel. A buy is taken when today's close is greater than the previous x closes, and a sell is taken when today's close is lower than the previous x day's closes. If a 40-day channel breakout strategy were employed, a buy signal would be generated every time the market's close was the highest of the past 40 days. Sell signals are generated when the market closes lower than any other close of the past 40 days. The longer the channel length, the less frequently the strategy will trade.

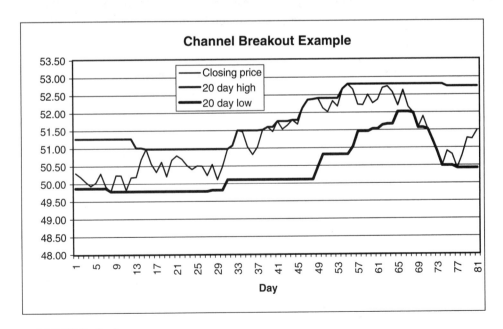

FIGURE   3.4

Channel Breakout Example. Price channels are created by calculating the highest and lowest closes over a specified range.

Channel Breakout Rules

- Buy if today's close is the highest close of the past x days
- Sell if today's close is the lowest close of the past x days

Not only are moving averages and channel breakouts popular, but they have generated substantial profits by riding long-term trends over the past 20 years. Due to this success, we will be spending much time with both trading methodologies. When evaluating performance of new trading strategies, we will always compare the results of any new systems to the performance of two specific variations of the moving average and channel breakout trading methodologies. This topic will be revisited in Chapter 4, "Evaluating Trading Strategy Performance."

Momentum

Momentum entries are perhaps the most simplistic techniques available to traders today. Momentum is calculated by taking a difference between one value and another value at some point in time.

$$\text{Momentum} = \text{Value}_{\text{today}} - \text{Value}_{x \text{ days ago}}$$

A typical example is price momentum (Figure 3.5). A 20-day momentum of closing prices would be calculated by taking the difference between today's close

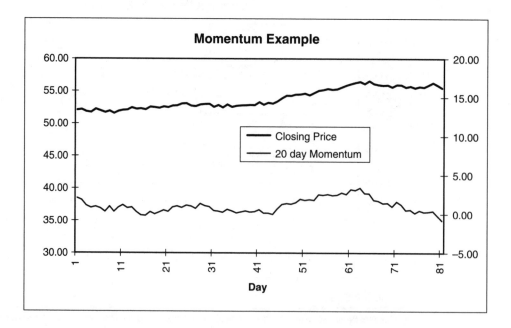

FIGURE 3.5

Momentum Example. Momentum is calculated by taking a price change over a specified range.

and the close 20 days before. Perhaps the most versatile indicator of all, momentum can be applied to prices, moving averages, oscillators, and other indicators. Typically, a buy signal is generated when momentum turns positive, and a sell is generated when momentum turns negative.

Momentum Rules

- Buy when today's close is greater than the close x days ago
- Sell when today's close is less than the close x days ago

Volatility Breakouts

Volatility breakouts are also a popular type of entry, commonly found as the basis of short-term systems that trade the S&P 500 and Treasury bond futures. Developed in the mid 1970s by Larry Williams, the premise behind the strategy is that large short-term price jumps tend to be precursors of further movement in the same direction.

There are a number of reasons why large price changes may be a signal to further movement in the same direction. First, trading costs are non-negligible, especially when committing large amounts of capital. When positive news breaks on a stock, it might take time for large institutions to make a decision to purchase shares. The transaction costs associated with buying or selling $100 million of assets is very costly, not only in terms of commissions, but also the slippage that is created from such large transaction sizes. Any institution willing to commit such large amounts of capital had better be sure it is the correct trade, otherwise the cost of reversing the trade could be enormous. This delay may allow the nimble quantitative trader to trade before the large institutions act. Another factor that can enhance the volatility breakout for traders is that all investors do not have equal information.

Sanford Grossman and Joseph Stiglitz (1980) first suggested the idea of information disequilibrium to explain the impossibility of truly efficient markets. Grossman and Stiglitz hypothesize that in every case, some investors have better information than others. The theory is based upon the significant costs associated with performing research. Hiring analysts to visit companies and dig through SEC filings can be expensive. If investors who spend this money on fundamental research cannot outperform uninformed investors, then the information gatherers will soon cease their research. As a result, markets will become inefficient until certain investors begin to do costly research again.

Chances are, when the informed investors take positions, they move markets to extremes due to their conviction. The volatility breakout strategy may be able to track the movement of these informed investors, identify these extremes, and exploit their profit potential. Volatility breakouts look for large single-day price moves and trade in the direction of the move.

The volatility breakout entry is comprised of three pieces: a *reference value*, a *volatility measure*, and a *volatility multiplier*. The reference value marks the measurement price of the move. The volatility measure computes the typical volatility of the market to separate significant movement from random price changes. The volatility multiplier determines the sensitivity of price movement required to trigger entry signals. The three components are combined into a trigger point. Buy entries are executed when prices close above the upper trigger, while sales are triggered when prices close below the lower trigger.

The reference value is the point from which we will measure the start of the move. This is typically measured using the previous day's close, today's opening, or a short-term moving average of closes. The three most common volatility measures are the standard deviation of price changes, the standard deviation of prices, and the average true range. The most logical volatility measure is to calculate a standard deviation of price returns. Remember, standard deviation measures the dispersion of returns and is a surrogate for market volatility. By calculating the standard deviation of returns, we can effectively determine significant market moves from random price action.

Another popular measure of volatility is to calculate the average true range. The true range is the largest of the following values:

- Today's high minus today's low
- Today's high minus yesterday's close
- Yesterday's close minus today's low

By averaging the true range over a set number of days, we can calculate a popular measure of market volatility called the average true range (ATR). The use of the previous day's close in some situations is to account for price gaps that may constitute the bulk of any day's volatility. If lumber, a futures market notorious for its trading halts due to daily price limits, opened limit-up and never traded lower during the day, the high-minus-low range would be zero. If this limit move continued for five days in a row, then taking a simple average of the high-to-low range would underestimate the true volatility of the market. By adjusting the high to low range for movement from the previous day's close, we create a more robust measure of volatility.

A third measure often used to calculate volatility is the standard deviation of market prices. Unlike the standard deviation of returns, this method does not allow strict interpretation using the normal distribution. It is nevertheless an effective measure of the volatility of prices. Despite the myriad methods to calculate market volatility, as we see in Figure 3.6, each dispersion calculation method yields reasonably similar values.

Volatility breakout entry points are derived by multiplying the volatility multiplier by the volatility measure and adding that value to the reference value.

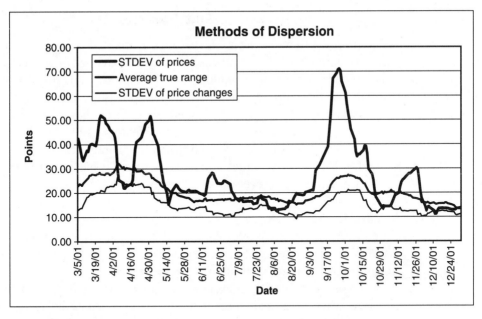

FIGURE 3.6

Methods of Dispersion. Calculating the standard deviation of prices, the standard deviation of price changes, and the average true range lead to very similar values.

Volatility Breakout Rules

- Upper trigger = *Reference Value* (yesterday's close, today's open, short-term moving average) plus the *Volatility Multiplier* times *Volatility Measure* (standard deviation of price returns, average true range, standard deviation of price). Buy when today's close is greater than the upper trigger.
- Lower trigger = *Reference Value* (yesterday's close, today's open, short-term moving average) plus the *Volatility Multiplier* times *Volatility Measure* (standard deviation of price returns, average true range, standard deviation of price). Sell when today's close is less than the lower trigger

For example, we could use yesterday's close as a reference value, the number one would be a volatility multiplier and a 10-day average true range calculation for a volatility measure. In this volatility breakout system, we would buy if today's close were greater than yesterday's close plus one times the average true range of the past 10 days. Conversely, if today's close were less than yesterday's close minus one times the average true range of the past 10 days, then we would sell the market.

Price Oscillators

Aside from the trend-following techniques mentioned above, there are numerous methods to define when a trend has become overextended or exhausted. These signals fall under a class of techniques called *oscillators*. The majority of oscillators use range statistics to explain where current prices are located within the recent range and attempt to generate sell signals when prices have risen too high and buy signals when prices are too low. Popular oscillators include the Relative Strength Index (RSI), %K stochastics, and Moving Average Convergence/Divergence (MACD). The premise behind standard oscillators is that once prices move to levels far from average, a reversal is eminent.

Relative Strength Index

Introduced by Welles Wilder in the 1978 classic *New Concepts in Technical Trading Systems,* the Relative Strength Index is perhaps the most popular overbought/oversold indicator used in the world today.

According to Wilder, market tops are often completed when the indicator rises above 70, while bottoms are formed during periods when the indicator falls below 30. Today, most practitioners prepare to buy the market on dips below 30, using a rise back above 30 on the indicator as a signal to buy. Conversely, traders will prepare to sell a market when the indicator moves above 70, entering on a cross below 70. The RSI sums the price changes of up days and compares them with price changes on down days to calculate the RSI value. (See Figure 3.7 for an example of the RSI.)

$$RSI = 100 - \frac{100}{1 + \dfrac{U}{D}}$$

where U is the average of all up moves and D is the average of all down moves

Stochastics

The *stochastic* indicator is another oscillator very popular with traders. Popularized by George Lane during the late 1970s and early 1980s, it compares current prices to the high and low range over a look-back period.

$$\text{Raw \%K Stochastics} = \frac{\text{Today's Close} - \text{Lowest Low}}{\text{Highest High} - \text{Lowest Low}}$$

The raw stochastic indicator is usually smoothed using a three-day moving average to form the fast %K stochastic. The fast %K stochastic is smoothed once again using another three-day moving average to form the fast %D stochastic. Long positions are typically taken when the fast %K stochastic rises above 30 and accompanied by a cross above the fast %D stochastic. Short positions are typically taken when the fast %K stochastic falls below 80 and is accompanied by a cross below the fast %D stochastic (see Figure 3.8).

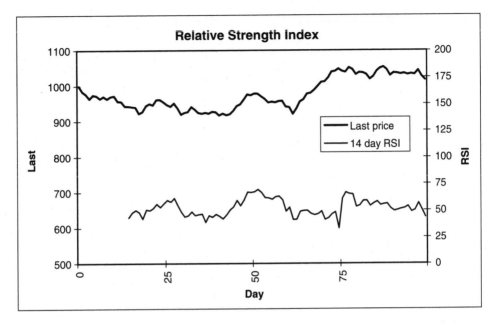

FIGURE 3.7

Relative Strength Index. The Relative Strength Index (RSI) rises and falls between 0 and 100.

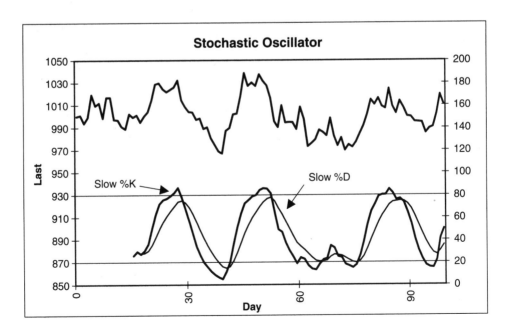

FIGURE 3.8

Stochastic Oscillator. The stochastic oscillator rises and falls between 0 and 100.

Moving Average Convergence/Divergence

The Moving Average Convergence/Divergence (Figure 3.9), developed by Gerald Appel during the 1980s, is an oscillator created by taking the difference between two exponential averages (a 12-day exponentially weighted average with $\alpha = 0.15$, and a 26-day exponential moving average with $\alpha = 0.075$). As the market rallies, the 12-day average will rise faster than the 26-day average, leading to increasing values of the MACD line. Declining markets will lead to declining values of the MACD, as the 12-day average will fall faster than the 26-day average.

An exponential moving average of the MACD (often referred to as the signal line) generates buy and sell signals from crossovers. As the MACD rallies, stalls, and then crosses below its signal line, it indicates that the trend is exhausted and short positions should be entered. Conversely, if the MACD falls, trades flat, and then rallies above the signal line, it indicates that the market is oversold and long positions should be entered.

$$\text{MACD} = \text{12-day EMA of close} - \text{26-day EMA of close}$$
$$\text{MACD Signal} = \text{9-day EMA of MACD}$$

The RSI, stochastics, and MACD are just a smattering of the many oscillators used to determine price exhaustion. Analyst Tom DeMark is a proponent of oscillators and has an interesting theory on their usefulness in identifying price exhaustion

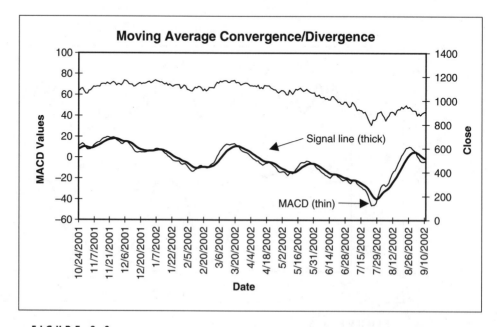

FIGURE 3.9

Moving Average Convergence/Divergence. The MACD and its signal line generate trading signals.

points. DeMark hypothesizes that uptrends continue until the last buyer has bought, and downtrends continue until the last seller has sold. At this point of exhaustion, prices must reverse due to a lack of further buyers or sellers. Using oscillators can help pinpoint these points of trend reversal.

One technique DeMark uses for generating trading signals is to only take signals if oscillators spend a short period of time in overbought or oversold territory. If prices rise and the 14-day RSI climbs above 65 and remains overbought for many days, then the market may be showing its underlying strength. Shorting such a strong market may not be prudent. On the other hand, if prices rise and then fall, with the RSI only remaining above 65 for a period of five days or less before declining and falling below 65, then the market has shown its weakness and short positions should be taken.

Price Patterns

Price pattern entries are the most difficult to define because they can encompass just about anything to generate trading signals. Some price patterns signal trend continuation, while others signal potential market reversals. Patterns can be composed of one or more days of price action.

One popular pattern, a key reversal day, indicates that the market may be turning. A key reversal sell signal is generated when today's high is greater than yesterday's high and today's close is lower than yesterday's close. A key reversal buy is generated when today's low is less than yesterday's low and today's close is higher than yesterday's close (see Figure 3.10).

Other patterns can include a reference to the day of week, in addition to a relationship between today's and previous days' opens, highs, lows, and closes. One of Larry Williams's patterns correctly forecasted the rally of April 17, 2001. The pattern includes two days of setups, with the trade made on the third day.

To enter the S&P 500 long, the close on Day one must be higher than the open. Day two must be Monday, Thursday, or Friday; the high must be lower than the high of the day before; and the low must be higher than the low of the day before. If on Day three the open is less than the high of Day three, then buy the market if prices rise above the high of Day one. While this price pattern is a bit more complex than most, do not be afraid to let your imagination run wild when creating your own pattern trading signals.

TRADING STRATEGY EXITS

Rarely do exits receive the attention they deserve within a complete trading system. In terms of creating a profitable system, they are responsible for converting the edge of entries into closed trade profits. While entries are responsible for creating profitable trades, we need signals to determine when to exit both profitable and unprofitable trades.

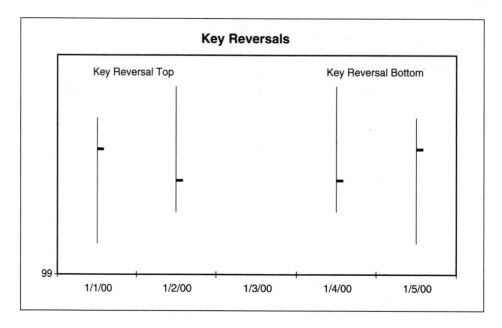

FIGURE 3.10

Key Reversals. Key reversals are one popular chart pattern that generates trading signals.

Typically, signals that close profitable trades are referred to as "exits," while signals that close unprofitable trades are called "stops" or "stop loss signals." Readers should note that I lump exits and stops together into the same category. That's because I believe they serve the same purpose: to maximize profits and minimize losses. A few popular exits include profit targets, trailing stops, and fixed value stop losses.

Profit Targets

Profit targets close profitable trades. They are usually calculated using a range statistic such as standard deviation of prices, standard deviation of closes, or average true range. For example, after buying IBM at $100, we might place a sell exit at three times the average true range of the past 20 days above the entry price of $100 to capture profits. If the average true range is $2, then we would sell IBM at $100 + (3)($2) = $106.

Trailing Exits

If our entry is immediately profitable, it's likely that the significant profits we generate will be at risk if the market turns. We might then give away all our profits and turn a winning trade into a losing one.

Trailing stops can lock in profits after trades start to turn against us. There are a number of methods to accomplish this task. For example, we can exit long positions when the market makes a five-day low. In this case, we are adapting the channel breakout entry into an exit. Also, we can exit long positions when the market closes below the previous pivot point low (see Figure 3.11). Pivot point lows are created when one day's low is lower than both the previous and following day's low. Pivots can be expanding to require multiple days, such that today's low must be lower than both the three days before and three days after.

Another example of a trailing exit is by following the best position profit. In this case, we might exit our trade when the market reversed a set amount from the maximum profit achieved in the trade (see Figure 3.12). The reversal amount can be based on the usual range statistics, such as standard deviation of prices, standard deviation of closes, or an average true range calculation.

For example, we might exit if prices fell three times the average true range of the past 20 days below the highest close while we were long. As long as prices rise while we are long, so too will our trailing stop. Once prices reverse, our trailing stop will become fixed (only changing based on the value of the true range), and if prices fall enough and decline below our stop level, we will exit the long position.

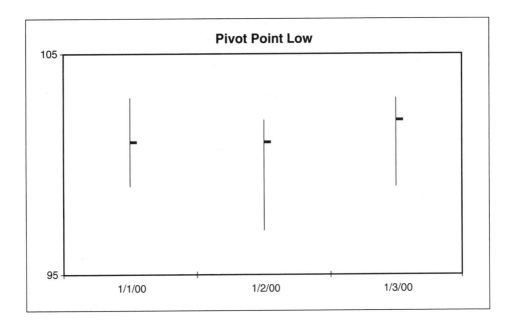

FIGURE 3.11

Pivot Point Low. A pivot point low is generated if the low immediately prior and the low immediately after are higher than the middle day's low.

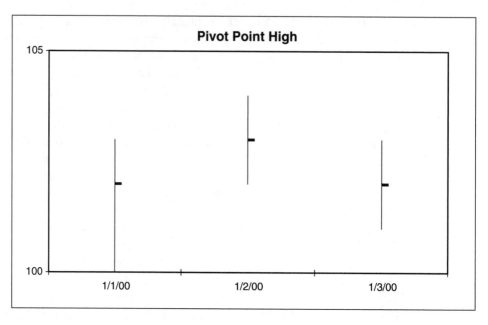

FIGURE 3.12

Pivot Point High. A pivot point high is generated if the high immediately prior and the high immediately after are lower than the middle day's high.

Fail-Safe Exits

Losing is a part of all trading. In the unfortunate event that we are unable to sell at our profit target and our trailing stops are not activated, we may need a fail-safe method of exiting unprofitable trades. We can place a sell order when the trade goes against us by an amount equal to two times the average true range of the past 20 days. If we buy IBM at 100 and the average true range is \$1.50, we would sell if IBM fell below \$97=$(100 - 2 \cdot 1.50)$ to minimize our losses and accept that our entry did not work.

Trading Strategy Filters

While entries and exits get us in and out of the market, there are better times than others to be trading the market. We use filters to determine those times when we should be on the sidelines and ignoring our entry signals. Filters either give the green light to trade or a red light that overrides buy and sell signals.

For example, we might use a trend filter to avoid trading during periods of consolidating markets. We might only take entry signals if the trend filter indicates the market is in trend mode. Popular trend filters include the Average Directional Movement Index (ADX) and the Vertical Horizontal Filter (VHF). Both measure the strength of a trend. A typical use of a filter is to only take signals when values of these filters are greater than some threshold.

CREATING NEW STRATEGIES

When creating new strategies, it's best to start with a trading premise and then mold this theory into concrete trading rules. A typical progression from theory to trading rule follows:

- *Theory*. Large moves are a result of new information entering the markets. This information may not be immediately digested by all market participants.
- *Trading rule*. Buy when today's price change is greater than two standard deviations of the 20-day standard deviation of price changes.

In the above example, we follow the process of formulating a theory, creating an experiment, and drawing conclusions. This scientific method is tremendously important to the development of trading strategy. Using logic to create trading methods helps to avoid the process of curve-fitting data to achieve a desired result, otherwise known as data mining. As we will see later, the pitfall of data mining is the need to overexplain market prices.

Traders are sometimes unsatisfied with profitable trading systems. Instead, they often feel the need to constantly improve strategies by adding complex rules to explain a larger proportion of price movement and thereby increase profitability. In the end, these models often break down in real-time trading due to the extra levels of unwarranted complexity. Throughout this book, we will diligently follow the scientific process of using logic to create, test, and then implement new trading strategies.

The Need for Trading Systems and Plans

In college, I began trading futures with two friends of mine. We opened an account with $3500 (mostly of student loan money) and began to trade multiple futures markets actively. Instead of using tested trading strategies similar to those in this chapter, we blindly chose to buy and sell contracts based on gut feel from price charts and tape reading. This lack of a trading plan hurt in many ways. Not only did we have no confidence that our ideas would be profitable, but we were not prepared for the day-to-day lifestyle associated with trading.

I remember one morning we were trading coffee futures the day of a finance final exam. With the exam stretching the opening of the coffee market, we recruited another dorm mate for trading and wrote detailed instructions to place our orders. The paper looked something like this:

1. At 9:45 call 1-800-xxx-xxxx.
2. Ask for the quote on July coffee.
3. If July coffee is above 155, say, "Buy 1 July coffee at 156 on a stop for account 1234."
4. If July coffee is below 153, say, "Sell 1 July coffee at 152 on a stop for account 1234."

Needless to say, this is not how one should be trading. Recruiting an 18-year-old college freshman (probably hung over from the night before) and asking him to enter important trading orders is downright unprofessional and incompetent. From this trading campaign I learned that following a detailed trading plan based on sound historical results is the only way to trade effectively. And oh yeah, make sure you're awake and sober when placing your trades.

CHAPTER 4

Evaluating Trading Strategy Performance

How to Correctly Assess Performance

Evaluation of a trading strategy can be a very tricky task because strategy performance can often be misleading. Quantitative traders need the correct tools to grade performance. To many traders, these tools are unknown or misunderstood. This chapter will examine the ideas of reward and risk. In the process, we'll introduce robust performance measures and expose the multitude of problems with popular performance statistics.

POPPER'S THEORIES APPLIED TO TRADING

While Karl Popper is regarded as one of the greatest philosophers of the 20th century, his influence on scientists today might be his most enduring legacy. Despite the time that has elapsed since his work, it is remarkable that scientists still praise Popper for the practicality of his philosophical work and the influence it has had in shaping their scientific thought processes.

Popper's main scientific theory focuses on the growth of human knowledge and the methods used in making new discoveries. He was very uneasy with the concept of absolute truth. Instead, he felt that theories, regardless of the scientific discipline, could never be proved. Rather, theories could only be falsified through experiment, with those that are not dispelled chosen as the best explanation available until either disproved or a better theory is discovered.

For example, most academics believe that the random walk is the best explanation of market behavior. Following Popper's lead, the best I can do to improve upon this theory is to show that certain quantitative trading strategies have generated trading profits in the past. But note that by doing so, I have not disproved the random walk theory. What's more, I cannot say for sure whether any strategy will be profitable in the future. If I show that my strategy is profitable over a number of markets and a number of parameter sets, I can then come closer to accepting a new theory that markets are predictable. Then, until I see more data that would refute my theory, or until a better theory comes along, this is the theory I will act upon. The proof of its efficacy is whether I make money in real-time trading.

I believe that Popper's approach is ideal for developing quantitative trading strategies. When developing new strategies, I start with the assumption that the idea will be unprofitable. If rigorous historical back-tests of the idea are profitable, then I'll reject my initial assumption and look closer at the historical back-test data. Similar to Popper's thinking, I can never accept that a strategy is going to be profitable in the future—the best I can do is assume the strategy will be profitable until I find a better strategy or discover problems with historical performance.

The entire process follows the scientific method from theory to hypothesis to experimentation to conclusion. Even when I complete the back-test, I have no guarantee that the strategy will continue to be profitable in the future. I test strategies and discard those with problems such as deteriorating performance over time, logical inconsistencies, or logistical issues in implementing the strategy. If I still have a profitable trading strategy after testing for all these problems, I can expect success in the future. Still, while continued success may be likely, I believe that no strategy will continue to be profitable forever. Markets may change, theories may no longer hold, and systems that were profitable once may have to be discarded for new and better ideas. I can never accept that my trading theory is truth. Popper would be proud.

FLAWS IN PERFORMANCE MEASURES

Today traders use a multitude of performance measures to evaluate trading strategies. Net profit, profit factor (gross profit divided by gross loss), profit to drawdown, and percentage of profitable trades are a few of the many statistics they employ. I believe that each of these measures is flawed. In fact, I rarely look at any of these measures when evaluating my own trading ideas. Let's look at each of these performance measures and critique their characteristics.

Net Profit

Net profit is one of the most widely quoted performance statistics. Simply put, net profit is the dollar profit earned or lost during the life of the back-test. In many ways, it is very important. After all, a strategy that makes money is more desirable than a strategy that loses money. But beyond simply stating whether a system is profitable, net profit does not clarify the performance picture. Without measuring the risk and consistency of the returns, using net profit to judge performance is akin to buying an antique sports car without looking under the hood to determine the engine's condition.

Consider two trading strategies, depicted in the chart in Figure 4.1, which produce the following distributions of weekly returns trading one contract of the S&P 500 futures.

Although both strategies produce an average profit of $500 per week, Strategy B is twice as risky as Strategy A when measured by standard deviation of returns. Some traders might say, "I can stomach risk, so I only care about returns." But with the capabilities of leverage in the stock and futures markets, we can leverage returns by factors often as high as 10:1. In the example shown in Figure 4.2, we again compare Strategy A and Strategy B, only this time by trading two contracts of Strategy A versus only one contract of Strategy B.

Clearly, Strategy A is preferable. Here, both strategies have the same risk, but Strategy A's average profit is now $1000 per week, compared with only $500 per week for Strategy B. The comparison above describes why we must care about risk and why traders who do not respect risk will always run into trouble. Whether we classify ourselves as traders or investors, we always want to maximize the return per unit of risk. Leverage then allows us to scale our risk to a desired level of return.

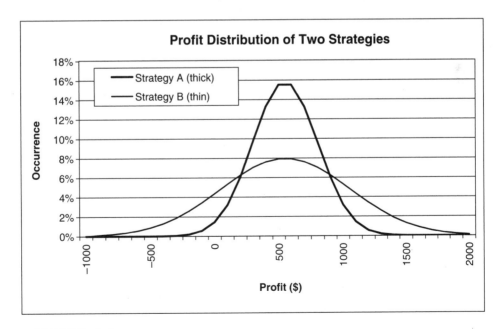

FIGURE 4.1

Profit Distribution of Two Strategies. Both Strategy A and Strategy B generate an average profit of $500 per week. The volatility of each strategy is different.

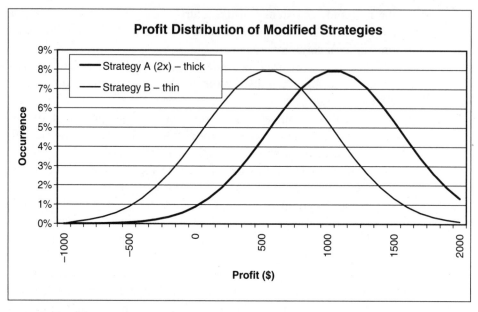

FIGURE 4.2

Profit Distribution of Modified Strategies. When we equalize the volatility by trading Strategy A with 2:1 leverage, we see that it is the preferred strategy.

There are many other reasons why absolute returns are not important. For example, consider two strategies that trade the S&P 500. One is always in the market, and the other attempts to time the market by holding a flat position from time to time. If both produced similar net profit, we would still prefer the latter strategy. It's less risky than the first, due to the smaller amount of time it's exposed to the market.

Another example of the flaw in solely considering net profit can be seen in comparing the returns of various futures contracts. A strategy that makes $50,000 trading one contract of corn might be better than a system that makes $100,000 trading one contract of T-bonds, due to the smaller volatility of the corn futures contract compared to the bond future. As we see in Figure 4.3, the average daily high-to-low range in corn is $200, compared to $800 for the average daily range of the T-bond contract. Since the volatility of the T-bond contract is roughly four times that of corn, one could argue that corn strategy performs much better compared to the overall volatility of each contract.

Profit Factor

Profit factor has also become a popular measure of trading strategy performance, due to its computational simplicity and its inclusion in popular computer programs such as TradeStation. Profit factor is calculated by dividing the total profit gained

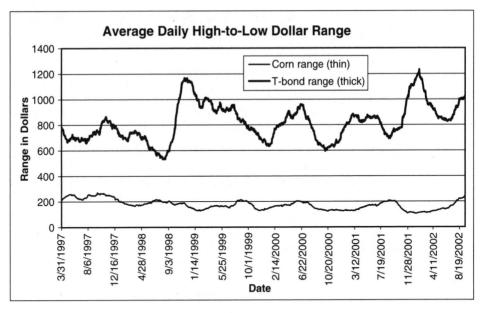

FIGURE 4.3

Average High-to-Low Dollar Range. The volatility of T-bonds and corn are not equivalent. As such, we must factor in a market's volatility when evaluating results.

on winning trades by the total loss on losing trades. If the strategy is profitable, then gross profit will be greater than gross loss and the corresponding profit factor will be greater than one. Unprofitable strategies produce profit factors of less than one. Consider the five trades in Figure 4.4:

Trade Number	Profit/Loss
1	+500
2	−750
3	+250
4	+1000
5	−750
Gross Profit	+1750
Gross Loss	−1500
Profit Factor	1.17

FIGURE 4.4

Calculating Profit Factor. Profit Factor is calculated by dividing Gross Profit by Gross Loss.

The gross profit, calculated by summing all the winning trades, is $1750. The gross loss on all losing trades is −$1500. These trades result in a net profit of

$250 (1750 – 1500). The profit factor is calculated by dividing the gross profit by the gross loss (1750/1500 = profit factor of 1.17).

$$\text{Profit Factor} = \frac{\text{Gross Profit}}{\text{Gross Loss}}$$

Many years ago I used the profit factor performance statistic to grade the system performance of over 100 strategies. After ranking each system by the profit factor statistic, I revisited the best systems and was disappointed with the results of the top ones. Very often, all the profits generated were the result of one large winner, while the bulk of the remaining trades were unprofitable. Many of the systems produced large profits, but the inconsistency of the results made me question each system's effectiveness. As a result, I began a search for a better measure of performance. Eventually, I created a new performance measure, the K-ratio, which we'll look at later in the chapter.

Profit to Drawdown

The ratio of net profit to maximum drawdown is also a popular measure of performance. A drawdown occurs when net profits falls from its highest point. This drawdown is calculated each trading day, and the maximum value is recorded as the maximum drawdown.

In Figure 4.5, the high in equity and the drawdown from that high is recorded each day. The maximum of the daily drawdown numbers will be reported as the maximum drawdown of the equity curve.

Figures 4.6 and 4.7 detail this process graphically. Each day of trading, we tally the highest profit achieved. Anytime the strategy suffers losses, the distance

Day	Equity	Equity High	Drawdown
0	0	0	0
1	−5	0	5
2	−7	0	7
3	−2	0	2
4	5	5	0
5	10	10	0
6	12	12	0
7	5	12	7
8	3	12	9

F I G U R E   4 . 5

Calculating Drawdown. Any day's drawdown is calculated by subtracting the current day's equity with the highest equity up to that point in time.

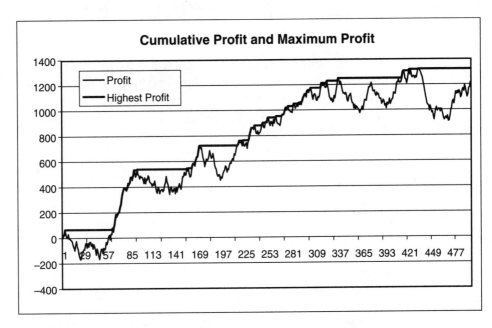

FIGURE 4.6

Cumulative Profit and Maximum Profit. We track the highest profit increases the life of the test. Any retreat from the highest profit is a drawdown.

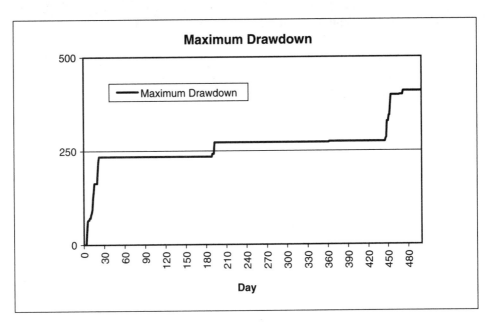

FIGURE 4.7

Maximum Drawdown. The maximum drawdown is computed each day, and it's increased when today's drawdown from an equity high is greater than any prior day's drawdown.

from current profits and maximum profit is recorded as drawdown. Over the life of the test, we keep a running tally of the maximum drawdown since the beginning of trading. Figure 4.6 depicts the current profit and maximum profit over the test. As the current profit declines from the maximum profit, a drawdown occurs. If the drawdown is greater than any before it, then the maximum drawdown in Figure 4.7 increases.

Dividing net profit by maximum drawdown creates a measure of reward to risk. Riskier strategies have larger maximum drawdowns and will lead to lower profit-to-drawdown ratios. There is, however, an overwhelming problem with using the profit-to-drawdown statistic to measure performance across strategies. In a consistent trading strategy, net profit will increase linearly over time. Each period should produce, on average, the same profit. Maximum drawdown, however, does not increase linearly with time.

To show how this works, I used a Monte Carlo simulator to generate the equity curve of 1000 random trials in which the average profit each day was $10, with a standard deviation of $1000. A Monte Carlo simulation involves using a random number generator to create values subject to a user's inputs, such as mean, standard deviation, and distribution of values.

The average of these 1000 trials is shown in Figure 4.8. Note that as expected, the net profit of the simulation rises linearly with time. On average, the test makes roughly the same amount of money each trading day when averaged over 1000 trials. The maximum drawdown, however, does not increase linearly with time. Figure 4.9 shows that the same strategy produces much different profit-to-drawdown ratios, depending on the number of days in the test. This graph details a very large flaw in the profit-to-drawdown ratio. Essentially, using more data in back-tests will lead to higher profit-to-drawdown ratios with all things staying the same. Traders should be aware of this inconsistency when comparing profit-to-drawdown ratios of different performance tests.

The profit-to-drawdown ratio will vary depending on the length of time in the test, despite the static characteristics of the underlying profitability. Due to this flaw, it becomes meaningless to compare profit-to-drawdown measures of strategies tested over differing lengths of time. The profit-to-drawdown ratios of a 5- and a 10-year back-test cannot be compared in an apples to apples manner. One of my requirements for performance measures is the ability to compare various strategies regardless of the time frame studied. Because the profit-to-drawdown statistic does not lend itself to this property, it should not be utilized when evaluating trading performance.

Percent of Profitable Trades

The percentage of profitable trades is another statistic that many use to gauge strategy success. It is the number of winning trades divided by the total number of

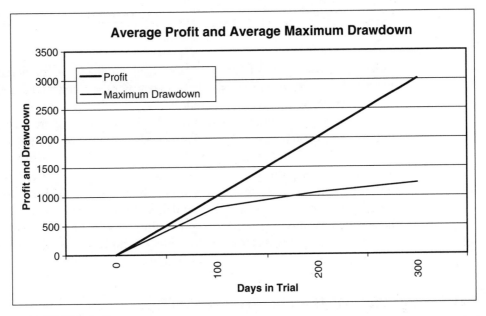

FIGURE 4.8

Average Profit and Maximum Drawdown. While our profit increases linearly with time, maximum drawdown does not.

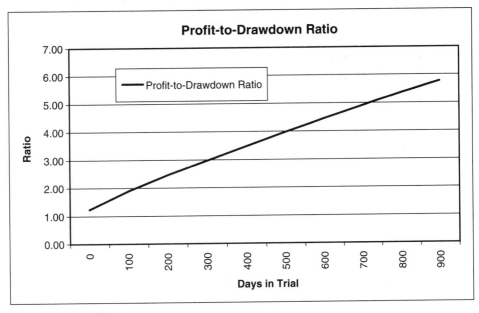

FIGURE 4.9

Profit-to-Drawdown Ratio. The more days, weeks, or months in our strategy test, the higher the profit to drawdown statistic. As such, we cannot compare profit to drawdown statistics for tests using differing numbers of days, weeks, and months.

trades in the back-test. Traders place too much emphasis on the percent of trades that are profitable, and I urge you to throw away the preconceived notion of maximizing the percent of profitable trades.

As we've seen from the studies of behavioral finance, there's a bias in human thinking that closing trades with a profit is good and that taking losses is bad. Personally, I am indifferent as to what percent of trades are profitable. It has no bearing on the performance of my portfolio or my strategies. I choose to think of my profits and losses in the dimension of time, and examine my profit and loss each day. In some ways, I hold the standards of my strategies to a higher level than those who attempt to maximize the probability of winning trades since my goal is to make money every day, rather than in every trade. As such, I use performance evaluation tools that examine my profit and loss on a daily basis.

BETTER MEASURES OF TRADING PERFORMANCE

The two main tools I use to evaluate trading performance are the Sharpe ratio and the K-ratio. Both measures compare reward to risk in order to assess strategy performance. Let's look at them one at a time.

The Sharpe Ratio

Developed by Nobel Laureate William Sharpe, the Sharpe ratio is a standard in the money management industry. The ratio is calculated using two statistical measures we introduced earlier: mean and standard deviation. The numerator—the return portion of the formula—is calculated by averaging returns over time using daily, weekly, or monthly returns. For each period's return, we subtract the return of a risk-free instrument such as short-term Treasury bills. The denominator—the risk portion of the Sharpe ratio—is the standard deviation of returns.

If returns are widely dispersed with both large winners and losers, the strategy would have a high standard deviation and would be considered risky. If returns are wrapped tightly around the mean, the strategy would have a smaller standard deviation and would be considered less risky.

Sharpe ratio = Average return / Standard deviation of returns · Scaling factor

The quotient of average returns and the standard deviation is then multiplied by a scaling factor equal to the square root of time periods in a year. If daily returns are used to calculate the Sharpe ratio, then the raw ratio would be multiplied by the square root of 252 (the approximate number of trading days in a year) to arrive at an annualized value of the Sharpe ratio. If monthly returns are used, the raw ratio would be multiplied by the square root of 12 (12 months in a year). This scaling is required because the expected return increases linearly with time, but standard deviation scales proportionally to the square root of time. After applying the scaling factor to create an annualized Sharpe ratio, the resulting statistic is an apples-to-apples measure of system performance that can compare strategies regardless of the markets traded or time period studied. Whenever testing strategies, a trader's first task should be to calculate the Sharpe ratio. Focus on finding strategies that produce Sharpe ratios greater than positive one.

The Sharpe ratio is not without its faults. Critics have argued (Schwager, 1995) that the performance statistic does not accurately describe performance if autocorrelation exists in returns. Positive autocorrelation exists when positive returns are generally followed by more positive returns and when negative returns are followed by more negative returns. The opposite situation, negative autocorrelation, exists when returns tend to alternate. That is, positive returns are followed by negative returns and negative returns are followed by positive returns.

To understand how this affects performance, consider two systems that both produce 10 months of +$1000 returns and 10 months of –$500 returns. The only difference between the two is the timing of the returns. The first system produces 10 returns of +$1000 followed by 10 returns of –$500—an example of positive autocorrelation. The second system has alternating returns of +$1000 and –$500—an example of negative autocorrelation.

Using just the Sharpe ratio, both systems would be deemed equal. But looking at the graph in Figure 4.10, which system would you rather trade? Clearly, the second system is preferable. The first system may have had its day in the sun, as recent returns have degraded substantially, while the second system is still performing strong.

The K-Ratio

Some years ago I realized that a measure was needed to complement and detect the flaws of the Sharpe ratio such as in the above example. The result was the creation of the K-ratio in 1996. Instead of looking at returns irrespective of when they occur, the K-ratio calculates performance based on the stability of the equity curve.

To calculate the K-ratio we first need to create an equity curve— that is, a graph of cumulative profits over time. To calculate the K-ratio correctly, the equity curve should increase linearly with respect to time. If strategy tests are performed using a constant number of contracts, shares, or dollar risk, we can cumulatively sum each period's return to create the equity curve.

Most traders test their performance in this manner, so no adjustments need to be made to the equity curve. Some traders, however, test performance by reinvesting profits. For systems that invest accumulated profits in new trades by adding contracts or shares as profits accumulate, the equity curve should increase exponentially with respect to time due to the effect of compounding returns. If we take the natural log of this exponentially rising equity curve, the result will be a new adjusted equity curve that will increase linearly with respect to time—exactly what we need for calculating

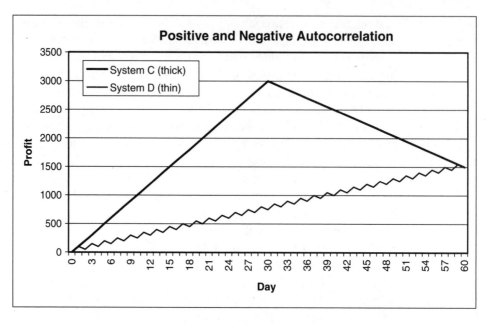

FIGURE 4.10

Positive and Negative Autocorrelation. System C suffers from positive autocorrelation, while System D suffers from negative autocorrelation. While System C and System D have equal Sharpe ratios, the autocorrelation in returns should be taken into account for performance evaluation.

the K-ratio. Again, if risk—dollars, shares, or contracts at risk or traded—is kept constant throughout the life of the test, no adjustments need to be made to the equity curve.

Both the linear and exponential equity curves are depicted in Figure 4.11.

We start by calculating a linear regression of the equity curve to a trend variable. A linear regression is a best fit line that minimizes the squared errors between the forecast and the actual values. The trend variable begins at 0 on the first day (or week or month) of the performance test and increases by one with each new day (or week or month). The slope of the regression line—b_1 in the equation below—is our proxy for reward in the K-ratio. It measures how quickly the equity curve rises over time. Naturally, steeper regression lines indicate a higher level of profitability than that indicated by flatter regression lines.

The regression equation:

$$\text{Equity Curve}_i = b_0 + b_1 \cdot \text{trend}_i$$

Risk in the K-ratio is measured by calculating the standard error of the b_1 regression coefficient. The standard error is a statistic that measures the reliability of the b_1 estimate calculated from the regression. Large standard errors indicate that the slope of the equity curve over time is inconsistent, while small standard errors

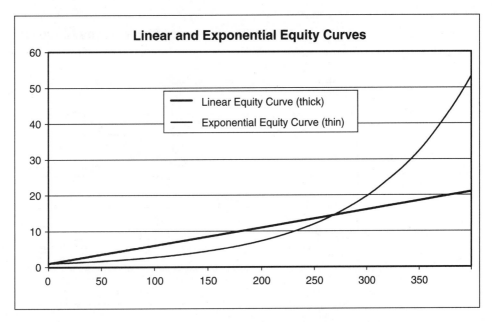

FIGURE 4.11

Linear and Exponential Equity Curves. A linear equity curves increases at a fixed rate by unit of time. An exponential equity curve rises in constant percentage terms and leads to a parabolic rise over time.

indicate a more consistent equity curve. If profits are due to one large winning trade, then standard error will likely be large due to the lack of steady returns.

In the charts following, both strategies produce similar net profit. Figure 4.12's returns are consistently positive over time while the bulk of Figure 4.13's returns are produced from strong periods before day 10. As a result, while the regression slope in the first graph (+0.58) is similar to regression slope in the second graph (+0.55), the standard error (0.02) of Figure 4.12 is much less than Figure 4.13's (0.07). The lower standard error suggests that the returns associated with Figure 4.12 are less risky than the returns associated with Figure 4.13.

The K-ratio is calculated by dividing the b_1 estimate by both the standard error of b_1 and the number of periods in the performance test. By dividing by the number of data points, we normalize the K-ratio to be consistent regardless of the periodicity used to calculate its components.

$$\text{K-ratio} = \frac{b_1}{\sigma_{b1}\, Obs}$$

This process can be completed in a strategy-testing software testing program such as TradeStation or in a spreadsheet such as Microsoft Excel. Figure 4.14 details the Microsoft Excel formulas for calculating the K-ratio.

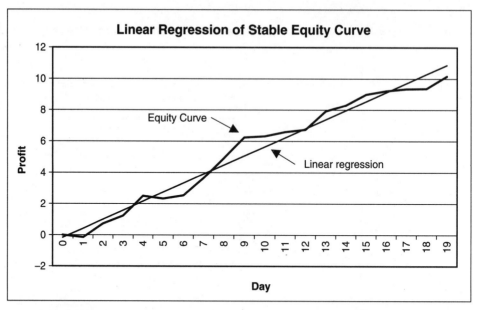

FIGURE 4.12

Linear Regression of Stable Equity Curve. We fit a best fit line to the path of the equity curve in order to generate statistics for calculating the K-ratio. The equity curve above appears to rise consistently over time.

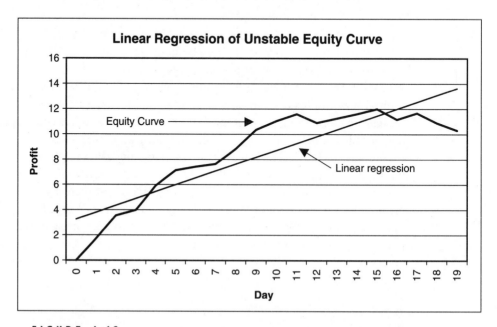

FIGURE 4.13

Linear Regression of Unstable Equity Curve. The equity curve above performs well in the first half but then flattens towards the end of the test.

Day	System 1	System 2
0	0.00	0.00
1	− 0.15	1.76
2	0.72	3.55
3	1.23	3.99
4	2.50	5.90
5	2.33	7.13
6	2.54	7.41
7	3.63	7.64
8	4.91	8.84
9	6.25	10.35
10	6.32	11.05
11	6.60	11.59
12	6.75	10.90
13	7.92	11.25
14	8.30	11.60
15	9.00	11.99
16	9.22	11.16
17	9.36	11.67
18	9.37	10.89
19	10.17	10.30
b1	=SLOPE(B2:B21,$A2:$A21)	=SLOPE(C2:C21,$A2:$A21)
s.e. b1	=STEYX(B2:B21,$A2:$A21) / SQRT(DEVSQ($A2:$A21))	=STEYX(C2:C21,$A2:$A21)/ SQRT(DEVSQ($A2:$A21))
Observations	20	20
K-ratio	=B22/(B23*A24)	=C22/(C23*A24)
b1	0.58	0.55
s.e. b1	0.02	0.07
K-ratio	1.32	0.40

FIGURE 4.14

Excel formulas for calculating the K-ratio. The K-ratio can be calculated in Excel using the above formulas.

The K-ratio is a unitless measure of performance that can be compared across markets and time periods. Weekly performance of corn futures can be compared with tick data performance of trading IBM. Traders should search for strategies yielding K-ratios greater than +0.50. Together, the Sharpe ratio and K-ratio are the most important measures when evaluating trading strategy performance.

Note: When I created the K-ratio in 1996, I thought I had created a robust measure to evaluate performance. In mid-2000, trader Bob Fuchs brought a small error to my attention regarding the scaling of the K-ratio. He was correct in his critique and I have corrected the error in this text. Publications prior to 2002 will show a different formula for the K-ratio. The updated formula in this book is correct.

COMPARISON OF BENCHMARK STRATEGIES

We've identified our primary measures of trading strategy performance: the Sharpe and K-ratios. In addition to these two, we will use a number of benchmark strategies to evaluate new ideas.

Channel breakouts and *moving average crossover* systems are among the most popular strategies used by traders today. The performance of both trend-following methods has been documented in trade publications and academic journals. When testing any new idea, we will always compare performance to these two strategies. In my *Comparison of Popular Trading Strategies,* I found that an overwhelming majority of new strategies actually underperformed the simple channel breakout and moving average crossover methodologies.

For the channel breakout, we use the following rules:

- Enter long if today's close is the highest close of the past 40 days.
- Exit long if today's close is the lowest close of the past 20 days.
- Enter short if today's close is the lowest close of the past 40 days.
- Exit short if today's close is the highest close of the past 20 days.

Similar parameters are used for the moving average crossover:

- Enter long if the 10-day simple moving average of closes crosses above the 40-day simple moving average of closes.
- Enter short if the 10-day simple moving average of closes crosses below the 40-day simple moving average of closes.

The channel breakout and moving average crossover systems are our benchmarks for any new strategy performance. We will calculate the Sharpe ratio and K-ratio of the channel breakout and moving average crossover strategies over a portfolio of markets for comparison to the new ideas we will create in the second half of this book.

PERFORMANCE EVALUATION TEMPLATES

Readers need to become accustomed to the performance evaluation templates that will be featured frequently throughout this book. Strategy performance will be presented in two sections using a combination of tables and graphs. The two sections are the Summary page and the Breakdown Statistics page, each of which we will examine in detail.

Summary Page

The name and description of the strategy tested, as well as the type of markets the strategy has been tested on (futures, stocks, or relative value), is located at the top of the Summary page (Figure 4.15a).

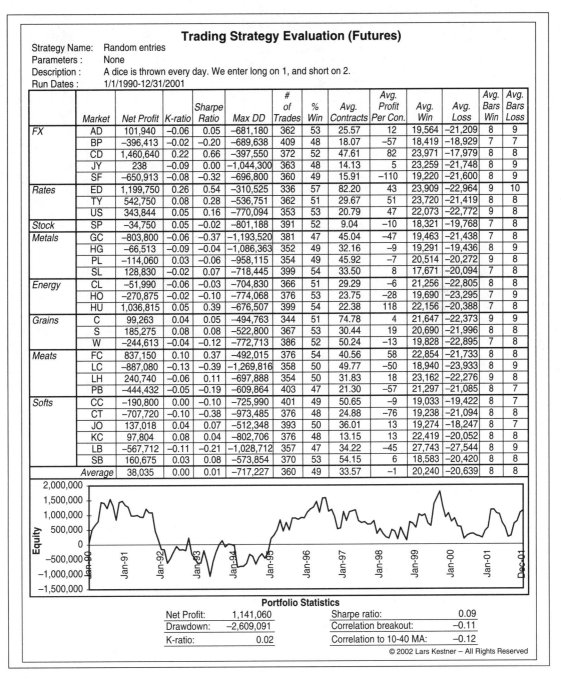

Trading Strategy Evaluation (Futures)

Strategy Name: Random entries
Parameters :   None
Description :   A dice is thrown every day. We enter long on 1, and short on 2.
Run Dates :   1/1/1990-12/31/2001

	Market	Net Profit	K-ratio	Sharpe Ratio	Max DD	# of Trades	% Win	Avg. Contracts	Avg. Profit Per Con.	Avg. Win	Avg. Loss	Avg. Bars Win	Avg. Bars Loss
FX	AD	101,940	−0.06	0.05	−681,180	362	53	25.57	12	19,564	−21,209	8	9
	BP	−396,413	−0.02	−0.20	−689,638	409	48	18.07	−57	18,419	−18,929	7	7
	CD	1,460,640	0.22	0.66	−397,550	372	52	47.61	82	23,971	−17,979	8	8
	JY	238	−0.09	0.00	−1,044,300	363	48	14.13	5	23,259	−21,748	8	9
	SF	−650,913	−0.08	−0.32	−696,800	360	49	15.91	−110	19,220	−21,600	8	9
Rates	ED	1,199,750	0.26	0.54	−310,525	336	57	82.20	43	23,909	−22,964	9	10
	TY	542,750	0.08	0.28	−536,751	362	51	29.67	51	23,720	−21,419	8	8
	US	343,844	0.05	0.16	−770,094	353	53	20.79	47	22,073	−22,772	9	8
Stock	SP	−34,750	0.05	−0.02	−801,188	391	52	9.04	−10	18,321	−19,768	7	8
Metals	GC	−803,800	−0.06	−0.37	−1,193,520	381	47	45.04	−47	19,463	−21,438	7	8
	HG	−66,513	−0.09	−0.04	−1,086,363	352	49	32.16	−9	19,291	−19,436	8	9
	PL	−114,060	0.03	−0.06	−958,115	354	49	45.92	−7	20,514	−20,272	9	8
	SL	128,830	−0.02	0.07	−718,445	399	54	33.50	8	17,671	−20,094	7	8
Energy	CL	−51,990	−0.06	−0.03	−704,830	366	51	29.29	−6	21,256	−22,805	8	8
	HO	−270,875	−0.02	−0.10	−774,068	376	53	23.75	−28	19,690	−23,295	7	9
	HU	1,036,815	0.05	0.39	−676,507	399	54	22.38	118	22,156	−20,388	7	8
Grains	C	99,263	0.04	0.05	−494,763	344	51	74.78	4	21,647	−22,373	9	9
	S	185,275	0.08	0.08	−522,800	367	53	30.44	19	20,690	−21,996	8	8
	W	−244,613	−0.04	−0.12	−772,713	386	52	50.24	−13	19,828	−22,895	7	8
Meats	FC	837,150	0.10	0.37	−492,015	376	54	40.56	58	22,854	−21,733	8	8
	LC	−887,080	−0.13	−0.39	−1,269,816	358	50	49.77	−50	18,940	−23,933	8	9
	LH	240,740	−0.06	0.11	−697,888	354	50	31.83	18	23,162	−22,276	9	8
	PB	−444,432	−0.05	−0.19	−609,864	403	47	21.30	−57	21,297	−21,085	8	7
Softs	CC	−190,800	0.00	−0.10	−725,990	401	49	50.65	−9	19,033	−19,422	8	7
	CT	−707,720	−0.10	−0.38	−973,485	376	48	24.88	−76	19,238	−21,094	8	8
	JO	137,018	0.04	0.07	−512,348	393	50	36.01	13	19,274	−18,247	8	7
	KC	97,804	0.08	0.04	−802,706	376	48	13.15	13	22,419	−20,052	8	8
	LB	−567,712	−0.11	−0.21	−1,028,712	357	47	34.22	−45	27,743	−27,544	8	9
	SB	160,675	0.03	0.08	−573,854	370	53	54.15	6	18,583	−20,420	8	8
	Average	38,035	0.00	0.01	−717,227	360	49	33.57	−1	20,240	−20,639	8	8

Portfolio Statistics

Net Profit:	1,141,060	Sharpe ratio:	0.09
Drawdown:	−2,609,091	Correlation breakout:	−0.11
K-ratio:	0.02	Correlation to 10-40 MA:	−0.12

© 2002 Lars Kestner – All Rights Reserved

F I G U R E   4 . 1 5 a

Sample performance evaluation. These sheets will be commonplace throughout the book.

Breakdown Statistics (Futures)

System Name: 0
Parameters: 0
Description: 0
Run Dates: 1/1/1990 – 12/31/2001

Breakdown by Market Sector

Market Sector	Average Net Profit	Average K-ratio	Average Sharpe Ratio	Average Max DD	Average Num Trades	Average % Win	Avg. Profit Per Contract	Average Win	Average Loss	Avg. Bars Win	Avg. Bars Loss
FX	103,099	-0.01	0.04	-701,894	373	50	-14	20,887	-20,293	8	8
Rates	521,586	0.10	0.24	-404,342	263	40	35	17,426	-16,789	6	6
Stock	-34,750	0.05	-0.02	-801,188	391	52	-10	18,321	-19,768	7	8
Metals	-213,886	-0.04	-0.10	-989,111	372	50	-14	19,235	-20,310	8	8
Energy	237,983	-0.01	0.09	-718,468	380	53	28	21,034	-22,163	8	8
Grains	13,308	0.03	0.00	-596,758	366	52	3	20,722	-22,421	8	8
Meats	-63,406	-0.03	-0.02	-767,396	373	50	-8	21,563	-22,257	8	8
Softs	-178,456	-0.01	-0.08	-769,516	379	49	-16	21,048	-21,130	8	8

Performance Breakdown by Year

Year	Net Profit	K-ratio	Sharpe Ratio
1990	1,267,751	.027	1.07
1991	-1,491,321	-0.30	-1.86
1992	-472,399	-0.03	-0.50
1993	586,055	0.26	0.56
1994	240,809	0.14	0.23
1995	896,329	0.43	1.10

Year	Net Profit	K-ratio	Sharpe Ratio
1996	10,522	-0.16	0.01
1997	-581,404	-0.35	-0.76
1998	35,610	0.11	0.04
1999	204,140	0.08	0.16
2000	-212,371	-0.17	-0.35
2001	586,720	-0.03	0.61

Length	Number of Windows	Num. of Profitable Windows	Percent Profitable
1 Month	144	75	52.08%
3 Months	142	74	52.11%
6 Months	139	72	51.80%
12 Months	133	62	46.62%
18 Months	127	61	48.03%
24 Months	121	55	45.45%

Net Profit by Year

© 2002 Lars Kestner – All Rights Reserved

F I G U R E   4 . 1 5 b

Sample performance evaluation. These sheets will be commonplace throughout the book.

Below the title and description are performance statistics of each individual market:

Net Profit: Total profit over the life of the test, including trades still open

K-ratio: K-ratio of that market's equity curve over the life of the test

Sharpe Ratio: Sharpe ratio of that market's returns over the life of the test

Max DD: Maximum dollar drawdown over the life of the test for that specific market.

# of Trades: Number of round-trip trades executed over the life of the test

% Win: Percentage of trades closed with a profit

Avg. Contracts: Average number of contracts or shares executed per trade

Avg. Profit per Contract: Net profit divided by the product of the number of trades and the average number of contracts or shares per trade; measures the average profit per trade per contract or share traded

Avg. Win: Average dollar profit on winning trades

Avg. Loss: Average dollar profit on losing trades

Avg. Bars Win: Average number of periods (usually days) winning trades were held

Avg. Bars Loss: Average number of periods (usually days) losing trades were held

Below the individual market statistics is a column labeled "Average," which averages each statistic over all markets. The bottom of the summary page contains a graph of the portfolio equity curve over the life of the test. The portfolio equity curve sums the individual equity curves over all markets tested. Along with the portfolio equity curve, the following portfolio performance statistics are also calculated:

Net Profit: Total profit across all markets

Drawdown: Maximum dollar drawdown the portfolio experienced over the life of the test

K-ratio: K-ratio of the portfolio's monthly equity curve

Sharpe ratio: Sharpe ratio of the portfolio's monthly returns

Note: The K-ratio and Sharpe ratio for the portfolio will typically be higher in absolute magnitude than the average of the markets individually. This occurs due to benefits of diversification, which we will discuss in the next chapter.

Correlation to breakout: Monthly returns from the system are compared with monthly returns from the 40-day/20-day channel breakout; the correlation among returns is calculated

Correlation to MA: Correlation of monthly returns between the system tested and the 10-day/40-day moving average crossover

Breakdown Statistics Page

The Breakdown Statistics page groups performance based on market themes:

Breakdown by Market Sector: An average of performance statistics across a sector of markets grouped by commodity type or stock industry. This allows for quick and easy analysis by market sector.

Performance Breakdown by Year: This table displays net profit, K-ratios, and Sharpe ratios of the portfolio for each year individually. These results allow us to judge the consistency of a strategy over time.

Profitability Windows: When performance is broken into time intervals, it's usually done by looking at calendar year returns. Why, though, do we use January-to-December returns instead of July-June returns? Or more specifically, why 12 months instead of six? Profitability windows break performance into tighter measurement intervals. For example, a three-month profitability window begins by summing the returns of months one, two, and three. The window is slid forward one month, and the net profit of months two, three, and four are summed. This number is recorded, and again the window moves one month forward. This process continues until the end of the performance test. The percentage profitable statistic measures the percentage of windows that were profitable. Windows are calculated with lengths of one, three, six, 12, 18, and 24 months.

Perhaps the most relevant information on the Breakdown Statistics page is the graph of Net Profit by Year, where we can examine the performance of the system on a year by year basis graphically. This graph can reveal if the strategy's edge is diminishing over time.

THE "HALF LIFE" OF STRATEGY PERFORMANCE

Some traders have questioned whether a strategy could work indefinitely or if all trading strategies are doomed to fail once enough traders begin to exploit the specific inefficiency. My best guess is that performance of any trading strategy will degrade over time, similar to a nuclear particle that decays exponentially over time.

"Half life" is a term borrowed from chemistry and physics. It refers to the length of time it takes for half the amount of a radioactive element to change into a nonradioactive substance through the nuclear decay process. I believe that the performance of trading strategies, like radioactive elements, is constantly decaying over time. With all the resources allocated to research, and enough people looking at trading strategies, sooner or later someone will find your Holy Grail. This diamond in the rough will be found by someone else, and eventually performance will suffer due to a crowding out effect.

Trend-following has been a mainstay for traders across the world for many years. The phase "always trade with the trend" is a trading mantra. Although history has shown trend-following to be profitable, can we expect it to continue? In the second edition of my *Comparison of Popular Trading Systems*, I predicted that trend-following traders might be in for some trouble in coming years. That was exactly the case. In fact, Barclays Systematic Traders Index had some of its worst returns in 1999 and 2001 (Figure 4.16).

How did I know subpar returns were ahead for trend followers? Look at the net profit by year for the channel breakout and moving average crossover strategies in Figures 4.17 and 4.18. Although almost every year between 1990 and 1998 was profitable, the size of the profits was decreasing. Actually, if we projected profits forward, annual net profit was expected to reach zero by 1999 or 2000. This below average profitability is exactly what occurred in 1998 through 2000.

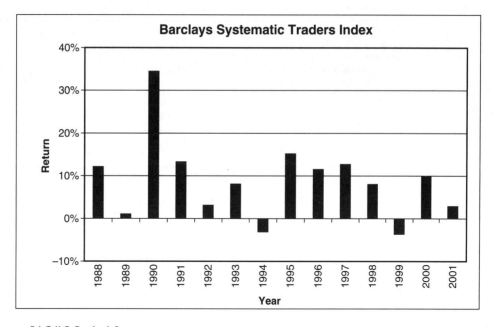

FIGURE 4.16

Barclays Systematic Traders Index. Systematic traders had below average returns during 1999 and 2001.

Why did the performance of trend-following systems run into trouble? It could be due to too much money trading trend-following strategies. It could be that in this information age, business cycles and price cycles have shortened, thereby causing trends to last weeks, not months. It could have been bad luck that caused the bad performance. Whatever the reason, our performance studies successfully predicted the rough time to come.

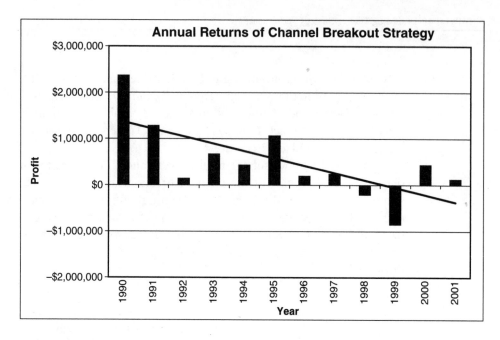

FIGURE 4.17

Annual Returns of Channel Breakout Strategy. Annual returns of a 40-day entry/20-day exit channel breakout declined throughout the 1990s.

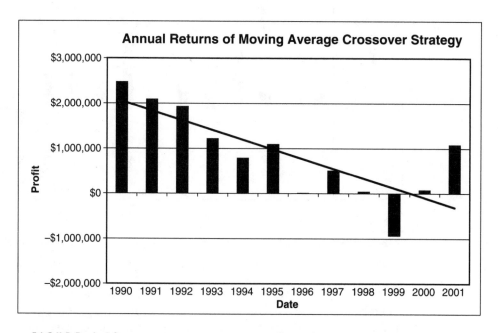

FIGURE 4.18

Annual Returns of Moving Average Crossover Strategy. Annual returns of a 10-day/40-day moving average crossover strategy decline throughout the 1990s.

WHAT TO DO WHEN STRATEGIES DETERIORATE

Even if a strategy's performance is deteriorating, it does not make that strategy useless. In many cases we will still want to trade the system, but closely monitor the continuing degradation of performance.

When do we stop using a system?

One method I use to determine cutoff points is to calculate a linear regression of the equity curve along with bands plotted two standard errors above and below the forecast's fit (see Figure 4.19). I use the standard error of the regression—a statistic which measures the goodness of the model's fit—to create these bands. When the equity curve breaks the lower channel, trading of the strategy should be halted and a decision must be made either to scrap the strategy or modify its workings to alleviate further performance deterioration.

GOLD MINES OF BAD PERFORMANCE

Often during the testing process, I'll find a strategy whose performance is so dreadful that I really get excited. Any strategy that performs poorly and produces trading losses can always be reversed to generate profits. To accomplish this, simply buy when the basic strategy signals a sale and sell when the system generates

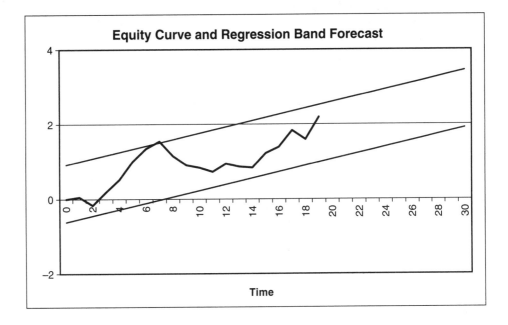

FIGURE 4.19

Equity Curve and Regression Band Forecast. We can forecast equity growth using past data. If equity falls below the lower band, we must reevaluate the potential of the strategy.

a buy. This is one reason I do not deduct charges for commissions and slippage in my strategy testing. I prefer to look at the true performance of a strategy first, and then scale down expectations due to trading costs in later performance tests.

OTHER TESTING METHODS

There are a few other methods for testing strategy performance I occasionally use in specific circumstances. Some trading strategies may produce profits due solely to an overall rising or falling underlying market. For example, many methods of trading the S&P 500 may profit because that market has a positive drift over time, not because the system is able to spot market inefficiencies.

The past few years aside, the S&P 500 has returned, on average, 8 to 12 percent per year. For a spot check to see if a strategy is outperforming the inherent returns of being long the S&P 500, I regress the strategy's returns on both the S&P 500's returns and squared returns. This method, first suggested by Jack Treynor and Kay Mazuy in 1956, measures the ability of a strategy to produce profits regardless of the market's overall drift.

$$\text{return}_{\text{strategy}} = b_0 + b_1\,\text{return}_{\text{market}} + b_2\,\text{return}_{\text{market}}{}^2 + \epsilon$$

I look at the significance of t-statistic of the b_2 coefficient to determine the validity of the system. If the t-statistic is less than +1, then chances are the strategy's performance is due only to the market's runup or decline. If the t-statistic is greater than one, then the strategy can be considered valid and not biased by the market's movement in one direction or another.

THE FALLACY OF MAGICAL THINKING

Psychologist B. F. Skinner (1948) carried out a number of experiments in which he noted a phenomenon called "magical thinking." Skinner fed pigeons on fixed 15-second intervals and noted changes in their behavior over time. He found that each bird would begin to repeat specific behaviors (head twitching, turning in circles), and theorized that it had to do with a learned response to the reception of food. Despite being fed at regular intervals, the birds associated the appearance of food with whatever random behavior they were performing at the time of the first feeding. As a result, they continued to perform this behavior. While the pigeons might believe that their "magical behavior" is the force creating the food, in reality the process is controlled by an entirely different power—the experimenter.

I have no doubt that there is much "magical thinking" in the markets as well. Many traders utilize trading strategies without evaluating their historical performance. Traders rationalize that if a strategy worked once or twice in the past, then the methodology must be valid. Inevitably, these methods cause large losses, since they possess no expected edge. The quantitative trader who carefully and rigorously evaluates his trading methodology should not suffer a similar fate.

CHAPTER 5

Performance of Portfolios

Maintaining Returns While Decreasing Risk

By diversifying our trading over multiple markets, multiple strategies, and multiple parameters within the same strategy, we can reduce the overall risk of our trading. While casinos have used the principles of diversification for hundreds of years, the finance community has only utilized these powerful tools for the past 50 years.

LESSONS LEARNED FROM A CASINO

Although I'm not a big gambler, I do make my way to Las Vegas or Atlantic City at least a couple times a year. Despite knowing that it's unlikely that I'll win, I still like to play blackjack. I do know that if I play correctly, I expect to lose 0.5 percent of the total money I bet on the tables in any given night; the fates and fortune are responsible in deciding which side actually prevails once the money is on the table.

Here's something to consider: If winning or losing at the tables is due to luck, then should the pit bosses (those super serious ladies and gentlemen employed by the casino to keep track of the amount of your bets) be worried that I walk away a winner? After all, if I have won, then their employer, the casino, has lost.

In fact, the pit bosses are completely indifferent as to whether I win or lose. Because of the principles of diversification, the casino is indifferent as to whether any single customer makes money. Each single bet is virtually irrelevant in the grand scheme of the casino's profit and loss. Because bets are uncorrelated with other bets, good luck and bad luck will tend to cancel over time and leave the house with the goodies—the natural edge in its negative expectancy betting games.

THE BENEFITS OF DIVERSIFICATION

In a simple game where we flip coins to determine winners and losers, I flip a coin in the air and record which side of the coin lands faceup. If the coin lands on heads, you pay me $1.00. If the coin lands on tails, I pay you $1.00.

To turn the percentages in my favor I'd need a magic coin. For example's sake, suppose I found a coin that would turn up as heads approximately 55 percent and tails 45 percent of the time.

First, let's calculate my expected edge of playing this game. In any game where there are two outcomes, we measure the edge by multiplying the probability of winning by the dollar amount of the winning payoff, then adding the probability of losing multiplied by the dollar amount of the losing payout:

Edge = Probability of winning · Amount if won + Probability of losing ·
    Amount if loss

In our game above, the probability of winning is 55 percent, the winning payout is $1.00, the probability of losing is 45 percent, and the losing payout is –$1.00. Plugging these values into our equation yields our edge on each coin flip:

Edge = Probability of winning · Amount if won + Probability of losing ·
    Amount if loss
Edge = 0.55 · 1 + 0.45 · –1 = 0.10

The expected edge of playing this game is $0.10. That is, I should expect to make $0.10 each time I play. However, on any given toss I have no idea if I'm going to win or lose. Now suppose we agree to play this coin game under three scenarios:

1. We play the game 10 times, betting $1.00 on each flip
2. We play the game 100 times, betting $0.10 on each flip
3. We play the game 1000 times, betting $.01 on each flip

At the end of each scenario, we tally up the wins and losses and settle up the cash value. Using statistics, I calculate that I have the identical edge under each scenario.

- In Game 1, my expected value for each flip is 55 percent · (+$1.00) + 45 percent · (–$1.00) = $0.10. Multiplied by the 10 times we agree to play, my total expected edge is $1.00.
- In Game 2, my expected value for each flip is 55 percent · (+$0.10) + 45 percent · (–$0.10) = $0.01. Multiplied by 100, my total expected edge is $1.00.
- In Game 3, my expected value for each flip is 55 percent · (+$0.01) + 45 percent · (–$0.01) = $0.001. Multiplied by 1000, my total expected edge is $1.00.

While my expected value in each strategy is equal, the risk of each strategy is not the same. After all the coin tosses are counted, I will win money 50 percent of the time playing Scenario 1, 82 percent of the time playing Scenario 2, and 99.9 percent of the time playing Scenario 3. The varying risks associated with each game have to do with the diversification of the risk of flipping the coin.

In Scenario 1, I have the ability to lose all ten coin flips, resulting in a loss of $10. The probability of this happening is 0.45^{10}, or 0.03 percent. In Scenario 2, I can also lose $10, but to do so I must lose 100 flips. The probability of this event is 0.45^{100}, which is so small that it requires scientific notation to express its value. In Scenario 3, it would take flipping 1000 tails in a row to lose $10. This probability ($0.45^{1000}$) is so small that calculating usually generates errors on most PCs. As you can see in Figure 5.1 below, by flipping more and more times, it becomes more and more unlikely that the adverse event of losing $10 occurs.

While the probability of losing $10 becomes less likely as the number of flips is increased and the bet size is decreased, so too does the probability of winning $10. The probability distributions of the winnings associated with the three games are displayed in Figure 5.2. As the number of flips increases and the size of each bet decreases, the distribution of our profit and loss narrows and eventually converges at $1. The casino mimics this example every day. Although any single bet is

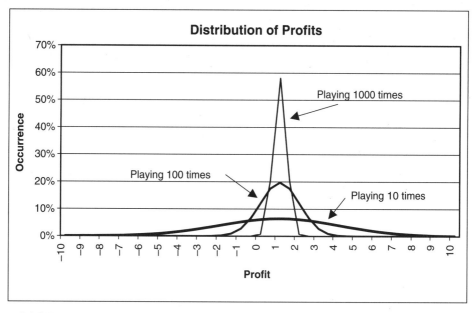

FIGURE 5.1

Distribution of Profits. The distribution of profits is higher depending on how many times we play the game.

Outcome	10 flips	100 flips	1000 filps
−10 to −8	0.4502%	0.0000%	0.0000%
−8 to −6	2.2890%	0.0000%	0.0000%
−6 to −4	7.4603%	0.0000%	0.0000%
−4 to −2	15.9568%	0.1820%	0.0000%
−2 to 0	23.4033%	18.0908%	0.0847%
0 to +2	23.8367%	68.3018%	99.8518%
+2 to +4	16.6478%	13.3494%	0.0635%
+4 to +6	7.6303%	0.0760%	0.0000%
+6 to +8	2.0724%	0.0000%	0.0000%
+8 to +10	0.2533%	0.0000%	0.0000%

FIGURE 5.2

Table of Distribution of Profits. The distribution of profits is higher depending on how many times we play the game.

largely random, the casino's edge is quite predictable when spread over many independent bets.

If each of the three scenarios generates the same expected return, then our true preference is to engage in the scenario with the least amount of risk. We see that as we spread our risk around many smaller bets, our risk is diminished. When I play blackjack at a casino, my bet is so inconsequential compared to all the money changing hands that night, that my good fortune is more than likely going to be canceled by some poor fellow's bad luck. Actually, the casino's biggest risk is a high roller whose bets are so large that they overwhelm the diversification of the smaller bettors. Sound familiar to trading?

DON'T PUT ALL YOUR EGGS IN ONE BASKET

Although the practice of diversification has been employed for thousands of years by casinos and betting houses, the concept is relatively new in the world of finance. In the early 1900s stocks with risky business outlooks and bonds with less than ideal credit standing were largely avoided due to their risk. Harry Markowitz, a University of Chicago graduate student, began to think about this problem in the 1950s within a completely quantitative framework. His work has led him to the title "Father of Modern Finance" and the 1990 Nobel Prize in Economics. In a nutshell, Markowitz asked the following:

> If stock A returns on average 10 percent per year with annualized standard deviation of 20 percent, and stock B returns on average 10 percent per year with annualized standard deviation of 20 percent, then what is the return and risk of holding a portfolio of 50 percent stock A and 50 percent stock B?

The expected return of the 50-50 portfolio is still 10 percent. As it turns out, if stock A and B are not correlated, then the risk of the 50-50 portfolio is reduced to a standard deviation of 14 percent, lower than the 20 percent standard deviation of any stock by itself.

Markowitz's work led to a complete rethinking of the value of risky assets. If we can package stocks with risky prospects into a diversified portfolio, then we might be able to reduce most of the risk due to any one company. The result is a portfolio with less risk than any single asset within the portfolio. In essence, we have accomplished exactly what the casino achieved by diversifying risk.

$$\text{Variance of a portfolio} = \sum_{i=1}^{n} \sum_{j=1}^{n} \omega_i \omega_j \sigma_i \sigma_j \rho_{i,j}$$

where ω_i is the percentage weight of asset i, ω_j is the percentage weight of asset j, σ_i is the standard deviation of asset i, σ_j is the standard deviation of asset j, and $\rho_{i,j}$ is the correlation between returns of asset i and asset j

The primary driver of diversification is the correlation among assets. If everyone in a casino wins when I win at the blackjack table, then the casino is in for a very long night. However, if my performance is completely independent of all other bettors' performance, then diversification is at its best.

Figure 5.3 illustrates the effectiveness of diversification. We analyze a portfolio containing anywhere from one to 1000 stocks, each with an annualized standard deviation of 20 percent. The correlation among all stocks in the portfolio ranges from 0.00 to 1.00.

Number of stocks	Correlation among stocks				
	1.00	0.75	0.50	0.25	0.00
1	20%	20%	20%	20%	20%
5	20%	18%	15%	13%	9%
10	20%	18%	15%	11%	6%
50	20%	17%	14%	10%	3%
100	20%	17%	14%	10%	2%
500	20%	17%	14%	10%	1%
1000	20%	17%	14%	10%	1%

FIGURE 5.3

Volatility of a Portfolio. As the number of stocks within a portfolio increase, the volatility of the portfolio decreases. As the correlation decreases among stocks, the volatility of the portfolio also decreases.

As we see, when correlation among stocks is 0.25 or lower, adding as few as 10 stocks can reduce overall portfolio volatility dramatically. However, with correlations of 0.75 and higher, the so-called benefits of diversification are muted.

The remainder of this chapter will focus on combining uncorrelated trading strategies with positive expected returns within a portfolio to minimize risk.

THE BEST DIVERSIFICATION: ACROSS MARKETS

The same logic and mathematics that Harry Markowitz applied to stocks can also be applied to quantitative strategies in the stock and futures markets. In a basic example, we will look at the performance of a moving average crossover strategy when tested on nine futures markets. Markets tested include Japanese yen, Swiss franc, eurodollars, T-bonds, crude oil, corn, cotton, coffee, and sugar. Buy signals are generated when today's 10-day simple moving average is greater than today's 40-day simple moving average. Shorts are entered when today's 10-day simple moving average is less than today's 40-day simple moving average. Figure 5.4 depicts both the individual market and portfolio performance statistics.

The portfolio produces reward-to-risk performance statistics superior to any of the individual markets. The K-ratio of the portfolio's equity curve (0.31) is greater than the K-ratio of all but one market (Japanese yen). The Sharpe ratio of the portfolio's equity curve (1.30) is greater than the Sharpe ratio of any single market contained in the portfolio.

These performance numbers show that even if we knew in advance which market would perform the best, we would still prefer to trade the portfolio over any single market since our risk-to-reward statistics are maximized by utilizing the benefits of diversification. The portfolio's results are achieved without any foresight as to which markets will perform best in the future. And as appealing as this

Market	Net Profit	K-ratio	Sharpe Ratio
JY	$1,582,763	0.52	0.77
SF	$673,875	0.13	0.35
ED	$2,865,075	0.17	1.00
US	$619,531	0.12	0.30
CL	$968,880	0.10	0.42
C	$741,025	0.16	0.30
CT	$629,190	0.06	0.30
KC	$1,033,564	0.15	0.34
SB	$360,606	0.04	0.19
Average	$1,052,723	0.16	0.44
Portfolio	$9,474,509	0.31	1.30

FIGURE 5.4

Performance of Varying Markets. The performance of the portfolio exceeds the performance of any individual markets.

Correlation	JY	SF	ED	US	CL	C	CT	KC	SB
JY	1.00								
SF	0.14	1.00							
ED	−0.01	0.13	1.00						
US	−0.13	0.11	0.22	1.00					
CL	0.12	−0.06	−0.25	−0.03	1.00				
C	−0.07	0.00	−0.06	0.09	0.06	1.00			
CT	0.07	0.01	0.11	−0.10	0.04	0.03	1.00		
KC	0.05	0.12	−0.03	−0.04	0.21	−0.03	0.05	1.00	
SB	−0.14	−0.03	0.07	−0.03	0.01	−0.06	−0.13	−0.08	1.00

FIGURE 5.5

Correlation of Selected Market Returns. Because the correlation of returns of many markets is near zero, benefits of diversification decrease return while maintaining returns.

approach is in this example, adding more uncorrelated markets could reduce risk further. The average correlation of monthly returns within the nine markets is less than +0.01, which suggests that the portfolio is realizing tremendous benefits of diversification.

Figure 5.5, above, shows a correlation matrix of monthly returns generated by the channel breakout strategy. While returns among markets within the same sector can be highly correlated, returns among markets within different sectors generally have small or no correlation. It is these noncorrelated returns that provide the risk-reducing diversification that our portfolio needs.

BETTER DIVERSIFICATION: ACROSS UNCORRELATED STRATEGIES

In an ideal world, we should trade our strategies on as many markets as possible to reduce the strategy's risk within a portfolio. By adding more markets—assuming each market added possesses similar expected edge—we reduce risk while maintaining expected returns. But why stop with adding markets to the portfolio for diversification? We can expand the diversification by adding other uncorrelated return streams to the portfolio. Instead of trading only one strategy, the next logical step is to trade multiple strategies on multiple markets. It is entirely possible to create two or more profitable strategies that are not correlated. One strategy might follow major market trends, while another may generate trading signals based on a particular price pattern.

To see if combining strategies improves our reward-to-risk characteristics, we will trade another strategy in addition to the 10-day/40-day moving average crossover on our nine-market portfolio. We combine the performance of our moving average crossover strategy with the performance generated by a 40-day

Moving Average Crossover	
K-ratio	0.31
Sharpe Ratio	1.30
Channel Breakout	
K-ratio	0.41
Sharpe Ratio	1.22
Combined Crossover and Breakout	
K-ratio	0.36
Sharpe Ratio	1.31

FIGURE 5.6

Performance of Varying Strategies. Trading multiple strategies helps our portfolio's reward to risk statistics.

entry/20-day exit channel breakout strategy. Figure 5.6 details the K-ratio and Sharpe ratio of each strategy on its own and then a combination of the two strategies into a new multistrategy portfolio.

We see that combining the moving average crossover with the channel breakout does not improve performance. Unlike the diversification of markets example above, where adding multiple markets produced a portfolio that was better than the performance of any single market, the combination of these two trend-following strategies does not lead to an improved trading program.

There are two reasons for this lack of improvement in performance. First, we are only combining two strategies. As more strategies are included in our trading program, we will pick up additional diversification. Second, and more important, the moving average crossover and channel breakout strategies are highly correlated. The correlation of monthly returns is +0.85. Remember, diversification only helps when combining noncorrelated returns. In this case, the high correlation of returns between the two strategies helps explain why the combination of the two did not produce better results. We will need to focus our attention on developing strategies with much lower correlation to each other.

By trading multiple strategies on multiple markets, we harness the power of diversification. Many professional money managers will trade as many as 10 to 15 uncorrelated strategies within their organization, all in order to smooth profits and reduce risk from their performance.

GOOD DIVERSIFICATION: ACROSS PARAMETERS WITHIN STRATEGIES

Why stop at adding multiple strategies to our portfolio when we can trade multiple parameter values for each strategy? In the channel breakout example above, we enter on 40-day highs and lows and exit on 20-day highs and lows. Instead of trading the 40- and 20-day parameters, we could add two additional parameter sets: a 20-day entry with a 10-day exit and an 80-day entry with a 40-day exit. If each strategy is equally profitable and the returns have zero correlation with each other, then we can retain our expected return and lower our risk by combining the four parameter sets into one trading portfolio.

In reality, the profit of different parameter sets tends to be highly correlated. As a result, we do not accomplish much by spreading our system across parameter sets. We tested the three parameter sets on our nine-market portfolio, comparing reward to risk statistics for each individual test to a combined portfolio of all three tests, and the results can be seen in Figure 5.7.

Much like the combination of the channel breakout and moving average crossover strategies, the combination of three parameter sets of a channel breakout strategy did not enhance the reward-to-risk statistics. Again, this occurs due to the highly correlated nature of using varying parameters within the same strategy. Because the actual entries and exits for a 20-day entry/10-day exit channel breakout strategy are similar to an 80-day entry/40-day exit strategy, the profit and loss numbers are highly correlated. The correlation of monthly returns from these three parameter sets range from +0.63 to +0.88, which is too high to realize any significant benefits of diversification.

THE TRADER'S HOLY GRAIL

Traders are fond of speaking of the "Holy Grail." In the world of quantitative trading, the Holy Grail is a magic potion of trading performance whose returns are perfectly consistent and never lose money.

Personally, I do not think the Holy Grail trading strategy exists. My half-life theory postulates that performance will decay over time to zero profitability.

20 day entry/10 day exit	
K-ratio	0.35
Sharpe Ratio	0.85
40-day entry/20-day exit	
K-ratio	0.41
Sharpe Ratio	1.22
80-day entry/40-day exit	
K-ratio	0.41
Sharpe Ratio	1.42
Combined three	
K-ratio	0.41
Sharpe Ratio	1.28

FIGURE 5.7

Performance of Varying Parameters. Trading multiple parameter sets slightly helps our portfolio's reward-to- risk statistics.

However, though there may be no Holy Grail trading strategy, the benefits of diversification are one type of Holy Grail that quantitative traders can enjoy. The ability to diversify across markets, strategies, and parameters improves reward-to-risk measures and may be a trader's only free lunch. Diversification is based on mathematical principles—its advantages are not subject to debate.

CHAPTER 6

Optimizing Parameters and Filtering Trading Signals

Improving the Basic Strategy

Optimization is one of the most controversial and discussed topics in quantitative trading. For some traders, optimization allows fine-tuning of a strategy to a market's ebb and flow. For others, optimization is the root of most problems in trading strategy performance. The latter believe that scrupulously fitting strategies to past data yields unrealistic expectations when real-time trading begins. Which side is correct? In this chapter we'll analyze the benefits and drawbacks of optimization using real-world results.

OPTIMIZING TRADING SIGNALS TO ENHANCE PROFITABILITY

Once we have identified a profitable trading system, we may wish to tweak its parameters. Parameters are any alterable inputs that are found in a trading system, such as the length of a moving average, the multiplier in a volatility breakout, or the look-back period for oscillators.

For example, if we buy at a 40-day channel breakout high only when a 10-day moving average is greater than a 40-day moving average, we have a trading system with three parameters: the number of days in the channel breakout (40 days), the length of the short moving average (10 days), and the length of the longer term moving average (40 days). If we filter these trades by only trading when a 14-day ADX is greater than 20, then we add two additional parameters: the length of the ADX (14 days) and the trigger to take positions (20 in the ADX). We already have five parameters in our system and we have yet to add an exit strategy. If we take the parameterization even further, we could use five values for short entries, which are different than long entries. You can see how a simple system can become very complex by adding just a few rules.

Some traders might test their trading strategy over a wide range of values for each parameter. This process is generally referred to as *optimization*. If we're trading a channel breakout where we enter on an x day highs and lows and exit on y day highs and lows, for instance, we could optimize the values of x and y. To do so, we could vary x from 11 to 80 in increments of one, and y from 11 to 30, recording the performance of each combination. This testing would lead to 1400 individual tests: 70 different x's and 20 different y's.

With the increased speed of personal computing, 1400 tests is certainly possible in one night's computing time. But if we optimize after adding another layer of complexity to our strategy, the process quickly becomes out of control. When we amend the strategy to only take our channel breakout trades when an a day ADX is greater than b, the total number of trials balloons to 560,000 if we run a between 11 and 30, and b from 21 to 40. This is a stretch for even today's fastest computers.

One method of simplification is to vary each parameter by more than one unit per test. If we increase each of the four parameters in increments of five instead of one, we reduce the total number of tests from 560,000 to 1875. Although this is manageable with today's computing power, what do we do with the results when we finish?

Optimization vs. Curve Fitting

Conventional wisdom is that optimization is an important technique to maximize the expected value of trading strategies. Popular thinking says parameter values that have performed best in the past are most likely to do so in the future. Whether or not this statement is true, if optimization is taken too far, the process turns into curve fitting of data.

Consider our optimization above with 560,000 trials. Suppose the parameter set of entering on 54-day highs and lows, exiting on 24-day highs and lows, while only taking trades when the 19-day ADX is greater than 18 ($x = 54$, $y = 24$, $a = 19$, and $b = 18$) is the best performing combination and produces a Sharpe ratio of 5.0. Meanwhile, the average Sharpe ratio for all 560,000 trials is 1.5.

Can we expect this specific set of parameters to perform three times as well as the average parameter set in the future? Chances are that it won't and the performance of any particular performance set will revert to the mean in the future. Of all the trials, approximately half will perform better than average and half will perform worse. A few of the 560,000 trials will produce spectacular winners, while a few will produce unbelievable losers. The distribution of the Sharpe ratios across all parameter sets might look similar to a bell curve normal distribution (see Figure 6.1). To a large degree, the dispersion of varying profits and losses is due to chance.

If the set of parameters ($x = 54$, $y = 24$, $a = 19$, and $b = 18$) created the best performance of the 560,000 sets, chances are much of the past performance was due to luck and performance will likely be much worse in the future. This is not to say the overall strategy will be unprofitable; rather, that blindly picking parameter sets based on past performance alone will usually overestimate true performance.

Let me give you an example of why optimization is misunderstood. Start with 100 coins and distribute one coin to 100 separate people. Have each person flip their coin five times and mark the number of times the coin comes up heads. Due to random chance, it's likely that at least one person will flip five heads in a row. Behold, that person has found a magic coin! Right? No. He just got lucky.

The same mistake can be made in optimization of trading systems. Traders will often perform complex trading simulations and pick the best performing parameter set without looking at other factors. That same trader will usually be tremendously disappointed when performance in real-time trading is not as profitable as the simulation. The trader will use idioms to explain the trading failure, such as "the market changed and my system fell apart." This is not why the trader

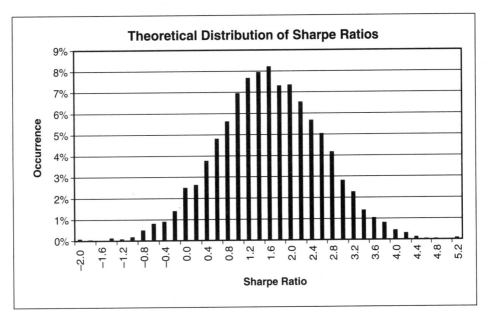

FIGURE 6.1

Theoretical Distribution of Sharpe Ratios. If we test 1000 parameter sets, the distribution of their performance ratios will likely fall under a normal distribution.

failed. The market did not change; rather, the performance of the trader's strategy reverted to results of the average overall parameter sets.

Measuring the Value of Optimization

At this point, some readers might be upset that I'm throwing cold water on the concept of optimization. Although I am not convinced that optimization is particularly useful, I can test its value through research.

Using the channel breakout, we will simulate trading on our stable of futures markets and stocks between the years 1990 and 2001. We test eight parameter sets by varying our channel breakout entry from 10 to 80 days in increments of 10. Our exit will always be half the length of the entry. At the end of each year, we'll rank the parameter sets by annual net profit. Over time, we'll compare the rank of one year's performance to the next. For example, if a 40-day entry channel breakout was the third best performing parameter in 1990 and the eighth best in 1991, we could plot the coordinate (3, 8) in a scatterplot like those in Figures 6.2a and 6.2b. Once the ranks of all combinations of parameters for all years are added to the graphs, we can determine if a relationship exists between successful performing parameters of one year compared to the performance the following year.

The results show a bias for parameters to be strong from one year to the next. Note that a best-fit trendline slopes upward, suggesting that the best ranking param-

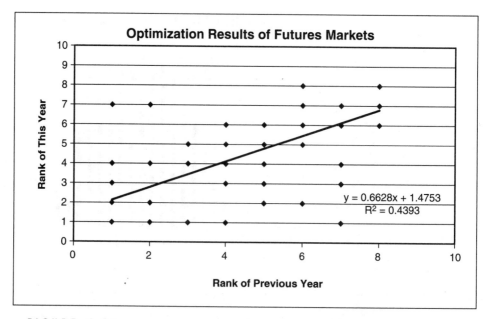

FIGURE 6.2a

Optimization Results of Futures Markets. The rank of one year's net profit plotted against the rank of the next year's net profit for all eight parameter sets.

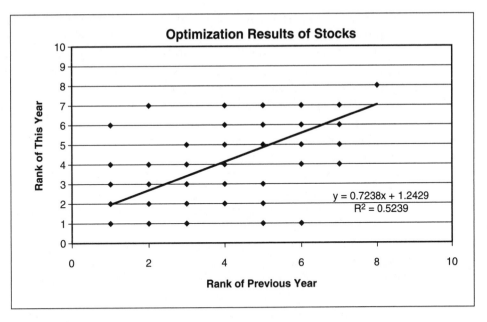

FIGURE 6.2b

Optimization Results of Stocks. The rank of one year's net profit plotted against the rank of next year's net profit for all eight parameter sets.

eters in one year are likely to be the best performing parameters during the next year. This phenomenon exists for the channel breakout when tested on both futures markets and individual stocks. The results above indicate that we want to stick with the best performing parameters and that performance from year to year is not random.

At the same time, other properties could be at work. In the test above, we gather performance data from eight variations of a channel breakout strategy. This could be explained by the fact that some parameters performed consistently better than others over the life of the test.

In the graphs in Figures 6.3a and 6.3b, we add a twist to our annual rankings. Instead of ranking net profit generated from one year's performance versus the previous year's performance, we normalized each year's profit versus the average over the life of the test. If the 10-day entry/5-day exit channel breakout averaged a profit of $100,000 over the 12 years of the test, then we subtract $100,000 from each year's profit to normalize the profit numbers over all parameter sets.

This normalization process will allow us to ask a different optimization question. After creating new scatterplots, we will be able to determine if this year's performance is above or below average, and what it might mean for next year's performance.

For the futures markets in Figure 6.3a, there does appear to be a slight bias in deviations of performance from year to year. The positive sloping trendline suggests that if this year's performance for any parameter set is above average, then next year's performance is also likely to be above average. While the slope and correlation of the best fit trendline is small, it's significant in a statistical sense. The results of the futures market performance data suggest that optimization of parameters from one year to the next will improve performance.

While the futures market performance gives credence to the notion of optimization, the stock performance data in Figure 6.3b does not. The slope of the trendline for stock performance ranks from one year to the next is slightly negative, indicating that a parameter that produced higher than average profits this year is likely to produce slightly less than average profits the following year. The correlation is small enough to suggest that no relationship—positive or negative— exists between this year's performance when compared to average performance and next year's performance.

While the above results are aggregated over an entire portfolio of markets, we can perform similar analysis on a single market. In this case, we choose General Electric to test for the value of optimization (Figures 6.4a and 6.4b).

Interestingly, we do not see the same results as for a portfolio of markets. When profit is ranked and one year's rank is plotted against the next, we see little relationship. The slope is slightly positive, but nowhere near the levels seen

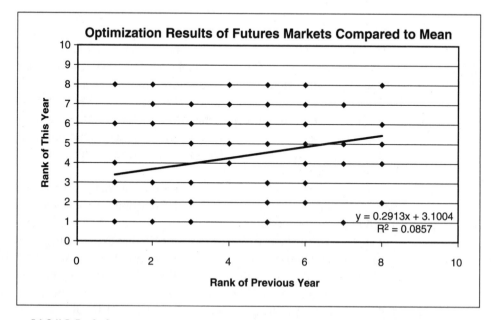

FIGURE 6.3a

Optimization Results of Futures Markets Compared to Mean. The normalized rank of one year's net profit plotted against the normalized rank of next year's net profit for all eight parameter sets. Ranks are normalized by subtracting the average annual profit for a parameter set from the annual return.

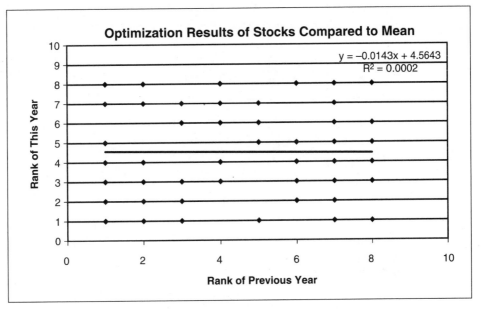

FIGURE 6.3b

Optimization Results of Stocks Compared to Mean. The normalized rank of one year's net profit plotted against the normalized rank of next year's net profit for all eight parameter sets. Ranks are normalized by subtracting the average annual profit for a parameter set from the annual return.

in the portfolio of futures or stocks. When we look at ranked deviations from average profit by parameter set, we find similar results. The slope for GE is slightly negative, indicating that a year with better than average performance will be followed by a year with less than average performance. Neither test concerning GE produces results that are statistically significant. While this study is certainly not the end of the argument, I think it does provide a clue about the benefits of optimization.

Leo Zamansky and James Goldcamp (2001) wrote an intriguing piece on the potential benefits of optimization. The two tested channel breakout strategies where parameters were optimized based on the past 60 and 120 days' performance. Two studies were run. The first would use parameters for the current period that had performed best in the prior period. The idea behind this strategy is that strings of past performance are likely to continue, and that as traders we want to stay with parameter sets that are performing the best. The second test selected parameter sets for the current period that performed the worst in the prior period. The idea behind this strategy is that performance is likely to mean revert over time. Parameter sets that have been "cold" and performing poorly are likely to revert and perform well in the future.

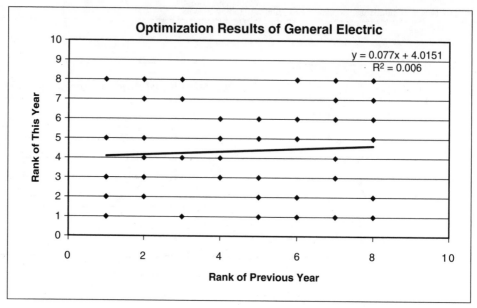

FIGURE 6.4a

Optimization Results for General Electric. The rank of one year's net profit plotted against the rank of next year's net profit for all eight parameter sets.

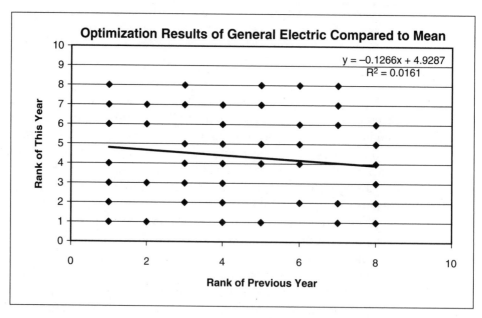

FIGURE 6.4b

Optimization Results for General Electric Compared to Mean. The normalized rank of one year's net profit plotted against the normalized rank of next year's net profit for all eight parameter sets. Ranks are normalized by subtracting the average annual profit for a parameter set from the annual return.

While the results of the study were mixed, Zamansky and Goldcamp's research did yield interesting information. In the longer performance look-back (120 days), parameter sets that were selected using the best performance of the prior period typically generated better results than the average of all parameter sets. These results mirror our own studies earlier in the chapter. However, the shorter performance look-back period (60 days) found that using parameter sets that had performed poorly did in fact enhance results.

The debate on optimization will not end soon. Some traders believe it is an absolute necessity, while others feel it is an avoidable evil. While I agree that it's important to optimize to test for parameter stability, the evidence above suggests that there is no clear answer. It does appear that some parameter sets perform better than others throughout the life of performance tests, but that optimizing parameters frequently based on "the hot hand" may not be better than sticking with the parameter set that has performed the best during a longer time frame.

FILTERING TO ENHANCE PROFITABILITY

Filtering, as we defined it in Chapter 3, is the process of deciding when to override trade signals. The most common use of filtering is within trend-following systems, where signals are only taken when a trend filter such as the ADX is rising or above a fixed point. Popular wisdom holds that when trend filters such as the ADX are rising, trend-following strategies will perform better than when falling. Although I have seen this trend filter argument time and again, I've never seen evidence that using a filter improves performance. Like other ideas in this book, we will examine whether using filters does indeed improve trading strategy performance.

Similarities of Trend Filters: ADX and VHF

While there are many ways of measuring whether a market is trending, most are remarkably similar to each other. Figure 6.5, below, is a chart of random price data along with two popular trend filters: a 14-day ADX and a 30-day Vertical Horizontal Filter (VHF). Note that the filters track each other very closely. In fact, many times they are virtually indistinguishable.

These filters do a good job of identifying when a trend has already developed, but what about identifying whether trends will continue? To answer that question we need to test the effectiveness of trend filters, which we will for one trend-following strategy.

Measuring the Value of Filtering

To test the effectiveness of filters, we return to the channel breakout strategy. We tested a 40-day entry/20-day exit channel breakout on stock and futures data from

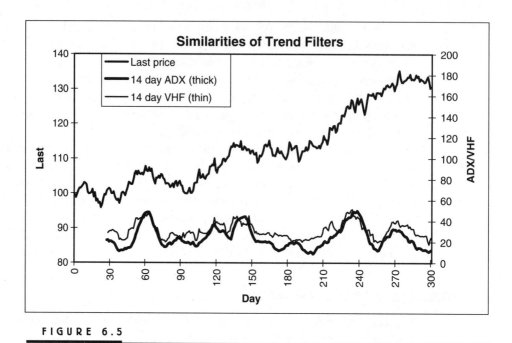

FIGURE   6.5

Similarities of Trend Filters. The movement of ADX and VHF are similar.

1990 through 2001. We filtered entries to take signals only when the 14-day ADX was between x and $x+5$ (where x runs from 15 to 30 increments of 5). In addition, we tested another run to take signals only when the 14-day ADX was between x and $x+5$ and the 14-day ADX was rising. The resulting charts are depicted in Figures 6.6 through 6.9.

The graphs tell two stories, depending on the type of market. For futures, we see that the results of the channel breakout might be improved by ignoring trading signals when the 14-day ADX is less than 20. These filtered signals produced Sharpe ratios that were much worse than entering trades with higher ADX values. The results are consistent whether we require the ADX to be rising or not.

For stocks, however, the opposite appears to hold true. Trades entered when the 14-day ADX value was less than 20 generated Sharpe ratios much better than trades entered during periods of higher ADX values. Essentially, the data are telling us to avoid trend-following signals when futures are caught in trading ranges but to take trend-following signals when stocks are in trading ranges.

Regime Switching Strategies

We can also use trend filters to pick the appropriate strategy to fit the current market regime. In these regime-switching models, we start by identifying market

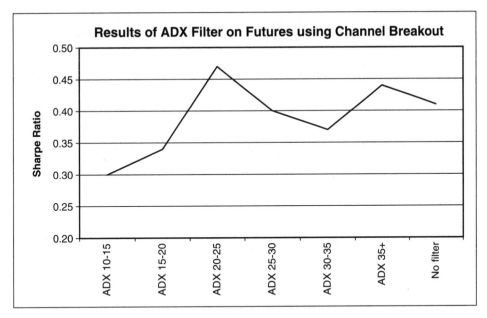

FIGURE 6.6

Results of ADX Filter on Futures Using Channel Breakout. The results of a 40-day entry/20-day exit tak-ing signals at varying 14-day ADX levels.

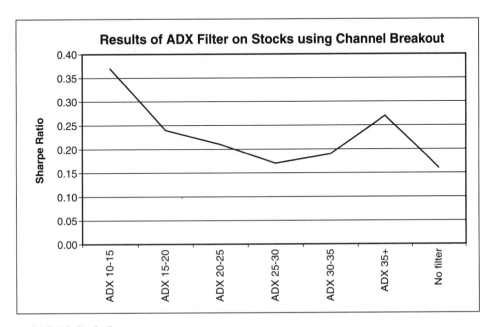

FIGURE 6.7

Results of ADX Filters on Stocks Using Channel Breakout. The results of a 40-day entry/20-day exit tak-ing signals at varying 14-day ADX levels.

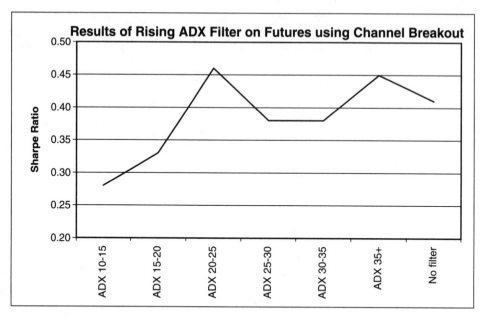

FIGURE 6.8

Results of Rising ADX on Stocks Using Channel Breakout. The results of a 40-day entry/20-day exit taking signals at varying 14-day rising ADX levels.

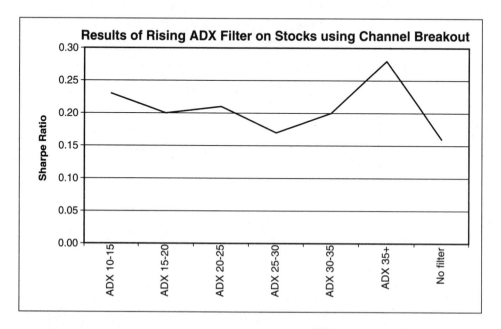

FIGURE 6.9

Results of Rising ADX on Stocks Using Channel Breakout. The results of a 40-day entry/20-day exit taking signals at varying 14-day rising ADX levels.

states based on a trend filter and apply the appropriate strategy, as seen in Figure 6.10:

Regime	Trend status	Strategy
ADX<15	Mean reverting prices	RSI oscillator to take counter trend signals
15<ADX>25	Random walk, no trend, no mean reversion in prices	No trading
ADX>25	Trending prices	40-day/20-day channel breakout

F I G U R E   6 . 1 0

Regime Switching Rules. Depending on the value of a 14-day ADX, we will either use a channel breakout or RSI strategy.

We test this relationship using historical data for one futures market (Treasury bonds, Figure 6.11) and one stock (Merrill Lynch, Figure 6.12). In addition to the 40-day/20-channel breakout, we test a standard 14-day RSI system that enters short on crosses above 65 and long on crosses below 35. For each day in the test, we measure the day's profit or loss for both strategies and the 14-day ADX value for each market. At the end of the test we aggregate the profit and loss based on values of the ADX. If today's ADX value is 23, then we add the day's profit or loss of the channel breakout to the 20–25 bin for the ADX. We do the same for the RSI strategy. At the end of the test, we average the daily profit and loss by the ADX bin.

Both the futures market (T-bonds) and the individual stock (Merrill Lynch) have well-defined profit and loss characteristics. The channel breakout strategy appears to perform best when the 14-day ADX is very low or very high (ADX values less than 20 and greater than 30). The 14-day RSI strategy appears to perform best when the 14-day ADX is anywhere between 20 and 30. Using these tendencies, we rewrite the rules to our regime strategy (Figure 6.13).

We can now create a more robust strategy using a combination of a channel breakout and RSI strategies to take advantage of the market's current state.

Filtering Using Profitability of the Last Trade

The tests above use price data to determine whether the market is trending or not trending and then selects an appropriate strategy to take advantage of the market's environment. We can also use data not associated with price to determine when to trade.

One popular filter that dates back to the mid 1980s is the concept of the last trade. Some traders theorize that winning trades are commonly followed by losing trades, and losers by winners. In essence, the idea is that trade by trade

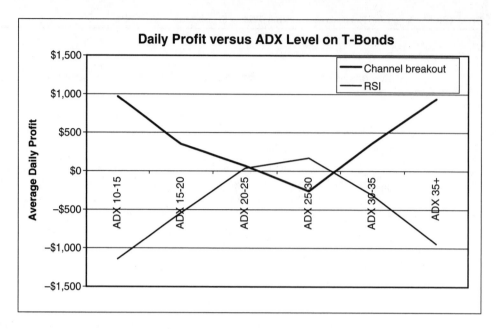

FIGURE 6.11

Daily Profit versus ADX Level on T-Bonds. A definitive pattern exists for the performance of the channel breakout and RSI strategies. The channel breakout performs best during extreme values of the 14-day ADX. while the RSI performs best during middle values.

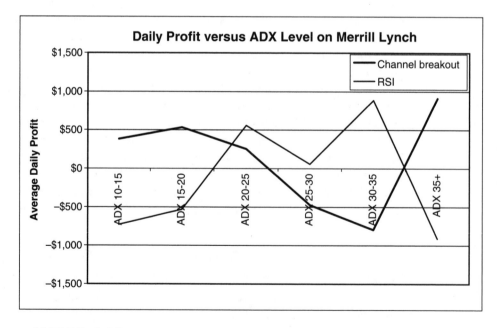

FIGURE 6.12

Daily Profit versus ADX Level on Merrill Lynch. Although not as pronounced as T-bonds, a similar pattern exists on the two strategies applied to Merrill Lynch.

Regime	Trend status	Strategy
ADX<20	Trend to begin soon	40-day/20-day channel breakout
20<ADX<30	Mean reversion in prices	14-day RSI strategy
ADX>30	Trending prices	40-day/20-day channel breakout

F I G U R E   6 . 1 3

Refined Regime Switching Rules. Based on the results above, we tweak our regime switching trading strategy.

profit is mean reverting over time. Others argue that strategies tend to get "hot," much like a shooter at a craps table, and that we should push full throttle in our trading when the last trade was a winner. Like most conflicting theories in this book, we can test performance historically to determine which, if any, of these two ideas has merit.

Using the 40-day entry/20-day exit channel breakout, we filter signals to only take entries when (1) the last trade was a winner and (2) the last trade was a loser.

The results, as seen in Figure 6.14, indicate that taking channel breakout trades after a winning trade has been closed is a losing proposition. While a standard channel breakout strategy produces profits, both futures and stocks produce losses if we only take trades after winning trades. On the flip side, taking trades only after losing trades is only a slight improvement to taking all channel breakout trades. In the futures market, taking signals after losing trades produces about half the profits as taking all trades with slightly lower reward-to-risk measures. On stocks, taking signals after losing trades produces only slightly lower profits with much higher reward-to-risk measures.

Trading the Equity Curve

Another possibility is that strategy returns are positively autocorrelated. In Chapter 2 we defined autocorrelation as the predictability of one period's values on the next. There are two states of autocorrelation: positive and negative. Positive autocorrelation exists when greater than average values tend to lead to greater than average values in the next period, and vice versa. Negative autocorrelation exists when greater than average values lead to less than average values. If autocorrelation exists in strategy returns, we can incorporate recent performance data into our trading signals as a filter. This process of filtering trades based on past performance is often referred to as "Trading the Equity Curve."

Using recent performance to filter trading signals is a new and exciting area of quantitative trading research. Such new thinking may put traders ahead of the

Futures			
	Profit	K-ratio	Sharpe Ratio
All trades	$5,971,279	0.12	0.41
Trades after winning trade	− $1,959,837	−0.18	−0.39
Trades after losing trade	$2,971,124	0.06	0.37
Stocks			
	Profit	K-ratio	Sharpe Ratio
All trades	$3,511,542	0.06	0.16
Trades after winning trade	−$5,752,819	−0.30	−0.77
Trades after losing trade	$3,373,470	0.17	0.27

FIGURE 6.14

Performance of Rules based on Last Trade. We see that taking signals after losing trades outperforms taking signals after winning trades.

curve in determining when to sit on the sidelines or when to have confidence in trading signals. This is one area of research that I will be spending much time on in the coming years.

HOW OFTEN DO MARKETS TREND?

I frequently hear that the market only trends 25 percent of the time. Quantifying how often a market trends is very vague since the results are entirely dependent on one's definition of a trend. If I define a trend to be 10 consecutive closes in any direction, then most markets spend years between trends. Similarly, if I define the trend as two consecutive closes in any direction, then markets are trending roughly 50 percent of the time. Clearly, one's definition of trend greatly influences how often markets do trend.

According to the random walk/efficient markets hypothesis, we would expect to be profitable roughly 50 percent of total trading days when we apply trend-following techniques. This 50 percent level is our benchmark hypothesis. To test it, we will apply our 40-day/20-day channel breakout to stock and futures markets. To measure the tendency to trend, we calculate the total number of days found in winning trades and compare that to the total number of days found in losing trades. That is, if a trade lasts 25 days from entry to exit, those 25 days would either be added to total winning days if the trade was profitable, or the 25 days would be added to the total losing days if the trade was unprofitable or breakeven.

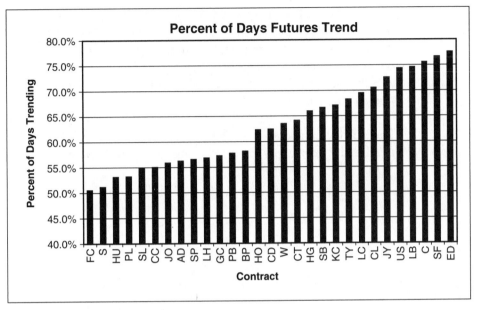

FIGURE 6.15

Percent of Days Futures Trend, Eurodollars Swiss franc, and corn trend most frequently, while feeder cattle, soybeans, and unleaded gas trend the least.

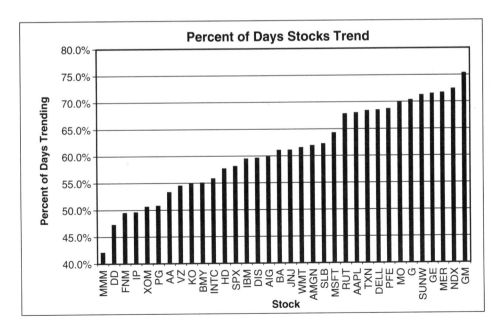

FIGURE 6.16

Percent of Days Stock Trend. General Motors, the Nasdaq 100, and Merrill trend most frequently, while MMM, Dupont, and Fannie Mae trend the least.

As we see from the results in Figures 6.15 and 6.16, the percent of profitable trading days averages much higher than our hypothesis of 50 percent. For futures, the average percent of profitable trading days is 63 percent. For stocks, the number is 61 percent. As might be expected, the highest values are recorded for markets that perform very well in the channel breakout and moving average crossover trading simulations.

Given these results, I suggest that markets trend roughly 60 percent of the time. The fact that the average falls greater than 50 percent suggests that markets do in fact trend, and we can apply trend-following strategies to exploit this inefficiency.

PART TWO

Harnessing the Power of Quantitative Techniques to Create a Trading Program

The second half of the book is designed to open the reader's eyes to new methods and markets never before discussed. I've developed new entries and exits over the past 15 years of trading, and I encourage the reader to explore these techniques in his or her own trading and research.

I will introduce a number of markets outside the realm of stocks and futures that are ideally suited for applying quantitative techniques. We will look at fixed income relative value arbitrage, commodity relative value trading, stock pairs trading, implied volatility trading, as well as stock index relative value arbitrage. Then we will explore some more simplistic strategies for trading the S&P 500—techniques computationally easy enough to trade effectively without software. I will also introduce a new tool for determining optimal leverage into our trading portfolios. Finally, all the new concepts of this book will be brought together to create a trading system for the futures markets.

CHAPTER 7

Dissecting Strategies Currently Available

What Works and What Doesn't

In this chapter we'll combine all the techniques studied thus far and apply them to test and evaluate trading strategies on stocks and futures. I consider this section unique in that few existent texts examine performance of trading strategies on both stock and futures markets in an apples-to-apples, side-by-side comparison. With the introduction of single stock futures, the lines are becoming blurred between these two asset classes.

TESTING STOCK AND FUTURES MARKETS

Each strategy will be tested on 29 domestically traded futures markets and 34 domestically traded stock and stock indices using the performance evaluation techniques described in Chapter 3.

The futures markets (Figure 7.1) hail from a wide variety of sectors: foreign exchange, interest rate products, stock indices, industrial and precious metals, energy, grains, meats, and soft commodities. Stocks (Figure 7.2) were classified based on sector classifications developed by Standard & Poor's. Single stocks representing the nine sectors were chosen: energy, materials, industrials, consumer discretionary, consumer staples, health care, financials, information technology, and telecommunications. In addition to single stocks, three popular stock indices are also tested. All strategy tests run from January 1, 1990, through December 31, 2001.

Sector	Symbol	Market
Foreign Exchange	AD	Australian Dollar
	BP	British Pound
	CD	Canadian Dollar
	JY	Japanese Yen
	SF	Swiss Franc
Interest Rates	ED	Eurodollar
	TY	Ten-Year Treasury Notes
	US	Thirty-Year Treasury Bonds
Stock Index	SP	Standard & Poor's 500 Stock Index
Metals	GC	Gold
	HG	Copper
	PL	Platinum
	SI	Silver
Energy	CL	Crude Oil
	HO	Heating Oil
	HU	Unleaded Gas
Grains	C	Corn
	S	Soybeans
	W	Wheat
Meats	FC	Feeder Cattle
	LC	Live Cattle
	LH	Live Hogs
	PB	Pork Bellies
Softs	CC	Cocoa
	CT	Cotton
	JO	Orange Juice
	KC	Coffee
	LB	Lumber
	SB	Sugar

FIGURE 7.1

Futures Markets Tested. Twenty-nine futures are tested in our performance evaluation.

CONSTRUCTING CONTINUOUS FUTURES CONTRACTS

A futures contract is an agreement to buy or sell the underlying security at a specified price at a specified date in the future. If I buy one March corn contract and hold until expiration, I will be required to pay for the value of and take delivery of 5000 bushels of corn housed at a warehouse in March.

In reality, this does not happen often. Very few of the futures contracts traded are held to maturity. The majority are either rolled into the next contract month or closed down prior to futures expiration. The measure of the number of futures

Sector	Symbol	Market
Energy	SLB	Schlumberger
	XOM	Exxon Mobil
Basic Materials	AA	Alcoa
	DD	Dupont
	IP	International Paper
Industrials	BA	Boeing
	GE	General Electric
	MMM	3M Company
Consumer Discretionary	DIS	Disney
	GM	General Motors
	HD	Home Depot
	WMT	Wal-Mart
Consumer Staples	G	Gilette
	KO	Coca Cola
	MO	Phillip Morris
	PG	Procter & Gamble
Healthcare	AMGN	Amgen
	BMY	Bristol Meyers
	JNJ	Johnson & Johnson
	PFE	Pfizer
Financials	AIG	AIG International
	FNM	Fannie Mae
	MER	Merrill Lynch
Information Technology	AAPL	Apple Computer
	DELL	Dell Computer
	IBM	IBM
	INTC	Intel
	MSFT	Microsoft
	SUNW	Sun Microsystems
	TXN	Texas Instruments
Telecommunications	VZ	Verizon
Stock Indices	SPX	Standard & Poor's 500
	NDX	Nasdaq 100
	RUT	Russell 2000

FIGURE 7.2

Stocks Tested. Thirty-four stocks are tested in our performance evaluation.

contracts outstanding, called the *open interest*, usually peaks some two to four weeks before a contract expires.

In our quantitative trading, we must create a methodology for splicing together futures contracts with finite lives. We will create a continuous price series

by piecing together price data associated with whichever futures contract possesses the most open interest. Because futures contracts have specific limited lives, we
must roll positions from one contract to the next as expiration nears. While there
are many methods to achieve this contract-rolling procedure, I have chosen the
back-adjusted method to create a consistent time series of futures prices.

When contracts expire and the front-month rolls from one month to the next,
gaps can occur in price action. Figure 7.3 depicts the gaps that occur when only
looking at front-month prices. Using front-month eurodollar prices, we see how
prices differ from one month to the next. It becomes impossible to resolve which
gaps are due to contract rolls and which price gaps are due to trading.

For an example of the back-adjusted method let's assume that we're trading
October cotton. As futures expiration nears, we will want to stop focusing on the
October contract and instead use the December contract as market participants
begin to close out their October positions and initiate December positions (see
Figure 7.4). This roll can present problems when analyzing price data since the
October and December contracts do not trade at the same price. December will
typically trade at a premium to October due to a mixture of carrying costs and stor-
age costs. We will need to adjust our data to account for the difference in prices
when we switch from the October to the December contract. The back-adjusted

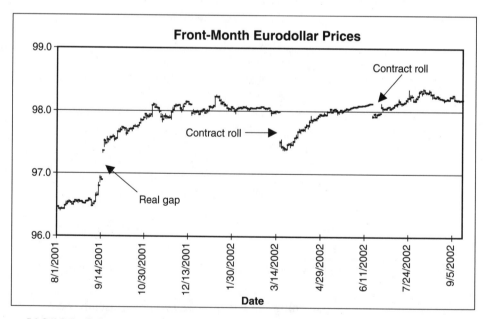

FIGURE 7.3

Front-month Eurodollar Prices. By looking at only front-month futures prices, we expose ourselves to
price gaps created when contracts expire.

Hypothetical Cotton Data - September 30						
Maturity	**Open**	**High**	**Low**	**Settle**	**Volume**	**Open Interest**
October	51.5	51.7	50.8	51	8,000	20,000
December	52.1	52.3	51.4	51.5	8,000	19,500

F I G U R E   7 . 4

Hypothetical Cotton Data. By adjusting our data by the difference between October and December set-tlement values, we can create a back-adjusted continuous contract.

method will calculate the difference between contracts and adjust all previous data to fill the gap between the two.

On September 30, October expiration cotton settles at 51.0, while December expiration cotton settles at 51.5. Let's assume this is the final day when the open interest of October outnumbers the open interest in December. Starting October 1, we will use December cotton prices for our trading and research purposes. We adjust all our previous data by adding 0.5 to all prices in order to compensate for the difference between our last recorded prices of October and December settlements. After the adjustment, we record December contract prices until the next contract roll. This process continues indefinitely. The result is that we maintain a record of most active contract prices and adjust for the difference between one contract and the next each time a futures contract approaches maturity.

Using the back-adjusted technique to adjust futures price data is not without flaws. As a result of continually adjusting for price gaps between contracts, our data will no longer be an accurate representation of actual prices traded. If we rolled our cotton contracts 10 times, and the average gap between contracts was 0.5, our first data points will be 5.0 higher than where prices actually traded at the time. In fact, in certain markets our adjustments can lead to negative prices, a trait that is certainly not possible in real life. Although our back-adjusted prices can be remarkably different than the actual recorded prices, the relative price movement is left intact.

This adjustment process is logically consistent because we are creating strategies to trade relative price movement. Strategies in which the absolute price level is used in trading decisions will not be applicable to our back adjusted data. Although this may sound like a dramatic flaw, there are very few strategies where actual levels are critical in generating trading signals. For example, a 40-day high is still a 40-day high, regardless of how prices have been adjusted.

NORMALIZING STOCK AND FUTURES VOLATILITY

The next issue to tackle is determining the number of futures contracts and shares of stock to trade in order to equalize each trading signal. As we saw in Chapter 2, the dollar value volatility of one S&P 500 contract is much larger than the dollar value volatility of one corn contract. One share of GE trading at $60 may be more or less volatile than one share of INTC trading at $30. Taken even further, $100 worth of CSCO stock is likely more volatile than $100 worth of MRK stock. We need to create a method of equalizing the volatility of all markets for our trading strategy evaluation, whether they are futures or stocks.

I cannot stress the importance of this concept in order to generate meaningful performance evaluation. Numerous tests on futures markets are completed in which strategies trade one contract each of the S&P 500, corn, wheat, and cotton. The results of this system will be relatively meaningless. The performance of the S&P 500 will dominate the results of the portfolio due to its overwhelming dollar volatility compared to the other three markets.

To illustrate this example of unbalanced risk, we examine two portfolios: one for stocks and another for futures. The stock portfolio contains two companies: Yahoo (YHOO) and Phillip Morris (MO). Yahoo is an Internet portal, a very volatile business over the past couple of years. Phillip Morris is a large diversified food and tobacco producer and marketer. Our portfolio begins on January 1, 1998, with $50 of each stock. Figure 7.5 presents a graph of our portfolio's value, with the value of YHOO and the value of MO.

When we compare the portfolio value against the values of the two component stocks, we notice that the portfolio moves in lockstep with the value of YHOO. It is

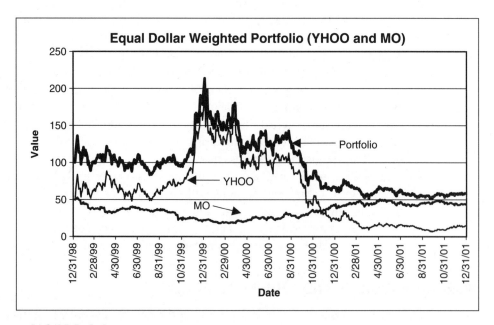

FIGURE 7.5

Equal Dollar Weighted Portfolio (YHOO and MO). Because YHOO is much more volatile than MO, the value of the portfolio is dominated by changes in YHOO share prices.

almost as if the MO portion of the portfolio is irrelevant. Such is life when we deal with stocks of varying volatility. Over the life of this portfolio, YHOO is almost three times as volatile as MO when compared using standard deviation of returns. In order to rebalance these stocks to have equal importance on the returns of our portfolio, we need to adjust the weightings based on some measure of volatility.

Adjusting the amount of money invested in each security at the beginning of the portfolio will not be enough to accomplish our desired result. A balanced portfolio one day becomes unbalanced the next, as some stocks outperform while others underperform. In the YHOO and MO example, let's suppose we invested $25 in YHOO and $75 in MO at the beginning of the portfolio. Because YHOO is roughly three times as volatile as MO, the risk to our portfolio from each stock is approximately the same. But if YHOO doubles and MO falls by 33 percent, then our YHOO stake will be worth $50 and our MO stake will be worth $50. Our portfolio is unchanged and still worth $100, but our risk has changed. Because YHOO is three times as volatile as MO, our effective exposure to YHOO is roughly three times as large as our exposure to MO. If we want to rebalance our exposure back to our original $75 for MO and $25 for YHOO, we will need to sell YHOO and buy MO. This is exactly how we manage quantitative portfolios using trading systems.

Similar problems arise in the futures markets when we trade on a single contract basis. Below is the profit and loss of being long one contract of the S&P 500 and one contract of corn since January 1, 1998 (Figure 7.6). It is evident that our performance is entirely dependent on the S&P 500. The profit and loss of the portfolio and the S&P 500 are indistinguishable. The profit and loss of the corn contract is virtually meaningless to the portfolio. Within our trading systems, we will want to treat each market as equal. We need to adjust the contract sizes depending on each market's volatility in order to equalize different contracts that we trade.

The tests in this book will not suffer the same fate as the examples above. Whether stocks, futures, or other, we will use intelligent weighting schemes that will dynamically weight each market based on recent market volatility. For futures, the number of contracts is calculated at the entry of each trade using the following formula:

$$\text{Number of contracts to trade} = \frac{\$10,000}{\sigma_{100daypricechanges} \ ContractMultiplier}$$

We determine the number of contracts to trade with each entry signal by dividing $10,000 by both the standard deviation of past 100 daily price changes and the contract multiplier of the futures contract. This formula uses recent market volatility to determine the number of contracts to trade on any given day. As volatility increases, measured by the standard deviation of price changes, the number of contracts is decreased. As volatility decreases, the number of contracts to trade is increased. The contract multiplier, found in the denominator of the equation, represents the dollar value of a base unit move for each contract. These numbers vary from futures contract to futures contract. For most grain contracts, the contract mul-

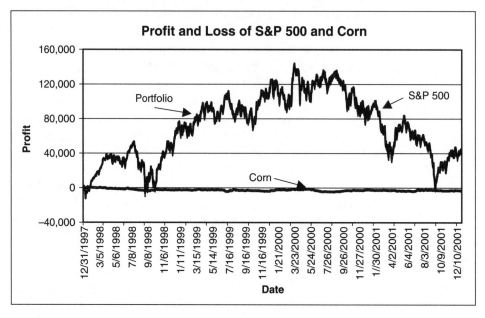

FIGURE 7.6

Profit and Loss of S&P 500 and Corn. Trading one contract of S&P 500 and corn leads to another unbalanced portfolio because the dollar volatility of an S&P 500 futures contract is much larger than that of a corn futures contract.

tiplier is $50. That is, a one penny increase or decrease is worth $50 per contract. In the S&P 500, the contract multiplier is $250. For T-bonds, this number is $1,000. Using a theoretical example, if the standard deviation of the past 100 price returns is eight points in the S&P 500, then our system would trade five contracts:

$$\text{Number of contracts to trade} = \frac{\$10,000}{8pts \cdot \$250 per contract} = 5 \text{ contracts}$$

As we see in the graph in Figure 7.7, the number of contracts to trade for S&P 500 futures has decreased over time, commensurate with an increase in both the price level and percentage volatility of the S&P 500.

This dynamically weighted contract size solves the futures market volatility mismatch. The beauty of this method is that every trade should have equal expected volatility as every past and future trade, regardless of the price level or notional size of the futures contract. When weighting contracts according to the formula above, the difference between contracts is minimized. Below, in Figure 7.8, we see the profit and loss of being long one S&P 500 future and one corn contract when weighted by our contract size formula. After the contract adjustment, the volatility of returns is roughly similar for the S&P 500 and corn.

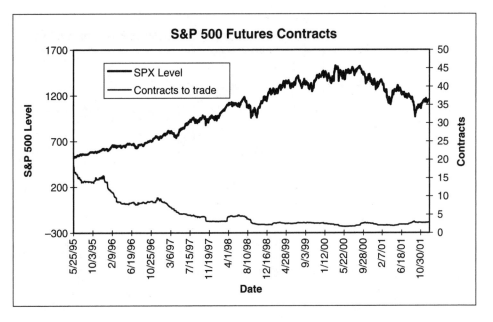

FIGURE 7.7

S&P 500 Futures Contracts. Our dynamically adjusting contract size will trade fewer contracts as prices and volatility rise.

On the equity side, we perform an analogous calculation to generate the number of shares to trade. Similar to the S&P 500 futures example, we trade fewer shares of stock as the price and volatility of that stock rises. The reason we weight share size by volatility instead of share price has to do with varying volatility among stocks in differing industries.

Technology firms such as Yahoo (YHOO) with risky business prospects and unstable cashflows are much more volatile than established, mature businesses with very predictable earnings streams such as McDonalds (MCD). Similar to the futures portfolio example above, trading a stock portfolio consisting of $10,000 each of YHOO, MCD, GE, and MRK is very inconsistent. The majority of the portfolio's performance will be determined by its most volatile component, YHOO. By weighting each stock by its volatility, we equalize the importance of all stocks in our performance evaluation. We determine the number of shares to trade in each entry signal by dividing $10,000 by the standard deviation of the stock's past 100 daily price changes.

$$\text{Number of shares to trade} = \frac{\$10,000}{\sigma_{100 \text{ days price return}}}$$

In Figure 7.9, below, we examine the number of shares per trade in General Electric (GE). We find that as the stock rallies between 1991 and 2001, we trade fewer shares.

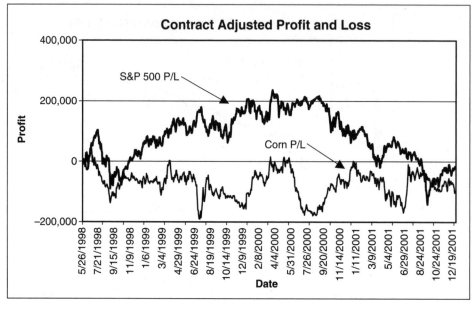

FIGURE 7.8

Contract Adjusted Profit and Loss. Once we adjust our portfolio to trade the dynamically adjusted contracts, the profit and loss of the S&P 500 and corn have similar volatility.

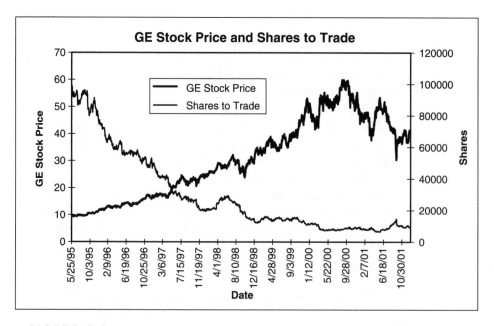

FIGURE 7.9

GE Stock Price and Shares to Trade. Our dynamically adjusting contract size will trade fewer shares as prices and volatility rise.

DEALING WITH COMMISSION AND SLIPPAGE

Perhaps the most controversial aspect of my approach to performance evaluation is that all trades are transacted without deducting any charges for transaction costs consisting of commission and slippage.

Commission is the fixed cost a trader pays to his broker for executing trades. Typical commission runs between $10 and $20 for round-turn futures trades and $0.02 to 0.03 for round-turn stock trades. Slippage is the difference between the price on a screen and the price at which trades are completed. These costs frequently outweigh commission costs and can run between $50 and $150, depending on the size and liquidity of the futures contract, and $0.05 and $0.15 per share on the stock side. I choose not to include such costs in order to focus on the pure profitability of each strategy.

Although I test without including trading costs, I never become excited about performance results until I factor in commission and slippage results. If a strategy is profitable but transaction costs take most of the trading profit, I may consider using the strategy as an entry or exit within another system. Another reason I do not deduct transaction costs is the chance that a system performs so poorly that I may consider taking signals exactly opposite of the original methodology in order to create a profitable strategy. You might be surprised just how many promising systems I have created by inverting the rules of unprofitable strategies.

PERFORMANCE OF POPULAR STRATEGIES

Let's examine some popular strategies and see how they perform in the stock and futures markets. We'll be looking at:

- Channel breakout
- Dual moving average crossover
- Momentum
- Volatility breakout
- Stochastics
- Relative Strength Index
- Moving Average Convergence/Divergence

As noted above, each strategy is tested on 29 futures markets and 34 stocks between January 1990 and December 2001. Signals are generated at the close of each trading day and executed on the next trading day's opening price.

Channel Breakout

The first strategy is a channel breakout that enters long when a market's close is the highest close of the past 40 days, and enters short when a market's close is the lowest close of the past 40 days. Longs are exited if today's close is the lowest close of the past 20 days. Shorts are exited if today's close is the highest close of the past 20 days.

The chart in Figure 7.10, below, depicts an example of the channel breakout strategy applied to American International Group (AIG). The solid lines represent the highest close and lowest close of the past 40 days. When prices rise above the upper channel, a long entry is generated. When prices fall below the lower channel, a short entry is generated.

There's a reason that the channel breakout is such a popular strategy among traders. As we see in the performance numbers (Figures 7.11a through 7.12b), it has been very profitable over the past 12 years. Ten of the 12 years tested produced profits on the futures markets, while 6 of the 12 years generated profits on the stock side. We see especially strong performance in the futures arena on currencies, interest rates, petroleum, and softs. On the stock side, the channel breakout performs especially well in technology stocks as well as some of the indices.

The major concern with the channel breakout is its recent deterioration of performance. If we examine the breakdown statistics for both stocks and futures, we see that recent performance has been less than stellar. These numbers may indicate that strategy performance has weakened enough to cause concern and alarm.

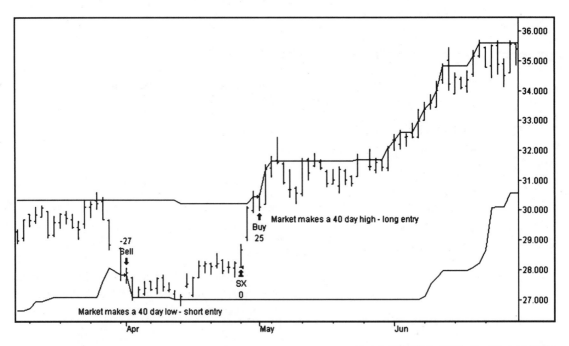

Created with TradeStation 2000i by Omega Research ® 1999

FIGURE 7.10

Channel Breakout Strategy Applied to AIG.

Trading Strategy Evaluation (Futures)

Strategy Name: 40 day entry/20 day exit channel breakout
Parameters: 40 day extreme for entry, 20 day extreme for exit
Description: Enter on a 40 day extreme close; exit on a 20 day extreme close
Run Dates: 1/1/1990 – 12/31/2001

	Market	Net Profit	K-ratio	Sharpe Ratio	Max DD	# of Trades	% Win	Avg. Contracts	Avg. Profit Per Con.	Avg. Win	Avg. Loss	Avg. Bars Win	Avg. Bars Loss
FX	AD	−272,840	−0.12	−0.18	−483,650	72	36	25.14	−151	47,395	−32,720	48	20
	BP	37,388	−0.04	0.02	−517,463	67	31	17.28	32	59,261	−26,241	52	22
	CD	−113,320	−0.03	−0.06	−479,190	70	34	46.63	−35	61,018	−34,299	47	19
	JY	1,269,550	0.29	0.67	−179,038	60	40	13.98	1,389	86,159	−25,074	62	20
	SF	852,838	0.29	0.51	−139,288	63	48	15.47	901	58,208	−26,317	54	19
Rates	ED	2,563,050	0.29	1.13	−168,925	55	53	89.82	519	115,653	−30,419	64	18
	TY	864,594	0.21	0.42	−173,953	63	43	29.41	457	71,770	−30,326	58	18
	US	456,844	0.10	0.26	−293,500	64	44	20.26	341	57,934	−32,771	56	18
Stock	SP	−525,075	−0.09	−0.32	−785,188	76	36	9.01	−767	44,358	−35,158	45	19
Metals	GC	56,740	−0.01	0.03	−468,870	68	35	46.00	18	62,783	−32,956	54	20
	HG	−297,838	−0.01	−0.18	−687,413	73	37	32.16	−127	43,378	−31,936	48	17
	PL	−1,080,215	−0.25	−0.66	−1,302,355	76	26	49.39	−300	44,647	−36,083	50	18
	SL	−629,135	−0.23	−0.40	−760,910	73	34	34.62	−267	32,762	−31,111	45	19
Energy	CL	888,760	0.17	0.42	−277,090	64	45	27.78	500	62,883	−26,710	49	21
	HO	486,003	0.12	0.21	−247,771	67	37	23.63	307	72,454	−31,556	51	22
	HU	−172,965	−0.02	−0.08	−491,480	79	38	22.21	−99	50,636	−34,531	44	19
Grains	C	925,163	0.19	0.45	−206,975	66	47	77.24	181	68,253	−34,019	51	19
	S	−92,275	−0.06	−0.05	−577,663	70	41	32.28	−48	38,934	−30,171	46	23
	W	162,725	0.07	0.08	−383,525	72	38	51.88	45	65,889	−35,773	52	19
Meats	FC	50,590	0.00	0.03	−438,020	67	39	40.01	17	48,903	−29,908	49	21
	LC	−154,676	−0.03	−0.09	−410,484	71	31	50.01	−44	53,697	−27,265	53	22
	LH	−134,704	0.03	−0.08	−360,008	71	30	31.44	−60	62,486	−28,938	56	21
	PB	−213,340	−0.07	−0.12	−565,640	68	37	20.49	−164	53,159	−36,233	51	20
Softs	CC	−465,190	−0.15	−0.27	−829,330	70	23	50.06	−152	62,602	−28,417	60	22
	CT	235,830	−0.01	0.13	−488,225	70	33	24.89	135	77,555	−32,935	58	19
	JO	−828,480	−0.14	−0.38	−1,264,553	73	25	35.88	−316	61,604	−35,225	52	21
	KC	1,022,948	0.12	0.32	−338,738	66	41	12.10	1,291	79,143	−28,350	53	19
	LB	1,398,328	0.13	0.49	−295,208	58	52	33.73	710	84,842	−41,297	53	19
	SB	−320,018	−0.11	−0.18	−622,171	72	31	53.41	−83	57,164	−31,553	50	20
	Average	199,043	0.02	0.07	−474,554	66	36	33.87	141	59,518	−30,610	50	19

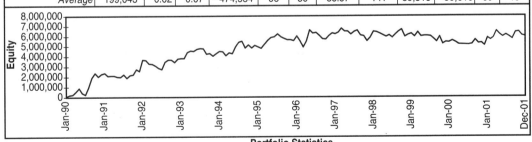

Portfolio Statistics

Net Profit:	5,971,279	Sharpe ratio:	0.41
Drawdown:	−1,710,956	Correlation to breakout:	1.00
K-ratio:	0.12	Correlation to 10-40 MA:	0.90

© 2002 Lars Kestner – All Rights Reserved

FIGURE 7.11a

Results of Channel Breakout Strategy Applied to Futures.

Breakdown Statistic (Futures)

System Name: 40 day entry/20 day exit channel breakout
Parameters: 40 day extreme for entry, 20 day extreme for exit
Description: Enter on 40 day extreme close; exit on a 20 day extreme close
Run Dates: 1/1/1990 – 12/31/2001

Breakdown by Market Sector

Market Sector	Average Net Profit	Average K-ratio	Average Sharpe Ratio	Average Max DD	Average Num Trades	Average % Win	Avg. Profit Per Contract	Average Win	Average Loss	Avg. Bars Win	Avg. Bars Loss
FX	354,723	0.08	0.19	-359,726	66	38	427	62,408	-28,930	52	20
Rates	971,122	0.15	0.45	-159,095	46	35	329	61,339	-23,379	45	14
Stock	-525,075	-0.09	-0.32	-785,188	76	36	-767	44,358	-35,158	45	19
Metals	-487,612	-0.13	-0.30	-804,887	73	33	-169	45,893	-33,021	49	19
Energy	400,600	0.09	0.18	-338,780	70	40	236	61,991	-30,932	48	21
Grains	331,871	0.07	0.16	-389,388	69	42	60	57,692	-33,321	50	20
Meats	-113,033	-0.02	-0.06	-443,538	69	34	-63	54,561	-30,586	52	21
Softs	173,903	-0.03	0.02	-639,704	68	34	264	70,485	-32,963	54	20

Performance Breakdown by Year

Year	Net Profit	K-ratio	Sharpe Ratio
1990	2,307,866	0.56	1.61
1991	1,291,201	0.19	0.94
1992	150,845	0.08	0.15
1993	681,499	0.07	0.72
1994	442,713	0.20	0.33
1995	1,075,741	0.20	1.20

Year	Net Profit	K-ratio	Sharpe Ratio
1996	202,431	0.11	0.12
1997	245,540	-0.15	0.20
1998	-216,622	-0.03	-0.21
1999	-857,497	-0.39	-0.48
2000	445,200	0.03	0.41
2001	132,049	0.08	0.11

Length	Number of Windows	Num. of Profitable Windows	Percent Profitable
1 Month	144	71	49.31%
3 Months	142	76	53.52%
6 Months	139	84	60.43%
12 Months	133	97	72.93%
18 Months	127	94	74.02%
24 Months	121	88	72.73%

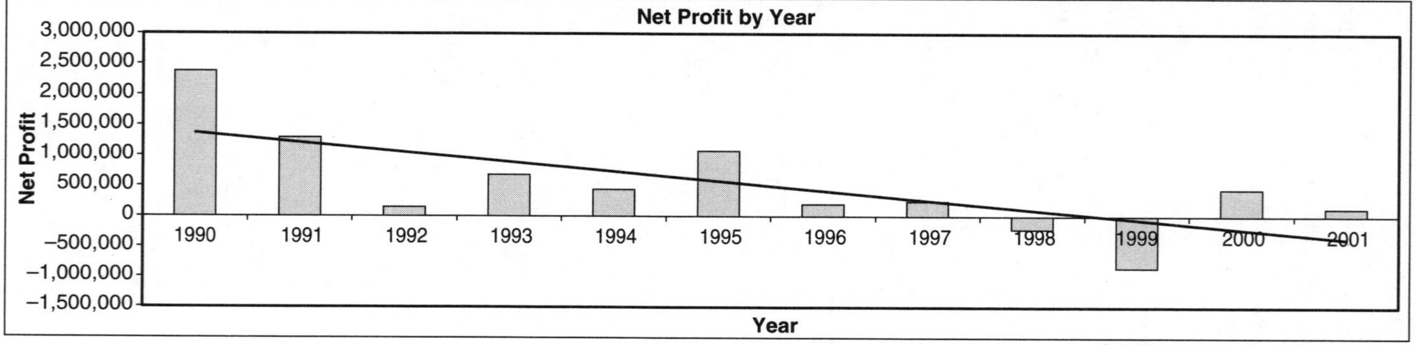

Net Profit by Year

© 2002 Lars Kestner – All Rights Reserved

FIGURE 7.11b

Results of Channel Breakout Strategy Applied to Futures.

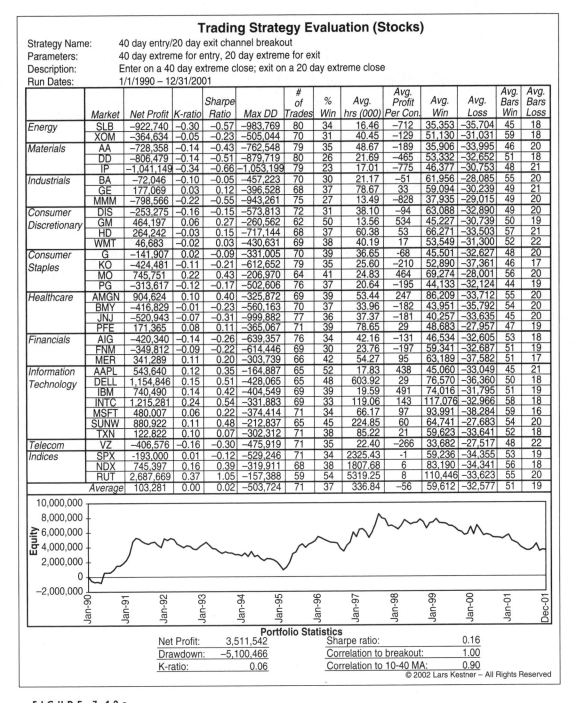

Trading Strategy Evaluation (Stocks)

Strategy Name: 40 day entry/20 day exit channel breakout
Parameters: 40 day extreme for entry, 20 day extreme for exit
Description: Enter on a 40 day extreme close; exit on a 20 day extreme close
Run Dates: 1/1/1990 – 12/31/2001

	Market	Net Profit	K-ratio	Sharpe Ratio	Max DD	# of Trades	% Win	Avg. hrs (000)	Avg. Profit Per Con.	Avg. Win	Avg. Loss	Avg. Bars Win	Avg. Bars Loss
Energy	SLB	−922,740	−0.30	−0.57	−983,769	80	34	16.46	−712	35,353	−35,704	45	18
	XOM	−364,634	−0.05	−0.23	−505,044	70	31	40.45	−129	51,130	−31,031	59	18
Materials	AA	−728,358	−0.14	−0.43	−762,548	79	35	48.67	−189	35,906	−33,995	46	20
	DD	−806,479	−0.14	−0.51	−879,719	80	26	21.69	−465	53,332	−32,652	51	18
	IP	−1,041,149	−0.34	−0.66	−1,053,199	79	23	17.01	−775	46,377	−30,753	48	21
Industrials	BA	−72,046	−0.10	−0.05	−457,223	70	30	21.17	−51	61,956	−28,085	55	20
	GE	177,069	0.03	0.12	−396,528	68	37	78.67	33	59,094	−30,239	49	21
	MMM	−798,566	−0.22	−0.55	−943,261	75	27	13.49	−828	37,935	−29,015	49	20
Consumer Discretionary	DIS	−253,275	−0.16	−0.15	−573,813	72	31	38.10	−94	63,088	−32,890	49	20
	GM	464,197	0.06	0.27	−260,562	62	50	13.56	534	45,227	−30,739	50	19
	HD	264,242	−0.03	0.15	−717,144	68	37	60.38	53	66,271	−33,503	57	21
	WMT	46,683	−0.02	0.03	−430,631	69	38	40.19	17	53,549	−31,300	52	22
Consumer Staples	G	−141,907	0.02	−0.09	−331,005	70	39	36.65	−68	45,501	−32,627	48	20
	KO	−424,481	−0.11	−0.21	−612,652	79	35	25.60	−210	52,890	−37,361	46	17
	MO	745,751	0.22	0.43	−206,970	64	41	24.83	464	69,274	−28,001	56	20
	PG	−313,617	−0.12	−0.17	−502,606	76	37	20.64	−195	44,133	−32,124	44	19
Healthcare	AMGN	904,624	0.10	0.40	−325,872	69	39	53.44	247	86,209	−33,712	55	20
	BMY	−416,829	−0.01	−0.23	−560,163	70	37	33.96	−182	43,951	−35,792	54	20
	JNJ	−520,943	−0.07	−0.31	−999,882	77	36	37.37	−181	40,257	−33,635	45	20
	PFE	171,365	0.08	0.11	−365,067	71	39	78.65	29	48,683	−27,957	47	19
Financials	AIG	−420,340	−0.14	−0.26	−639,357	76	34	42.16	−131	46,534	−32,605	53	18
	FNM	−349,812	−0.09	−0.22	−614,446	69	30	23.76	−197	59,341	−32,687	51	19
	MER	341,289	0.11	0.20	−303,739	66	42	54.27	95	63,189	−37,582	51	17
Information Technology	AAPL	543,640	0.12	0.35	−164,887	65	52	17.83	438	45,060	−33,049	45	21
	DELL	1,154,846	0.15	0.51	−428,065	65	48	603.92	29	76,570	−36,360	50	18
	IBM	740,490	0.14	0.42	−404,549	69	39	19.59	491	74,016	−31,795	51	19
	INTC	1,215,281	0.24	0.54	−331,883	69	33	119.06	143	117,076	−32,966	58	18
	MSFT	480,007	0.06	0.22	−374,414	71	34	66.17	97	93,991	−38,284	59	16
	SUNW	880,922	0.11	0.48	−212,837	65	45	224.85	60	64,741	−27,683	54	20
	TXN	122,822	0.10	0.07	−302,312	71	38	85.22	21	59,623	−33,641	52	18
Telecom	VZ	−406,576	−0.16	−0.30	−475,919	71	35	22.40	−266	33,682	−27,517	48	22
Indices	SPX	−193,000	0.01	−0.12	−529,246	71	34	2325.43	−1	59,236	−34,355	53	19
	NDX	745,397	0.16	0.39	−319,911	68	38	1807.68	6	83,190	−34,341	56	18
	RUT	2,687,669	0.37	1.05	−157,388	59	54	5319.25	8	110,446	−33,623	55	20
	Average	103,281	0.00	0.02	−503,724	71	37	336.84	−56	59,612	−32,577	51	19

Portfolio Statistics

Net Profit:	3,511,542	Sharpe ratio:	0.16
Drawdown:	−5,100,466	Correlation to breakout:	1.00
K-ratio:	0.06	Correlation to 10-40 MA:	0.90

© 2002 Lars Kestner – All Rights Reserved

FIGURE 7.12a

Results of Channel Breakout Strategy Applied to Stocks.

Breakdown Statistics (Stocks)

System Name: 40 day entry/20 day exit channel breakout
Parameters: 40 day extreme for entry, 20 day extreme for exit
Description: Enter on a 40 day extreme close; exit on a 20 day extreme close
Run Dates: 1/1/1990 – 12/31/2001

Breakdown by Market Sector

Market Sector	Average Net Profit	Average K-ratio	Average Sharpe Ratio	Average Max DD	Average Num Trades	Average % Win	Avg. Profit Per Contract	Average Win	Average Loss	Avg. Bars Win	Avg. Bars Loss
Energy	-643,687	-0.17	-0.40	-744,407	75	33	-421	43,242	-33,368	52	18
Materials	-858,662	-0.21	-0.53	-898,489	79	28	-476	45,205	-32,466	49	20
Industrials	-231,181	-0.10	-0.16	-599,004	71	31	-282	52,995	-29,113	51	20
Discretionary	130,462	-0.04	0.07	-495,538	68	39	128	57,034	-32,108	52	20
Staples	-33,564	0.00	-0.01	-413,308	72	38	-2	52,949	-32,528	48	19
Healthcare	34,554	0.03	-0.01	-562,746	72	38	-22	54,775	-32,774	50	20
Financials	-142,954	-0.04	-0.10	-519,181	70	36	-78	56,355	-34,291	51	18
Info. Tech.	734,001	0.13	0.37	-316,992	68	41	183	75,868	-33,397	53	19
Telecom	-406,576	-0.16	-0.30	-475,919	71	35	-266	33,682	-27,517	48	22
Indices	1,080,022	0.18	0.44	-335,515	66	42	4	84,291	-34,106	54	19

Performance Breakdown by Year

Year	Net Profit	K-ratio	Sharpe Ratio
1990	2,211,334	0.55	1.29
1991	2,908,152	0.12	1.25
1992	-790,907	-0.33	-0.73
1993	-1,569,699	-0.69	-1.96
1994	-1,315,095	-0.41	-0.92
1995	3,892,735	0.76	2.29
1996	-62,333	-0.02	-0.03
1997	1,306,090	0.17	0.48
1998	669,032	0.09	0.39
1999	-635,023	-0.42	-0.26
2000	-1,086,564	-0.27	-0.53
2001	-2,089,440	-0.32	-1.37

Profitability Windows

Length	Number of Windows	Num of Profitable Windows	Percent Profitable
1 Month	144	62	43.06%
3 Months	142	62	43.66%
6 Months	139	65	46.76%
12 Months	133	54	40.60%
18 Months	127	63	49.61%
24 Months	121	64	52.89%

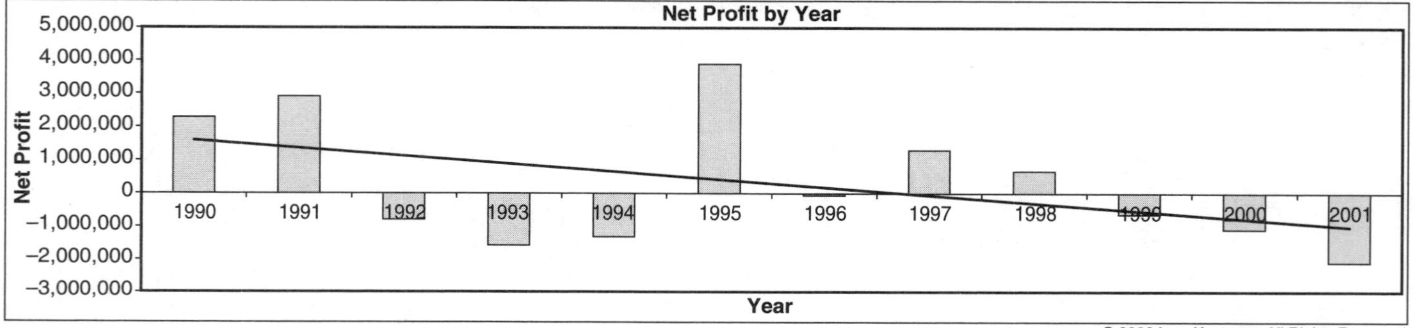

Net Profit by Year

© 2002 Lars Kestner – All Rights Reserved

FIGURE 7.12 b

Results of Channel Breakout Strategy Applied to Stocks.

Dual Moving Average Crossover

We use crosses of two moving averages for creating trading signals. A 10-day and 40-day simple moving average are calculated every day. Long entries are established if the 10-day average crosses above the 40-day average. Short entries are established if the 10-day average crosses below the 40-day average. Positions are exited on an entry signal in the opposite direction.

The chart below (Figure 7.13) applies the dual moving average crossover to Dell Computer (DELL). In mid-January the 10-day moving average falls below the 40-day moving average. This break generates a short entry. Later, in the beginning of March, prices rally and the 10-day average crosses above the 40-day average. This cross causes us to close short positions and establish a long position.

The dual moving average crossover also shows strong performance over the basket of markets tested (Figures 7.14a through 7.15b). Eleven of the 12 years produced profits on the futures side, while six of the 12 years produced profits on the stock side. The dual moving average crossover outperforms the channel breakout strategy above, producing higher Sharpe ratios and higher K-ratios on both futures markets and stocks. The similarity between the channel breakout and moving average crossover is noted by the high correlation in returns. Correlation is 0.90 for both futures and stocks. Performance in the moving average crossover

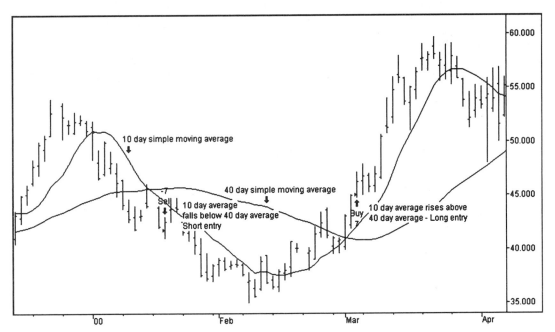

Created with TradeStation 2000i by Omega Research © 1999

FIGURE 7.13

Moving Average Crossover Strategy Applied to Dell.

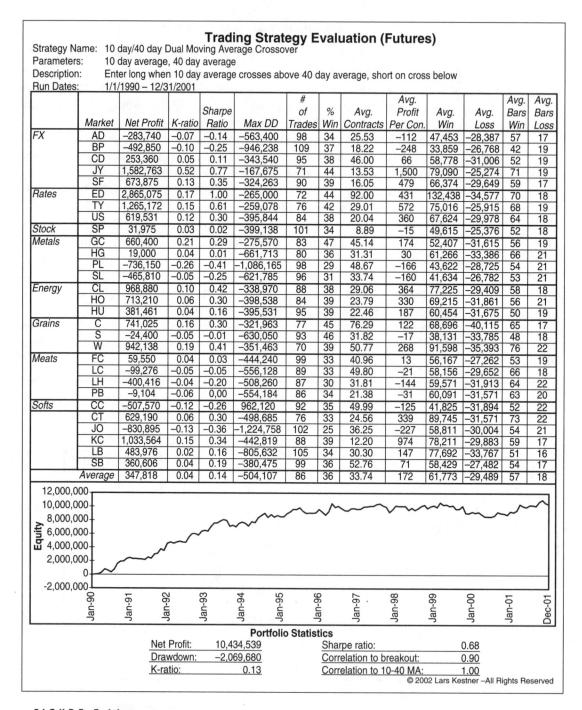

Trading Strategy Evaluation (Futures)

Strategy Name: 10 day/40 day Dual Moving Average Crossover
Parameters: 10 day average, 40 day average
Description: Enter long when 10 day average crosses above 40 day average, short on cross below
Run Dates: 1/1/1990 – 12/31/2001

	Market	Net Profit	K-ratio	Sharpe Ratio	Max DD	# of Trades	% Win	Avg. Contracts	Avg. Profit Per Con.	Avg. Win	Avg. Loss	Avg. Bars Win	Avg. Bars Loss
FX	AD	–283,740	–0.07	–0.14	–563,400	98	34	25.53	–112	47,453	–28,387	57	17
	BP	–492,850	–0.10	–0.25	–946,238	109	37	18.22	–248	33,859	–26,768	42	19
	CD	253,360	0.05	0.11	–343,540	95	38	46.00	66	58,778	–31,006	52	19
	JY	1,582,763	0.52	0.77	–167,675	71	44	13.53	1,500	79,090	–25,274	71	19
	SF	673,875	0.13	0.35	–324,263	90	39	16.05	479	66,374	–29,649	59	17
Rates	ED	2,865,075	0.17	1.00	–265,000	72	44	92.00	431	132,438	–34,577	70	18
	TY	1,265,172	0.15	0.61	–259,078	76	42	29.01	572	75,016	–25,915	68	19
	US	619,531	0.12	0.30	–395,844	84	38	20.04	360	67,624	–29,978	64	18
Stock	SP	31,975	0.03	0.02	–399,138	101	34	8.89	–15	49,615	–25,376	52	18
Metals	GC	660,400	0.21	0.29	–275,570	83	47	45.14	174	52,407	–31,615	56	19
	HG	19,000	0.04	0.01	–661,713	80	36	31.31	30	61,266	–33,386	66	21
	PL	–736,150	–0.26	–0.41	–1,086,165	98	29	48.67	–166	43,622	–28,725	54	21
	SL	–465,810	–0.05	–0.25	–621,785	96	31	33.74	–160	41,634	–26,782	53	21
Energy	CL	968,880	0.10	0.42	–338,970	88	38	29.06	364	77,225	–29,409	58	18
	HO	713,210	0.06	0.30	–398,538	84	39	23.79	330	69,215	–31,861	56	21
	HU	381,461	0.04	0.16	–395,531	95	39	22.46	187	60,454	–31,675	50	19
Grains	C	741,025	0.16	0.30	–321,963	77	45	76.29	122	68,696	–40,115	65	17
	S	–24,400	–0.05	–0.01	–630,050	93	46	31.82	–17	38,131	–33,785	48	18
	W	942,138	0.19	0.41	–351,463	70	39	50.77	268	91,598	–35,393	76	22
Meats	FC	59,550	0.04	0.03	–444,240	99	33	40.96	13	56,167	–27,262	53	19
	LC	–99,276	–0.05	–0.05	–556,128	89	33	49.80	–21	58,156	–29,652	66	18
	LH	–400,416	–0.04	–0.20	–508,260	87	30	31.81	–144	59,571	–31,913	64	22
	PB	–9,104	–0.06	0,00	–554,184	86	34	21.38	–31	60,091	–31,571	63	20
Softs	CC	–507,570	–0.12	–0.26	962,120	92	35	49.99	–125	41,825	–31,894	52	22
	CT	629,190	0.06	0.30	–498,685	76	33	24.56	339	89,745	–31,571	73	22
	JO	–830,895	–0.13	–0.36	–1,224,758	102	25	36.25	–227	58,811	–30,004	54	21
	KC	1,033,564	0.15	0.34	–442,819	88	39	12.20	974	78,211	–29,883	59	17
	LB	483,976	0.02	0.16	–805,632	105	34	30.30	147	77,692	–33,767	51	16
	SB	360,606	0.04	0.19	–380,475	99	36	52.76	71	58,429	–27,482	54	17
	Average	347,818	0.04	0.14	–504,107	86	36	33.74	172	61,773	–29,489	57	18

Portfolio Statistics

Net Profit:	10,434,539		Sharpe ratio:	0.68
Drawdown:	–2,069,680		Correlation to breakout:	0.90
K-ratio:	0.13		Correlation to 10-40 MA:	1.00

© 2002 Lars Kestner –All Rights Reserved

FIGURE 7.14a

Results of Moving Average Crossover Strategy Applied to Futures.

Breakdown Statistics (Futures)

System Name: 10 day/40 day Dual Moving Average Crossover
Parameters: 10 day average, 40 day average
Description: Enter long when 10 day average crosses above 40 day average, short on cross below
Run Dates: 1/1/1990 – 12/31/2001

Breakdown by Market Sector

Market Sector	Average Net Profit	Average K-ratio	Average Sharpe Ratio	Average Max DD	Average Num Trades	Average % Win	Avg. Profit Per Contract	Average Win	Average Loss	Avg. Bars Win	Avg. Bars Loss
FX	346,682	0.10	0.17	-469,023	93	38	337	57,111	-28,217	56	18
Rates	1,187,445	0.11	0.48	-229,980	58	31	341	68,769	-22,618	50	14
Stock	31,975	0.03	0.02	-399,138	101	34	-15	49,615	-25,376	52	18
Metals	-130,640	-0.01	-0.09	-661,308	89	36	-30	49,732	-30,127	57	20
Energy	687,850	0.07	0.29	-377,680	89	39	294	68,964	-30,981	55	19
Grains	552,921	0.10	0.23	-434,492	80	43	124	66,142	-36,431	63	19
Meats	-112,312	-0.03	-0.06	-515,703	90	32	-46	58,496	-30,100	61	20
Softs	194,812	0.00	0.06	-719,081	94	34	196	67,452	-30,767	57	19

Performance Breakdown by Year

Year	Net Profit	K-ratio	Sharpe Ratio	Year	Net Profit	K-ratio	Sharpe Ratio
1990	2,509,780	0.77	2.36	1996	15,802	0.06	0.01
1991	2,097,781	0.38	1.49	1997	514,921	-0.01	0.42
1992	1,932,274	0.60	1.77	1998	47,906	0.01	0.05
1993	1,223,970	0.13	0.86	1999	-940,824	-0.32	-0.40
1994	794,525	0.32	0.54	2000	82,997	0.01	0.09
1995	1,100,609	0.12	1.07	2001	1,086,424	0.38	0.79

Length	Number of Windows	Num. of Profitable Windows	Percent Profitable
1 Month	144	81	56.25%
3 Months	142	96	67.61%
6 Months	139	99	71.22%
12 Months	133	106	79.70%
18 Months	127	99	77.95%
24 Months	121	95	78.51%

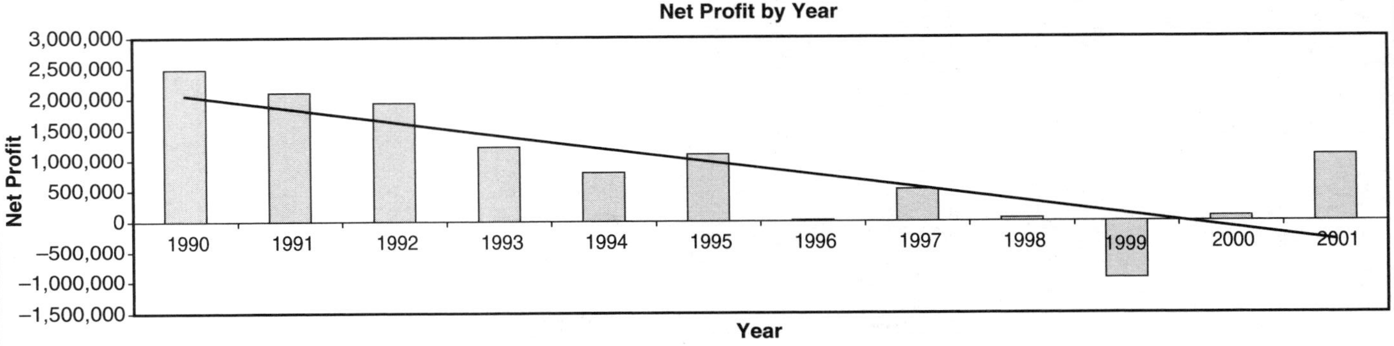

Net Profit by Year

© 2002 Lars Kestner – All Rights Reserved

FIGURE 7.14 b

Results of Moving Average Crossover Strategy Applied to Futures.

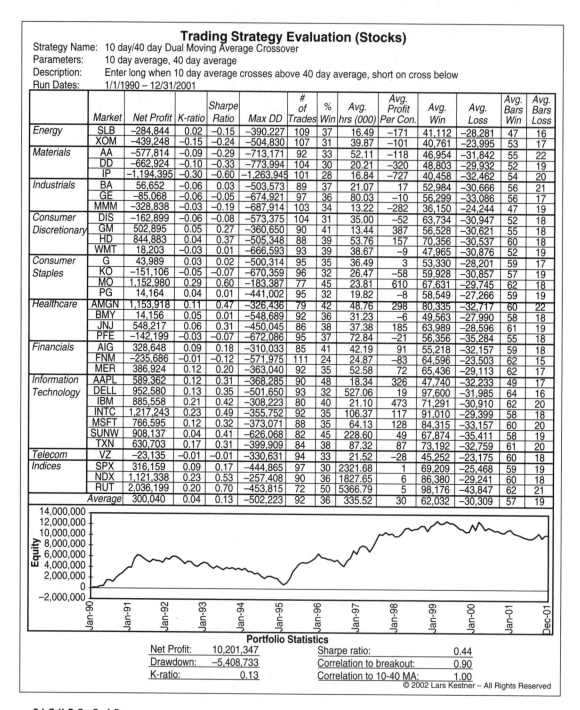

Trading Strategy Evaluation (Stocks)

Strategy Name: 10 day/40 day Dual Moving Average Crossover
Parameters: 10 day average, 40 day average
Description: Enter long when 10 day average crosses above 40 day average, short on cross below
Run Dates: 1/1/1990 – 12/31/2001

	Market	Net Profit	K-ratio	Sharpe Ratio	Max DD	# of Trades	% Win	Avg. hrs (000)	Avg. Profit Per Con.	Avg. Win	Avg. Loss	Avg. Bars Win	Avg. Bars Loss
Energy	SLB	−284,844	0.02	−0.15	−390,227	109	37	16.49	−171	41,112	−28,281	47	16
	XOM	−439,248	−0.15	−0.24	−504,830	107	31	39.87	−101	40,761	−23,995	53	17
Materials	AA	−577,814	−0.09	−0.29	−713,171	92	33	52.11	−118	46,954	−31,842	55	22
	DD	−662,924	−0.10	−0.33	−773,994	104	30	20.21	−320	48,803	−29,932	52	19
	IP	−1,194,395	−0.30	−0.60	−1,263,945	101	28	16.84	−727	40,458	−32,462	54	20
Industrials	BA	56,652	−0.06	0.03	−503,573	89	37	21.07	17	52,984	−30,666	56	21
	GE	−85,068	−0.06	−0.05	−674,921	97	36	80.03	−10	56,299	−33,086	56	17
	MMM	−328,838	−0.03	−0.19	−687,914	103	34	13.22	−282	36,150	−24,244	47	19
Consumer Discretionary	DIS	−162,899	−0.06	−0.08	−573,375	104	31	35.00	−52	63,734	−30,947	52	18
	GM	502,895	0.05	0.27	−360,650	90	41	13.44	387	56,528	−30,621	55	18
	HD	844,883	0.04	0.37	−505,348	88	39	53.76	157	70,356	−30,537	60	18
	WMT	18,203	−0.03	0.01	−666,593	93	39	38.67	−9	47,965	−30,876	52	19
Consumer Staples	G	43,989	0.03	0.02	−500,314	95	35	36.49	3	53,330	−28,201	59	17
	KO	−151,106	−0.05	−0.07	−670,359	96	32	26.47	−58	59,928	−30,857	57	19
	MO	1,152,980	0.29	0.60	−183,387	77	45	23.81	610	67,631	−29,745	62	18
	PG	14,164	0.04	0.01	−441,002	95	32	19.82	−8	58,549	−27,266	59	19
Healthcare	AMGN	1,153,918	0.11	0.47	−326,436	79	42	48.76	298	80,335	−32,717	60	22
	BMY	14,156	0.05	0.01	−548,689	92	36	31.23	−6	49,563	−27,990	58	18
	JNJ	548,217	0.06	0.31	−450,045	86	38	37.38	185	63,989	−28,596	61	19
	PFE	−142,199	−0.03	−0.07	−672,086	95	37	72.84	−21	56,356	−35,284	55	18
Financials	AIG	328,648	0.09	0.18	−310,033	85	41	42.19	91	55,218	−32,157	59	18
	FNM	−235,686	−0.01	−0.12	−571,975	111	24	24.87	−83	64,596	−23,503	62	15
	MER	386,924	0.12	0.20	−363,040	92	35	52.58	72	65,436	−29,113	62	17
Information Technology	AAPL	589,362	0.12	0.31	−368,285	90	48	18.34	326	47,740	−32,233	49	17
	DELL	952,580	0.13	0.35	−501,650	93	32	527.06	19	97,600	−31,985	64	16
	IBM	885,558	0.21	0.42	−308,223	80	40	21.10	473	71,291	−30,910	62	20
	INTC	1,217,243	0.23	0.49	−355,752	92	35	106.37	117	91,010	−29,399	58	18
	MSFT	766,595	0.12	0.32	−373,071	88	35	64.13	128	84,315	−33,157	60	20
	SUNW	908,137	0.04	0.41	−626,068	82	45	228.60	49	67,874	−35,411	58	19
	TXN	630,703	0.17	0.31	−399,909	84	38	87.32	87	73,192	−32,759	61	20
Telecom	VZ	−23,135	−0.01	−0.01	−330,631	94	33	21.52	−28	45,252	−23,175	60	18
Indices	SPX	316,159	0.09	0.17	−444,865	97	30	2321.68	1	69,209	−25,468	59	19
	NDX	1,121,338	0.23	0.53	−257,408	90	36	1827.65	6	86,380	−29,241	60	18
	RUT	2,036,199	0.20	0.70	−453,815	72	50	5366.79	5	98,176	−43,847	62	21
	Average	300,040	0.04	0.13	−502,223	92	36	335.52	30	62,032	−30,309	57	19

Portfolio Statistics

Net Profit:	10,201,347	Sharpe ratio:	0.44
Drawdown:	−5,408,733	Correlation to breakout:	0.90
K-ratio:	0.13	Correlation to 10-40 MA:	1.00

© 2002 Lars Kestner – All Rights Reserved

FIGURE 7.15a

Results of Moving Average Crossover Strategy Applied to Stocks.

Breakdown Statistics (Stocks)

System Name: 10 day/40 day Dual Moving Average Crossover
Parameters: 10 day average, 40 day average
Description: Enter long when 10 day average crosses above 40 day average, short on cross below
Run Dates: 1/1/19990 – 12/31/2001

Breakdown by Market Sector

Market Sector	Average Net Profit	Average K-ratio	Average Sharpe Ratio	Average Max DD	Average Num Trades	Average % Win	Avg. Profit Per Contract	Average Win	Average Loss	Avg. Bars Win	Avg. Bars Loss
Energy	-362,046	-0.06	-0.20	-447,529	108	34	-136	40,937	-26,138	50	17
Materials	-811,711	-0.16	-0.41	-917,037	99	30	-388	45,405	-31,412	54	20
Industrials	-119,085	-0.05	-0.07	-622,136	96	36	-92	48,478	-29,332	53	19
Discretionary	300,771	0.00	0.14	-526,492	94	37	121	59,645	-30,745	55	18
Staples	265,007	0.08	0.14	-448,766	91	36	137	59,860	-29,017	59	18
Healthcare	393,523	0.05	0.18	-499,314	88	38	114	62,561	-31,147	58	19
Financials	159,962	0.07	0.09	-415,016	96	33	26	61,750	-28,258	61	17
Info. Tech.	850,025	0.15	0.37	-418,994	87	39	171	76,146	-32,265	59	19
Telecom	-23,135	-0.01	-0.01	-330,631	94	33	-28	45,252	-23,175	60	18
Indices	1,157,899	0.17	0.47	-385,363	86	38	4	84,588	-32,852	60	19

Performance Breakdown by Year

Year	Net Profit	K-ratio	Sharpe Ratio
1990	3,973,593	1.03	3.00
1991	1,708,961	0.07	0.77
1992	-739,200	-0.34	-0.51
1993	-1,405,681	-0.32	-1.17
1994	-2,191,573	-0.71	-1.79
1995	5,294,085	0.88	3.17

Year	Net Profit	K-ratio	Sharpe Ratio
1996	-8,458	0.02	0.00
1997	3,292,301	0.45	1.26
1998	2,316,182	0.35	1.29
1999	4,560	-0.25	0.00
2000	-938,830	-0.25	-0.39
2001	-1,074,375	-0.12	-0.67

Profitability Windows

Length	Number of Windows	Num. of Profitable Windows	Percent Profitable
1 Month	144	70	48.61%
3 Months	142	72	50.70%
6 Months	139	74	53.24%
12 Months	133	68	51.13%
18 Months	127	70	55.12%
24 Months	121	75	61.98%

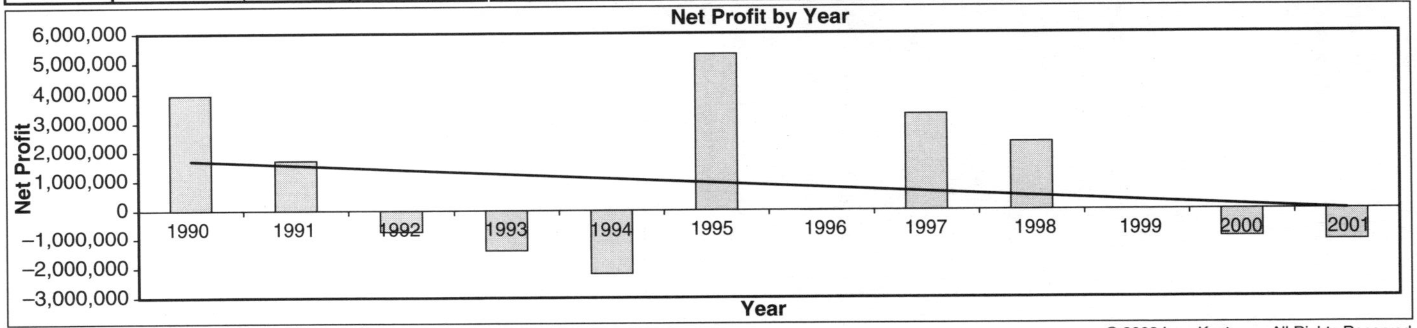

Net Profit by Year

© 2002 Lars Kestner – All Rights Reserved

FIGURE 7.15 b

Results of Moving Average Crossover Strategy Applied to Stocks.

149

is also dominated by similar sectors as in the channel breakout. Currencies, interest rates, petroleum, softs, technology, and stock indices all perform strongly.

Momentum

Perhaps the simplest strategy visited in this chapter is one that utilizes price momentum to generate long and short entries. Two parameter sets are tested—a shorter term 20-day momentum and a longer term 80-day momentum.

In the 20-day momentum strategy, long entries are established if today's close is greater than the close 20 days ago. Short entries are established if today's close is less than the close 20 days ago. In the 80-day momentum strategy, long entries are established if today's close is greater than the close 80 days ago. Short entries are established if today's close is less than the close 80 days ago.

Figure 7.16 is an example of the 20-day momentum strategy applied to the heating oil market. The indicator plotted in the lower half of the chart is a 20-day momentum. When prices begin to rise in early September, the 20-day momentum turns above zero and generates a long entry. Later in October, prices begin to fall. Short entries are established as the 20-day momentum crosses below zero.

The 20-day momentum produces strong results on futures markets but inconsistent results on stocks (Figures 7.17a through 7.18b). Profitable in 11 of the 12

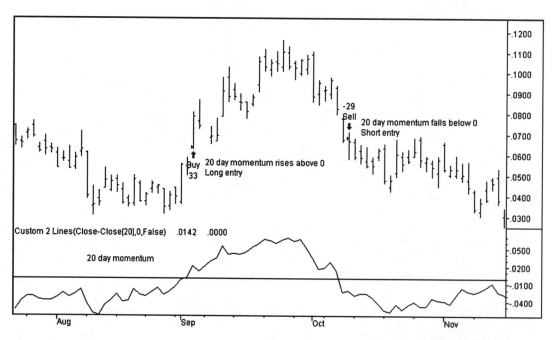

Created with TradeStation 2000i by Omega Research © 1999

FIGURE 7.16

Momentum Strategy Applied to Heating Oil.

Trading Strategy Evaluation (Futures)

Strategy Name: | 20 day momentum
Parameters: | 20 day momentum triggers entries and exits
Description: | Buy if today's close > close of 20 days ago; exit if today's close < close of 20 days ago
Run Dates: | 1/1/1990 – 12/31/2001

	Market	Net Profit	K-ratio	Sharpe Ratio	Max DD	# of Trades	% Win	Avg. Contracts	Avg. Profit Per Con.	Avg. Win	Avg. Loss	Avg. Bars Win	Avg. Bars Loss
FX	AD	−240,110	−0.11	−0.13	−657,880	277	34	25.59	−36	27,399	−15,721	20	6
	BP	272,363	0.04	0.14	−345,500	304	37	18.21	47	24,007	−12,835	16	6
	CD	−16,550	0.01	−0.01	−537,360	259	36	45.72	0	30,982	−17,050	21	6
	JY	1,208,800	0.27	0.56	−225,625	288	41	13.33	282	29,137	−13,608	17	6
	SF	840,975	0.16	0.40	−230,538	279	40	15.53	200	29,526	−14,617	19	5
Rates	ED	2,237,200	0.29	0.91	−340,725	211	41	85.21	125	52,017	−17,868	26	6
	TY	1,056,375	0.25	0.50	−252,438	246	38	29.53	140	36,936	−15,792	23	6
	US	690,281	0.22	0.33	−196,125	270	37	20.24	115	30,719	−14,365	21	5
Stock	SP	−339,700	−0.07	−0.17	−660,300	314	34	9.37	−115	25,473	−14,603	18	6
Metals	GC	301,520	0.16	0.14	−393,510	261	39	46.48	25	27,116	−15,763	20	6
	HG	−3,175	−0.05	0.00	−534,525	290	31	31.13	−3	29,372	−13,545	21	6
	PL	60,715	0.01	0.03	−399,160	301	41	45.86	−1	20,719	14,375	16	6
	SL	−549,855	−0.23	−0.30	−712,590	341	33	33.75	−55	18,669	−12,155	16	5
Energy	CL	1,604,530	0.32	0.69	−201,190	244	39	28.37	232	39,177	−14,575	23	6
	HO	1,009,915	0.17	0.41	−357,504	286	36	21.66	166	33,865	−13,709	19	6
	HU	657,989	0.09	0.26	−585,220	252	40	22.86	113	31,992	−16,773	20	6
Grains	C	985,675	0.20	0.43	−447,763	283	41	77.82	44	31,830	−16,371	19	5
	S	22,400	0.02	0.01	−561,575	308	36	30.86	−1	24,921	−14,099	18	5
	W	356,750	0.10	0.16	−515,825	250	37	52.97	28	32,099	−16,689	23	6
Meats	FC	−71,725	0.03	−0.04	−617,485	282	37	41.82	−6	27,201	−16,062	19	6
	LC	−452,296	−0.05	−0.22	−663,588	336	36	50.51	−26	23,855	−15,316	16	5
	LH	482,992	0.08	0.25	−386,912	245	36	31.94	61	32,863	−15,094	25	6
	PB	−213,316	−0.04	−0.10	−575,804	299	34	20.11	−44	29,489	−16,605	18	6
Softs	CC	−1,078,630	−0.21	−0.49	−1,290,390	307	27	50.20	−78	25,108	−14,500	21	6
	CT	−37,475	−0.07	−0.02	−566,855	298	32	25.31	−5	31,714	−14,799	20	6
	JO	−644,798	−0.17	−0.27	−1,096,418	283	31	36.15	−67	26,734	−15,372	19	7
	KC	794,805	0.17	0.31	−316,538	263	39	12.83	230	30,870	−14,726	20	6
	LB	142,136	−0.02	0.04	−1,185,224	250	32	31.25	16	46,316	−21,045	24	6
	SB	−486,697	−0.13	−0.24	−797,127	328	31	53.28	−26	27,319	−14,544	18	5
	Average	286,370	0.05	0.12	−521,723	272	35	33.60	45	29,248	−14,753	19	6

Portfolio Statistics

Net Profit:	8,591,095	Sharpe ratio:	0.53
Drawdown:	−1,631,559	Correlation to breakout:	0.86
K-ratio:	0.32	Correlation to 10-40 MA:	0.80

© 2002 Lars Kestner – All Rights Reserved

FIGURE 7.17a

Results of 20-day Momentum Strategy Applied to Futures.

Breakdown Statistics (Futures)

System Name: 20 day momentum
Parameters: 20 day momentum triggers entries and exits
Description: Buy if today's close > close of 20 days ago; exit if today's close < close of 20 days ago
Run Dates: 1/1/1990 – 12/31/2001

Breakdown by Market Sector

Market Sector	Average Net Profit	Average K-ratio	Average Sharpe Ratio	Average Max DD	Average Num Trades	Average % Win	Avg. Profit Per Contract	Average Win	Average Loss	Avg. Bars Win	Avg. Bars Loss
FX	413,096	0.08	0.19	-399,381	281	38	99	28,210	-14,766	19	6
Rates	995,964	0.19	0.44	-197,322	182	29	95	29,918	-12,006	17	4
Stock	-339,700	-0.07	-0.17	-660,300	314	34	-115	25,473	-14,603	18	6
Metals	-47,699	-0.03	-0.03	-509,946	298	36	-8	23,969	-13,960	18	6
Energy	1,090,811	0.20	0.45	-381,304	261	38	170	35,011	-15,019	21	6
Grains	454,942	0.11	0.20	-508,388	280	38	23	29,617	-15,720	20	5
Meats	-63,586	0.00	-0.02	-560,947	291	35	-4	28,352	-15,769	19	6
Softs	-218,443	-0.07	-0.11	-875,425	288	32	12	31,344	-15,831	20	6

Performance Breakdown by Year

Year	Net Profit	K-ratio	Sharpe Ratio
1990	970,061	0.31	0.76
1991	882,541	0.15	0.54
1992	1,177,523	0.29	1.17
1993	909,262	0.10	0.68
1994	308,412	0.12	0.20
1995	1,646,924	0.43	1.66

Year	Net Profit	K-ratio	Sharpe Ratio
1996	61,749	0.10	0.04
1997	1,734,574	0.32	1.42
1998	379,823	0.18	0.29
1999	-524,422	-0.10	-0.49
2000	736,747	-0.02	0.49
2001	170,648	0.23	0.13

Length	Number of Windows	Num. of Profitable Windows	Percent Profitable
1 Month	144	82	56.94%
3 Months	142	90	63.38%
6 Months	139	99	71.22%
12 Months	133	110	82.71%
18 Months	127	113	88.98%
24 Months	121	111	91.74%

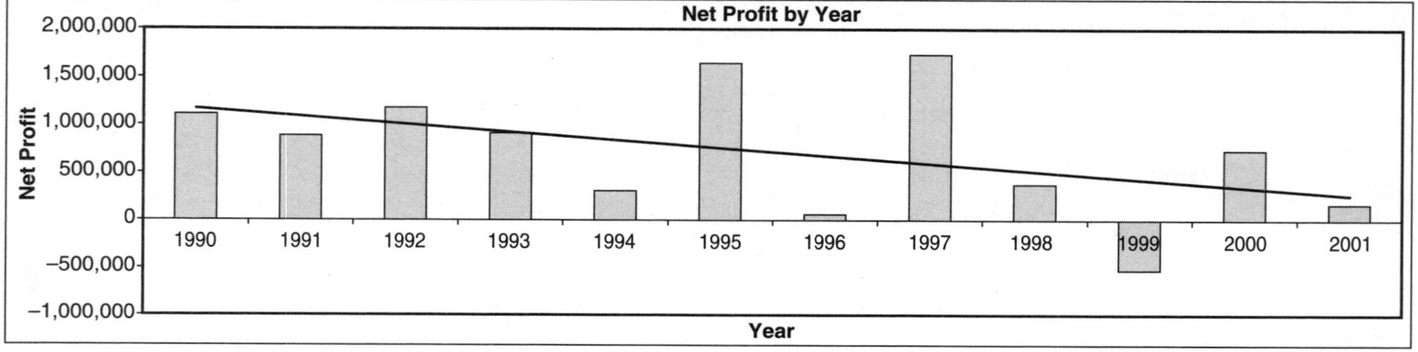

Net Profit by Year

© 2002 Lars Kestner – All Rights Reserved

FIGURE 7.17b

Results of 20-day Momentum Strategy Applied to Futures.

Trading Strategy Evaluation (Stocks)

Strategy Name: 20 day momentum
Parameters: 20 day momentum triggers entries and exits
Description: Buy if today's close > close of 20 days ago; exit if today's close < close of 20 days ago
Run Dates: 1/1/1990 – 12/31/2001

	Market	Net Profit	K-ratio	Sharpe Ratio	Max DD	# of Trades	% Win	Avg. hrs (000)	Avg. Profit Per Con.	Avg. Win	Avg. Loss	Avg. Bars Win	Avg. Bars Loss
Energy	SLB	−955,125	−0.30	−0.46	−997,275	324	34	15.31	−200	21,433	−15,833	16	6
	XOM	−1,359,121	−0.25	−0.76	−1,435,131	360	33	42.29	−91	16,705	−13,863	16	5
Materials	AA	−294,627	−0.04	−0.16	−486,388	62	35	51.37	−89	48,930	−33,972	56	25
	DD	−299,668	−0.09	−0.16	−504,303	285	35	19.95	−53	24,129	−14,469	19	6
	IP	−599,662	−0.13	−0.34	−750,473	310	35	15.64	−123	22,255	−15,033	17	6
Industrials	BA	−417,500	−0.15	−0.21	−1,029,025	289	37	20.55	−75	23,302	−16,351	18	6
	GE	−379,773	−0.14	−0.21	−655,041	346	35	76.68	−14	22,737	−14,048	16	5
	MMM	−722,739	−0.23	−0.39	−1,169,792	362	36	12.75	−170	18,099	−13,669	14	5
Consumer Discretionary	DIS	2,565	−0.06	0.00	−829,661	283	33	34.93	1	29,713	−14,277	19	7
	GM	−344,289	−0.16	−0.17	−672,231	321	35	13.01	−83	25,014	−14,875	17	5
	HD	−63,952	−0.05	−0.03	−640,216	303	36	59.54	−8	28,098	−16,550	18	5
	WMT	47,186	0.02	0.02	−375,945	280	39	38.91	3	25,740	−15,993	18	6
Consumer Staples	G	−1,169,342	−0.27	−0.58	−1,248,970	313	29	36.55	−106	26,412	−16,471	18	6
	KO	−221,768	−0.08	−0.10	−657,747	296	34	27.85	−25	27,554	−15,121	19	6
	MO	748,299	0.29	0.39	−208,049	302	40	23.14	107	25,937	−13,218	18	5
	PG	−1,252,387	−0.32	−0.58	−1,514,795	338	31	21.62	−170	22,422	−15,611	17	5
Healthcare	AMGN	532,002	0.04	0.22	−594,800	316	32	56.59	29	35,220	−13,884	20	5
	BMY	−688,343	−0.03	−0.36	−823,276	329	36	36.23	−59	20,605	−15,027	16	5
	JNJ	−865,251	−0.15	−0.41	−1,243,533	312	36	37.99	−72	22,709	−17,183	17	6
	PFE	322,112	0.12	0.17	−281,875	286	38	80.46	13	25,068	−13,960	19	6
Financials	AIG	632,361	0.19	0.35	−330,226	278	40	37.11	61	27,213	−14,577	18	6
	FNM	−928,974	−0.24	−0.49	−933,024	317	32	24.48	−119	23,351	−15,179	18	6
	MER	443,794	0.11	0.22	−323,894	253	35	48.54	36	34,065	−15,464	23	6
Information Technology	AAPL	1,000,862	0.18	0.54	−289,070	285	39	17.92	195	28,675	−12,336	19	5
	DELL	1,278,125	0.22	0.53	−367,356	250	39	540.00	9	39,541	−17,505	21	6
	IBM	1,485,401	0.27	0.70	−445,355	241	39	18.39	305	37,257	−14,277	23	6
	INTC	1,970,394	0.36	0.82	−259,640	250	41	112.51	70	41,264	−15,177	21	6
	MSFT	643,405	0.08	0.28	−346,784	285	33	66.20	31	35,008	−14,382	20	6
	SUNW	227,258	0.01	0.10	−439,377	283	36	201.46	4	31,610	−16,834	21	5
	TXN	222,272	0.11	0.10	−437,504	260	37	79.31	9	32,991	−17,835	21	6
Telecom	VZ	−1,452,631	−0.38	−0.76	−1,607,757	318	31	20.17	−225	20,695	−15,944	18	6
Indices	SPX	178,843	0.05	0.09	−541,793	298	31	2366.38	0	32,051	−13,195	20	6
	NDX	1,089,513	0.21	0.53	−272,123	319	37	1686.54	2	31,797	−13,421	18	5
	RUT	3,354,420	0.43	1.34	−228,710	199	39	4852.00	3	67,372	−16,443	28	6
Average		63,637	−0.01	0.01	−674,739	290	36	317.42	−24	29,264	−15,646	20	6

Portfolio Statistics

Net Profit:	2,163,659	Sharpe ratio:	0.10
Drawdown:	−6,983,168	Correlation to breakout:	0.87
K-ratio:	0.03	Correlation to 10-40 MA:	0.79

© 2002 Lars Kestner – All Rights Reserved

FIGURE 7.18a

Results of 20-day Momentum Strategy Applied to Stocks.

Breakdown Statistics (Stocks)

System Name: 20 day momentum
Parameters: 20 day momentum triggers entries and exits
Description: Buy if today's close > close of 20 days ago; exit if today's close < close of 20 days ago
Run Dates: 1/1/1990 – 12/31/2001

Breakdown by Market Sector

Market Sector	Average Net Profit	Average K-ratio	Average Sharpe Ratio	Average Max DD	Average Num Trades	Average % Win	Avg. Profit Per Contract	Average Win	Average Loss	Avg. Bars Win	Avg. Bars Loss
Energy	-1,157,123	-0.28	-0.61	-1,216,203	342	34	-146	19,069	-14,848	16	5
Materials	-397,986	-0.09	-0.22	-580,388	219	35	-88	31,771	-21,158	31	12
Industrials	-506,671	-0.17	-0.27	-951,286	332	36	-86	21,379	-14,690	16	5
Discretionary	-89,623	-0.06	-0.04	-629,513	297	35	-22	27,141	-15,424	18	6
Staples	-473,800	-0.10	-0.22	-907,390	312	34	-49	25,581	-15,105	18	5
Healthcare	-174,870	-0.01	-0.10	-735,871	311	36	-22	25,900	-15,014	18	5
Financials	49,060	0.02	0.03	-529,048	283	36	-7	28,210	-15,073	20	6
Info. Tech.	975,388	0.18	0.44	-369,298	265	38	89	35,192	-15,478	21	6
Telecom	-1,452,631	-0.38	-0.76	-1,607,757	318	31	-225	20,695	-15,944	18	6
Indices	1,540,925	0.23	0.65	-347,542	272	36	2	43,740	-14,353	22	6

Performance Breakdown by Year

Year	Net Profit	K-ratio	Sharpe Ratio
1990	2,158,278	0.50	1.09
1991	3,712,911	0.23	1.60
1992	-578,265	-0.33	-0.44
1993	-1,228,554	-0.49	-0.92
1994	-827,251	-0.15	-0.61
1995	2,414,329	0.40	1.62
1996	-1,031,018	-0.07	-0.42
1997	2,041,296	0.25	0.65
1998	581,269	0.10	0.26
1999	-1,483,106	-0.42	-0.75
2000	-2,013,818	-0.47	-1.08
2001	-1,444,220	-0.24	-0.86

Profitability Windows

Length	Number of Windows	Num. of Profitable Windows	Percent Profitable
1 Month	144	68	47.22%
3 Months	142	65	45.77%
6 Months	139	62	44.60%
12 Months	133	61	45.86%
18 Months	127	63	49.61%
24 Months	121	59	48.76%

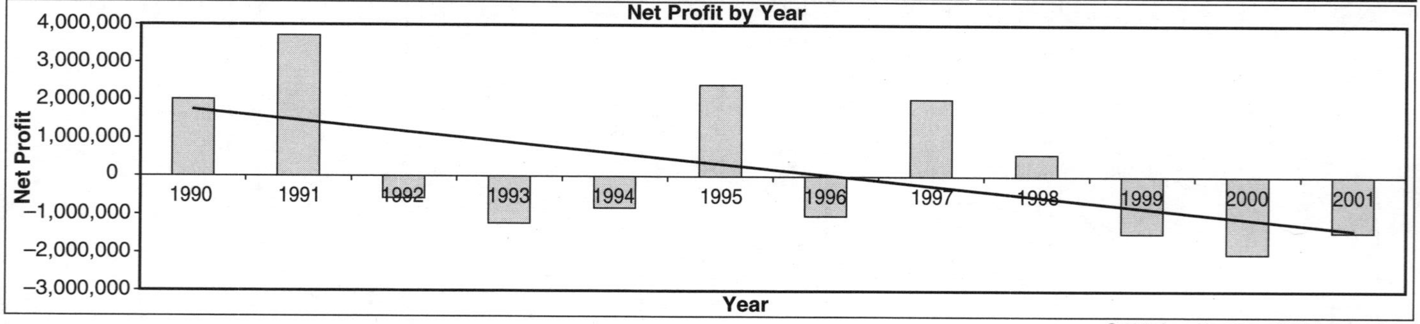

Net Profit by Year

© 2002 Lars Kestner – All Rights Reserved

FIGURE 7.18 b

Results of 20-day Momentum Strategy Applied to Stocks.

years on futures but only five of 12 years on stocks, the 20-day momentum strategy's returns are highly correlated to both the 40-day entry/20-day exit channel breakout and a 10-day/40-day moving average crossover strategy.

Note the dichotomy of performance on the stock side. Very strong performance is generated on technology stocks and on stock indices, with every market producing profits. Yet when we look at the energy, materials, and industrial sectors, all eight markets led to losses. This split performance is becoming very prevalent and leads me to believe that some sectors are more apt to trend than other sectors.

In addition to the 20-day momentum, an 80-day momentum strategy was also tested (Figures 7.19a through 7.20b). In both futures markets and stocks, the 80-day momentum strategy produces higher Sharpe ratios and higher K-ratios. This improved performance is due to the enhanced profitability of the petroleum and soft sectors in the tests of futures, and health care and consumer discretionary sectors in the stock tests.

Volatility Breakout

We also test the performance of a volatility breakout strategy. In this version, we enter long if today's price change is greater than twice the standard deviation of price changes over the past 100 days. We enter short if today's price change is less than negative two times the standard deviation of price changes over the past 100 days. There are no other entry rules and no rules for exiting positions, except for an entry in the other direction.

The chart below (Figure 7.21) of Fannie Mae (FNM) details entries generated by our volatility breakout strategy. The strong one-day rise in late March was the only day strong enough to generate a trading signal in this example. The rise was large enough that a buy order was placed for the next morning's opening.

The performance of the volatility breakout strategy leads to results somewhat backward to the tests examined thus far (Figures 7.22a through 7.23b). Profitability on stocks is somewhat strong, while tests on futures barely eke out a profit over the 12 years of the back-test. Correlation to the channel breakout and moving average crossover strategies is on average about 0.50, suggesting that we may incorporate some benefits of diversification by adding this strategy to our trading program.

Stochastics

Oscillators are also tested in our performance details. The first uses a 14-day Slow %K stochastic to generate long and short entries (refer to Chapter 3 for a detailed explanation on the derivation of the Slow %K, RSI, and MACD oscillators). Long entries are established when today's 14-day Slow %K stochastic falls below 20 and then crosses back above 20. Short entries are established when today's 14-day

Trading Strategy Evaluation (Futures)

Strategy Name: 80 day momentum
Parameters: 80 day momentum triggers entries and exits
Description: Buy if today's close > close of 80 days ago; exit if today's close < close 80 days ago
Run Dates: 1/1/1990 – 12/31/2001

	Market	Net Profit	K-ratio	Sharpe Ratio	Max DD	# of Trades	% Win	Avg Contracts	Avg. Profit Per Con.	Avg. Win	Avg. Loss	Avg. Bars Win	Avg. Bars Loss
FX	AD	−53,390	0.05	−0.03	−369,570	165	34	25.72	−15	28,760	−15,343	36	9
	BP	−207,750	−0.11	−0.10	−890,925	182	36	17.72	−80	24,698	−16,272	29	10
	CD	108,550	0.06	0.05	−320,690	135	37	46.51	6	32,743	−18,846	43	9
	JY	1,480,200	0.34	0.73	−215,013	93	53	13.03	1,139	46,165	−20,042	52	10
	SF	382,513	0.06	0.20	−215,963	107	34	14.97	254	45,470	−17,316	57	13
Rates	ED	2,171,300	0.15	0.90	−306,575	88	32	79.91	140	71,313	−16,813	79	8
	TY	731,469	0.27	0.32	−230,719	135	37	28.10	197	41,759	−15,770	50	6
	US	887,375	0.28	0.44	−380,125	111	42	21.25	376	42,355	−17,252	53	8
Stock	SP	−218,825	0.01	−0.11	−698,850	153	30	8.95	−154	38,173	−18,377	46	8
Metals	GC	109,890	0.05	0.05	−515,420	124	33	44.60	19	34,419	−15,718	52	11
	HG	567,225	0.10	0.30	−398,325	120	32	33.68	135	49,671	−16,355	54	11
	PL	178,875	−0.02	0.08	−877,635	154	29	50.75	19	47,832	−18,420	39	11
	SL	−645,880	−0.18	−0.31	−956,165	193	27	30.75	−117	25,455	−14,298	37	8
Energy	CL	2,266,660	0.31	0.88	−184,980	97	41	29.73	725	75,627	−16,391	57	12
	HO	1,767,402	0.21	0.60	−276,864	133	32	25.51	462	66,900	−14,531	49	9
	HU	1,673,839	0.29	0.61	−263,802	113	40	21.93	627	56,174	−14,330	48	12
Grains	C	1,547,663	0.16	0.45	−469,350	129	40	75.38	157	58,349	−19,588	43	10
	S	−322,500	−0.07	−0.16	−470,413	152	36	30.22	−76	25,199	−17,871	31	13
	W	840,038	0.15	0.39	−197,363	102	36	51.89	156	56,656	−19,537	63	10
Meats	FC	−167,295	−0.02	−0.08	−832,785	165	29	39.87	−30	40,651	−18,353	36	10
	LC	74,576	−0.03	0.04	−494,868	165	28	47.04	−9	36,125	−14,964	43	8
	LH	477,696	0.10	0.22	−449,308	107	37	32.99	132	43,936	−19,257	59	9
	PB	−161,740	0.00	−0.07	−525,592	147	31	20.36	−55	35,759	−17,382	39	12
Softs	CC	174,230	−0.02	0.00	−672,420	113	31	48.18	6	40,789	−17,860	62	10
	CT	797,555	0.08	0.40	−469,535	130	30	24.08	106	47,246	−16,597	50	9
	JO	−139,043	−0.01	−0.06	−439,710	166	35	36.65	−23	26,068	−15,319	36	8
	KC	1,453,515	0.19	0.45	−275,794	136	34	10.86	843	54,439	−13,981	37	11
	LB	1,193,984	0.19	0.37	−318,136	119	33	36.19	257	62,003	−16,389	61	7
	SB	157,236	0.04	0.08	−373,173	131	29	53.93	23	41,171	−15,049	61	7
	Average	570,846	0.09	0.22	−436,336	129	33	33.36	174	43,197	−16,274	47	9

Portfolio Statistics

Net Profit:	17,125,366	Sharpe ratio:	1.01
Drawdown:	−1,302,645	Correlation to breakout:	0.71
K-ratio:	0.53	Correlation to 10-40 MA:	0.65

© 2002 Lars Kestner – All Rights Reserved

FIGURE 7.19a

Results of 80-day Momentum Strategy Applied to Futures.

Breakdown Statistics (Futures)

System Name: 80 day momentum
Parameters: 80 day momentum triggers entries and exits
Description: Buy if today's close > close of 80 days ago; exit if today's close < close of 80 days ago
Run Dates: 1/1/1990 – 12/31/2001

Breakdown by Market Sector

Market Sector	Average Net Profit	Average K-ratio	Average Sharpe Ratio	Average Max DD	Average Num Trades	Average % Win	Avg. Profit Per Contract	Average Win	Average Loss	Avg. Bars Win	Avg. Bars Loss
FX	342,025	0.08	0.17	-402,432	136	39	261	35,567	-17,564	43	10
Rates	947,536	0.18	0.41	-229,355	84	28	178	38,857	-12,459	45	5
Stock	-218,825	0.01	-0.11	-698,850	153	30	-154	38,173	-18,377	46	8
Metals	52,528	-0.01	0.03	-686,886	148	30	14	39,344	-16,198	46	10
Energy	1,902,633	0.27	0.70	-241,882	114	38	605	66,234	-15,084	51	11
Grains	688,400	0.08	0.23	-379,042	128	38	79	46,735	-18,998	46	11
Meats	55,809	0.01	0.03	-575,638	146	31	10	39,118	-17,489	44	10
Softs	606,246	0.08	0.22	-424,795	133	32	202	45,286	-15,866	51	9

Performance Breakdown by Year

Year	Net Profit	K-ratio	Sharpe Ratio	Year	Net Profit	K-ratio	Sharpe Ratio
1990	1,944,570	0.64	1.39	1996	2,312,252	0.53	1.33
1991	1,421,135	0.19	0.89	1997	828,593	0.02	0.78
1992	-53,122	0.04	-0.04	1998	2,331,234	0.71	1.81
1993	697,802	0.01	0.56	1999	508,325	0.09	0.20
1994	2,479,142	0.65	1.67	2000	2,546,629	0.81	2.10
1995	1,815,731	0.61	1.93	2001	346,263	0.13	0.16

Length	Number of Windows	Num. of Profitable Windows	Percent Profitable
1 Month	144	86	59.72%
3 Months	142	102	71.83%
6 Months	139	118	84.89%
12 Months	133	126	94.74%
18 Months	127	124	97.64%
24 Months	121	120	99.17%

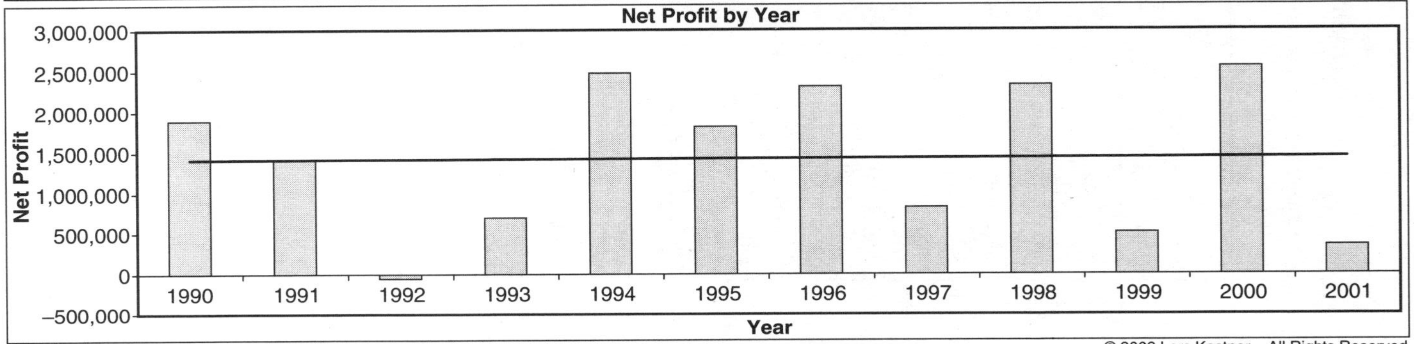

Net Profit by Year

© 2002 Lars Kestner – All Rights Reserved

FIGURE 7.19b

Results of 80-day Momentum Strategy Applied to Futures.

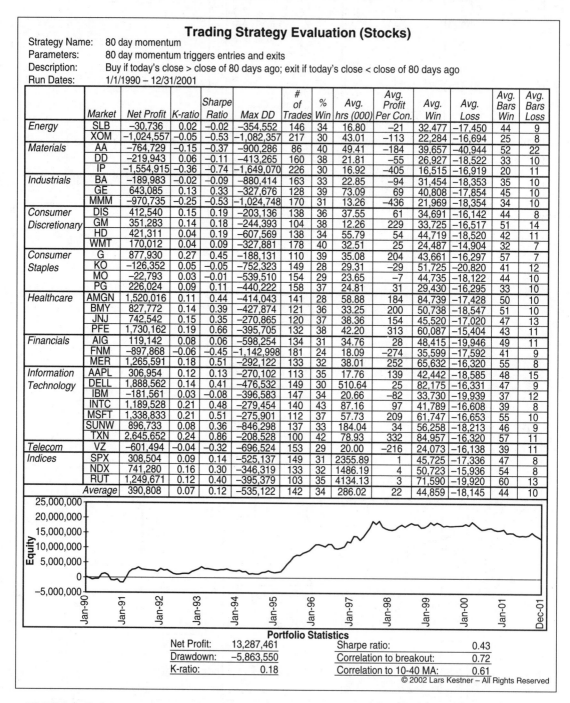

Trading Strategy Evaluation (Stocks)

Strategy Name: 80 day momentum
Parameters: 80 day momentum triggers entries and exits
Description: Buy if today's close > close of 80 days ago; exit if today's close < close of 80 days ago
Run Dates: 1/1/1990 – 12/31/2001

	Market	Net Profit	K-ratio	Sharpe Ratio	Max DD	# of Trades	% Win	Avg. hrs (000)	Avg. Profit Per Con.	Avg. Win	Avg. Loss	Avg. Bars Win	Avg. Bars Loss
Energy	SLB	−30,736	0.02	−0.02	−354,552	146	34	16.80	−21	32,477	−17,450	44	9
	XOM	−1,024,557	−0.05	−0.53	−1,082,357	217	30	43.01	−113	22,284	−16,694	25	8
Materials	AA	−764,729	−0.15	−0.37	−900,286	86	40	49.41	−184	39,657	−40,944	52	22
	DD	−219,943	0.06	−0.11	−413,265	160	38	21.81	−55	26,927	−18,522	33	10
	IP	−1,554,915	−0.36	−0.74	−1,649,070	226	30	16.92	−405	16,515	−16,919	20	11
Industrials	BA	−189,983	−0.02	−0.09	−880,414	163	33	22.85	−94	31,454	−18,353	35	10
	GE	643,085	0.13	0.33	−327,676	128	39	73.09	69	40,808	−17,854	45	10
	MMM	−970,735	−0.25	−0.53	−1,024,748	170	31	13.26	−436	21,969	−18,354	34	10
Consumer Discretionary	DIS	412,540	0.15	0.19	−203,136	138	36	37.55	61	34,691	−16,142	44	8
	GM	351,283	0.14	0.18	−244,393	104	38	12.26	229	33,725	−16,517	51	14
	HD	421,311	0.04	0.19	−607,569	138	34	55.79	54	44,719	−18,520	42	11
	WMT	170,012	0.04	0.09	−327,881	178	40	32.51	25	24,487	−14,904	32	7
Consumer Staples	G	877,930	0.27	0.45	−188,131	110	39	35.08	204	43,661	−16,297	57	7
	KO	−126,352	0.05	−0.05	−752,323	149	28	29.31	−29	51,725	−20,820	41	12
	MO	−22,793	0.03	−0.01	−539,510	154	29	23.65	−7	44,735	−18,122	44	10
	PG	226,024	0.09	0.11	−440,222	158	37	24.81	31	29,430	−16,295	33	10
Healthcare	AMGN	1,520,016	0.11	0.44	−414,043	141	28	58.88	184	84,739	−17,428	50	10
	BMY	827,772	0.14	0.39	−427,874	121	36	33.25	200	50,738	−18,547	51	10
	JNJ	742,542	0.15	0.35	−270,865	120	37	38.36	154	45,520	−17,020	47	13
	PFE	1,730,162	0.19	0.66	−395,705	132	38	42.20	313	60,087	−15,404	43	11
Financials	AIG	119,142	0.08	0.06	−598,254	134	31	34.76	28	48,415	−19,946	49	11
	FNM	−897,868	−0.06	−0.45	−1,142,998	181	24	18.09	−274	35,599	−17,592	41	9
	MER	1,265,591	0.18	0.51	−292,122	133	32	38.01	252	65,632	−16,320	55	8
Information Technology	AAPL	306,954	0.12	0.13	−270,102	113	35	17.76	139	42,442	−18,585	48	15
	DELL	1,888,562	0.14	0.41	−476,532	149	30	510.64	25	82,175	−16,331	47	9
	IBM	−181,561	0.03	−0.08	−396,583	147	34	20.66	−82	33,730	−19,939	37	12
	INTC	1,189,528	0.21	0.48	−279,454	140	43	87.16	97	41,789	−16,608	39	8
	MSFT	1,338,833	0.21	0.51	−275,901	112	37	57.73	209	61,747	−16,653	55	10
	SUNW	896,733	0.08	0.36	−846,298	137	33	184.04	34	56,258	−18,213	46	9
	TXN	2,645,652	0.24	0.86	−208,528	100	42	78.93	332	84,957	−16,320	57	11
Telecom	VZ	−601,494	−0.04	−0.32	−696,524	153	29	20.00	−216	24,073	−16,138	39	11
Indices	SPX	308,504	0.09	0.14	−525,137	149	31	2355.89	1	45,725	−17,336	47	8
	NDX	741,280	0.16	0.30	−346,319	133	32	1486.19	4	50,723	−15,936	54	8
	RUT	1,249,671	0.12	0.40	−395,379	103	35	4134.13	3	71,590	−19,920	60	13
	Average	390,808	0.07	0.12	−535,122	142	34	286.02	22	44,859	−18,145	44	10

Portfolio Statistics

Net Profit:	13,287,461	Sharpe ratio:	0.43
Drawdown:	−5,863,550	Correlation to breakout:	0.72
K-ratio:	0.18	Correlation to 10-40 MA:	0.61

© 2002 Lars Kestner – All Rights Reserved

FIGURE 7.20a

Results of 80-day Momentum Strategy Applied to Stocks.

159

Breakdown Statistics (Stocks)

System Name: 80 day momentum
Parameters: 80 day momentum triggers entries and exits
Description: Buy if today's close > close of 80 days ago; exit if today's close < close of 80 days ago
Run Dates: 1/1/1990 – 12/31/2001

Breakdown by Market Sector

Market Sector	Average Net Profit	Average K-ratio	Average Sharpe Ratio	Average Max DD	Average Num Trades	Average % Win	Avg. Profit Per Contract	Average Win	Average Loss	Avg. Bars Win	Avg. Bars Loss
Energy	-527,647	-0.01	-0.27	-718,455	182	32	-67	27,380	-17,072	35	9
Materials	-846,529	-0.15	-0.40	-987,540	157	36	-215	27,700	-25,462	35	14
Industrials	-172,544	-0.05	-0.10	-744,279	154	34	-154	31,410	-18,187	38	10
Discretionary	338,787	0.09	0.16	-345,745	140	37	92	34,405	-16,521	42	10
Staples	238,702	0.11	0.13	-480,047	143	33	50	42,388	-17,883	44	10
Healthcare	1,205,123	0.15	0.46	-377,122	129	35	213	60,271	-17,100	48	11
Financials	162,288	0.07	0.04	-677,791	149	29	2	49,882	-17,953	49	9
Info. Tech.	1,154,957	0.15	0.38	-393,343	128	36	108	57,585	-17,521	47	11
Telecom	-601,494	-0.04	-0.32	-696,524	153	29	-216	24,073	-16,138	39	11
Indices	766,485	0.12	0.28	-422,279	128	33	3	56,013	-17,731	53	10

Performance Breakdown by Year

Year	Net Profit	K-ratio	Sharpe Ratio
1990	-1,889,995	-0.14	-0.68
1991	4,643,077	0.19	1.69
1992	-88,700	-0.04	-0.06
1993	-625,273	-0.30	-0.56
1994	-524,972	-0.05	-0.39
1995	8,422,657	1.31	4.97

Year	Net Profit	K-ratio	Sharpe Ratio
1996	1,770,088	0.06	0.64
1997	4,296,308	0.30	0.90
1998	1,393,734	0.15	0.62
1999	610,535	-0.09	0.13
2000	-1,843,270	-0.38	-0.84
2001	-3,119,418	-0.29	-1.58

Profitability Windows

Length	Number of Windows	Num. of Profitable Windows	Percent Profitable
1 Month	144	76	52.78%
3 Months	142	75	52.82%
6 Months	139	71	51.08%
12 Months	133	77	57.89%
18 Months	127	86	67.72%
24 Months	121	86	71.07%

Net Profit by Year

© 2002 Lars Kestner – All Rights Reserved

FIGURE 7.20b

Results of 80-day Momentum Strategy Applied to Stocks.

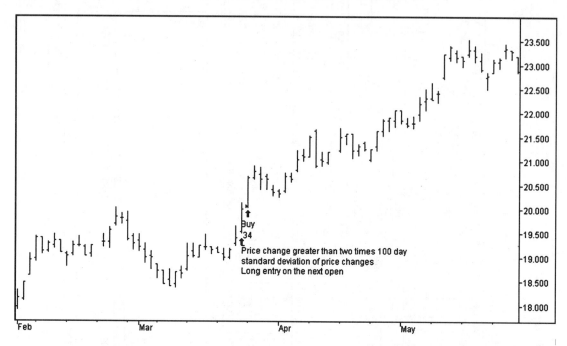

Buy
34
Price change greater than two times 100 day
standard deviation of price changes
Long entry on the next open

Created with TradeStation 2000i by Omega Research © 1999

FIGURE 7.21

Volatility Breakout Strategy Applied to Fannie Mae.

Slow %K stochastic rises above 80 and then crosses below 80. There are no other rules and no rules for exiting positions, except for an entry in the other direction.

Sample entries and exits are applied to Home Depot (HD) in the graph below (Figure 7.24). The stochastic oscillator is adept at picking tops and bottoms in mean reverting markets. In early October, prices become overbought, leading to a stochastic level greater than 80. Short entries are established as the 14-day Slow %K stochastic falls back below 80. Long entries are established in late October as the stochastic indicator falls below and then rises above 20.

Results of the 14-day slow %K stochastics leave much to be desired (see Figures 7.25a through 7.26b). Performance on futures is dreadful, as the strategy produces profits in only two of the 12 years in the test. Stock performance is not quite as bad, with profits coming in 5 out of the 12 years. On the futures side, sectors that perform poorly under standard trend-following rules (metals, meats, cocoa) perform very well using the stochastics strategy.

Returns from this stochastics strategy are negatively correlated to returns from channel breakout and moving average crossover. This should not be surprising. In the stochastics strategy, we buy as prices fall and sell as prices rise—exactly opposite to the other two trend-following strategies.

Trading Strategy Evaluation (Futures)

Strategy Name: Volatility breakout
Parameters: 1 day returns, 2 sigmas of past 100 day price returns
Description: Enter long if today's price return is greater than twice the 100 day sigma; opposite for shorts
Run Dates: 1/1/1990 – 12/31/2001

	Market	Net Profit	K-ratio	Sharpe Ratio	Max DD	# of Trades	% Win	Avg. Contracts	Avg. Profit Per Con.	Avg. Win	Avg. Loss	Avg. Bars Win	Avg. Bars Loss
FX	AD	−374,390	−0.06	−0.21	−996,300	85	29	26.14	−173	62,710	−32,553	52	27
	BP	−312,888	−0.05	−0.14	−865,825	100	39	17.94	−170	49,506	−36,652	40	23
	CD	428,410	0.03	0.19	−752,590	72	49	47.66	126	63,784	−48,609	49	35
	JY	468,563	0.02	0.24	−412,688	86	44	13.80	264	54,336	−36,477	42	28
	SF	−631,538	−0.12	−0.33	−943,825	92	36	16.15	−417	55,508	−41,552	49	24
Rates	ED	1,832,900	0.19	0.88	−398,875	74	49	84.12	301	94,512	−40,198	61	22
	TY	−482,313	−0.06	−0.24	−717,188	90	40	30.56	−176	55,945	−46,250	44	26
	US	−172,125	0.04	−0.08	−519,281	80	40	21.46	−167	57,770	−44,501	44	32
Stock	SP	−172,025	−0.12	−0.08	−619,950	97	33	8.29	−344	58,113	−32,858	41	25
Metals	GC	572,370	0.13	0.27	−490,410	68	40	49.16	170	81,809	−40,000	66	27
	HG	−321,000	−0.19	−0.17	−834,600	77	38	33.67	−148	47,465	−36,691	44	35
	PL	338,455	0.12	0.19	−312,435	68	47	48.93	118	53,973	−37,046	56	32
	SL	428,675	0.08	0.25	−326,220	75	47	35.42	157	51,235	−34,380	60	19
Energy	CL	−221,580	0.02	−0.10	−624,280	90	36	28.12	−83	64,288	−39,108	40	30
	HO	74,907	−0.01	0.04	−430,563	78	40	24.16	49	71,158	−44,979	43	36
	HU	−258,972	−0.10	−0.12	−958,482	86	44	22.41	−128	51,450	−45,874	38	33
Grains	C	378,138	0.01	0.17	−484,100	104	45	82.07	49	58,423	−40,895	47	13
	S	−796,213	−0.17	−0.38	−1,478,475	99	35	30.28	−315	43,760	−38,691	41	22
	W	946,350	0.13	0.48	−507,750	65	45	50.30	293	84,234	−41,217	69	28
Meats	FC	−101,330	−0.06	−0.06	−476,230	81	47	41.32	−61	39,733	−39,840	51	24
	LC	−885,980	−0.18	−0.46	−1,092,340	83	33	50.10	−224	55,677	−43,445	41	33
	LH	−685,152	−0.04	−0.33	−987,076	89	35	32.87	−220	54,893	−40,411	48	26
	PB	−403,588	−0.09	−0.19	−881,188	41	34	25.38	−329	75,357	−51,742	83	42
Softs	CC	180,870	−0.03	0.10	−613,240	70	43	51.15	20	51,699	−36,993	53	29
	CT	19,270	−0.09	0.01	−756,815	90	32	24.34	17	72,654	−33,935	66	17
	JO	−463,995	−0.15	−0.23	−1,286,288	89	31	36.99	−145	58,975	−34,916	56	23
	KC	777,825	0.18	0.40	−299,869	87	45	14.18	629	63,351	−35,317	50	21
	LB	−45,176	−0.09	−0.02	−734,256	48	50	51.69	−70	73,016	−80,302	46	75
	SB	223,171	−0.01	0.12	−625,823	77	38	56.60	36	65,634	−36,376	63	22
	Average	11,388	−0.02	0.01	−680,899	78	39	35.18	−31	59,032	−39,727	49	28

Portfolio Statistics

Net Profit:	341,640	Sharpe ratio:	0.02
Drawdown:	−5,802,061	Correlation to breakout:	0.51
K-ratio:	−0.09	Correlation to 10-40 MA:	0.43

© 2002 Lars Kestner – All Rights Reserved

FIGURE 7.22a

Results of Volatility Breakout Strategy Applied to Futures.

Breakdown Statistics (Futures)

System Name: Volatility breakout
Parameters: 1 day returns, 2 sigmas of past 100 day price returns
Description: Enter long if today's price return is greater than twice the 100 day sigma; opposite for shorts
Run Dates: 1/1/1990 – 12/31/2001

Breakdown by Market

Market Sector	Average Net Profit	Average K-ratio	Average Sharpe Ratio	Average Max DD	Average Num Trades	Average % Win	Avg. Profit Per Contract	Average Win	Average Loss	Avg. Bars Win	Avg. Bars Loss
FX	-84,369	-0.04	-0.05	-794,246	87	39	-74	57,169	-39,168	46	28
Rates	294,616	0.04	0.14	-408,836	61	32	-11	52,057	-32,737	37	20
Stock	-172,025	-0.12	-0.08	-619,950	97	33	-344	58,113	-32,858	41	25
Metals	254,625	0.03	0.13	-490,916	72	43	74	58,621	-37,029	57	28
Energy	-135,215	-0.03	-0.06	-671,108	85	40	-54	62,299	-43,320	40	33
Grains	176,092	-0.01	0.09	-823,442	89	42	9	62,139	-40,268	52	21
Meats	-519,013	-0.09	-0.26	-859,209	74	37	-208	56,415	-43,860	56	31
Softs	115,328	-0.03	0.06	-719,382	77	40	81	64,222	-42,973	56	31

Performance Breakdown by Year

Year	Net Profit	K-ratio	Sharpe Ratio	Year	Net Profit	K-ratio	Sharpe Ratio
1990	1,745,638	0.40	1.52	1996	-1,260,219	-0.20	-1.06
1991	215,864	-0.07	0.25	1997	103,774	0.04	0.12
1992	-983,659	-0.31	-1.28	1998	-611,764	-0.11	-0.58
1993	-385,093	-0.07	-0.40	1999	352,827	0.12	0.38
1994	-831,783	-0.37	-0.92	2000	1,221,088	0.41	1.40
1995	-342,973	-0.16	-0.29	2001	1,039,355	0.45	0.74

Length	Number of Windows	Num. of Profitable Windows	Percent Profitable
1 Month	144	75	52.08%
3 Months	142	69	48.59%
6 Months	139	68	48.92%
12 Months	133	62	46.62%
18 Months	127	49	38.58%
24 Months	121	31	25.62%

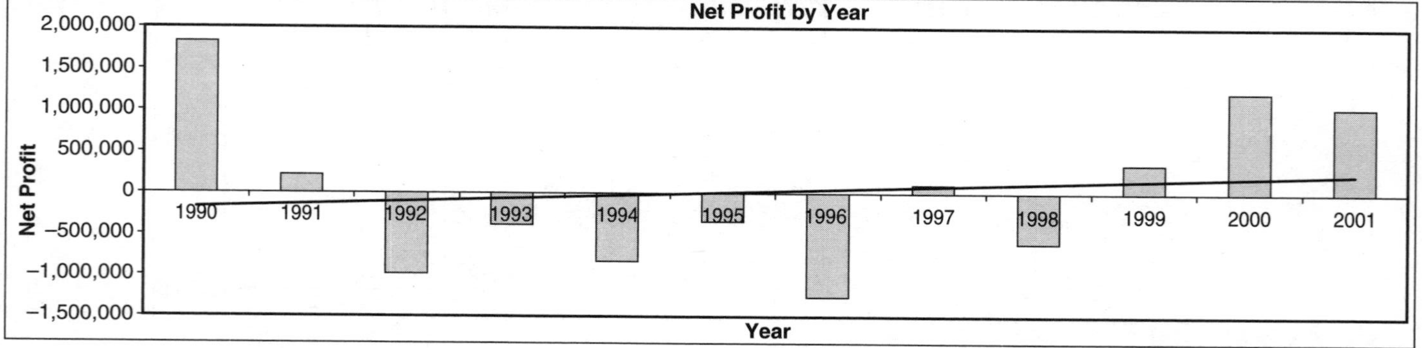

Net Profit by Year

© 2002 Lars Kestner – All Right Reserved

FIGURE 7.22b

Results of Volatility Breakout Strategy Applied to Futures.

162

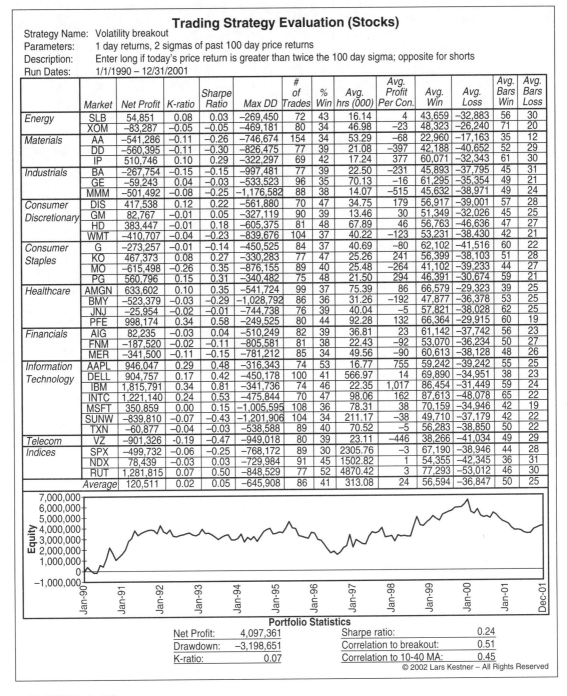

Trading Strategy Evaluation (Stocks)

Strategy Name: Volatility breakout
Parameters: 1 day returns, 2 sigmas of past 100 day price returns
Description: Enter long if today's price return is greater than twice the 100 day sigma; opposite for shorts
Run Dates: 1/1/1990 – 12/31/2001

	Market	Net Profit	K-ratio	Sharpe Ratio	Max DD	# of Trades	% Win	Avg. hrs (000)	Avg. Profit Per Con.	Avg. Win	Avg. Loss	Avg. Bars Win	Avg. Bars Loss
Energy	SLB	54,851	0.08	0.03	−269,450	72	43	16.14	4	43,659	−32,883	56	30
	XOM	−83,287	−0.05	−0.05	−469,181	80	34	46.98	−23	48,323	−26,240	71	20
Materials	AA	−541,286	−0.11	−0.26	−746,674	154	34	53.29	−68	22,960	−17,163	35	12
	DD	−560,395	−0.11	−0.30	−826,475	77	39	21.08	−397	42,188	−40,652	52	29
	IP	510,746	0.10	0.29	−322,297	69	42	17.24	377	60,071	−32,343	61	30
Industrials	BA	−267,754	−0.15	−0.15	−997,481	77	39	22.50	−231	45,893	−37,795	45	31
	GE	−59,243	0.04	−0.03	−533,523	96	35	70.13	−16	61,295	−35,354	49	21
	MMM	−501,492	−0.08	−0.25	−1,176,582	88	38	14.07	−515	45,632	−38,971	49	24
Consumer Discretionary	DIS	417,538	0.12	0.22	−561,880	70	47	34.75	179	56,917	−39,001	57	28
	GM	82,767	−0.01	0.05	−327,119	90	39	13.46	30	51,349	−32,026	45	25
	HD	383,447	−0.01	0.18	−605,375	81	48	67.89	46	56,763	−46,636	47	27
	WMT	−410,707	−0.04	−0.23	−839,676	104	37	40.22	−123	53,231	−38,430	42	21
Consumer Staples	G	−273,531	−0.01	−0.14	−450,525	84	37	40.69	−80	62,102	−41,516	60	22
	KO	467,373	0.08	0.27	−330,283	77	47	25.26	241	56,399	−38,103	51	28
	MO	−615,498	−0.26	0.35	−876,155	89	40	25.48	−264	41,102	−39,233	44	27
	PG	560,796	0.15	0.31	−340,482	75	48	21.50	294	46,391	−30,674	59	21
Healthcare	AMGN	633,602	0.10	0.35	−541,724	99	37	75.39	86	66,579	−29,323	39	25
	BMY	−523,379	−0.03	−0.29	−1,028,792	86	36	31.26	−192	47,877	−36,378	53	25
	JNJ	−25,954	−0.02	−0.01	−744,738	76	39	40.04	−5	57,821	−38,028	62	25
	PFE	998,174	0.34	0.58	−249,525	80	44	92.28	132	66,364	−29,915	60	19
Financials	AIG	82,235	−0.03	0.04	−510,249	82	39	36.81	23	61,142	−37,742	56	23
	FNM	−187,520	−0.02	−0.11	−805,581	81	38	22.43	−92	53,070	−36,234	50	27
	MER	−341,500	−0.11	−0.15	−781,212	85	34	49.56	−90	60,613	−38,128	48	26
Information Technology	AAPL	946,047	0.29	0.48	−316,343	74	53	16.77	755	59,242	−39,242	55	25
	DELL	904,757	0.17	0.42	−450,178	100	41	566.97	14	69,890	−34,951	38	23
	IBM	1,815,791	0.34	0.81	−341,736	74	46	22.35	1,017	86,454	−31,449	59	24
	INTC	1,221,140	0.24	0.53	−475,844	70	47	98.06	162	87,613	−48,078	65	22
	MSFT	350,859	0.00	0.15	−1,005,595	108	36	78.31	38	70,159	−34,946	42	19
	SUNW	−839,810	−0.07	−0.43	−1,201,906	104	34	211.17	−38	49,710	−37,179	42	22
	TXN	−60,877	−0.04	−0.03	−538,588	89	40	70.52	−5	56,283	−38,850	50	22
Telecom	VZ	−901,326	−0.19	−0.47	−949,018	80	39	23.11	−446	38,266	−41,034	49	29
Indices	SPX	−499,732	−0.06	−0.25	−768,172	89	30	2305.76	−3	67,190	−38,946	44	28
	NDX	78,439	−0.03	0.03	−729,984	91	45	1502.82	1	54,355	−42,345	36	31
	RUT	1,281,815	0.07	0.50	−848,529	77	52	4870.42	3	77,293	−53,012	46	30
	Average	120,511	0.02	0.05	−645,908	86	41	313.08	24	56,594	−36,847	50	25

Portfolio Statistics

Net Profit:	4,097,361	Sharpe ratio:	0.24
Drawdown:	−3,198,651	Correlation to breakout:	0.51
K-ratio:	0.07	Correlation to 10-40 MA:	0.45

© 2002 Lars Kestner – All Rights Reserved

FIGURE 7.23a

Results of Volatility Breakout Strategy Applied to Stocks.

Breakdown Statistics (Stock)

System Name: Volatility breakout
Parameters: 1 day returns, 2 sigmas of past 100 day price returns
Description: Enter long if today's price return is greater than twice the 100 day sigma; opposite for shorts
Run Dates: 1/1/1990 – 12/31/2001

Breakdown by Market Sector

Market Sector	Average Net Profit	Average K-ratio	Average Sharpe Ratio	Average Max DD	Average Num Trades	Average % Win	Avg. Profit Per Contract	Average Win	Average Loss	Avg. Bars Win	Avg. Bars Loss
Energy	-14,218	0.02	-0.01	-369,316	76	38	-9	45,991	-29,562	64	25
Materials	-196,978	-0.04	-0.09	-631,815	100	38	-29	41,740	-30,052	49	24
Industrials	-276,163	-0.06	-0.14	-902,529	87	37	-254	50,940	-37,373	47	25
Discretionary	118,261	0.02	0.05	-583,513	86	43	33	54,565	-39,023	48	25
Staples	34,854	-0.01	0.02	-499,361	81	43	47	51,499	-37,382	53	24
Healthcare	270,611	0.10	0.16	-641,195	85	39	5	59,660	-33,411	54	24
Financials	-148,928	-0.06	-0.07	-699,014	83	37	-53	58,275	-37,368	51	25
Info. Tech.	619,701	0.13	0.27	-618,599	88	42	278	68,479	-37,814	50	22
Telecom	-901,326	-0.19	-0.47	-949,018	80	39	-446	38,266	-41,034	49	29
Indices	286,841	-0.01	0.09	-782,228	86	42	0	66,279	-44,768	42	30

Performance Breakdown by Year

Year	Net Profit	K-ratio	Sharpe Ratio
1990	1,644,585	0.34	0.89
1991	2,647,021	0.40	1.92
1992	-824,894	-0.18	-0.85
1993	-421,725	-0.30	-0.44
1994	464,799	0.20	0.32
1995	-4,753	-0.12	0.00

Year	Net Profit	K-ratio	Sharpe Ratio
1996	-1,328,496	-0.09	-0.68
1997	1,063,112	0.23	0.70
1998	1,477,134	0.40	0.84
1999	1,888,414	0.79	1.21
2000	-2,147,773	-0.33	-1.44
2001	-319,913	-0.07	-0.47

Profitability Windows

Length	Number of Windows	Num. of Profitable Windows	Percent Profitable
1 Month	144	76	52.78%
3 Months	142	73	51.41%
6 Months	139	74	53.24%
12 Months	133	66	49.62%
18 Months	127	71	55.91%
24 Months	121	69	57.02%

Net Profit by Year

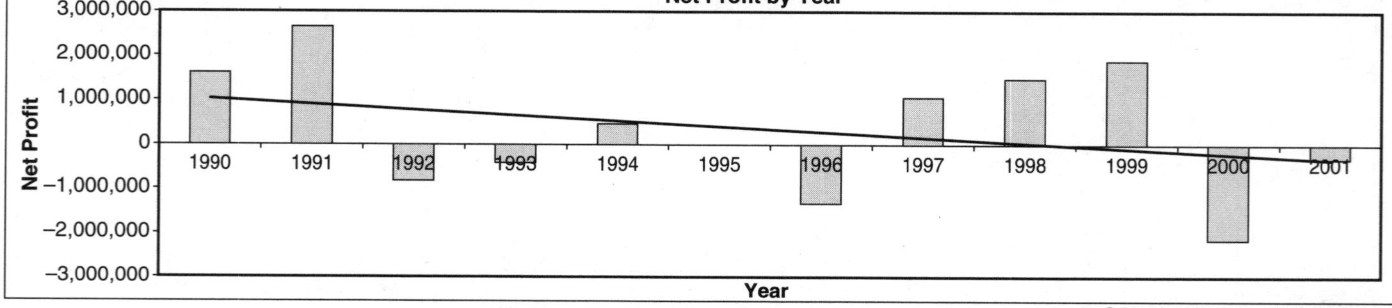

© 2002 Lars Kestner – All Rights Reserved

FIGURE 7.23b

Results of Volatility Breakout Strategy Applied to Stocks.

164

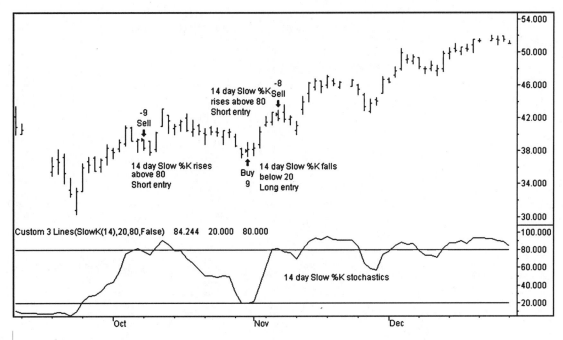

FIGURE 7.24

Stochastic Strategy Applied to Home Depot.

One point of interest: Although returns on both futures and stocks were less than perfect, both the profitable years on futures and two of the five profitable years on stocks have occurred over the past three years. This could be a sign that the markets are trending less and that the strategies of the future may involve exhaustion methods such as stochastics or RSI to generate trading signals.

Relative Strength Index

The next oscillator tested is a 14-day Relative Strength Index (RSI). Long entries are established if today's 14-day RSI falls below 35. Short entries are established if today's 14-day RSI rises above 65. There are no other rules and no rules for exiting positions, except for an entry in the other direction.

The RSI generates signals common with similar oscillators such as stochastics. Sample entries for Microsoft (MSFT) are detailed in Figure 7.28. In early October, prices rally from a bottom, causing the 14-day RSI to fall below 35 and generating a long entry. In later October, after a three week rally, a quick sell-off causes the RSI to fall below 65. Our long position is exited and a short position is established.

Trading Strategy Evaluation (Futures)

Strategy Name: 14 day Slow %K stochastics
Parameters: 14 days in stochastic calculation
Description: Enter long when %K crosses above 20, enter short when %K crosses below 80
Run Dates: 1/1/1990 – 12/31/2001

Market	Net Profit	K-ratio	Sharpe Ratio	Max DD	# of Trades	% Win	Avg. Contracts	Avg. Profit Per Con.	Avg. Win	Avg. Loss	Avg. Bars Win	Avg. Bars Loss
FX AD	898,980	0.14	0.44	−490,760	109	67	25.63	317	35,215	−46,796	17	49
BP	210,638	0.11	0.11	−423,888	100	61	17.76	132	32,381	−44,619	18	48
CD	−107,910	−0.07	−0.05	−996,850	101	67	45.85	−25	28,297	−61,872	21	49
JY	−1,068,175	−0.22	−0.51	−1,291,713	88	59	13.83	−792	30,636	−71,023	19	55
SF	−518,475	−0.05	−0.26	−850,238	88	60	15.38	−401	30,045	−61,018	19	57
Rates ED	−3,391,050	−0.20	−1.16	−3,740,525	69	58	86.37	−567	28,959	−156,376	21	75
TY	−582,953	−0.16	−0.26	−871,297	96	61	29.27	−194	31,501	−64,975	18	53
US	−158,719	−0.06	−0.08	−702,656	106	63	20.29	−55	32,007	−58,010	16	48
Stock SP	297,725	0.03	0.15	−565,013	91	65	8.28	365	33,412	−52,995	19	59
Metals GC	−377,760	−0.08	−0.17	−739,520	89	60	45.54	−93	33,594	−59,951	18	56
HG	159,200	0.02	0.08	−617,238	97	66	32.60	60	31,795	−55,912	17	58
PL	249,925	0.06	0.14	−787,975	96	64	45.31	66	30,466	−44,898	22	47
SL	14,375	0.05	0.01	−394,765	85	62	32.90	28	30,168	−47,531	22	57
Energy CL	−1,145,260	−0.22	−0.47	−1,219,770	97	59	29.89	−364	29,408	−68,275	17	49
HO	−763,585	−0.21	−0.29	−1,011,104	94	61	22.94	−362	29,920	−67,189	18	53
HU	−644,423	−0.10	−0.25	−921,278	94	62	23.06	−303	29,234	−65,337	19	52
Grains C	−734,463	−0.15	−0.33	−975,075	86	63	74.62	−109	31,872	−75,720	19	61
S	−29,563	0.03	−0.01	−547,513	96	64	30.29	−2	30,539	−53,366	20	51
W	−420,538	−0.11	−0.17	−1,106,063	92	63	50.97	−90	35,108	−72,240	19	56
Meats FC	464,740	0.00	0.22	−636,485	111	65	41.29	102	33,305	−49,506	17	46
LC	1,863,092	0.42	0.88	−338,628	136	79	50.20	272	30,473	−48,291	15	49
LH	65,868	−0.02	0.03	−584,808	102	65	31.33	23	34,664	−61,475	19	50
PB	953,960	0.20	0.43	−400,512	112	67	20.95	428	37,991	−49,877	17	45
Softs CC	1,288,880	0.20	0.63	−577,440	111	73	49.02	231	33,209	−47,713	17	52
CT	−324,655	0.03	−0.16	−536,310	90	69	24.74	−150	30,632	−79,763	20	63
JO	1,203,015	0.29	0.49	−443,640	113	74	35.62	301	31,563	−49,589	19	47
KC	−937,271	−0.13	−0.34	−1,430,715	97	64	12.07	−800	27,365	−75,243	18	52
LB	−287,344	−0.01	−0.09	−1,242,616	119	67	32.71	−77	34,847	−79,206	16	44
SB	68,511	0.00	0.03	−517,910	97	64	51.93	8	31,256	−54,217	18	54
Average	−125,108	−0.01	−0.03	−832,077	95	62	33.35	−68	30,662	−60,766	18	51

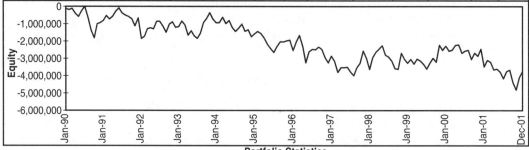

Portfolio Statistics

Net Profit:	−3,753,234	Sharpe ratio:	−0.23
Drawdown:	−4,817,779	Correlation to breakout:	−0.84
K-ratio:	−0.15	Correlation to 10-40 MA:	−0.79

© 2002 Lars Kestner – All Rights Reserved

FIGURE 7.25a

Stochastic Strategy Applied to Futures.

Breakdown Statistics (Futures)

System Name: 14 day Slow %K stochastics
Parameters: 14 days in stochastic calculation
Description: Enter long when %K crosses above 20, enter short when %K crosses below 80
Run Dates: 1/1/1990 – 12/31/2001

Breakdown by Market Sector

Market Sector	Average Net Profit	Average K-ratio	Average Sharpe Ratio	Average Max DD	Average Num Trades	Average % Win	Avg. Profit Per Contract	Average Win	Average Loss	Avg. Bars Win	Avg. Bars Loss
FX	−116,989	−0.02	−0.05	−810,690	97	63	−154	31,315	−57,066	19	52
Rates	−1,033,180	−0.10	−0.37	−1,328,620	68	46	−204	23,117	−69,840	14	44
Stock	297,725	0.03	0.15	−565,013	91	65	365	33,412	−52,995	19	59
Metals	11,435	0.01	0.02	−634,874	92	63	15	31,506	−52,073	20	54
Energy	−851,089	−0.18	−0.33	−1,050,717	95	60	−343	29,521	−66,934	18	51
Grains	−394,854	−0.07	−0.17	−876,217	91	63	−67	32,507	−67,108	19	56
Meats	836,915	0.15	0.39	−490,108	115	69	206	34,108	−52,287	17	47
Softs	168,523	0.06	0.09	−791,439	105	69	−81	31,479	−64,289	18	52

Performance Breakdown by Year

Year	Net Profit	K-ratio	Sharpe Ratio	Year	Net Profit	K-ratio	Sharpe Ratio
1990	−694,621	−0.25	−0.46	1996	−315,211	−0.17	−0.19
1991	−1,030,055	−0.14	−0.68	1997	−771,352	0.02	−0.52
1992	683,328	0.18	0.68	1998	361,326	−0.07	0.23
1993	224,322	0.12	0.18	1999	991,753	0.22	0.82
1994	−638,956	−0.37	−0.65	2000	−1,201,215	−0.23	−0.82
1995	−971,455	−0.18	−1.01	2001	−270,136	−0.25	−0.18

Length	Number of Windows	Num. of Profitable Windows	Percent Profitable
1 Month	144	73	50.69%
3 Months	142	57	40.14%
6 Months	139	54	38.85%
12 Months	133	46	34.59%
18 Months	127	47	37.01%
24 Months	121	36	29.75%

Net Profit by Year

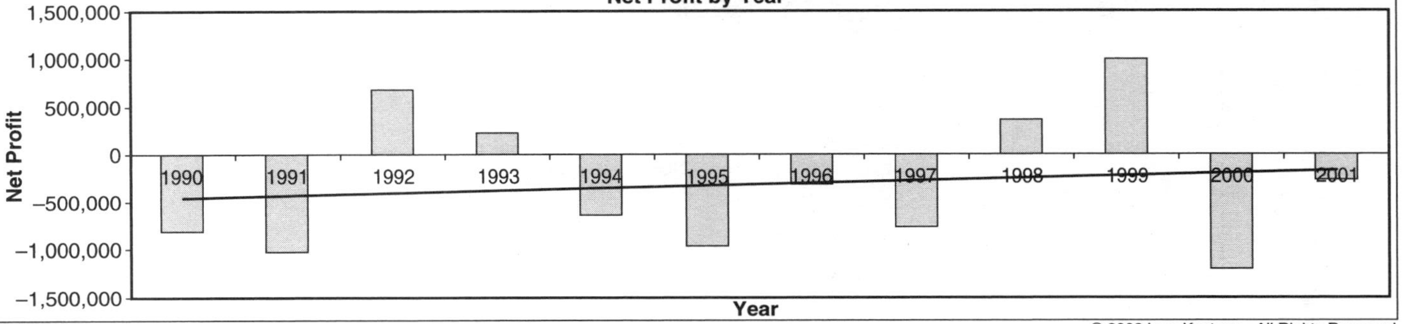

© 2002 Lars Kestner – All Rights Reserved

FIGURE 7.25b

Stochastic Strategy Applied to Futures.

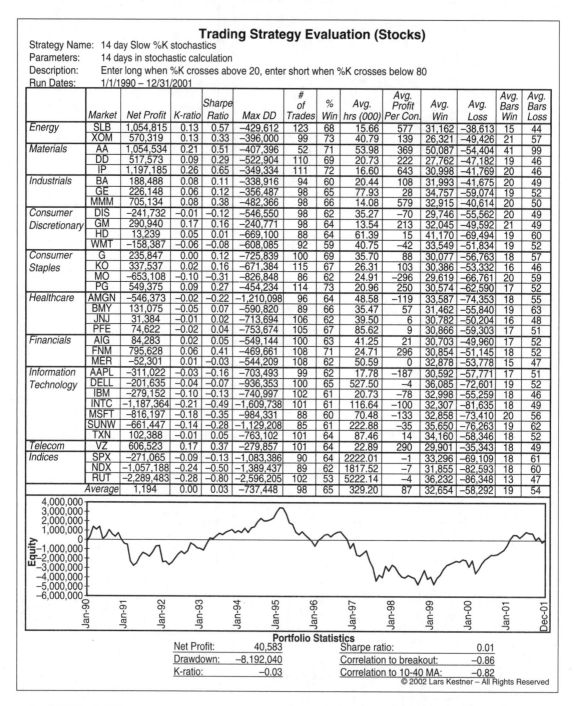

Trading Strategy Evaluation (Stocks)

Strategy Name: 14 day Slow %K stochastics
Parameters: 14 days in stochastic calculation
Description: Enter long when %K crosses above 20, enter short when %K crosses below 80
Run Dates: 1/1/1990 – 12/31/2001

	Market	Net Profit	K-ratio	Sharpe Ratio	Max DD	# of Trades	% Win	Avg. hrs (000)	Avg. Profit Per Con.	Avg. Win	Avg. Loss	Avg. Bars Win	Avg. Bars Loss
Energy	SLB	1,054,815	0.13	0.57	−429,612	123	68	15.66	577	31,162	−38,613	15	44
	XOM	570,319	0.13	0.33	−396,000	99	73	40.79	139	26,321	−49,426	21	57
Materials	AA	1,054,534	0.21	0.51	−407,396	52	71	53.98	369	50,087	−54,404	41	99
	DD	517,573	0.09	0.29	−522,904	110	69	20.73	222	27,762	−47,182	19	46
	IP	1,197,185	0.26	0.65	−349,334	111	72	16.60	643	30,998	−41,769	20	46
Industrials	BA	188,488	0.08	0.11	−338,916	94	60	20.44	108	31,993	−41,675	20	49
	GE	226,148	0.06	0.12	−356,487	98	65	77.93	28	34,757	−59,074	19	52
	MMM	705,134	0.08	0.38	−482,366	98	66	14.08	579	32,915	−40,614	20	50
Consumer Discretionary	DIS	−241,732	−0.01	−0.12	−546,550	98	62	35.27	−70	29,746	−55,562	20	49
	GM	290,940	0.17	0.16	−240,771	98	64	13.54	213	32,045	−49,592	21	49
	HD	13,239	0.05	0.01	−669,100	88	64	61.39	15	41,170	−69,494	19	60
	WMT	−158,387	−0.06	−0.08	−608,085	92	59	40.75	−42	33,549	−51,834	19	52
Consumer Staples	G	235,847	0.00	0.12	−725,839	100	69	35.70	88	30,077	−56,763	18	57
	KO	337,537	0.02	0.16	−671,384	115	67	26.31	103	30,386	−53,332	16	46
	MO	−653,108	−0.10	−0.31	−826,848	86	62	24.91	−296	29,619	−66,761	20	59
	PG	549,375	0.09	0.27	−454,234	114	73	20.96	250	30,574	−62,590	17	52
Healthcare	AMGN	−546,373	−0.02	−0.22	−1,210,098	96	64	48.58	−119	33,587	−74,353	18	55
	BMY	131,075	−0.05	0.07	−590,820	89	66	35.47	57	31,462	−55,840	19	63
	JNJ	31,384	−0.01	0.02	−713,694	106	62	39.50	6	30,782	−50,204	16	48
	PFE	74,622	−0.02	0.04	−753,674	105	67	85.62	9	30,866	−59,303	17	51
Financials	AIG	84,283	0.02	0.05	−549,144	100	63	41.25	21	30,703	−49,960	17	52
	FNM	795,628	0.06	0.41	−469,661	108	71	24.71	296	30,854	−51,145	18	52
	MER	−52,301	0.01	−0.03	−544,209	108	62	50.59	0	32,878	−53,778	15	47
Information Technology	AAPL	−311,022	−0.03	−0.16	−703,493	99	62	17.78	−187	30,592	−57,771	17	51
	DELL	−201,635	−0.04	−0.07	−936,353	100	65	527.50	−4	36,085	−72,601	19	52
	IBM	−279,152	−0.10	−0.13	−740,997	102	61	20.73	−78	32,998	−55,259	18	46
	INTC	−1,187,364	−0.21	−0.49	−1,609,738	101	61	116.64	−100	32,307	−81,635	18	49
	MSFT	−816,197	−0.18	−0.35	−984,331	88	60	70.48	−133	32,858	−73,410	20	56
	SUNW	−661,447	−0.14	−0.28	−1,129,208	85	61	222.88	−35	35,650	−76,263	19	62
	TXN	102,388	−0.01	0.05	−763,102	101	64	87.46	14	34,160	−58,346	18	52
Telecom	VZ	606,523	0.17	0.37	−279,857	101	64	22.89	290	29,901	−35,343	18	49
Indices	SPX	−271,065	−0.09	−0.13	−1,083,386	90	64	2222.01	−1	33,296	−69,109	18	61
	NDX	−1,057,188	−0.24	−0.50	−1,389,437	89	62	1817.52	−7	31,855	−82,593	18	60
	RUT	−2,289,483	−0.28	−0.80	−2,596,205	102	53	5222.14	−4	36,232	−86,348	13	47
	Average	1,194	0.00	0.03	−737,448	98	65	329.20	87	32,654	−58,292	19	54

Portfolio Statistics

Net Profit:	40,583	Sharpe ratio:	0.01
Drawdown:	−8,192,040	Correlation to breakout:	−0.86
K-ratio:	−0.03	Correlation to 10-40 MA:	−0.82

© 2002 Lars Kestner – All Rights Reserved

FIGURE 7.26a

Stochastic Strategy Applied to Stocks.

Breakdown Statistics (Stocks)

System Name: 14 day Slow %K stochastics
Parameters: 14 days in stochastic calculation
Description: Enter long when %K crosses above 20, enter short when %K crosses below 80
Run Dates: 1/1/1990 – 12/31/2001

Breakdown by Market Sector

Market Sector	Average Net Profit	Average K-ratio	Average Sharpe Ratio	Average Max DD	Average Num Trades	Average % Win	Avg. Profit Per Contract	Average Win	Average Loss	Avg. Bars Win	Avg. Bars Loss
Energy	812,567	0.13	0.45	-412,806	111	71	358	28,741	-44,019	18	51
Materials	923,097	0.19	0.48	-426,545	91	71	411	36,282	-47,785	27	64
Industrials	373,257	0.07	0.20	-392,590	97	64	239	33,222	-47,121	20	51
Discretionary	-23,985	0.04	-0.01	-516,127	94	62	29	34,127	-56,620	20	53
Staples	117,413	0.00	0.06	-669,576	104	68	37	30,164	-59,862	18	53
Healthcare	-77,323	-0.02	-0.02	-817,072	99	65	-12	31,674	-59,925	18	54
Financials	275,870	0.03	0.14	-521,005	105	65	106	31,478	-51,628	17	50
Info. Tech.	-479,204	-0.10	-0.21	-981,032	97	62	-75	33,521	-67,898	18	52
Telecom	606,523	0.17	0.37	-279,857	101	64	290	29,901	-35,343	18	49
Indices	-1,205,912	-0.20	-0.48	-1,689,676	94	60	-4	33,794	-79,350	17	56

Performance Breakdown by Year

Year	Net Profit	K-ratio	Sharpe Ratio
1990	-218,783	-0.08	-0.09
1991	-1,943,596	0.00	-0.68
1992	1,424,585	0.53	1.10
1993	1,913,059	0.55	1.77
1994	2,022,781	0.65	1.64
1995	-3,660,423	-0.93	-2.52
1996	332,322	-0.02	0.21
1997	-2,297,717	-0.28	-0.79
1998	-1,270,173	-0.17	-0.68
1999	1,076,264	0.39	0.30
2000	2,268,662	0.50	1.23
2001	585,539	0.00	0.41

Profitability Windows

Length	Number of Windows	Num. of Profitable Windows	Percent Profitable
1 Month	144	79	54.86%
3 Months	142	78	54.93%
6 Months	139	79	56.83%
12 Months	133	75	56.39%
18 Months	127	67	52.76%
24 Months	121	60	49.59%

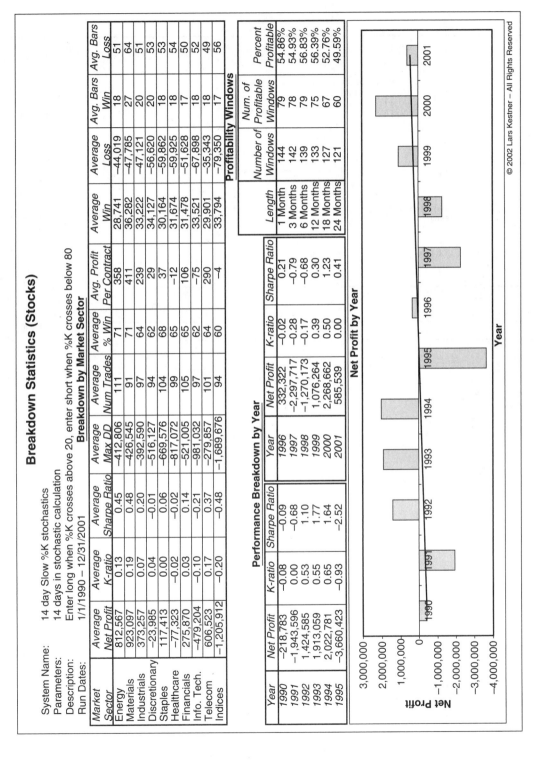

Net Profit by Year

© 2002 Lars Kestner – All Rights Reserved

FIGURE 7.26b

Stochastic Strategy Applied to Stocks.

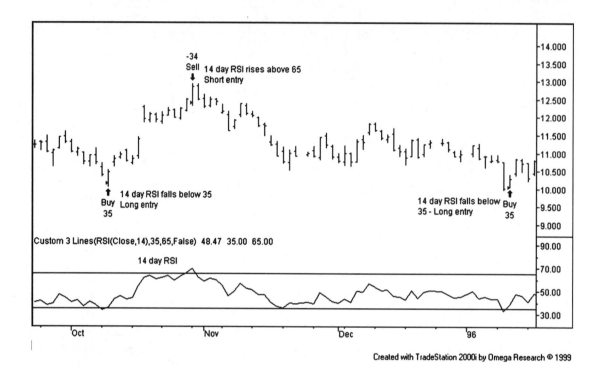

-34
Sell 14 day RSI rises above 65
      Short entry

14 day RSI falls below 35
Buy Long entry
35

14 day RSI falls below Buy
35 - Long entry   35

Custom 3 Lines(RSI(Close,14),35,65,False) 48.47 35.00 65.00

14 day RSI

Created with TradeStation 2000i by Omega Research © 1999

FIGURE 7.27

RSI Strategy Applied to Microsoft.

The 14-day RSI strategy performs very poorly on both futures markets and stocks (Figures 7.28a through 7.29b). Both sets of markets produce strong negative Sharpe ratios and K-ratios. Tests on futures markets produce profits in only 4 of 12 years. While stocks produce profits in 7 of the 12 years tested, the five years of losses overwhelm the seven years of gains. As was seen in the stochastics tests, returns from the 14-day RSI strategy are negatively correlated to basic trend-following returns. Weakest performance is generated by interest rates, petroleum futures, and technology stocks.

Moving Average Convergence/Divergence

Our final strategy tested in this chapter is the popular Moving Average Convergence/Divergence strategy. The MACD is constructed by calculating the difference between a 12-day and 26-day exponential moving average. The signal line is generated by calculating a nine-day exponential moving average of the MACD. Long entries are established when the MACD rises above the signal line. Short entries are established when the MACD falls below the signal line.

Trading Strategy Evaluation (Futures)

Strategy Name: 14 day RSI
Parameters: 14 days in RSI calculation
Description: Enter long when %K falls below 35, enter short when %K rises above 65
Run Dates: 1/1/1990 – 12/31/2001

	Market	Net Profit	K-ratio	Sharpe Ratio	Max DD	# of Trades	% Win	Avg. Contracts	Avg. Profit Per Con.	Avg. Win	Avg. Loss	Avg. Bars Win	Avg. Bars Loss
FX	AD	123,340	−0.03	0.07	−514,700	42	69	24.65	99	44,549	−91,481	46	127
	BP	37,375	0.02	0.02	−870,775	42	76	17.72	50	41,875	−130,288	53	132
	CD	782,490	0.10	0.33	−373,980	51	67	48.58	308	54,981	−65,079	43	92
	JY	−1,777,938	−0.53	−0.85	−1,780,538	30	37	14.06	−3,937	47,739	−115,066	32	138
	SF	−851,700	−0.14	−0.45	−1,071,288	36	53	15.78	−1,392	45,363	−97,218	36	131
Rates	ED	−1,954,150	−0.15	−0.79	−2,150,825	41	63	87.19	−210	44,528	−127,298	37	112
	TY	−1,112,906	−0.28	−0.52	−1,216,969	34	59	28.94	−1,112	40,666	−136,261	43	151
	US	−1,033,281	−0.18	−0.50	−1,177,938	34	47	20.31	−1,475	45,234	−96,811	37	133
Stock	SP	594,263	0.06	0.30	−642,013	40	70	8.24	1,800	58,092	−86,094	42	151
Metals	GC	467,280	0.15	0.20	−521,380	42	69	42.00	255	47,802	−72,094	52	114
	HG	−403,213	−0.10	−0.22	−951,700	38	63	34.97	−339	43,403	−106,580	47	131
	PL	572,640	0.13	0.29	−642,530	41	73	48.69	302	50,171	−81,999	54	126
	SL	852,720	0.26	0.42	−396,970	43	72	33.52	616	46,163	−45,233	51	119
Energy	CL	−1,415,590	−0.28	−0.55	−1,598,220	37	51	29.08	−1,259	45,643	−123,423	43	118
	HO	−395,560	−0.09	−0.14	−1,115,990	41	61	25.98	−308	60,185	−114,564	44	114
	HU	−49,640	−0.04	−0.02	−563,732	43	58	21.84	−12	54,341	−76,092	41	107
Grains	C	−829,975	−0.13	−0.34	−1,117,675	36	64	75.68	−285	45,504	−140,225	52	135
	S	325,913	−0.01	0.14	−633,738	40	65	29.66	313	51,286	−68,693	47	123
	W	−521,313	−0.11	−0.22	−1,070,925	37	59	50.53	−300	52,377	−114,268	46	131
Meats	FC	−177,885	−0.05	−0.08	−987,890	35	69	40.64	−119	47,614	−119,313	45	167
	LC	−424,944	−0.04	−0.21	−568,600	31	58	48.13	−180	50,319	−90,344	45	163
	LH	152,904	0.04	0.08	−452,392	43	63	30.91	111	49,195	−73,783	41	116
	PB	177,992	0.06	0.09	−399,556	37	73	20.53	255	43,918	−99,207	55	151
Softs	CC	357,260	0.09	0.17	−441,400	38	63	49.54	248	53,860	−58,956	41	140
	CT	−1,243,350	−0.23	−0.67	−1,349,980	28	54	24.62	−1,825	45,831	−149,676	55	162
	JO	342,458	0.07	0.14	−676,140	42	64	36.70	224	53,708	−73,614	41	123
	KC	−1,227,281	−0.15	−0.41	−2,120,419	35	60	12.22	−2,574	41,313	−140,605	49	118
	LB	−606,544	−0.08	−0.20	−1,416,288	44	68	35.73	−395	52,937	−157,754	36	138
	SB	−335,474	−0.12	−0.16	−801,002	38	55	53.90	−180	47,763	−80,645	49	116
	Average	−319,137	−0.06	−0.14	−920,852	37	60	33.68	−377	46,879	−97,756	43	126

Portfolio Statistics

Net Profit:	−9,574,109	Sharpe ratio:	−0.57
Drawdown:	−11,206,636	Correlation to breakout:	−0.84
K-ratio:	−0.17	Correlation to 10-40 MA:	−0.80

© 2002 Lars Kestner – All Rights Reserved

FIGURE 7.28a

RSI Strategy Applied to Futures.

Breakdown Statistics (Futures)

System Name: 14 day RSI
Parameters: 14 days in RSI calculation
Description: Enter long when %K falls below 35, enter short when %K rises above 65
Run Dates: 1/1/1990 – 12/31/2001

Breakdown by Market Sector

Market Sector	Average Net Profit	Average K-ratio	Average Sharpe Ratio	Average Max DD	Average Num Trades	Average % Win	Avg. Profit Per Contract	Average Win	Average Loss	Avg. Bars Win	Avg. Bars Loss
FX	-337,287	-0.11	-0.17	-922,256	40	60	-974	46,901	-99,826	42	124
Rates	-1,025,084	-0.15	-0.45	-1,136,433	27	42	-699	32,607	-90,093	29	99
Stock	594,263	0.06	0.30	-642,013	40	70	1,800	58,092	-86,094	42	151
Metals	372,357	0.11	0.17	-628,145	41	69	208	46,885	-76,477	51	122
Energy	-620,263	-0.14	-0.24	-1,092,648	40	57	-526	53,390	-104,693	43	113
Grains	-341,792	-0.09	-0.14	-940,779	38	63	-91	49,723	-107,729	48	130
Meats	-67,983	0.00	-0.03	-602,110	37	66	-17	47,761	-95,662	47	149
Softs	-452,155	-0.07	-0.19	-1,134,205	38	61	-750	49,235	-110,208	45	133

Performance Breakdown by Year

Year	Net Profit	K-ratio	Sharpe Ratio	Year	Net Profit	K-ratio	Sharpe Ratio
1990	-1,969,512	-0.53	-1.11	1996	-1,255,660	-0.18	-0.60
1991	-897,463	-0.15	-0.64	1997	454,089	0.36	0.42
1992	-767,682	-0.37	-0.87	1998	-255,003	-0.10	-0.18
1993	-1,445,818	-0.12	-0.97	1999	1,047,970	0.34	0.47
1994	-2,789,276	-0.73	-1.97	2000	-967,716	-0.20	-1.00
1995	-933,726	-0.15	-0.81	2001	252,452	0.05	0.18

Length	Number of Windows	Num. of Profitable Windows	Percent Profitable
1 Month	144	69	47.92%
3 Months	142	53	37.32%
6 Months	139	52	37.41%
12 Months	133	33	24.81%
18 Months	127	21	16.54%
24 Months	121	26	21.49%

Net Profitability by Year

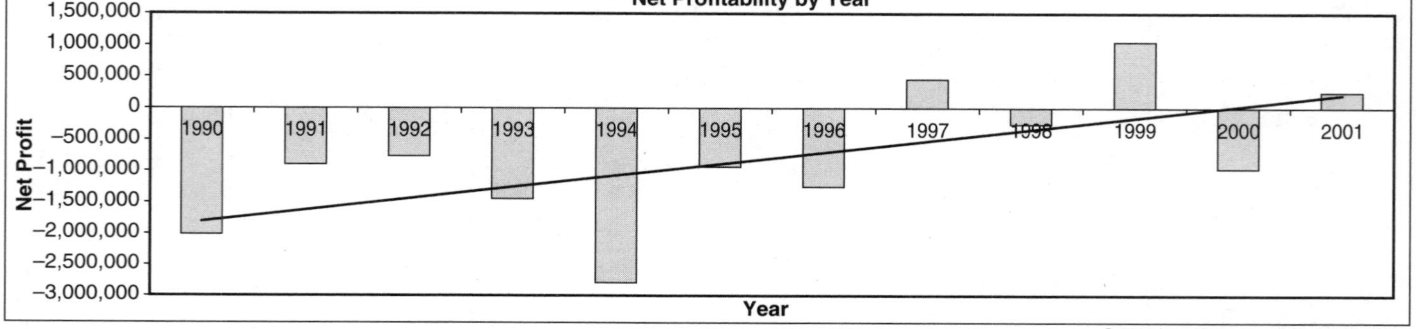

© 2002 Lars Kestner – All Rights Reserved

FIGURE 7.28b

RSI Strategy Applied to Futures.

172

Trading Strategy Evaluation (Stocks)

Strategy Name: 14 day RSI
Parameters: 14 days in RSI calculation
Description: Enter long when %K falls below 35, enter short when %K rises above 65
Run Dates: 1/1/1990 – 12/31/2001

	Market	Net Profit	K-ratio	Sharpe Ratio	Max DD	# of Trades	% Win	Avg. hrs (000)	Avg. Profit Per Con.	Avg. Win	Avg. Loss	Avg. Bars Win	Avg. Bars Loss
Energy	SLB	−338,453	−0.07	−0.17	−669,830	32	56	18.42	−553	46,952	−83,652	37	161
	XOM	576,238	0.04	0.30	−723,344	29	83	39.50	477	55,814	−158,628	71	243
Materials	AA	940,140	0.05	0.46	−612,178	121	69	51.89	151	30,288	−41,170	17	41
	DD	940,788	0.11	0.46	−337,832	44	77	20.24	1,076	51,186	−78,152	53	116
	IP	1,455,155	0.38	0.69	−244,463	44	82	18.22	1,817	51,855	−51,211	57	120
Industrials	BA	−81,798	−0.01	−0.04	−710,955	38	71	21.92	−96	45,156	−118,099	51	146
	GE	−551,274	−0.09	−0.30	−679,624	30	50	78.90	−238	59,853	−97,452	57	144
	MMM	1,256,945	0.23	0.72	−255,750	44	82	13.49	2,145	50,744	−69,209	53	137
Consumer Discretionary	DIS	172,303	0.02	0.08	−578,416	44	61	39.31	93	49,850	−69,682	36	116
	GM	−304,259	−0.14	−0.16	−711,318	37	51	13.34	−615	44,459	−63,793	44	120
	HD	−983,966	−0.07	−0.43	−1,316,118	32	69	55.70	−528	41,461	−185,386	57	169
	WMT	643,434	0.14	0.31	−498,086	46	72	39.00	388	54,871	−85,774	40	126
Consumer Staples	G	300,226	0.01	0.16	−477,593	40	68	35.78	244	51,192	−79,512	42	141
	KO	438,645	0.03	0.19	−833,272	44	80	23.56	403	52,233	−156,723	44	163
	MO	−651,657	−0.17	−0.31	−939,039	36	61	22.81	−807	43,501	−115,686	49	137
	PG	−58,300	−0.04	−0.03	−907,456	38	66	25.03	−45	49,854	−99,195	44	146
Healthcare	AMGN	−1,232,585	−0.07	−0.40	−1,863,956	34	68	58.09	−628	60,944	−240,130	56	156
	BMY	205,247	−0.01	0.09	−801,860	38	71	32.79	176	51,677	−106,913	49	147
	JNJ	140,269	0.01	0.06	−1,157,350	39	72	41.13	63	56,835	−135,465	42	167
	PFE	−628,071	−0.15	−0.25	−1,205,406	34	59	85.86	−212	53,348	−120,330	49	143
Financials	AIG	−424,471	−0.09	−0.19	−782,154	37	59	43.26	−285	48,553	−101,642	40	139
	FNM	411,906	0.04	0.22	−707,419	34	74	24.66	497	62,351	−126,929	57	167
	MER	−583,673	−0.11	−0.23	−1,308,586	37	62	60.50	−261	58,048	−137,047	40	147
Information Technology	AAPL	−94,655	0.01	−0.04	−805,320	43	60	19.55	−102	48,804	−79,674	48	103
	DELL	−2,425,660	−0.20	−0.49	−3,287,845	33	64	719.82	−101	48,595	−284,390	51	157
	IBM	−36,081	−0.02	−0.02	−750,866	42	64	18.12	73	48,849	−84,250	51	104
	INTC	−1,099,569	−0.19	−0.43	−1,334,885	36	61	126.27	−233	43,441	−144,024	46	139
	MSFT	−431,214	−0.07	0.16	−1,234,359	40	70	59.59	−171	56,176	−165,046	37	160
	SUNW	−408,737	−0.10	−0.15	−857,301	42	67	215.23	−45	56,813	−142,506	44	125
	TXN	−1,511,004	−0.17	−0.47	−2,437,998	32	56	104.64	−449	50,028	−171,651	40	158
Telecom	VZ	−36,979	−0.09	−0.02	−623,148	35	54	23.61	9	42,645	−50,185	51	123
Indices	SPX	2,845	−0.04	0.00	−850,971	36	69	2344.05	0	54,205	−122,371	49	160
	NDX	−1,212,027	−0.18	−0.51	−1,594,825	33	52	1961.44	−18	59,048	−136,820	39	144
	RUT	−1,422,463	−0.19	−0.48	−1,937,955	53	60	5820.52	−4	46,719	−136,678	33	92
	Average	−206,846	−0.03	−0.05	−1,001,102	41	66	361.07	65	50,775	−118,805	46	140

Portfolio Statistics

Net Profit:	−7,032,755	Sharpe ratio:	−0.26
Drawdown:	−13,381,024	Correlation to breakout:	−0.85
K-ratio:	−0.13	Correlation to 10-40 MA:	−0.77

© 2002 Lars Kestner – All Rights Reserved

FIGURE 7.29a

RSI Strategy Applied to Stocks.

Breakdown Statistics (Stocks)

System Name:
Parameters: 14 day RSI
Description: 14 days in RSI calculation
Enter long when %K falls below 35, enter short when %K rises above 65
Run Dates: 1/1/1990 – 12/31/2001

Breakdown by Market Sector

Market Sector	Average Net Profit	Average K-ratio	Average Sharpe Ratio	Average Max DD	Average Num Trades	Average % Win	Avg. Profit Per Contract	Average Win	Average Loss	Avg. Bars Win	Avg. Bars Loss
Energy	118,893	-0.01	0.07	-696,587	31	70	-38	51,383	-121,140	54	202
Materials	1,112,028	0.18	0.53	-398,158	70	76	1,015	44,443	-56,844	42	92
Industrials	207,958	0.04	0.13	-548,776	37	68	604	51,918	-94,920	54	143
Discretionary	-118,122	-0.01	-0.05	-775,985	40	63	-166	47,660	-101,159	44	133
Staples	7,229	-0.04	0.00	-789,340	40	68	-51	49,195	-112,779	45	147
Healthcare	-378,785	-0.06	-0.12	-1,257,143	36	67	-150	55,701	-150,709	49	153
Financials	-198,746	-0.05	-0.07	932,720	36	65	-16	56,317	-121,873	46	151
Info. Tech.	-858,131	-0.09	-0.25	-1,529,796	38	63	-147	50,387	-153,077	45	135
Telecom	-36,979	-0.09	-0.02	-623,148	35	54	9	42,645	-50,185	51	123
Indices	-877,215	-0.13	-0.33	-1,461,250	41	60	-8	53,324	-131,956	41	132

Performance Breakdown by Year

Year	Net Profit	K-ratio	Sharpe Ratio
1990	-1,125,428	-0.36	-0.55
1991	-2,937,935	-0.14	-1.28
1992	1,144,756	0.34	0.93
1993	996,449	0.41	0.88
1994	1,080,710	0.24	1.03
1995	-7,161,716	-1.00	-3.63

Year	Net Profit	K-ratio	Sharpe Ratio
1996	-82,598	0.11	-0.04
1997	-1,533,516	-0.15	-0.35
1998	-641,549	-0.07	-0.26
1999	-1,125,253	0.04	-0.26
2000	1,823,557	0.42	0.75
2001	2,582,246	0.53	1.65

Profitability Windows

Length	Number of Windows	Num. of Profitable Windows	Percent Profitable
1 Month	144	75	52.08%
3 Months	142	78	54.93%
6 Months	139	70	50.36%
12 Months	133	66	49.62%
18 Months	127	59	46.46%
24 Months	121	50	41.32%

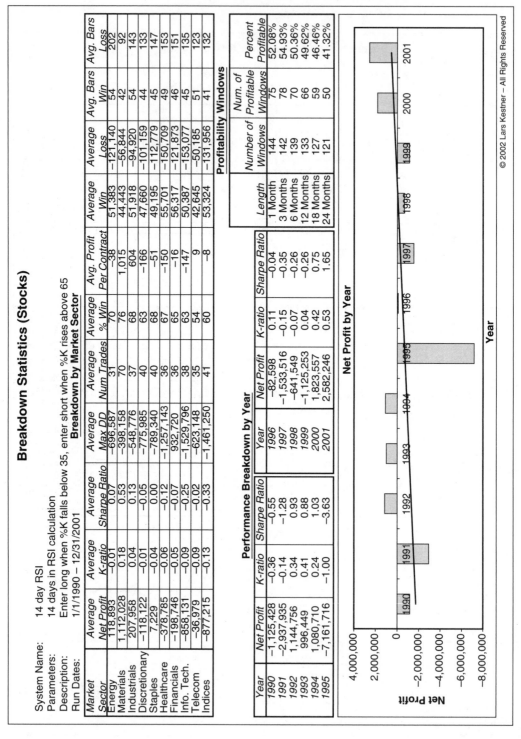

Net Profit by Year

© 2002 Lars Kestner – All Rights Reserved

FIGURE 7.29b

RSI Strategy Applied to Stocks.

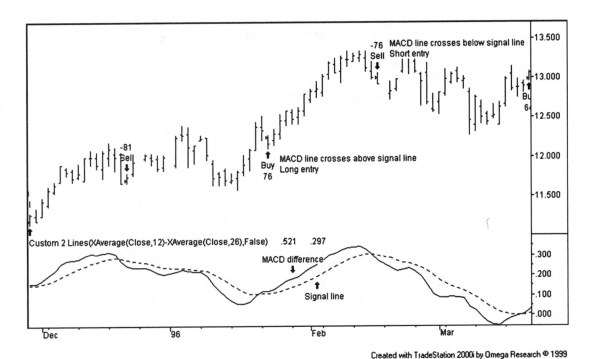

FIGURE 7.30

MACD Strategy Applied to General Electric.

The MACD strategy is applied to General Electric (GE) in Figure 7.30. In late December the stock begins to roll over and the MACD crosses below its nine-day exponential moving average. A short position is established based on this cross. Prices then rally in mid-January. This rally causes the MACD to rally and cross above its signal line. At this point, our short positions are exited and a long position is established.

The MACD strategy leads to interesting performance results (Figures 7.31a through 7.32b). MACD trading signals are almost half trend-following/half oscillator. The premise is to buy on periods of strength after declines and sell periods of weakness after rallies. This hybrid strategy performs favorably on futures markets, leading to profits in 9 of 12 years. Currencies and softs produce the strongest gains. Stock performance is awful with the MACD strategy, generating losses in all 12 years of the test. Notably weak are the energy, health care, and financial sectors.

A BASELINE FOR FUTURE TRADING STRATEGIES

Standard trend-following strategies appear to work well on futures markets—especially currencies, interest rates, petroleum, and softs.

Trading Strategy Evaluation (Futures)

Strategy Name: MACD
Parameters: 12 day minus 26 day exponential moving averages; 9 day EMA for signal line
Description: Buy when MACD crosses above signal line, sell when MACD crosses below signal line
Run Dates: 1/1/1990 – 12/31/2001

	Market	Net Profit	K-ratio	Sharpe Ratio	Max DD	# of Trades	% Win	Avg. Contracts	Avg. Profit Per Con.	Avg. Win	Avg. Loss	Avg. Bar Win	Avg. Bars Loss
FX	AD	499,100	0.05	0.28	–347,580	234	41	25.10	83	32,449	–18,691	21	7
	BP	994,700	0.15	0.59	–376,750	234	42	18.46	220	33,947	–17,849	19	8
	CD	1,217,070	0.32	0.62	–196,410	230	43	46.65	111	37,889	–19,956	20	8
	JY	683,088	0.14	0.35	–365,288	207	41	13.77	203	39,742	–22,946	23	9
	SF	202,963	0.10	0.11	–276,350	229	36	16.10	62	39,256	–20,756	21	9
Rates	ED	–60,025	0.00	–0.02	–516,775	230	35	81.71	–3	46,250	–25,480	21	9
	TY	–593,688	–0.07	–0.28	–764,016	253	36	29.36	–80	33,672	–22,584	20	7
	US	–132,250	–0.04	–0.07	–555,156	251	35	20.74	–25	36,660	–20,601	21	7
Stock	SP	–464,725	–0.16	–0.25	–670,450	252	36	8.64	–209	30,665	–20,159	21	7
Metals	GC	146,450	0.00	0.07	–560,360	238	35	45.18	13	38,750	–20,242	21	8
	HG	733,675	0.23	0.39	–228,488	223	38	32.28	98	38,099	–18,363	20	9
	PL	–978,775	–0.15	–0.49	–1,236,220	229	33	47.57	–90	33,042	–22,851	22	9
	SL	–286,210	–0.03	–0.17	–688,155	246	35	35.40	–42	30,761	–18,830	20	8
Energy	CL	39,360	0.10	0.02	–507,140	226	37	27.74	6	39,706	–23,237	22	8
	HO	234,705	0.14	0.11	–417,526	252	33	23.03	39	43,251	–19,902	21	7
	HU	993,350	0.23	0.44	–320,107	224	40	22.55	193	42,116	–21,018	22	7
Grains	C	872,888	0.23	0.43	–287,738	224	38	76.85	49	43,037	–19,804	21	9
	S	313,038	0.01	0.18	–424,700	218	43	31.57	42	31,604	–21,619	21	8
	W	–309,400	0.02	–0.13	–569,363	256	35	51.82	–24	36,157	–21,527	20	7
Meats	FC	-290,030	–0.03	–0.15	–510,045	246	34	41.45	–29	37,891	–21,084	21	8
	LC	–1,176,116	–0.16	–0.58	–1,288,976	266	29	50.55	–90	31,242	–19,367	20	8
	LH	166,792	0.08	0.08	–612,732	231	39	32.41	17	39,172	–24,093	22	7
	PB	100,016	–0.05	0.05	–542,488	246	35	21.08	16	40,168	–21,463	20	8
Softs	CC	-77,850	0.00	–0.04	–584,930	247	39	51.73	–5	28,137	–18,325	19	8
	CT	–301,615	–0.15	–0.14	–768,190	238	32	24.69	–54	42,303	–21,419	21	9
	JO	53,453	–0.03	0.02	–667,253	221	37	36.32	5	34,447	–20,008	21	9
	KC	1,002,731	0.16	0.43	–372,690	228	41	13.45	329	38,259	–18,879	20	8
	LB	1,436,816	0.19	0.54	–381,496	217	41	34.86	189	49,938	–23,001	21	9
	SB	33,162	–0.03	0.02	–551,287	240	36	53.93	2	33,926	–18,795	21	8
	Average	168,422	0.04	0.08	–519,622	228	36	33.83	34	36,085	–20,095	20	8

Portfolio Statistics

Net Profit:	5,052,672	Sharpe ratio:	0.39
Drawdown:	–2,371,700	Correlation to breakout:	0.34
K-ratio:	0.18	Correlation to 10-40 MA:	0.29

© 2002 Lars Kestner – All Rights Reserved

FIGURE 7.31a

MACD Strategy Applied to Futures.

Breakdown Statistics (Futures)

System Name: MACD
Parameters: 12 day minus 26 day exponential moving averages; 9 day EMA for signal line
Description: Buy when MACD crosses above signal line, sell when MACD crosses below signal line
Run Dates: 1/1/1990 – 12/31/2001

Breakdown by Market Sector

Market Sector	Average Net Profit	Average K-ratio	Average Sharpe Ratio	Average Max DD	Average Num Trades	Average % Win	Avg. Profit Per Contract	Average Win	Average Loss	Avg. Bars Win	Avg. Bars Loss
FX	719,384	0.15	0.39	-312,476	227	41	136	36,657	-20,040	21	8
Rates	-196,491	-0.03	-0.09	-458,987	184	27	-22	29,146	-17,166	16	6
Stock	-464,725	-0.16	-0.25	-670,450	252	36	-209	30,665	-20,159	21	7
Metals	-96,215	0.02	-0.05	-678,306	234	35	-5	35,163	-20,072	21	8
Energy	422,472	0.16	0.19	-414,924	234	37	79	41,691	-21,386	22	8
Grains	292,175	0.09	0.16	-427,267	233	39	22	36,932	-20,984	21	8
Meats	-299,835	-0.04	-0.15	-738,560	247	34	-21	37,118	-21,502	21	8
Softs	357,783	0.02	0.14	-554,308	232	37	78	37,835	-20,071	21	8

Performance Breakdown by Year

Year	Net Profit	K-ratio	Sharpe Ratio
1990	854,003	0.37	0.80
1991	1,856,272	0.24	1.11
1992	147,206	0.02	0.17
1993	86,160	0.14	0.09
1994	-446,822	-0.22	-0.42
1995	-850,935	-0.60	-1.20
1996	1,792,444	0.54	2.04
1997	1,310,569	0.24	1.08
1998	1,094,260	0.54	1.16
1999	823,637	0.43	3.86
2000	155,987	-0.17	0.15
2001	-1,787,280	-0.80	-1.53

Length	Number of Windows	Num. of Profitable Windows	Percent Profitable
1 Month	144	73	50.69%
3 Months	142	81	57.04%
6 Months	139	86	61.87%
12 Months	133	90	67.67%
18 Months	127	95	74.80%
24 Months	121	89	73.55%

Net Profit by Year

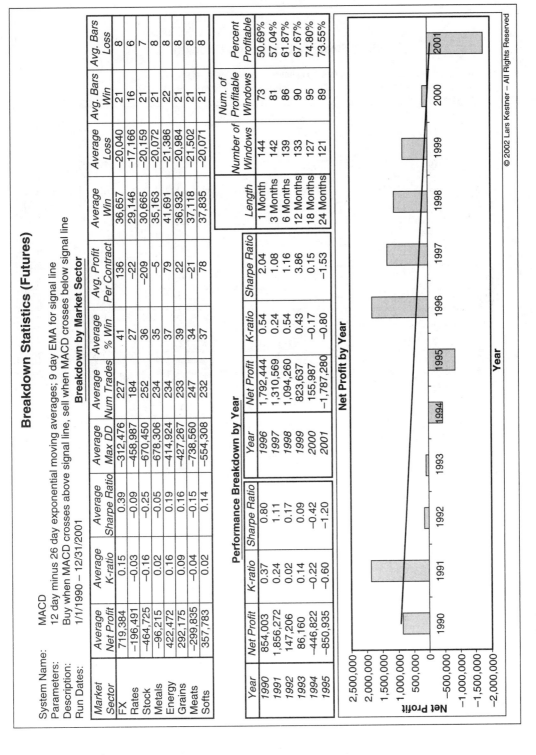

© 2002 Lars Kestner – All Rights Reserved

FIGURE 7.31b

MACD Strategy Applied to Futures.

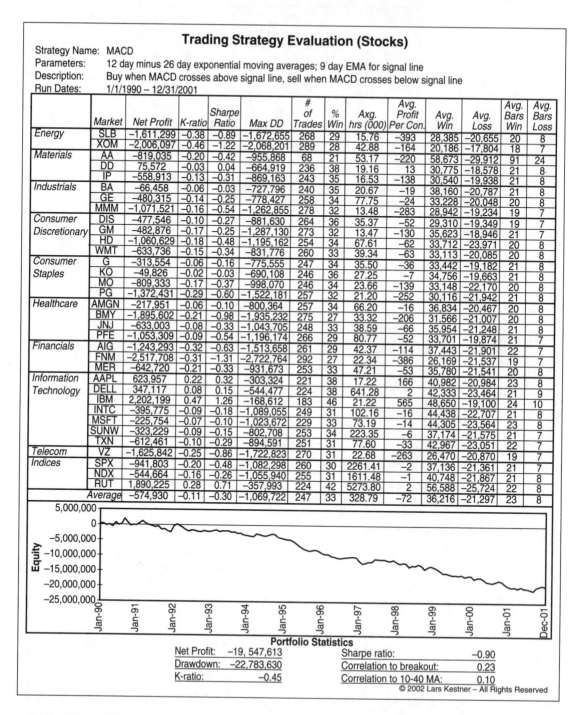

Trading Strategy Evaluation (Stocks)

Strategy Name: MACD
Parameters: 12 day minus 26 day exponential moving averages; 9 day EMA for signal line
Description: Buy when MACD crosses above signal line, sell when MACD crosses below signal line
Run Dates: 1/1/1990 – 12/31/2001

	Market	Net Profit	K-ratio	Sharpe Ratio	Max DD	# of Trades	% Win	Axg. hrs (000)	Avg. Profit Per Con.	Avg. Win	Avg. Loss	Avg. Bars Win	Avg. Bars Loss
Energy	SLB	−1,611,299	−0.38	−0.89	−1,672,655	268	29	15.76	−393	28,385	−20,655	20	8
	XOM	−2,006,097	−0.46	−1.22	−2,068,201	289	28	42.88	−164	20,186	−17,804	18	7
Materials	AA	−819,035	−0.20	−0.42	−955,868	68	21	53.17	−220	58,673	−29,912	91	24
	DD	75,572	−0.03	0.04	−664,919	236	38	19.16	13	30,775	−18,578	21	8
	IP	−558,913	−0.13	−0.31	−869,163	243	35	16.53	−138	30,540	−19,938	21	8
Industrials	BA	−66,458	−0.06	−0.03	−727,796	240	35	20.67	−19	38,160	−20,787	21	8
	GE	−480,315	−0.14	−0.25	−778,427	258	34	77.75	−24	33,228	−20,048	20	8
	MMM	−1,071,521	−0.16	−0.54	−1,262,855	278	32	13.48	−283	28,942	−19,234	19	7
Consumer Discretionary	DIS	−477,546	−0.10	−0.27	−881,630	264	36	35.37	−52	29,310	−19,349	19	7
	GM	−482,876	−0.17	−0.25	−1,287,130	273	32	13.47	−130	35,623	−18,946	21	7
	HD	−1,060,629	−0.18	−0.48	−1,195,162	254	34	67.61	−62	33,712	−23,971	20	8
	WMT	−633,736	−0.15	−0.34	−831,776	260	33	39.34	−63	33,113	−20,085	20	8
Consumer Staples	G	−313,554	−0.06	−0.16	−775,555	247	34	35.50	−36	33,442	−19,182	21	8
	KO	−49,826	−0.02	−0.03	−690,108	246	36	27.25	−7	34,756	−19,663	21	8
	MO	−809,333	−0.17	−0.37	−998,070	246	34	23.66	−139	33,148	−22,170	20	8
	PG	−1,372,431	−0.29	−0.60	−1,522,181	257	32	21.20	−252	30,116	−21,942	21	8
Healthcare	AMGN	−217,951	−0.06	−0.10	−800,364	257	34	66.20	−16	36,834	−20,467	20	8
	BMY	−1,895,602	−0.21	−0.98	−1,935,232	275	27	33.32	−206	31,566	−21,007	20	8
	JNJ	−633,003	−0.08	−0.33	−1,043,705	248	33	38.59	−66	35,954	−21,248	21	8
	PFE	−1,053,309	−0.09	−0.54	−1,196,174	266	29	80.77	−52	33,701	−19,874	21	7
Financials	AIG	−1,243,293	−0.32	−0.63	−1,513,658	261	29	42.37	−114	37,443	−21,901	22	7
	FNM	−2,517,708	−0.31	−1.31	−2,722,764	292	27	22.34	−386	26,169	−21,537	19	7
	MER	−642,720	−0.21	−0.33	−931,673	253	33	47.21	−53	35,780	−21,541	20	8
Information Technology	AAPL	623,957	0.22	0.32	−303,324	221	38	17.22	166	40,982	−20,984	23	8
	DELL	347,117	0.08	0.15	−544,477	224	38	641.28	2	42,333	−23,464	21	9
	IBM	2,202,199	0.47	1.26	−168,612	183	46	21.22	565	48,650	−19,100	24	10
	INTC	−395,775	−0.09	−0.18	−1,089,055	249	31	102.16	−16	44,438	−22,707	21	8
	MSFT	−225,754	−0.07	−0.10	−1,023,672	229	33	73.19	−14	44,305	−23,564	23	8
	SUNW	−323,229	−0.09	−0.15	−802,708	253	34	223.35	−6	37,174	−21,575	21	7
	TXN	−612,461	−0.10	−0.29	−894,591	251	31	77.60	−33	42,967	−23,051	22	7
Telecom	VZ	−1,625,842	−0.25	−0.86	−1,722,823	270	31	22.68	−263	26,470	−20,870	19	7
Indices	SPX	−941,803	−0.20	−0.48	−1,082,298	260	30	2261.41	−2	37,136	−21,361	21	7
	NDX	−544,664	−0.16	−0.26	−1,055,940	255	31	1611.48	−1	40,748	−21,867	21	8
	RUT	1,890,225	0.28	0.71	−357,993	224	42	5273.80	2	56,588	−25,724	22	8
	Average	−574,930	−0.11	−0.30	−1,069,722	247	33	328.79	−72	36,216	−21,297	23	8

Portfolio Statistics

Net Profit: −19, 547,613
Drawdown: −22,783,630
K-ratio: −0.45

Sharpe ratio: −0.90
Correlation to breakout: 0.23
Correlation to 10-40 MA: 0.10

© 2002 Lars Kestner – All Rights Reserved

FIGURE 7.32a

MACD Strategy Applied to Stocks.

Breakdown Statistics (stocks)

System Name: MACD
Parameters: 12 day minus 26 day exponential moving averages; 9 day EMA for signal line
Description: Buy when MACD crosses above signal line, sell when MACD crosses below signal line
Run Dates: 1/1/1990 – 12/31/2001

Breakdown by Market Sector

Market Sector	Average Net Profit	Average K-ratio	Average Sharpe Ratio	Average Max DD	Average Num Trades	Average % Win	Avg. Profit Per Contract	Average Win	Average Loss	Avg. Bars Win	Avg. Bars Loss
Energy	-1,808,698	-0.42	-1.05	-1,870,428	279	29	-279	24,286	-19,230	19	7
Materials	-434,125	-0.12	-0.23	-829,983	182	31	-115	39,996	-22,809	44	13
Industrials	-539,431	-0.12	-0.27	-923,026	259	34	-109	33,443	-20,023	20	7
Discretionary	-663,697	-0.15	-0.33	-1,048,925	263	34	-77	32,939	-20,588	20	7
Staples	-636,286	-0.13	-0.29	-996,479	249	34	-108	32,866	-20,739	21	8
Healthcare	-949,966	-0.11	-0.49	-1,243,869	262	31	-85	34,514	-20,649	20	8
Financials	-1,467,907	-0.28	-0.76	-1,722,698	269	30	-185	33,131	-21,659	20	7
Info. Tech.	230,865	0.06	0.14	-689,491	230	36	95	42,978	-22,064	22	8
Telecom	-1,625,842	-0.25	-0.86	-1,722,823	270	31	-263	26,470	-20,870	19	7
Indices	134,586	-0.03	-0.01	-832,077	246	34	0	44,824	-22,984	21	8

Performance Breakdown by Year

Year	Net Profit	K-ratio	Sharpe Ratio
1990	-456,863	0.02	-0.15
1991	-282,931	-0.32	-0.10
1992	-1,696,271	-0.42	-0.12
1993	-1,211,538	-0.40	-1.14
1994	-1,131,160	-0.13	-0.71
1995	-4,602,830	-0.85	-3.79

Year	Net Profit	K-ratio	Sharpe Ratio
1996	-2,494,832	-0.33	-1.76
1997	-297,395	0.12	-0.18
1998	-1,599,932	-0.29	-0.74
1999	-2,700,304	-0.48	-4.47
2000	-3,375,565	-0.46	-1.89
2001	-33,242	0.03	-0.02

Profitability Windows

Length	Number of Windows	Num. of Profitable Windows	Percent Profitable
1 Month	144	55	38.19%
3 Months	142	40	28.17%
6 Months	139	27	19.42%
12 Months	133	9	6.77%
18 Months	127	2	1.57%
24 Months	121	0	0.00%

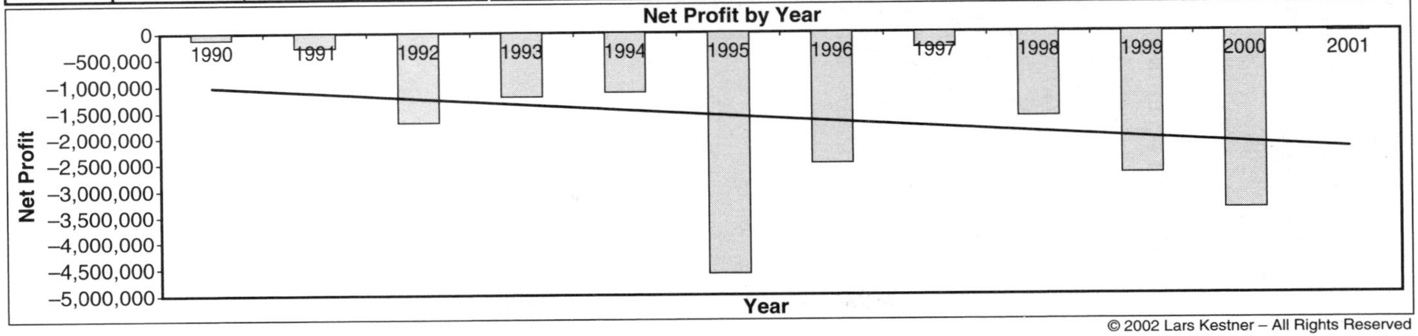

Net Profit by Year

© 2002 Lars Kestner – All Rights Reserved

FIGURE 7.32b

MACD Strategy Applied to Stocks.

The major worry with these trend-following models is relying on markets to continue their trending ways. While performance in the early 1990s was very strong, recent annual profits have been less than average. This is one area for systematic traders to monitor. The results may suggest that exhaustion strategies could be favored over trend-following strategies during the next 10 to 20 years.

We found that stock performance was very mixed. Trend-following strategies performed beautifully on specific sectors such as technology and stock indices, but overall, trend following performance was mixed. If we remove the small batch of stocks that produced profits, we find that the majority of stocks do not respond well to trend-following strategies. Removing technology and indices, the 14-day Slow %K strategy produced profits in 19 out the 24 remaining markets. This phenomenon is grounds for further study.

By evaluating today's popular trading strategies, we have established a baseline to compare new trading strategies that we will create later in the book. This level playing field approach allows traders to see exactly where they stand in the world of trading success. The performance results of the strategies in this chapter can be analyzed to gain a better understanding of how markets work.

CHAPTER 8

New Ideas on Entries, Exits, and Filters

Enhancing Trading Performance Using Cutting Edge Techniques

There are a number of new trading strategies for use with stocks and futures markets that I will introduce in this section. These ideas are not simply rehashes of currently used techniques; they are unique. Each strategy details the exact rules for buy and sell signals, and presents a price graph that plots sample buy and sell signals applied to real market data in addition to performance statistics for a portfolio of stocks and futures.

A WOLF IN SHEEP'S CLOTHING

The focus of my trading ideas is adapting indicators to prevailing market conditions. If a market is volatile, we want our entries and exits to be less sensitive to prices changes. We never want to use a fixed dollar stop or other such nonsense which is not derived from market statistics. Every idea is based on logic and rigorous statistical principles.

I've seen a number of "groundbreaking" strategies introduced in magazines such as *Technical Analysis of Stocks and Commodities* or sold as $3000 systems to the public. Very often, these methods consist of nothing more than the channel breakout and dual moving average crossover strategies that we have used in this book. More times than not, the core strategy will be wrapped with a number of filters that do not enhance strategy performance, and rarely even influence buy and sell signals. An example might be:

Setup 1: An inside day, a pattern where both today's high is less than yesterday's high and today's low is greater than yesterday's low, occurred within the last 10 trading days.

Setup 2: An outside day, a pattern where both today's high is greater than yesterday's high and today's low is less than yesterday's low, occurred within the last 10 trading days.

Setup 3: Today's close is the highest close of the past 40 days.

Setup 4: Today's close is the lowest close of the past 40 days.

If Setup 1, 2, and 3 are fulfilled, then buy the market.

If Setup 1, 2, and 4 are fulfilled, then sell the market.

You might see this strategy dubbed as the "Wiggle-Waggle Entry Mechanism," or some other catchy title. The wiggle and waggle (the inside and outside day filter) likely have nothing to do with the performance of the system. I see no reason why having an inside and outside day would affect the performance of a channel breakout system. It is a nonsensical trend filter. Despite the irrelevance of Setup 1 and Setup 2, this strategy is profitable. Why? Because the 40-day channel breakout that drives the performance of this strategy is inherently profitable. Although performance may actually be better without the wiggle and waggle setups, chances are the strategy creator will not tell you that.

One method to gauge the similarity of strategies is to calculate a correlation matrix of returns. Remember, systems with low correlation can be combined to utilize benefits of diversification, while highly correlated systems (such as the wiggle-waggle example above, and the 40-day/20-day channel breakout) do not provide any benefit to the trader. Keep an eye on the correlation statistics featured at the bottom of my performance templates. These numbers are an easy way to detect this high correlation to popular trend-following strategies.

THE SONG REMAINS THE SAME: SIMILARITIES OF OSCILLATORS

Trading strategies are not the only piece of the trading puzzle that suffers from severe correlation. Indicators—specifically overbought/oversold price oscillators such as the Relative Strength Index and %K stochastics—face similar problems due to the similarities in their calculation. As a result, their movements track each other very closely (Figure 8.1), so using one particular oscillator versus another may not be terribly important in trading decisions.

11 NEW TRADING TECHNIQUES

Why do I point out the similarities in oscillators and overspecified trading strategies? In the following pages, I will present 11 new ideas that are not a rehash of

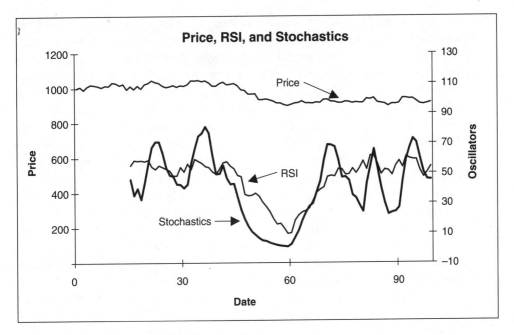

FIGURE 8.1

Price, RSI, and Stochastics. Moves in a 14-day RSI and 14-day Slow %K stochastics are very similar.

the old and overused. Nor are these techniques copycats of current trading logic. While many are variations of current methodologies, they're applied in a way that will generate entirely new and improved trading signals. The 11 are:

- Kestner's Moving Average system
- Second Order Breakout
- MACD histogram replacement
- Divergence Index
- Moving Average Confluence method
- Normalized Envelope Indicator
- Multiple Entry Oscillator system
- Adjusted stochastic
- Three in a row
- Volume Reversal strategy
- Saitta's Support and Resistance strategy

Kestner's Moving Average System

The first system I ever designed involved improving an already popular moving average crossover system. In the traditional single moving average crossover, buy signals are generated when prices close above the moving average, while sell signals are generated when prices close below the moving average. The most problematic feature of the single moving average crossover is the whipsaws caused by frequent crossings of price and the moving average. As explained in Chapter 4, if a market oscillates between strength and weakness with little follow-through, the typical moving average strategy can be whipsawed as it buys after periods of strength and sells after periods of weakness. This usually is the main driver to losses or failure of a moving average strategy's performance.

One way to alleviate these whipsaws is to create a channel using two separate averages. I accomplish this by calculating two averages: one using daily highs and another using daily lows. I require prices to close above the moving average of highs to generate buy signals, while prices must close below the moving average of lows to generate sell signals. In addition, I filter these signals by only taking buys when today's moving average is greater than the moving average x days ago, and only taking sell signals when today's moving average is less than the moving average x days ago. Typically, the x parameter used in the filtering process is equal to the length of the moving average.

The graph in Figure 8.2, shows the Kestner Moving Average System using a 20-day moving average when applied to General Electric (GE). In early June, both conditions are met to generate a long entry: prices rally above the 20-day moving average of highs, and the 20-day moving average is greater than the prior day's value. In late July, prices begin to fall leading to a decline below the 20-day moving average of lows and a falling 20-day moving average of closes. At this point we exit our long positions and enter short.

I generate trading signals by combining two separate systems—using a 20-day moving average and an 80-day moving average. Positions are taken when both systems are in agreement. That is, if the new moving average strategy using a 20-day moving average is long and the new strategy using an 80-day moving average is also long, we will enter a long position in the market tested. If the new moving average strategy using a 20-day moving average is short and the new strategy using an 80-day moving average is also short, we will enter a short position in the market tested. Long positions are exited if today's close falls below the 80-day simple moving average of lows. Short positions are exited if today's close rises above the 80-day simple moving average of highs.

Kestner's Moving Average system performs very well on our stable of futures markets (Figures 8.3a and 8.3b). A Sharpe ratio of 0.95 and K-ratio of 0.43 are two of the highest we will see. This strategy is profitable in 11 out of 12 years tested. Performance on stocks is not as impressive, but still generates profits in seven of 12 years (Figures 8.4a and 8.4b). The trading logic yields high correlation to standard trend-following strategies for both stocks and futures.

Second Order Breakout

This strategy was designed to distinguish between the strength of varying length channel breakouts. In a typical 20-day channel breakout, a long position is established

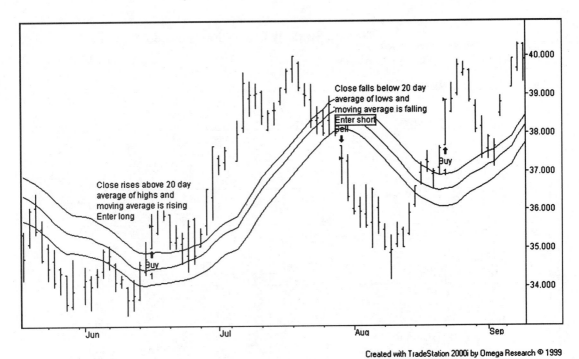

Close rises above 20 day
average of highs and
moving average is rising
Enter long

Close falls below 20 day
average of lows and
moving average is falling
Enter short

Created with TradeStation 2000i by Omega Research © 1999

FIGURE 8.2

Kestner's Moving Average System Applied to General Electric.

when the market makes a 20-day high. By definition, a 40-day high is also a 20-day high, since a market making a longer-term high is always making a shorter-term high. As such, the 40-day high would be considered a buy signal in our 20-day channel breakout strategy. Perhaps we need to distinguish the two by saying that a 40-day high is more significant than a 20-day high. Likewise, an 80-day high is more significant than a 40-day high. I developed the second order breakout to determine the significance of each new high and low.

Each day, we determine the significance of that day's close compared to the close of the past 80 days. By comparing today's close to the past 80, we determine the degree of breakout that is occurring today. If today's close is the highest of the past five days' closes, then today is a five-day high. If today's close is the highest of the past 20 days' closes, then today is a 20-day high. We search up to 80 days prior to determine the extent of today's breakout. The number of days high or low is recorded as the Second Order Breakout statistic. Highs are recorded as positive values and lows are recorded as negative values. For example, if today were the highest close of the past 40 days, then today's Second Order Breakout statistic would have a value of 40. If today were the lowest close of the past 35 days, then today's Second Order Breakout statistic would have a value of –35. We generate trading signals using the typical channel breakout methodology instead of enter-

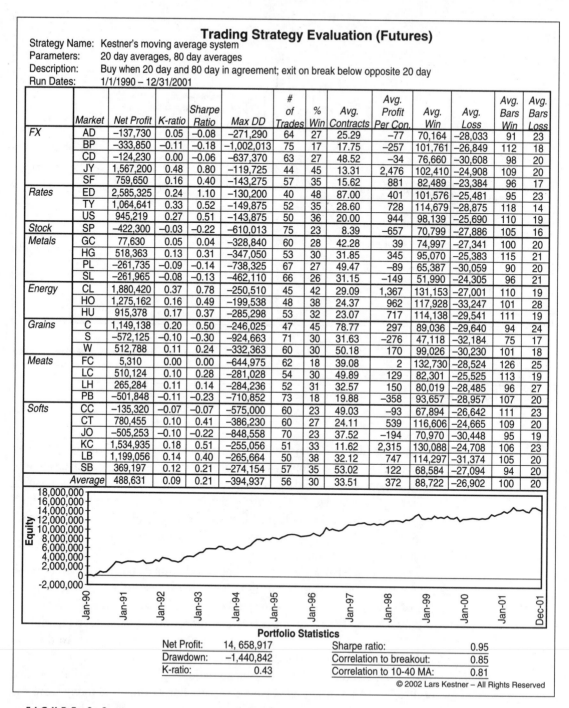

Trading Strategy Evaluation (Futures)

Strategy Name: Kestner's moving average system
Parameters: 20 day averages, 80 day averages
Description: Buy when 20 day and 80 day in agreement; exit on break below opposite 20 day
Run Dates: 1/1/1990 – 12/31/2001

	Market	Net Profit	K-ratio	Sharpe Ratio	Max DD	# of Trades	% Win	Avg. Contracts	Avg. Profit Per Con.	Avg. Win	Avg. Loss	Avg. Bars Win	Avg. Bars Loss
FX	AD	-137,730	0.05	-0.08	-271,290	64	27	25.29	-77	70,164	-28,033	91	23
	BP	-333,850	-0.11	-0.18	-1,002,013	75	17	17.75	-257	101,761	-26,849	112	18
	CD	-124,230	0.00	-0.06	-637,370	63	27	48.52	-34	76,660	-30,608	98	20
	JY	1,567,200	0.48	0.80	-119,725	44	45	13.31	2,476	102,410	-24,908	109	20
	SF	759,650	0.16	0.40	-143,275	57	35	15.62	881	82,489	-23,384	96	17
Rates	ED	2,585,325	0.24	1.10	-130,200	40	48	87.00	401	101,576	-25,481	95	23
	TY	1,064,641	0.33	0.52	-149,875	52	35	28.60	728	114,679	-28,875	118	14
	US	945,219	0.27	0.51	-143,875	50	36	20.00	944	98,139	-25,690	110	19
Stock	SP	-422,300	-0.03	-0.22	-610,013	75	23	8.39	-657	70,799	-27,886	105	16
Metals	GC	77,630	0.05	0.04	-328,840	60	28	42.28	39	74,997	-27,341	100	20
	HG	518,363	0.13	0.31	-347,050	53	30	31.85	345	95,070	-25,383	115	21
	PL	-261,735	-0.09	-0.14	-738,325	67	27	49.47	-89	65,387	-30,059	90	20
	SL	-261,965	-0.08	-0.13	-462,110	66	26	31.15	-149	51,990	-24,305	96	21
Energy	CL	1,880,420	0.37	0.78	-250,510	45	42	29.09	1,367	131,153	-27,001	110	19
	HO	1,275,162	0.16	0.49	-199,538	48	38	24.37	962	117,928	-33,247	101	28
	HU	915,378	0.17	0.37	-285,298	53	32	23.07	717	114,138	-29,541	111	19
Grains	C	1,149,138	0.20	0.50	-246,025	47	45	78.77	297	89,036	-29,640	94	24
	S	-572,125	-0.10	-0.30	-924,663	71	30	31.63	-276	47,118	-32,184	75	17
	W	512,788	0.11	0.24	-332,363	60	30	50.18	170	99,026	-30,230	101	18
Meats	FC	5,310	0.00	0.00	-644,975	62	18	39.08	2	132,730	-28,524	126	25
	LC	510,124	0.10	0.28	-281,028	54	30	49.89	129	82,301	-25,525	113	19
	LH	265,284	0.11	0.14	-284,236	52	31	32.57	150	80,019	-28,485	96	27
	PB	-501,848	-0.11	-0.23	-710,852	73	18	19.88	-358	93,657	-28,957	107	20
Softs	CC	-135,320	-0.07	-0.07	-575,000	60	23	49.03	-93	67,894	-26,642	111	23
	CT	780,455	0.10	0.41	-386,230	60	27	24.11	539	116,606	-24,665	109	20
	JO	-505,253	-0.10	-0.22	-848,558	70	23	37.52	-194	70,970	-30,448	95	19
	KC	1,534,935	0.18	0.51	-255,056	51	33	11.62	2,315	130,088	-24,708	106	23
	LB	1,199,056	0.14	0.40	-265,664	50	38	32.12	747	114,297	-31,374	105	20
	SB	369,197	0.12	0.21	-274,154	57	35	53.02	122	68,584	-27,094	94	20
	Average	488,631	0.09	0.21	-394,937	56	30	33.51	372	88,722	-26,902	100	20

Portfolio Statistics

Net Profit:	14, 658,917	Sharpe ratio:	0.95
Drawdown:	-1,440,842	Correlation to breakout:	0.85
K-ratio:	0.43	Correlation to 10-40 MA:	0.81

© 2002 Lars Kestner – All Rights Reserved

FIGURE 8.3a

Kestner's Moving Average System Applied to Futures.

Breakdown Statistics (Futures)

System Name: Kestner's moving average system
Parameters: 20 day averages, 80 day averages
Description: Buy when 20 day and 80 day in agreement; exit on break below opposite 20 day
Run Dates: 1/1/1990 – 12/31/2001

Breakdown by Market Sector

Market Sector	Average Net Profit	Average K-ratio	Average Sharpe Ratio	Average Max DD	Average Num Trades	Average % Win	Avg. Profit Per Contract	Average Win	Average Loss	Avg. Bars Win	Avg. Bars Loss
FX	346,208	0.11	0.18	-434,735	61	30	598	86,697	-26,756	101	20
Rates	1,148,796	0.21	0.53	-105,988	36	30	518	78,599	-20,012	81	14
Stock	-422,300	-0.03	-0.22	-610,013	75	23	-657	70,799	-27,886	105	16
Metals	18,073	0.00	0.02	-469,081	62	28	36	71,861	-26,772	100	21
Energy	1,356,987	0.23	0.55	-245,115	49	37	1,016	121,073	-29,930	107	22
Grains	363,267	0.07	0.15	-501,017	59	35	64	78,393	-30,685	90	20
Meats	69,718	0.03	0.05	-480,273	60	24	-19	97,176	-27,873	110	23
Softs	540,512	0.06	0.20	-434,110	58	30	573	94,740	-27,488	103	21

Performance Breakdown by Year

Year	Net Profit	K-ratio	Sharpe Ratio	Year	Net Profit	K-ratio	Sharpe Ratio
1990	2,896,322	0.80	2.20	1996	1,846,725	0.41	1.03
1991	1,015,345	0.11	0.77	1997	946,459	0.15	1.05
1992	1,172,679	0.24	1.02	1998	619,292	0.23	0.44
1993	1,296,009	0.19	1.13	1999	-149,373	-0.10	-0.08
1994	1,941,894	0.61	1.52	2000	1,771,296	0.48	1.83
1995	1,167,284	0.25	1.42	2001	104,071	0.09	0.06

Length	Number of Windows	Num. of Profitable Windows	Percent Profitable
1 Month	144	82	56.94%
3 Months	142	95	66.90%
6 Months	139	112	80.58%
12 Months	133	121	90.98%
18 Months	127	123	96.85%
24 Months	121	120	99.17%

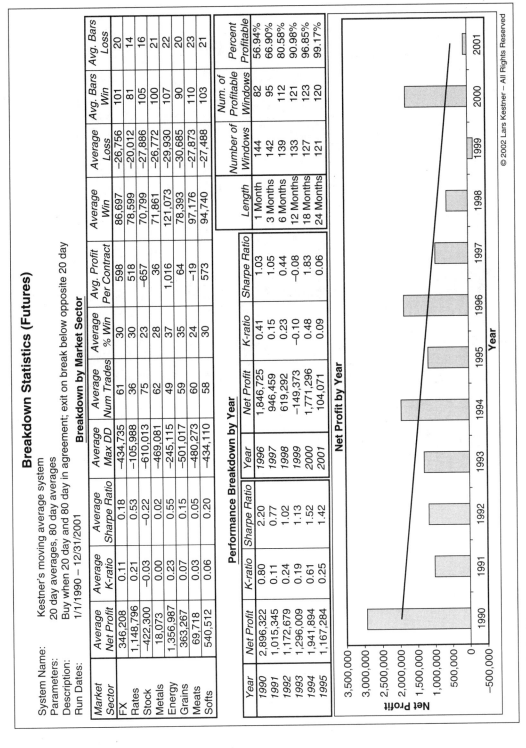

Net Profit by Year

© 2002 Lars Kestner – All Rights Reserved

FIGURE 8.3b

Kestner's Moving Average System Applied to Futures.

Trading Strategy Evaluation (Stocks)

Strategy Name: Kestner's moving average system
Parameters: 20 day averages, 80 day averages
Description: Buy when 20 day and 80 day in agreement; exit on break below opposite 20 day
Run Dates: 1/1/1990 – 12/31/2001

	Market	Net Profit	K-ratio	Sharpe Ratio	Max DD	# of Trades	% Win	Avg. hrs (000)	Avg. Profit Per Con.	Avg. Win	Avg. Loss	Avg. Bars Win	Avg. Bars Loss
Energy	SLB	12,214	0.02	0.01	−366,403	67	27	15.88	−3	68,403	−25,185	96	18
	XOM	−447,922	−0.02	−0.26	−541,961	76	25	41.51	−142	52,154	−25,243	86	19
Materials	AA	721,966	0.12	0.40	−250,884	235	40	48.10	61	35,536	−18,836	20	8
	DD	−265,376	0.02	−0.14	−479,546	73	23	22.97	−141	72,089	−26,109	95	18
	IP	−1,112,854	−0.30	−0.65	−1,148,649	79	15	17.70	−795	61,491	−27,615	97	22
Industrials	BA	4,860	0.00	0.00	−385,808	59	27	20.20	4	75,617	−28,024	99	26
	GE	349,766	0.10	0.20	−364,851	64	34	79.63	71	71,585	−28,926	94	14
	MMM	−1,016,660	−0.24	−0.57	−1,068,669	77	23	12.79	−1,066	41,279	−30,389	83	19
Consumer	DIS	326,890	0.12	0.17	−191,997	63	33	36.77	141	70,385	−27,409	89	19
Discretionary	GM	522,145	0.15	0.30	−131,960	50	48	12.51	835	46,691	−23,017	87	20
	HD	425,147	0.05	0.21	−407,104	68	21	61.55	98	123,029	−24,306	117	18
	WMT	216,902	0.04	0.12	−367,950	62	29	35.19	73	76,994	−27,854	101	17
Consumer	G	53,686	0.08	0.03	−263,338	58	34	38.31	2	68,186	−35,745	98	15
Staples	KO	−202,256	0.03	−0.09	−693,084	66	20	23.79	−129	121,941	−33,726	129	18
	MO	362,990	0.12	0.19	−387,817	59	27	24.75	253	101,668	−29,226	109	21
	PG	−197,343	−0.01	−0.09	−546,069	77	22	22.92	−143	88,192	−29,195	93	17
Healthcare	AMGN	1,300,388	0.13	0.52	−369,204	53	28	48.35	510	152,821	−25,916	111	25
	BMY	331,151	0.11	0.18	−411,910	57	26	32.05	167	97,871	−27,691	115	22
	JNJ	199,063	0.05	0.09	−728,386	63	25	35.58	94	98,255	−28,959	104	20
	PFE	1,398,474	0.22	0.62	−393,704	49	31	59.60	475	146,145	−23,650	119	26
Financials	AIG	3,885	0.04	0.00	−380,118	70	21	39.63	11	97,927	−26,134	108	18
	FNM	−779,473	−0.06	−0.43	−1,076,581	83	20	19.19	−486	67,667	−29,156	95	16
	MER	817,597	0.13	0.38	−284,852	56	29	49.81	297	122,951	−28,487	110	21
Information	AAPL	639,949	0.16	0.30	−192,795	53	32	18.41	628	85,244	−23,229	88	29
Technology	DELL	2,171,902	0.17	0.45	−345,975	57	30	547.31	69	191,668	−27,503	115	17
	IBM	198,592	0.08	0.10	−453,018	60	28	18.38	120	81,820	−29,265	90	24
	INTC	1,148,675	0.21	0.50	−348,956	65	26	84.70	202	132,157	−23,686	98	19
	MSFT	1,191,043	0.17	0.46	−393,357	61	30	56.31	343	140,155	−31,254	108	16
	SUNW	746,528	0.10	0.32	−418,119	57	33	214.84	61	100,118	−30,413	95	19
	TXN	1,105,334	0.20	0.47	−275,614	56	36	97.26	204	99,957	−24,606	97	19
Telecom	VZ	−441,685	−0.01	−0.27	−508,096	61	28	21.47	−381	50,430	−30,815	96	22
Indices	SPX	−110,761	0.04	−0.06	−569,651	73	23	2275.32	−1	85,035	−27,627	105	16
	NDX	987,273	0.27	0.46	−201,943	52	40	1610.30	12	97,629	−33,229	100	19
	RUT	1,582,679	0.24	0.56	−168,291	53	38	5270.06	6	127,551	−29,641	90	20
	Average	360,140	0.07	0.13	−444,608	68	29	323.92	43	92,666	−27,708	98	19

Portfolio Statistics

Net Profit:	12,244,768	Sharpe ratio:	0.44
Drawdown:	−5,487,815	Correlation to breakout:	0.85
K-ratio:	0.18	Correlation to 10-40 MA:	0.75

© 2002 Lars Kestner – All Rights Reserved

FIGURE 8.4a

Kestner's Moving Average System Applied to Stocks.

Breakdown Statistics (Stocks)

System Name: Kestner's moving average system
Parameters: 20 day averages, 80 day averages
Description: Buy when 20 day and 80 day in agreement; exit on break below opposite 20 day
Run Dates: 1/1/2001 – 13/31/2001

Breakdown by Market Sector

Market Sector	Average Net Profit	Average K-ratio	Average Sharpe Ratio	Average Max DD	Average Num Trades	Average % Win	Avg. Profit Per Contract	Average Win	Average Loss	Avg. Bars Win	Avg. Bars Loss
Energy	-217,854	0.00	-0.13	-454,182	72	26	-72	60,279	-25,214	91	18
Materials	-218,755	-0.05	-0.13	-626,360	129	26	-292	56,372	-24,187	71	16
Industrials	-220,678	-0.05	-0.12	-606,443	67	28	-330	62,827	-29,113	92	20
Discretionary	372,771	0.09	0.20	-274,753	61	33	287	79,275	-25,647	98	19
Staples	4,269	0.06	0.01	-472,577	65	26	-4	94,997	-31,973	107	18
Healthcare	807,269	0.13	0.35	-475,801	56	28	312	123,773	-26,554	113	23
Financials	14,003	0.04	-0.02	-580,517	70	23	-59	96,182	-27,926	104	18
Info. Tech.	1,028,860	0.16	0.37	-346,833	58	31	233	118,731	-27,137	99	20
Telecom	-441,685	-0.01	-0.27	-508,096	61	28	-381	50,430	-30,815	96	22
Indices	819,730	0.18	0.32	-313,295	59	34	6	103,405	-30,166	98	19

Performance Breakdown by Year

Year	Net Profit	K-ratio	Sharpe Ratio
1990	669,156	0.21	0.29
1991	4,485,590	0.24	1.86
1992	-781,404	-0.14	-0.64
1993	-684,393	-0.41	-0.59
1994	-867,500	-0.21	-0.73
1995	7,419,158	1.20	3.97
1996	881,730	0.00	0.37
1997	3,063,863	0.23	0.70
1998	1,986,832	0.21	0.87
1999	444,131	-0.15	0.11
2000	-1,151,191	-0.30	-0.55
2001	-3,309,846	-0.49	-1.87

Profitability Windows

Length	Number of Windows	Num. of Profitable Windows	Percent Profitable
1 Month	144	73	50.69%
3 Months	142	70	49.30%
6 Months	139	73	52.52%
12 Months	133	80	60.15%
18 Months	127	86	67.72%
24 Months	121	76	62.81%

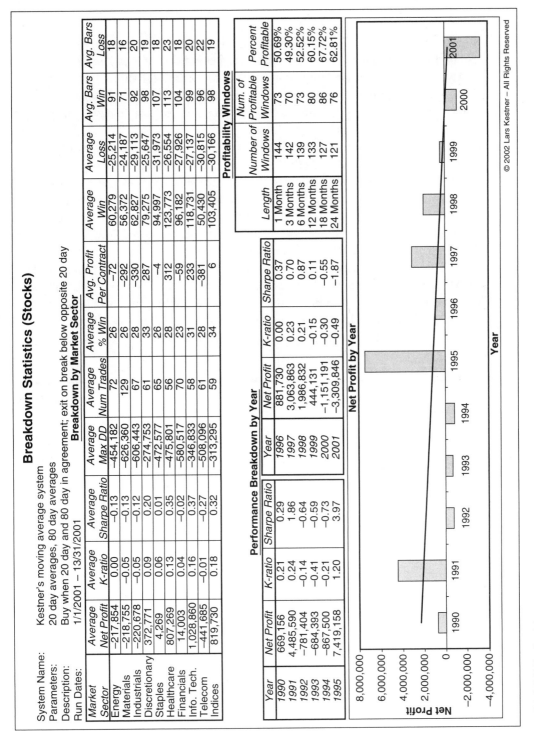

Net Profit by Year

© 2002 Lars Kestner – All Rights Reserved

FIGURE 8.4 b

Kestner's Moving Average System Applied to Stocks.

ing on breakouts of prices, we create signals based on channel breakouts of the Second Order Breakout statistic. The logic behind this strategy is as follows: If today's Second Order Breakout statistic is both the highest value over the past 40 days and greater than 20, then long positions are established. If today's Second Order Breakout statistic is both the lowest value over the past 40 days and less than –20, then short positions are established.

The beauty of the Second Order Breakout is that price moves of varying degrees are assessed and ranked. If a 40-day high was recently made, then today's 20-day high is somewhat discounted. For the 20-day high not to be a 40-day high, prices must be consolidating and the trend could be changing. As such, we may wish to take a pass on a typical channel breakout buy signal because the market appears to be consolidating, losing steam, and prone to reversal. The Second Order Breakout helps to spot these trend changes.

The chart in Figure 8.5, below, displays signals generated on Intel (INTC). In May, a rally resulted in a 20-day high, as indicated by a Second Order Breakout statistic value of 20. In addition, because the 20-day high was the most extreme high over the past 40 days, we enter long. This rally had legs, extending the 20-day highs to 80-day highs in mid-July. Again, this is indicated by the Second Order

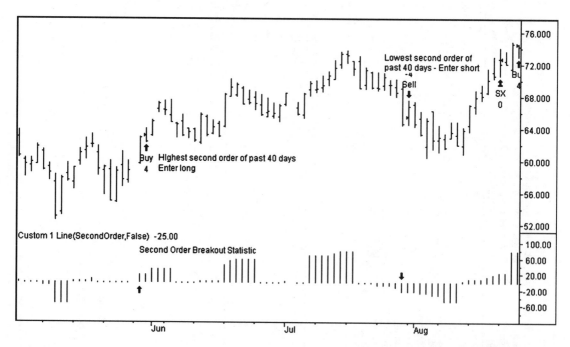

Created with TradeStation 2000i by Omega Research ℗ 1999

FIGURE 8.5

Second Order Breakout Strategy Applied to Intel.

Breakout statistic value of 80. A sell-off in late July causes the market to make a 20-day low and a corresponding Second Order Breakout statistic value of -20. Because the Second Order Breakout statistic was the lowest value of the past 40 days, we enter short.

The unique idea of the Second Order Breakout does not transfer to bottom-line performance. While I think there is merit in its logic, the second order strategy underperforms standard trend-following strategies. The standard 40-day entry/20-day exit channel breakout from Chapter 7 (see Figures 7.11a through 7.12b) produced a Sharpe ratio of 0.41 on futures, 0.16 on stocks, a K-ratio of 0.12 on futures, and 0.06 on stocks. Each of these reward-to-risk measures outperforms the corresponding measures of the Second Order Breakout strategy seen in Figures 8.6a through 8.7b. We'll have to take the Second Order Breakout back to the drawing board for more work before employing it in our trading

MACD Histogram Retracement

The third new technique involves the widely used Moving Average Convergence/ Divergence indicator (MACD), created by Gerald Appel. The MACD is itself an oscillator created by taking the difference between two exponential moving averages. An exponential moving average of the MACD—often referred to as the "signal line"—generates buy and sell signals from crossovers. When the MACD crosses above its signal line, we buy the market. When the MACD falls below its signal line, we sell the market. The default parameters are a 12- and 26-day EMA for the MACD and a 9-day EMA for the signal line. The MACD histogram is plotted by subtracting the value of the MACD signal line from the MACD value. Often, the histogram will generate early warning signals when trends are about to change.

MACD = 12-day exponential moving average of close $-$ 26-day exponential moving average of close

MACD Signal = 9-day exponential moving average of MACD

MACD Histogram = MACD $-$ MACD Signal

The MACD histogram retracement system uses the MACD histogram's ability to spot trend reversal early and turns that ability into profitable trading signals. The strategy generates a buy signal when the histogram retraces x percent of its prior trough when below zero. It generates a sell signal if the histogram retraces x percent of its prior peak when above zero. To avoid whipsaws, we require the histogram to reach some minimum threshold above zero before taking short entry signals, and some minimum threshold below zero before taking long entries. We are using the early warning power of the MACD histogram, and harnessing it by trading once it reverses a set amount from its last peak or trough.

Trading Strategy Evaluation (Futures)

Strategy Name: Second order breakout
Parameters: Check 20 to 80 day breakouts
Description: Enter on 40 day breakout of second order indicator
Run Dates: 1/1/1990 – 12/31/2001

	Market	Net Profit	K-ratio	Sharpe Ratio	Max DD	# of Trades	% Win	Avg. Contracts	Avg. Profit Per Con.	Avg. Win	Avg. Loss	Avg. Bars Win	Avg. Bars Loss
FX	AD	−431,470	−0.12	−0.24	−754,450	87	34	25.52	−195	47,617	−32,661	47	21
	BP	159,700	−0.01	0.09	−359,250	83	35	17.32	103	53,846	−26,164	50	21
	CD	−179,170	−0.03	−0.08	−487,980	87	33	46.03	−45	57,786	−31,982	47	21
	JY	978,763	0.22	0.47	−234,725	81	38	13.96	773	73,932	−28,351	55	19
	SF	755,388	0.22	0.40	−175,113	84	44	15.73	591	55,276	−26,913	51	16
Rates	ED	2,609,000	0.28	1.09	−278,150	70	49	89.59	416	111,070	−32,427	62	17
	TY	636,516	0.11	0.30	−334,984	79	42	29.45	257	62,847	−32,063	56	18
	US	297,750	0.07	0.16	−360,000	80	41	20.28	158	56,289	−34,055	54	18
Stock	SP	−777,238	−0.16	−0.44	−917,850	95	32	8.99	−884	45,666	−32,691	45	20
Metals	GC	115,150	0.01	0.05	−566,000	85	38	46.95	28	56,141	−31,810	50	20
	HG	−259,338	−0.01	−0.15	−597,725	89	36	31.81	−92	46,099	−30,430	48	17
	PL	−1,226,845	−0.21	−0.67	−1,468,055	98	30	49.87	−261	39,921	−35,247	45	17
	SL	−858,465	−0.23	−0.48	−980,175	97	30	35.22	−272	38,691	−30,192	47	18
Energy	CL	502,850	0.06	0.21	−310,190	84	42	28.21	217	61,765	−33,640	49	20
	HO	490,152	0.10	0.18	−320,544	82	39	23.95	255	70,185	−34,907	51	20
	HU	−233,835	−0.02	−0.09	−533,610	96	38	22.40	−103	51,200	−34,415	44	19
Grains	C	695,363	0.17	0.31	−345,913	83	45	78.08	107	63,417	−35,893	52	17
	S	−925	−0.06	0.00	−462,763	84	43	31.61	−6	39,461	−29,942	47	22
	W	202,225	0.09	0.09	−429,088	86	38	52.28	48	63,001	−35,191	52	17
Meats	FC	74,980	0.05	0.04	−357,745	81	43	40.68	21	47,051	−34,286	48	20
	LC	−427,096	−0.05	−0.22	−617,336	87	31	51.22	−95	51,901	−30,424	52	21
	LH	−81,364	0.05	−0.04	−530,700	87	33	31.49	−33	56,003	−29,557	54	20
	PB	−4,068	−0.03	0.00	−425,644	83	39	20.99	−31	56,497	−36,507	52	20
Softs	CC	−643,040	−0.17	−0.33	−1,064,280	91	23	50.46	−155	58,096	−27,582	57	21
	CT	96,690	−0.04	0.05	−561,180	89	28	25.04	43	83,553	−31,127	58	19
	JO	−872,835	−0.19	−0.38	−1,397,813	91	26	35.38	−276	54,908	−32,914	49	20
	KC	1,028,269	0.14	0.31	−303,881	84	35	12.22	1,009	81,991	−24,386	54	20
	LB	1,250,184	0.11	0.42	−278,952	77	43	33.38	483	85,908	−36,231	54	19
	SB	−610,467	−0.16	−0.31	−837,738	90	31	54.68	−118	54,505	−34,006	50	19
	Average	109,561	0.01	0.02	−543,061	83	35	34.09	65	57,487	−30,866	49	19

Portfolio Statistics

Net Profit:	3,286,823	Sharpe ratio:	0.21
Drawdown:	−2,627,541	Correlation to breakout:	0.95
K-ratio:	0.07	Correlation to 10-40 MA:	0.87

© 2002 Lars Kestner – All Rights Reserved

FIGURE 8.6a

Second Order Breakout Strategy Applied to Futures.

Breakdown Statistics (Futures)

System Name: Second order breakout
Parameters: Check 20 to 80 day breakouts
Description: Enter on 40 day breakout of second order indicator
Run Dates: 1/1/1990 – 12/31/2001

Breakdown by Market Sector

Market Sector	Average Net Profit	Average K-ratio	Average Sharpe Ratio	Average Max DD	Average Num Trades	Average % Win	Avg. Profit Per Contract	Average Win	Average Loss	Avg. Bars Win	Avg. Bars Loss
FX	256,642	0.05	0.13	-402,304	84	37	245	57,691	-29,214	50	20
Rates	885,816	0.11	0.39	-243,284	57	33	208	57,551	-24,636	43	13
Stock	-777,238	-0.16	-0.44	-917,850	95	32	-884	45,666	-32,691	45	20
Metals	-557,374	-0.11	-0.31	-902,989	92	33	-149	45,213	-31,920	47	18
Energy	253,056	0.05	0.10	-388,115	87	39	123	61,050	-34,321	48	20
Grains	298,888	0.07	0.13	-412,588	84	42	50	55,293	-33,675	50	19
Meats	-109,387	0.00	-0.06	-482,856	85	37	-34	52,863	-32,694	51	20
Softs	41,467	-0.05	-0.04	-740,641	87	31	164	69,827	-31,041	54	19

Length	Number of Windows	Num. of Profitable Windows	Percent Profitable
1 Month	144	72	50.00%
3 Months	142	78	54.93%
6 Months	139	76	54.68%
12 Months	133	86	64.66%
18 Months	127	80	62.99%
24 Months	121	79	65.29%

Performance Breakdown by Year

Year	Net Profit	K-ratio	Sharpe Ratio	Year	Net Profit	K-ratio	Sharpe Ratio
1990	1,495,478	0.39	1.01	1996	-80,293	0.12	-0.04
1991	1,028,123	0.16	0.68	1997	225,670	-0.11	0.17
1992	310,111	0.11	0.27	1998	-282,394	0.00	-0.22
1993	355,555	0.01	0.31	1999	-1,147,752	-0.31	-0.64
1994	111,099	0.07	0.07	2000	238,855	-0.03	0.18
1995	1,071,309	0.16	1.18	2001	-113,283	0.04	-0.13

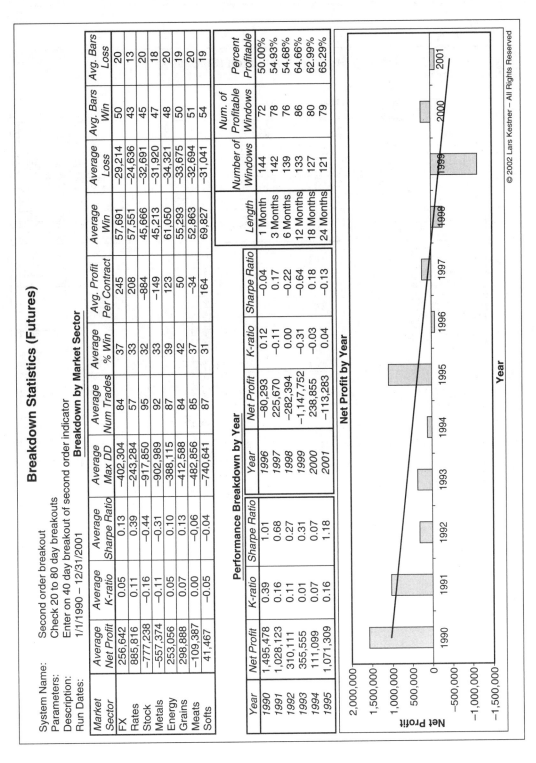

Net Profit by Year

© 2002 Lars Kestner – All Rights Reserved

FIGURE 8.6b

Second Order Breakout Strategy Applied to Futures.

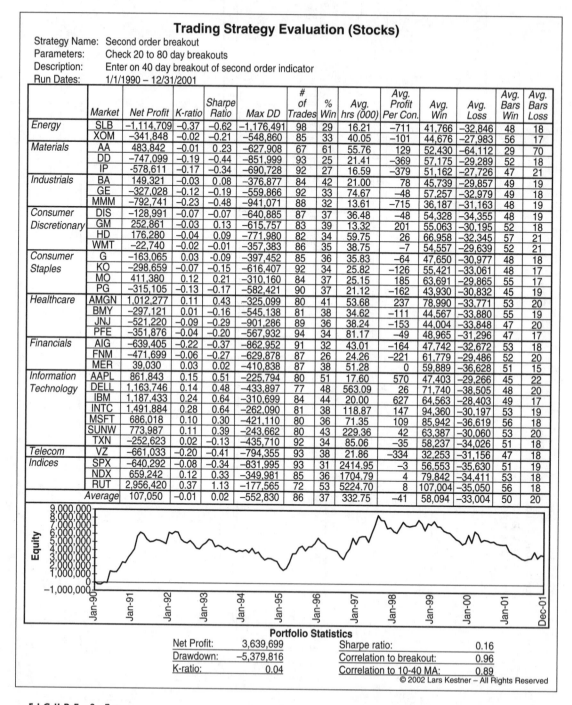

Trading Strategy Evaluation (Stocks)

Strategy Name: Second order breakout
Parameters: Check 20 to 80 day breakouts
Description: Enter on 40 day breakout of second order indicator
Run Dates: 1/1/1990 – 12/31/2001

	Market	Net Profit	K-ratio	Sharpe Ratio	Max DD	# of Trades	% Win	Avg. hrs (000)	Avg. Profit Per Con.	Avg. Win	Avg. Loss	Avg. Bars Win	Avg. Bars Loss
Energy	SLB	−1,114,709	−0.37	−0.62	−1,176,491	98	29	16.21	−711	41,766	−32,846	48	18
	XOM	−341,848	−0.02	−0.21	−548,860	85	33	40.05	−101	44,676	−27,983	56	17
Materials	AA	483,842	−0.01	0.23	−627,908	67	61	55.76	129	52,430	−64,112	29	70
	DD	−747,099	−0.19	−0.44	−851,999	93	25	21.41	−369	57,175	−29,289	52	18
	IP	−578,611	−0.17	−0.34	−690,728	92	27	16.59	−379	51,162	−27,726	47	21
Industrials	BA	149,321	−0.03	0.08	−376,877	84	42	21.00	78	45,739	−29,857	49	19
	GE	−327,028	−0.12	−0.19	−559,866	92	33	74.67	−48	57,257	−32,979	49	18
	MMM	−792,741	−0.23	−0.48	−941,071	88	32	13.61	−715	36,187	−31,163	48	19
Consumer	DIS	−128,991	−0.07	−0.07	−640,885	87	37	36.48	−48	54,328	−34,355	48	19
Discretionary	GM	252,861	−0.03	0.13	−615,757	83	39	13.32	201	55,063	−30,195	52	18
	HD	176,280	−0.04	0.09	−771,980	82	34	59.75	26	66,958	−32,345	57	21
	WMT	−22,740	−0.02	−0.01	−357,383	86	35	38.75	−7	54,557	−29,639	52	21
Consumer	G	−163,065	0.03	−0.09	−397,452	85	36	35.83	−64	47,650	−30,977	48	18
Staples	KO	−298,659	−0.07	−0.15	−616,407	92	34	25.82	−126	55,421	−33,061	48	17
	MO	411,380	0.12	0.21	−310,160	84	37	25.15	185	63,691	−29,865	55	17
	PG	−315,105	−0.13	−0.17	−582,421	90	37	21.12	−162	43,930	−30,832	45	19
Healthcare	AMGN	1,012,277	0.11	0.43	−325,099	80	41	53.68	237	78,990	−33,771	53	20
	BMY	−297,121	0.01	−0.16	−545,138	81	38	34.62	−111	44,567	−33,880	55	19
	JNJ	−521,220	−0.09	−0.29	−901,286	89	36	38.24	−153	44,004	−33,848	47	20
	PFE	−351,876	−0.04	−0.20	−567,932	94	34	81.17	−49	48,965	−31,296	47	17
Financials	AIG	−639,405	−0.22	−0.37	−862,952	91	32	43.01	−164	47,742	−32,672	53	18
	FNM	−471,699	−0.06	−0.27	−629,878	87	26	24.26	−221	61,779	−29,486	52	20
	MER	39,030	0.03	0.02	−410,838	87	38	51.28	0	59,889	−36,628	51	15
Information	AAPL	861,843	0.15	0.51	−225,794	80	51	17.60	570	47,403	−29,266	45	22
Technology	DELL	1,163,746	0.14	0.48	−433,897	77	48	563.09	26	71,740	−38,505	48	20
	IBM	1,187,433	0.24	0.64	−310,699	84	44	20.00	627	64,563	−28,403	49	17
	INTC	1,491,884	0.28	0.64	−262,090	81	38	118.87	147	94,360	−30,197	53	19
	MSFT	686,018	0.10	0.30	−421,110	80	36	71.35	109	85,942	−36,619	56	18
	SUNW	773,987	0.11	0.39	−243,662	80	43	229.36	42	63,387	−30,060	53	20
	TXN	−252,623	0.02	−0.13	−435,710	92	34	85.06	−35	58,237	−34,026	51	18
Telecom	VZ	−661,033	−0.20	−0.41	−794,355	93	38	21.86	−334	32,253	−31,156	47	18
Indices	SPX	−640,292	−0.08	−0.34	−831,995	93	31	2414.95	−3	56,553	−35,630	51	19
	NDX	659,242	0.12	0.33	−349,981	85	36	1704.79	4	79,842	−34,411	53	18
	RUT	2,956,420	0.37	1.13	−177,565	72	53	5224.70	8	107,004	−35,050	56	18
	Average	107,050	−0.01	0.02	−552,830	86	37	332.75	−41	58,094	−33,004	50	20

Portfolio Statistics

Net Profit:	3,639,699	Sharpe ratio:	0.16
Drawdown:	−5,379,816	Correlation to breakout:	0.96
K-ratio:	0.04	Correlation to 10-40 MA:	0.89

© 2002 Lars Kestner – All Rights Reserved

FIGURE 8.7a

Second Order Breakout Strategy Applied to Stocks.

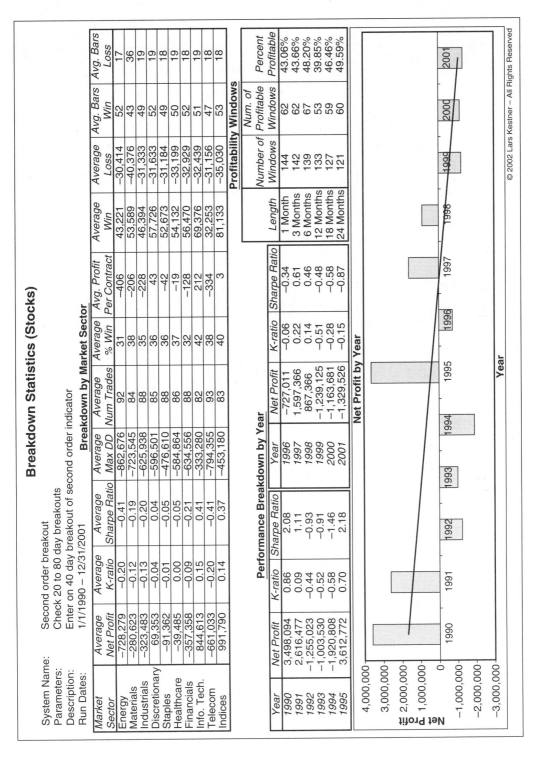

FIGURE 8.7b

Second Order Breakout Strategy Applied to Stocks.

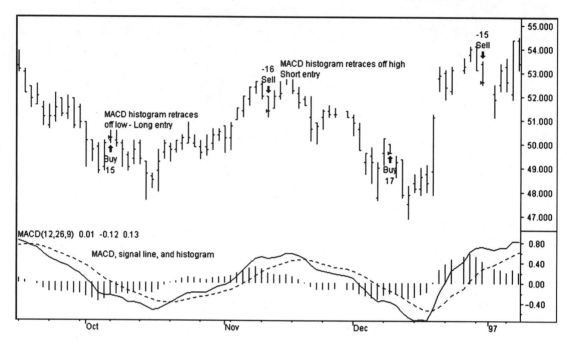

Created with TradeStation 2000i by Omega Research ® 1999

FIGURE 8.8

MACD Histogram Retracement Strategy Applied to Coca-Cola.

Our version of the MACD histogram retracement requires the histogram to exceed one-half of the standard deviation of price changes over the past 20 days before taking short signals. We require the histogram to be less than negative one-half times the standard deviation of price changes over the past 20 days before taking long signals. Long signals are entered if the histogram retraces 25 percent of its minimum value since its last cross below zero. Short signals are entered if the histogram retraces 25 percent of its maximum value since its last cross above zero.

The chart in Figure 8.8, above, depicts MACD histogram retracement signals applied to Coca-Cola (KO). In early October, a rally off a short-term low causes the MACD histogram to rise from its short term low of –0.32. When the histogram rises above 75 percent of –0.32 (75% of –0.32 is –0.23), we enter long positions. A short entry is established in mid-November as the MACD histogram retraces 25 percent of its maximum value—falling from 0.40 to 0.30.

Performance of the MACD retracement strategy will not get anyone excited. Although better than most oscillator-type strategies, futures markets produce profits in only 5 of the 12 years tested (Figures 8.9a and 8.9b). Stocks produce profits in only two of the 12 years tested (Figures 8.10a and 8.10b). Note, however, that four out of the past five years have been profitable on futures markets. Although not ready to be traded today, the MACD retracement strategy may be one to keep an eye on in later years.

Divergence Index

Buying pullbacks in uptrends and selling rallies in downtrends is one of my favorite trading techniques. I created the Divergence Index to measure the strength of such pullbacks. I believe that strong pullbacks within the context of even stronger trends make the best entries. The Divergence Index measures pullbacks by multiplying two momentum indicators. We divide the product of the two momentum measures by the variance of recent price changes in order to scale the indicator so results can be compared regardless of the market studied.

Divergence Index = 10 day momentum · 40-day momentum / (40-day standard deviation of price changes)^2

One feature of charting the Divergence Index is that trading opportunities are extremely obvious. More times than not, the 10-day and 40-day trend are the same when measured by simple momentum. When both momentum values are of the same sign (positive or negative), it leads to positive values for the Divergence Index. If we multiply two positive numbers together, the product is positive. Multiplying two negative numbers also leads to a positive value. We focus on the negative values of the Divergence Index for establishing new entries. If one momentum measure is positive while the other is negative, it suggests that a short-term divergence in the longer term trend is occurring. When the Divergence Index is negative, we want to make trades in the direction of the longer term trend.

Long entries are established when the Divergence Index is less than –10 and 40-day momentum is greater than zero. Sell signals are generated when the Divergence Index is less than –10 and 40-day momentum is less than zero.

Figure 8.11 details signals generated on Phillip Morris (MO). In late October the uptrend begins to stall as prices trade lower. While the 10-day momentum turns negative, the 40-day momentum is still positive. This leads to negative values for the Divergence Index. When the Divergence Index falls below –10, we enter long, attempting to buy the pullback in the longer term trend. This long position coincided with a short-term market bottom.

It's interesting to note that further research may also be able to identify trend exhaustion by using the Divergence Index. Large positive values might coincide with market tops and bottoms, or, at a minimum, they may lead to market congestion. If a market is overextended, both long-term and short-term momentum measures will show extreme values, leading to large positive values of the Divergence Index. An example of this trend exhaustion can be seen in the above chart during late September, when the Divergence Index rose above 150.

Trading Strategy Evaluation (Futures)

Strategy Name: MACD histogram retracement
Parameters: 12 day/26 day/9 day MACD; retrace 25% of extreme
Description: Enter long when MACD histogram retraces 25% of extreme move; opp. for shorts
Run Dates: 1/1/1990 – 12/31/2001

	Market	Net Profit	K-ratio	Sharpe Ratio	Max DD	# of Trades	% Win	Avg. Contracts	Avg. Profit Per Con.	Avg. Win	Avg. Loss	Avg. Bars Win	Avg. Bars Loss
FX	AD	77,660	−0.02	0.04	−742,670	51	53	25.21	66	56,696	−60,235	53	63
	BP	547,650	0.11	0.28	−400,000	50	66	16.84	662	47,723	−59,853	47	86
	CD	−571,480	−0.18	−0.27	−936,010	57	44	46.78	−229	49,422	−57,689	50	53
	JY	−965,038	−0.22	−0.43	−1,191,775	53	49	14.28	−1,447	42,796	−81,761	33	78
	SF	156,775	0.00	0.08	−715,288	53	60	16.33	206	58,521	−80,698	40	76
Rates	ED	−845,550	−0.19	−0.36	−1,429,175	49	51	87.58	−207	68,902	−108,827	53	65
	TY	−1,036,750	−0.30	−0.50	−1,504,016	54	46	30.36	−629	51,854	−80,271	34	73
	US	−765,094	−0.12	−0.39	−956,500	54	43	21.35	−635	53,174	−63,074	41	66
Stock	SP	270,713	0.07	0.15	−489,813	45	58	9.11	792	56,709	−60,515	54	81
Metals	GC	293,850	0.05	0.13	−600,440	51	47	47.58	125	75,804	−56,156	44	70
	HG	10,325	−0.02	0.01	−909,838	50	62	33.59	22	53,506	−85,354	57	64
	PL	810,680	0.19	0.40	−323,695	55	64	48.59	330	51,191	−45,485	48	59
	SL	873,135	0.15	0.48	−202,330	46	65	30.55	577	52,889	−48,488	56	78
Energy	CL	−844,400	−0.07	−0.35	−1,487,060	55	49	27.54	−514	51,028	−77,000	44	63
	HO	−816,904	−0.12	−0.34	−1,089,682	50	54	23.04	−641	48,270	−88,769	50	69
	HU	−833,226	−0.11	−0.35	−1,113,563	60	53	22.34	−592	42,819	−77,272	37	62
Grains	C	−255,750	−0.03	−0.12	−508,213	56	46	76.26	−65	60,792	−61,883	41	63
	S	120,488	−0.01	0.06	−538,700	52	50	29.32	52	50,914	−47,855	48	65
	W	676,563	0.14	0.35	−445,638	57	60	48.81	238	61,980	−62,783	49	55
Meats	FC	173,005	−0.04	0.09	−509,600	62	60	39.67	57	45,552	−61,828	36	66
	LC	−8,220	−0.04	0.00	−831,324	44	61	49.93	3	49,835	−78,814	43	108
	LH	−513,352	−0.22	−0.26	−833,136	54	50	31.67	−291	44,270	−62,732	39	72
	PB	−202,960	0.04	−0.09	−531,900	60	53	20.72	−110	47,413	−59,073	44	56
Softs	CC	1,056,490	0.15	0.56	−316,140	50	60	49.47	428	64,446	−43,729	52	69
	CT	−664,015	−0.09	−0.38	−752,025	42	60	24.00	−662	47,626	−109,320	48	103
	JO	−1,253	0.04	0.00	−482,213	59	58	33.48	26	40,626	−53,211	44	59
	KC	384,570	0.09	0.15	−641,618	50	66	11.90	623	58,052	−90,879	55	65
	LB	−596,960	−0.04	−0.20	−1,030,408	72	60	32.79	−239	48,822	−91,858	30	58
	SB	358,377	0.09	0.19	−544,264	45	53	54.43	144	63,475	−55,785	59	69
	Average	−103,689	−0.02	−0.04	−735,234	51	53	33.45	−64	51,504	−67,040	44	67

Portfolio Statistics

Net Profit:	−3,110,671	Sharpe ratio:	−0.23
Drawdown:	−7,011,997	Correlation to breakout:	−0.49
K-ratio:	−0.04	Correlation to 10-40 MA:	−0.51

© 2002 Lars Kestner – All Rights Reserved

FIGURE 8.9a

MACD Histogram Retracement Strategy Applied to Futures.

Breakdown Statistics (Futures)

System Name: MACD histogram retracement
Parameters: 12 day/26 day/9 day MACD; retrace 25% of extreme
Description: Enter long when MACD histogram retraces 25% of extreme move; opp. for shorts
Run Dates: 1/1/1990 – 12/31/2001

Breakdown by Market Sector

Market Sector	Average Net Profit	Average K-ratio	Average Sharpe Ratio	Average Max DD	Average Num Trades	Average % Win	Avg. Profit Per Contract	Average Win	Average Loss	Avg. Bars Win	Avg. Bars Loss
FX	-150,887	-0.06	-0.06	-797,149	53	54	-148	51,032	-68,047	45	71
Rates	-661,848	-0.15	-0.31	-972,423	39	35	-368	43,483	-63,043	32	51
Stock	270,713	0.07	0.15	-489,813	45	58	792	56,709	-60,515	54	81
Metals	496,998	0.09	0.25	-509,076	51	59	263	58,347	-58,870	51	68
Energy	-831,510	-0.10	-0.35	-1,230,102	55	52	-582	47,372	-81,014	44	64
Grains	180,433	0.03	0.10	-497,517	55	52	75	57,895	-57,507	46	61
Meats	-137,882	-0.07	-0.07	-676,490	55	56	-86	46,767	-65,612	40	76
Softs	89,535	0.04	0.05	-627,778	53	59	53	53,841	-74,130	48	71

Performance Breakdown by Year

Year	Net Profit	K-ratio	Sharpe Ratio		Year	Net Profit	K-ratio	Sharpe Ratio
1990	-2,050,949	-0.56	-1.32		1996	-1,052,815	-0.36	-0.80
1991	348,342	-0.02	0.32		1997	412,551	0.37	0.54
1992	-780,411	-0.50	-0.76		1998	506,933	0.17	0.56
1993	-2,038,258	-0.25	-1.36		1999	2,227,351	0.90	1.96
1994	-356,741	0.02	-0.36		2000	369,908	0.30	0.37
1995	-483,338	-0.03	-0.47		2001	-213,243	-0.12	-0.30

Length	Number of Windows	Num. of Profitable Windows	Percent Profitable
1 Month	144	77	53.47%
3 Months	142	74	52.11%
6 Months	139	68	48.92%
12 Months	133	55	41.35%
18 Months	127	51	40.16%
24 Months	121	44	36.36%

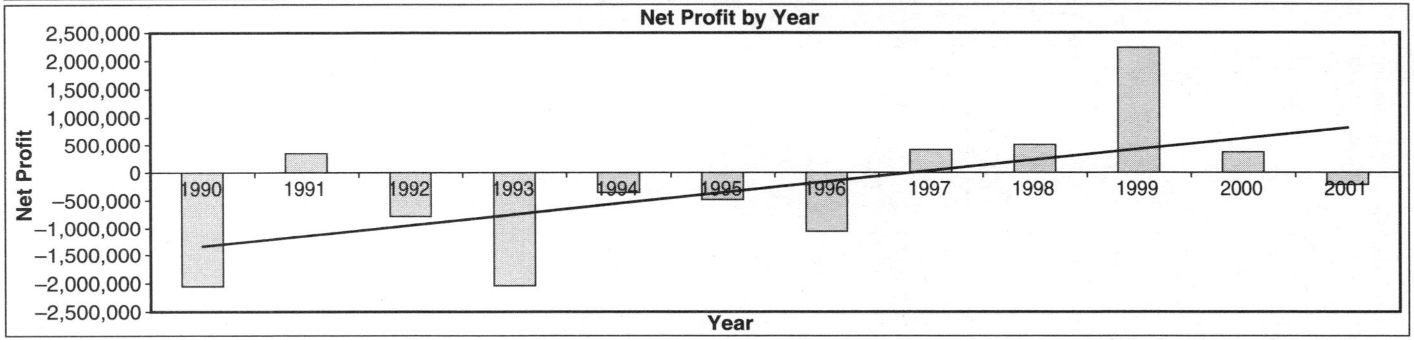

Net Profit by Year

©2002 Lars Kestner – All Rights Reserved

FIGURE 8.9 b

MACD Histogram Retracement Strategy Applied to Futures.

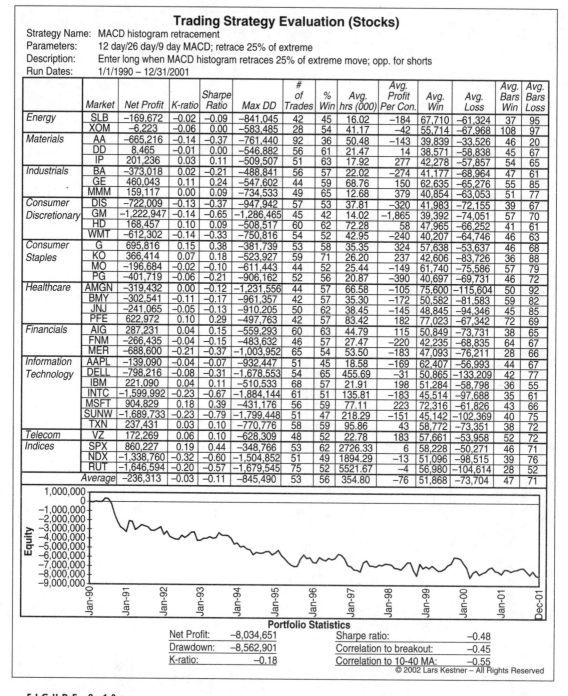

Trading Strategy Evaluation (Stocks)

Strategy Name: MACD histogram retracement
Parameters: 12 day/26 day/9 day MACD; retrace 25% of extreme
Description: Enter long when MACD histogram retraces 25% of extreme move; opp. for shorts
Run Dates: 1/1/1990 – 12/31/2001

	Market	Net Profit	K-ratio	Sharpe Ratio	Max DD	# of Trades	% Win	Avg. hrs (000)	Avg. Profit Per Con.	Avg. Win	Avg. Loss	Avg. Bars Win	Avg. Bars Loss
Energy	SLB	−169,672	−0.02	−0.09	−841,045	42	45	16.02	−184	67,710	−61,324	37	95
	XOM	−6,223	−0.06	0.00	−583,485	28	54	41.17	−42	55,714	−67,968	108	97
Materials	AA	−665,216	−0.14	−0.37	−761,440	92	36	50.48	−143	39,839	−33,526	46	20
	DD	8,465	−0.01	0.00	−546,882	56	61	21.47	14	38,571	−58,838	45	67
	IP	201,236	0.03	0.11	−509,507	51	63	17.92	277	42,278	−57,857	54	65
Industrials	BA	−373,018	0.02	−0.21	−488,841	56	57	22.02	−274	41,177	−68,964	47	61
	GE	460,043	0.11	0.24	−547,602	44	59	68.76	150	62,635	−65,276	55	85
	MMM	159,117	0.00	0.09	−734,533	49	65	12.68	379	40,854	−63,053	51	77
Consumer	DIS	−722,009	−0.13	−0.37	−947,942	57	53	37.81	−320	41,983	−72,155	39	67
Discretionary	GM	−1,222,947	−0.14	−0.65	−1,286,465	45	42	14.02	−1,865	39,392	−74,051	57	70
	HD	168,457	0.10	0.09	−508,517	60	62	72.28	58	47,965	−66,252	41	61
	WMT	−612,302	−0.14	−0.33	−750,816	54	52	42.95	−240	40,207	−64,746	46	63
Consumer	G	695,816	0.15	0.38	−381,739	53	58	35.35	324	57,638	−53,637	46	68
Staples	KO	366,414	0.07	0.18	−523,927	59	71	26.20	237	42,606	−83,726	36	88
	MO	−196,684	−0.02	−0.10	−611,443	44	52	25.44	−149	61,740	−75,586	57	79
	PG	−401,719	−0.06	−0.21	−906,162	52	56	20.87	−390	40,697	−69,731	46	72
Healthcare	AMGN	−319,432	0.00	−0.12	−1,231,556	44	57	66.58	−105	75,600	−115,604	50	92
	BMY	−302,541	−0.11	−0.17	−961,357	42	57	35.30	−172	50,582	−81,583	59	82
	JNJ	−241,065	−0.05	−0.13	−910,205	50	62	38.45	−145	48,845	−94,346	45	85
	PFE	622,972	0.10	0.29	−497,763	42	57	83.42	182	77,023	−67,342	72	69
Financials	AIG	287,231	0.04	0.15	−559,293	60	63	44.79	115	50,849	−73,731	38	65
	FNM	−266,435	−0.04	−0.15	−483,632	46	57	27.47	−220	42,235	−68,835	64	67
	MER	−688,600	−0.21	−0.37	−1,003,952	65	54	53.50	−183	47,093	−76,211	28	66
Information	AAPL	−139,090	−0.04	−0.07	−932,447	51	45	18.58	−169	62,407	−56,993	44	67
Technology	DELL	−798,216	−0.08	−0.31	−1,678,553	54	65	455.69	−31	50,865	−133,209	42	77
	IBM	221,090	0.04	0.11	−510,533	68	57	21.91	198	51,284	−58,798	36	55
	INTC	−1,599,992	−0.23	−0.67	−1,884,144	61	51	135.81	−183	45,514	−97,688	35	61
	MSFT	904,829	0.18	0.39	−431,176	56	59	77.11	223	72,316	−61,826	43	66
	SUNW	−1,689,733	−0.23	−0.79	−1,799,448	51	47	218.29	−151	45,142	−102,369	40	75
	TXN	237,431	0.03	0.10	−770,776	58	59	95.86	43	58,772	−73,351	38	72
Telecom	VZ	172,269	0.06	0.10	−628,309	48	52	22.78	183	57,661	−53,958	52	72
Indices	SPX	860,227	0.19	0.44	−348,766	53	62	2726.33	6	58,228	−50,271	46	71
	NDX	−1,338,760	−0.32	−0.60	−1,504,852	51	49	1894.29	−13	51,096	−98,515	39	76
	RUT	−1,646,594	−0.20	−0.57	−1,679,545	75	52	5521.67	−4	56,980	−104,614	28	52
	Average	−236,313	−0.03	−0.11	−845,490	53	56	354.80	−76	51,868	−73,704	47	71

Portfolio Statistics

Net Profit:	−8,034,651	Sharpe ratio:	−0.48
Drawdown:	−8,562,901	Correlation to breakout:	−0.45
K-ratio:	−0.18	Correlation to 10-40 MA:	−0.55

© 2002 Lars Kestner – All Rights Reserved

FIGURE 8.10a

MACD Histogram Retracement Strategy Applied to Stocks.

Breakdown Statistics (Stocks)

System Name: MACD histogram retracement
Parameters: 12 day/26 day/9 day MACD; retrace 25% of extreme
Description: Enter long when MACD histogram retraces 25% of extreme move; opp. for shorts
Run Dates: 1/1/1990 – 12/31/2001

Breakdown by Market Sector

Market Sector	Average Net Profit	Average K-ratio	Average Sharpe Ratio	Average Max DD	Average Num Trades	Average % Win	Avg. Profit Per Contract	Average Win	Average Loss	Avg. Bars Win	Avg. Bars Loss
Energy	-87,948	-0.04	-0.05	-712,265	35	49	-113	61,712	-64,646	72	96
Materials	-151,838	-0.04	-0.09	-605,943	66	53	50	40,230	-50,074	48	51
Industrials	82,047	0.04	0.04	-590,325	50	61	85	48,222	-65,764	51	75
Discretionary	-597,200	-0.07	-0.32	-873,435	54	52	-592	42,387	-69,301	46	65
Staples	115,957	0.04	0.06	-605,818	52	59	5	50,670	-70,670	46	77
Healthcare	-60,017	-0.02	-0.03	-900,220	45	58	-60	63,012	-89,719	56	82
Financials	-222,601	-0.07	-0.12	-682,292	57	58	-96	46,726	-72,926	43	66
Info. Tech.	-409,097	-0.05	-0.18	-1,143,868	57	55	-10	55,186	-83,462	40	67
Telecom	172,269	0.06	0.10	-628,309	48	52	183	57,661	-53,958	52	72
Indices	-708,376	-0.11	-0.25	-1,177,721	60	54	-4	55,435	-84,467	38	66

Performance Breakdown by Year

Year	Net Profit	K-ratio	Sharpe Ratio	Year	Net Profit	K-ratio	Sharpe Ratio
1990	-3,293,470	-0.43	-2.28	1996	-444,312	-0.02	-0.35
1991	-273,648	-0.13	-0.14	1997	281,832	0.14	0.21
1992	-600,043	-0.06	-0.43	1998	-252,022	-0.05	-0.13
1993	-285,611	-0.06	-0.28	1999	329,010	0.25	0.28
1994	-1,074,985	-0.33	-1.17	2000	-1,136,280	-0.05	-0.71
1995	-996,098	-0.10	-0.68	2001	-289,024	-0.13	-0.28

Profitability Windows

Length	Number of Windows	Num of Profitable Windows	Percent Profitable
1 Month	144	62	43.06%
3 Months	142	64	45.07%
6 Months	139	51	36.69%
12 Months	133	35	26.32%
18 Months	127	19	14.96%
24 Months	121	18	14.88%

Net Profit by Year

© 2002 Lars Kestner – All Rights Reserved

FIGURE 8.10b

MACD Histogram Retracement Strategy Applied to Stocks.

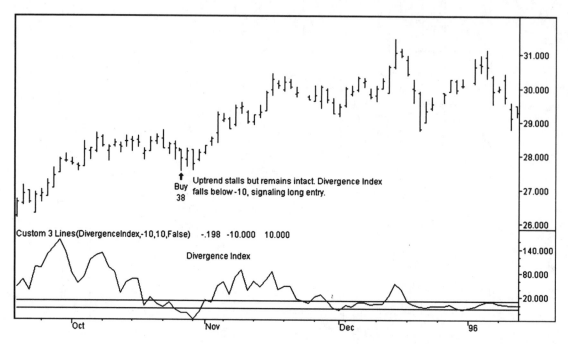

Custom 3 Lines(DivergenceIndex,-10,10,False)   -.198 -10.000 10.000

Divergence Index

Uptrend stalls but remains intact. Divergence Index
falls below -10, signaling long entry.

Buy
38

Created with TradeStation 2000i by Omega Research © 1999

FIGURE 8.11

Divergence Index Strategy Applied to Phillip Morris.

Divergence Index strategy performance is strong, especially on futures markets (Figures 8.12a and 8.12b). With a Sharpe ratio of 0.73 and a K-ratio of 0.26, futures markets generate profits in 11 out of 12 years tested. The strongest markets are not those typically associated with trend-following strategies. Stock indices, grains, and softs are the strongest performing sectors. When tested on stocks (Figures 8.13a and 8.13b), profits are generated in 7 of the 12 years tested. Health care, technology, and stock indices perform the best. Unlike typical trend-following strategies, performance of the Divergence Index does not deteriorate to the same extent over time. This property bodes well for future performance.

Moving Average Confluence Method

Optimization is an important enough topic that half of an entire chapter has been devoted to its concepts within this text. I have created a moving average trading method that simplifies the need to optimize parameter values. Instead of attempting to find optimal parameter values, the Moving Average Confluence method scans all parameter possibilities and enters trades only when a minimum number of parameter sets are in agreement.

Trading Strategy Evaluation (Futures)

Strategy Name: Divergence Index
Parameters: 10 day and 40 day momentum to calculate Divergence Index
Description: Enter when Divergence Index falls below −10
Run Dates: 1/1/1990 − 12/31/2001

	Market	Net Profit	K-ratio	Sharpe Ratio	Max DD	# of Trades	% Win	Avg. Contracts	Avg. Profit Per Con.	Avg. Win	Avg. Loss	Avg. Bars Win	Avg. Bars Loss
FX	AD	−350,390	−0.05	−0.32	−401,680	39	31	24.35	−369	34,153	−28,156	47	18
	BP	56,663	−0.06	0.05	−388,463	39	36	17.58	83	46,066	−23,531	37	13
	CD	−302,010	−0.05	−0.24	−469,970	42	29	48.51	−148	55,324	−32,197	43	15
	JY	918,763	0.27	0.56	−198,013	38	47	13.38	1,528	70,372	−24,473	64	16
	SF	427,425	0.18	0.31	−211,575	39	46	15.50	707	54,926	−26,726	54	14
Rates	ED	1,077,575	0.08	0.66	−309,000	36	47	87.49	128	57,140	−29,961	57	13
	TY	652,984	0.24	0.40	−144,859	39	46	28.10	596	60,001	−20,335	59	15
	US	572,281	0.22	0.44	−149,156	38	47	19.72	764	56,887	−22,584	54	12
Stock	SP	285,113	0.09	0.24	−298,275	35	34	8.08	1,008	69,830	−24,037	65	13
Metals	GC	123,110	0.04	0.08	−351,130	37	27	43.42	77	79,053	−24,719	59	23
	HG	−63,163	0.02	−0.05	−364,025	36	47	34.14	−26	36,600	−34,461	43	15
	PL	−494,655	−0.30	−0.49	−545,255	39	31	45.03	−282	16,045	−25,452	43	16
	SL	92,460	0.06	0.06	−202,765	35	40	31.33	84	43,819	−24,810	45	15
Energy	CL	127,400	0.03	0.09	−176,300	44	36	29.00	92	47,092	−22,730	47	14
	HO	−154,942	−0.06	−0.12	−338,898	41	32	25.17	−158	42,078	−25,370	42	14
	HU	−129,671	−0.03	−0.10	−291,988	46	37	22.34	−143	35,272	−25,737	40	19
Grains	C	525,813	0.10	0.32	−258,488	35	37	75.06	200	78,351	−22,398	59	18
	S	84,825	0.05	0.07	−152,013	41	46	31.79	50	31,675	−24,390	42	15
	W	473,525	0.14	0.30	−165,938	35	37	48.42	279	78,255	−24,718	70	15
Meats	FC	317,540	0.04	0.22	−200,335	44	41	39.51	183	56,980	−27,235	51	18
	LC	369,084	0.14	0.38	−91,308	35	63	49.17	181	28,917	−24,976	39	16
	LH	88,692	0.03	0.06	−221,360	48	46	30.88	60	38,629	−29,274	46	12
	PB	−127,548	−0.09	−0.09	−479,168	43	42	20.32	−146	46,440	−38,539	49	16
Softs	CC	−126,010	−0.10	−0.10	−387,710	42	36	51.47	−72	37,591	−26,676	39	10
	CT	635,915	0.05	0.47	−308,995	35	40	24.58	728	85,051	−26,872	63	12
	JO	−149,475	−0.07	−0.15	−219,353	35	34	35.67	−87	37,937	−24,529	41	15
	KC	1,069,988	0.22	0.50	−164,644	40	43	11.41	2,343	91,341	−20,992	63	16
	LB	822,632	0.10	0.31	−212,984	43	33	34.11	561	117,132	−28,180	55	17
	SB	374,853	0.08	0.29	−182,974	37	41	54.66	182	55,477	−21,139	50	16
	Average	239,959	0.05	0.14	−262,887	38	38	33.34	280	52,948	−25,173	49	15

Portfolio Statistics

Net Profit:	7,198,775	Sharpe ratio:	0.73
Drawdown:	−1,550,895	Correlation to breakout:	0.63
K-ratio:	0.26	Correlation to 10-40 MA:	0.56

© 2002 Lars Kestner – All Rights Reserved

FIGURE 8.12a

Divergence Index Strategy Applied to Futures.

Breakdown Statistics (Futures)

System Name: Divergence Index
Parameters: 10 day and 40 day momentum to calculate Divergence Index
Description: Enter when Divergence Index falls below −10
Run Dates: 1/1/1990 – 12/31/2001

Breakdown by Market Sector

Market Sector	Average Net Profit	Average K-ratio	Average Sharpe Ratio	Average Max DD	Average Num Trades	Average % Win	Avg. Profit Per Contract	Average Win	Average Loss	Avg. Bars Win	Avg. Bars Loss
FX	150,090	0.06	0.07	−333,940	39	38	360	52,168	−27,016	49	15
Rates	575,710	0.14	0.38	−150,754	28	35	372	43,507	−18,220	43	10
Stock	285,113	0.09	0.24	−298,275	35	34	1,008	69,830	−24,037	65	13
Metals	−85,562	−0.05	−0.10	−365,794	37	36	−37	43,879	−27,361	47	17
Energy	−52,404	−0.02	−0.04	−269,062	44	35	−70	41,481	−24,612	43	16
Grains	361,388	0.10	0.23	−192,146	37	40	177	62,760	−23,835	57	16
Meats	161,942	0.03	0.14	−248,043	43	48	69	42,741	−30,006	46	15
Softs	437,984	0.05	0.22	−246,110	39	38	609	70,755	−24,731	52	14

Performance Breakdown by Year

Year	Net Profit	K-ratio	Sharpe Ratio	Year	Net Profit	K-ratio	Sharpe Ratio
1990	1,643,266	1.07	2.10	1996	762,460	0.15	0.85
1991	438,228	−0.02	0.44	1997	493,611	−0.10	0.64
1992	316,037	0.28	0.44	1998	652,202	0.26	0.73
1993	1,673,517	0.46	1.96	1999	−902,079	−0.60	−2.05
1994	20,336	0.11	0.03	2000	515,743	0.18	0.82
1995	879,776	0.39	1.20	2001	712,044	0.40	0.67

Length	Number of Windows	Num. of Profitable Windows	Percent Profitable
1 Month	144	85	59.03%
3 Months	142	90	63.38%
6 Months	139	102	73.38%
12 Months	133	110	82.71%
18 Months	127	110	86.61%
24 Months	121	106	87.60%

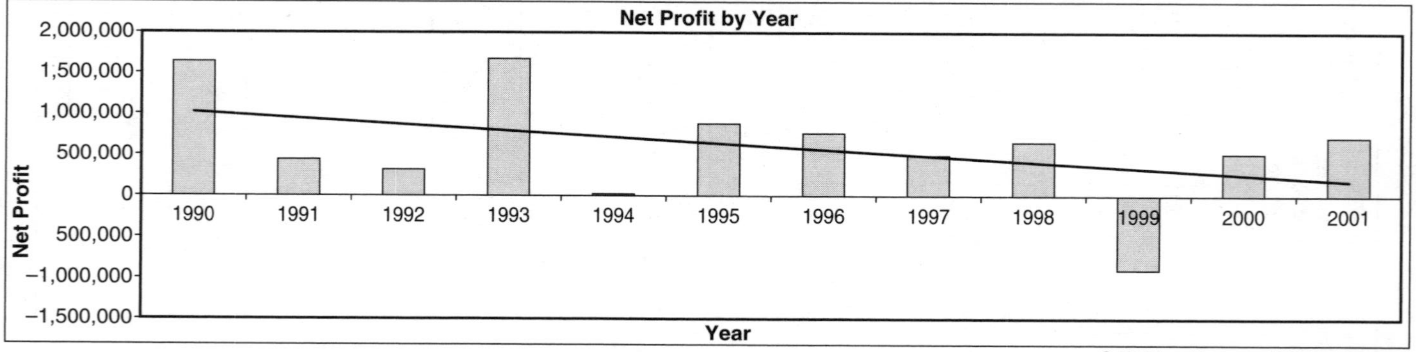

Net Profit by Year

© 2002 Lars Kestner – All Rights Reserved

FIGURE 8.12b

Divergence Index Strategy Applied to Futures.

Trading Strategy Evaluation (Stocks)

Strategy Name: Divergence Index
Parameters: 10 day and 40 day momentum to calculate Divergence Index
Description: Enter when Divergence Index falls below −10
Run Dates: 1/1/1990 − 12/31/2001

	Market	Net Profit	K-ratio	Sharpe Ratio	Max DD	# of Trades	% Win	Avg. hrs (000)	Avg. Profit Per Con.	Avg. Win	Avg. Loss	Avg. Bars Win	Avg. Bars Loss
Energy	SLB	51,368	0.06	0.04	−256,145	34	38	16.40	92	53,060	−30,401	54	14
	XOM	−443,474	−0.39	−0.66	−468,469	27	22	46.29	−355	14,060	−25,135	35	17
Materials	AA	−488,370	−0.03	−0.26	−633,194	64	38	49.74	−157	49,173	−41,963	78	28
	DD	−295,009	−0.08	−0.34	−398,076	38	34	20.36	−381	28,330	−26,532	35	12
	IP	−415,874	−0.21	−0.38	−526,065	44	32	16.29	−595	32,398	−29,346	39	12
Industrials	BA	166,355	0.00	0.12	−298,679	41	32	19.12	212	72,736	−27,829	57	15
	GE	217,269	0.09	0.18	−243,538	35	43	71.11	87	55,550	−30,799	56	15
	MMM	−271,950	−0.09	−0.25	−319,835	36	31	12.59	−600	31,714	−24,832	44	16
Consumer Discretionary	DIS	22,902	−0.01	0.02	−221,771	39	31	37.00	14	59,431	−25,688	50	15
	GM	−201,470	−0.08	−0.17	−271,613	37	32	13.53	−418	34,223	−24,799	49	20
	HD	928,008	0.08	0.60	−338,473	33	36	55.94	503	127,461	−28,644	84	13
	WMT	87,663	0.00	0.07	−348,214	33	45	41.06	65	48,748	−35,753	52	17
Consumer Staples	G	202,314	0.06	0.16	−174,740	37	46	35.29	124	37,277	−23,619	48	19
	KO	−282,288	−0.08	−0.28	−367,034	38	34	25.38	−293	31,297	−27,566	36	17
	MO	435,219	0.20	0.34	−196,571	31	45	24.66	569	57,414	−21,681	61	19
	PG	−164,772	−0.03	−0.14	−256,831	41	39	19.95	−230	28,924	−26,049	36	13
Healthcare	AMGN	629,482	0.08	0.39	−170,184	34	41	62.83	295	80,532	−24,898	57	16
	BMY	−234,205	−0.07	−0.23	−258,740	36	31	36.70	−177	34,833	−24,695	37	17
	JNJ	561,514	0.15	0.40	−106,686	38	42	46.23	320	67,554	−23,607	54	10
	PFE	426,258	0.15	0.29	−156,378	32	47	73.82	180	59,355	−27,298	56	17
Financials	AIG	−62,377	−0.04	−0.06	−220,007	38	42	41.26	−40	35,394	−28,577	42	14
	FNM	314,278	0.12	0.28	−158,375	33	42	26.85	355	50,742	−20,848	49	16
	MER	234,389	0.00	0.17	−383,969	43	35	42.27	117	69,338	−29,577	56	14
Information Technology	AAPL	−54,746	−0.04	−0.04	−323,193	44	41	18.27	−79	32,728	−25,090	46	17
	DELL	1,383,436	0.28	0.66	−241,445	33	55	575.44	72	100,130	−28,671	68	19
	IBM	−44,537	0.02	−0.03	−375,134	36	36	18.95	−124	59,255	−37,181	56	21
	INTC	181,141	0.05	0.11	−418,837	39	38	116.70	43	58,534	−28,390	42	16
	MSFT	796,838	0.12	0.48	−471,525	33	33	57.74	409	125,115	−27,178	73	16
	SUNW	648,152	0.09	0.42	−179,443	38	42	213.77	81	67,409	−19,022	53	19
	TXN	−15,753	0.04	−0.01	−383,180	43	33	76.77	−5	51,463	−25,387	46	18
Telecom	VZ	63,749	0.08	0.05	−205,669	35	49	22.72	80	35,264	−29,763	48	15
Indices	SPX	458,209	0.12	0.36	−285,347	36	31	2217.62	6	93,451	−22,790	63	14
	NDX	738,586	0.28	0.52	−118,447	35	57	1735.86	12	55,048	−23,558	51	18
	RUT	627,018	0.17	0.33	−238,292	44	36	5142.38	3	94,902	−32,655	63	17
	Average	182,333	0.03	0.09	−294,532	38	39	324.44	5	56,848	−27,348	52	16

Portfolio Statistics

Net Profit:	6,199,323	Sharpe ratio:	0.40
Drawdown:	−2,377,389	Correlation to breakout:	0.73
K-ratio:	0.15	Correlation to 10-40 MA:	0.62

© 2002 Lars Kestner – All Rights Reserved

FIGURE 8.13a

Divergence Index Strategy Applied to Stocks.

Breakdown Statistics (Stocks)

System Name: Divergence Index
Parameters: 10 day and 40 day momentum to calculate Divergence Index
Description: Enter when Divergence Index falls below –10
Run Dates: 1/1/1990 – 12/31/2001

Breakdown by Market Sector

Market Sector	Average Net Profit	Average K-ratio	Average Sharpe Ratio	Average Max DD	Average Num Trades	Average % Win	Avg. Profit Per Contract	Average Win	Average Loss	Avg. Bars Win	Avg. Bars Loss
Energy	-196,053	-0.17	-0.31	-362,307	31	30	-131	33,560	-27,768	45	16
Materials	-399,751	-0.11	-0.33	-519,112	49	35	-378	36,634	-32,614	51	17
Industrials	37,225	0.00	0.02	-287,351	37	35	-100	53,333	-27,820	52	15
Discretionary	209,276	0.00	0.13	-295,018	36	36	41	67,466	-28,721	59	16
Staples	47,618	0.04	0.02	-248,794	37	41	42	38,728	-24,729	45	17
Healthcare	345,762	0.08	0.21	-172,997	35	40	154	60,568	-25,124	51	15
Financials	162,097	0.03	0.13	-254,117	38	40	144	51,825	-26,334	49	15
Info. Tech.	413,504	0.08	0.23	-341,822	38	40	57	70,662	-27,274	55	18
Telecom	63,749	0.08	0.05	-205,669	35	49	80	35,264	-29,763	48	15
Indices	607,938	0.19	0.40	-214,029	38	41	7	81,134	-26,334	59	16

Performance Breakdown by Year

Year	Net Profit	K-ratio	Sharpe Ratio
1990	-16,309	0.13	-0.01
1991	3,129,578	0.27	2.04
1992	150,768	0.05	0.18
1993	-95,390	-0.12	-0.14
1994	-961,333	-0.49	-1.90
1995	4,114,823	1.12	3.50

Year	Net Profit	K-ratio	Sharpe Ratio
1996	993,139	0.09	0.62
1997	705,830	0.07	0.36
1998	-603,424	-0.33	-0.68
1999	294,386	-0.11	0.20
2000	-58,461	-0.07	-0.06
2001	-1,555,907	-0.52	-1.54

Profitability Windows

Length	Number of Windows	Num. of Profitable Windows	Percent Profitable
1 Month	144	72	50.00%
3 Months	142	68	47.89%
6 Months	139	65	46.76%
12 Months	133	67	50.38%
18 Months	127	77	60.63%
24 Months	121	79	65.29%

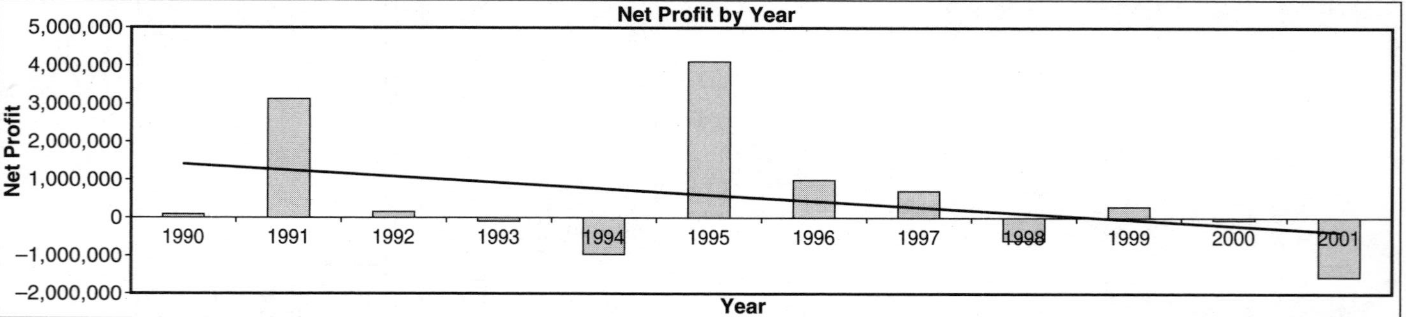

Net Profit by Year

© 2002 Lars Kestner – All Rights Reserved

FIGURE 8.13b

Divergence Index Strategy Applied to Stocks.

I look at moving average crossovers between one and 20 days, where the longer average is always four times the length of the shorter average. Each trading day, I determine if the one-day/four-day, two-day/eight-day, and so on, to the 20-day/80-day moving average crossovers are generating long or short trading signals. Any single parameter set generates a long signal if the shorter length average is greater than the longer length average, and generates a short signal if the shorter length moving average is less than the longer length moving average. Each day, I calculate the percentage of the 20 pairs that are signaling long positions in the market. This percentage is plotted as the Moving Average Confluence Statistic (MACS). That is, we start with the one day/four day moving average pair. If the one day average is greater than the four-day average, then we add +5 to the MACS statistic. This process is continued for the 20 pairs of moving averages and results in an indicator that oscillates between zero and 100. Long signals are generated when the MACS is 60 or above, and shorts are initiated when the MACS is 40 or below.

The chart in Figure 8.14 depicts signals generated on the S&P 500. From late February to early April, virtually all the moving average pairs were in agreement to be short. This is indicated by the zero and near zero values of the Moving

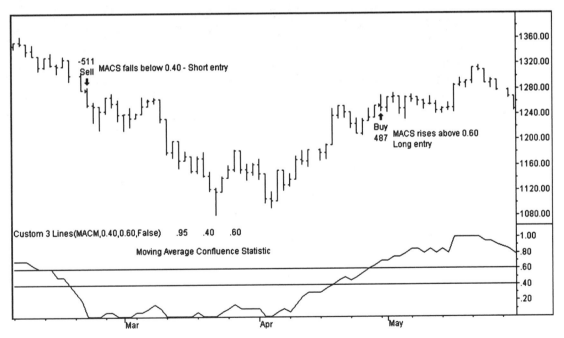

Created with TradeStation 2000i by Omega Research © 1999

FIGURE 8.14

Moving Average Confluence Method Strategy Applied to the S&P 500.

Average Confluence Statistic in the bottom half of the chart. As a result, our strategy was short between February and April. As the market rallied toward the end of April, many of the moving average pairs began to signal long positions. As a result, the MACS rose above 60 around the beginning of May and we entered long.

The Moving Average Confluence method performs well on both futures and stock data (Figures 8.15a through 8.16b). Futures markets generate profits in 11 out of the 12 years tested. Strong sectors include currencies, interest rates, and petroleum. Stock performance is not as strong, with profits accruing in 8 of the 12 years tested. Strong stock sectors include health care, technology, and stock indices.

Most moving averages are in agreement when strong trends emerge. The MACS shows when signals are in confluence by producing values near zero or 100. Future research could add some complexity to the strategy by entering on crosses of the 25 and 75 thresholds, while exiting and maintaining neutral positions between MACS values of 25 and 75, or by using a crossover of the 50 level as an exit signal.

Normalized Envelope Indicator

Some of the oldest trading strategies involved using simple moving averages to generate buy and sell signals. But as quantitative trading strategies increased in popularity, traders began to look for more complex methods to capture profits. As research progressed, traders became interested in taking advantage of price extremes away from the moving average. In order to do this, they needed a method of judging when prices had wandered too far from their average.

Ideally, the moving average would act like a rubber band, drawing prices closer to the average when stretched either way. As a result, the moving average envelope was created. Envelopes are formed by plotting two bands around the moving average—one above and one below. Historically this had been accomplished by multiplying the average by two constants. Typically, the moving average is multiplied by 105 percent to arrive at the upper band and 95 percent to calculate the lower band. The idea of the envelope was that as prices ran far above or below the moving average, they would correct themselves and return toward the average. This would create a profitable opportunity for traders, as they would buy when prices touched the lower price band and sell at the upper price band.

Traders have used this approach for many years with some success. One problem with these moving average bands is determining optimal displacement. Hours of trial and error had been the trader's only method of fitting a market with a good envelope. Should 95 and 105 percent be used, or are 90 and 110 percent more ideal? I figured there had to be a better way other than arbitrarily guessing, so I developed the Normalized Envelope Indicator. The NEI draws two envelopes automatically, based on the recent optimal displacement.

Trading Strategy Evaluation (Futures)

Strategy Name: Moving average confluence method
Parameters: 1 day/4 day, 2day/8 day, ..., to 20 day/80 day
Description: Enter long when MACS > 60, enter short when MACD < 40
Run Dates: 1/1/1990 – 12/31/2001

	Market	Net Profit	K-ratio	Sharpe Ratio	Max DD	# of Trades	% Win	Avg. Contracts	Avg. Profit Per Con.	Avg. Win	Avg. Loss	Avg. Bars Win	Avg. Bars Loss
FX	AD	-127,600	0.00	-0.07	-376,330	62	35	25.89	-74	59,941	-35,927	84	28
	BP	-33,788	-0.07	-0.02	-742,963	62	27	18.17	-37	74,260	-28,979	96	31
	CD	140,160	0.03	0.06	-425,460	62	39	47.59	65	73,770	-41,507	82	27
	JY	1,632,863	0.42	0.77	-154,638	46	50	13.57	2,395	94,096	-29,086	105	24
	SF	1,136,625	0.25	0.62	-229,650	45	44	15.52	1,630	95,204	-30,628	114	29
Rates	ED	3,383,675	0.22	1.20	-148,050	41	49	93.71	427	117,724	-34,026	108	28
	TY	932,109	0.16	0.43	-282,438	52	38	28.60	635	103,526	-35,175	105	28
	US	561,531	0.08	0.28	-450,156	57	37	20.16	461	89,970	-37,760	97	27
Stock	SP	-554,988	-0.06	-0.30	-694,025	72	25	8.45	-941	79,418	-37,075	89	26
Metals	GC	857,480	0.19	0.35	-227,780	51	47	42.77	391	77,924	-37,676	90	30
	HG	-49,000	0.03	-0.03	-652,688	63	37	30.98	2	67,910	-38,957	87	24
	PL	-389,605	-0.14	-0.19	-931,880	63	33	48.95	-144	56,597	-38,842	86	28
	SL	-391,445	-0.03	-0.18	-680,895	61	31	31.66	-216	61,210	-37,627	95	29
Energy	CL	1,190,880	0.24	0.51	-309,060	57	47	29.19	683	84,801	-38,440	81	25
	HO	618,748	0.12	0.25	-313,194	57	42	24.53	387	81,189	-42,644	88	25
	HU	418,198	0.06	0.19	-374,136	65	35	23.53	249	76,724	-32,930	78	28
Grains	C	1,111,700	0.18	0.46	-323,963	50	46	73.29	287	89,370	-37,184	92	31
	S	-500,313	-0.08	-0.27	-996,988	62	34	31.59	-296	48,479	-38,968	76	33
	W	887,400	0.17	0.40	-373,300	53	42	51.81	329	95,539	-38,682	100	26
Meats	FC	483,225	0.04	0.24	-340,435	62	37	40.52	191	74,095	-31,370	85	27
	LC	-34,488	-0.08	-0.02	-534,596	61	31	48.00	-66	73,057	-37,651	98	26
	LH	-30,448	0.06	-0.01	-413,196	59	31	31.88	-22	86,306	-38,888	93	32
	PB	-205,988	-0.08	-0.09	-698,408	59	31	21.25	-177	77,294	-39,341	98	30
Softs	CC	205,200	0.00	0.11	-427,850	49	43	49.24	54	57,120	-38,224	106	26
	CT	417,975	0.00	0.21	-701,855	57	30	24.43	322	114,048	-37,256	110	28
	JO	-486,480	-0.05	-0.21	-1,191,150	68	24	35.22	-205	89,746	-37,036	101	26
	KC	1,582,489	0.18	0.53	-345,300	45	44	11.93	2,656	118,394	-37,657	106	30
	LB	563,920	0.03	0.18	-692,048	64	34	33.20	261	112,033	-45,503	91	24
	SB	225,680	0.06	0.11	-295,030	53	43	53.96	77	70,576	-46,770	96	25
	Average	451,524	0.06	0.18	-477,582	55	36	33.65	311	80,011	-36,060	91	27

Portfolio Statistics

Net Profit:	13,545,716	Sharpe ratio:	0.87
Drawdown:	-1,788,611	Correlation to breakout:	0.86
K-ratio:	0.18	Correlation to 10-40 MA:	0.86

© 2002 Lars Kestner – All Rights Reserved

FIGURE 8.15a

Moving Average Confluence Method Strategy Applied to Futures.

Breakdown Statistics (Futures)

System Name: Moving average confluence method
Parameters: 1 day/4 day, 2 day/8 day, ..., to 20 day/80 day
Description: Enter long when MACS > 60, enter short when MACD < 40
Run Dates: 1/1/1990 – 12/31/2001

Breakdown by Market Sector

Market Sector	Average Net Profit	Average K-ratio	Average Sharpe Ratio	Average Max DD	Average Num Trades	Average % Win	Avg. Profit Per Contract	Average Win	Average Loss	Avg. Bars Win	Avg. Bars Loss
FX	549,652	0.13	0.27	-385,808	55	39	796	79,454	-33,225	96	28
Rates	1,219,329	0.11	0.48	-220,161	38	31	381	77,805	-26,740	78	21
Stock	-554,988	-0.06	-0.30	-694,025	72	25	-941	79,418	-37,075	89	26
Metals	6,858	0.01	-0.01	-623,311	60	37	8	65,910	-38,275	90	28
Energy	742,609	0.14	0.31	-332,130	60	42	440	80,904	-38,005	82	26
Grains	499,596	0.09	0.20	-564,750	55	40	107	77,796	-38,278	90	30
Meats	53,075	-0.02	0.03	-496,659	60	32	-18	77,688	-36,813	94	29
Softs	418,131	0.04	0.16	-608,872	56	36	527	93,653	-40,408	102	26

Performance Breakdown by Year

Year	Net Profit	K-ratio	Sharpe Ratio
1990	3,612,628	0.91	2.64
1991	1,670,730	0.24	1.04
1992	1,269,081	0.33	1.03
1993	2,564,749	0.40	1.96
1994	683,215	0.37	0.65
1995	1,568,564	0.33	1.69
1996	23,015	-0.02	0.01
1997	835,068	0.00	0.79
1998	317,949	0.11	0.33
1999	-798,958	-0.33	-0.34
2000	622,926	0.07	0.63
2001	1,100,376	0.34	0.68

Length	Number of Windows	Num. of Profitable Windows	Percent Profitable
1 Month	144	86	59.72%
3 Months	142	91	64.08%
6 Months	139	107	76.98%
12 Months	133	110	82.71%
18 Months	127	108	85.04%
24 Months	121	107	88.43%

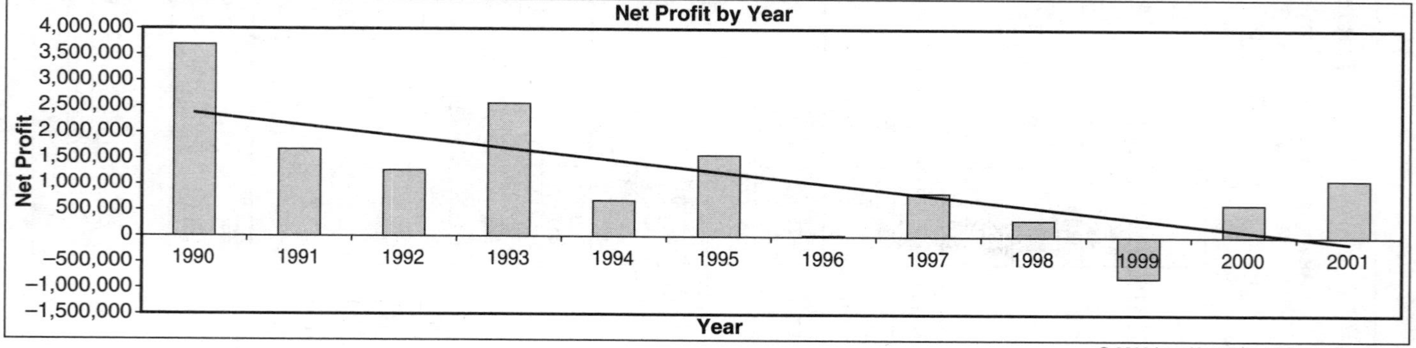

Net Profit by Year

© 2002 Lars Kestner – All Rights Reserved

FIGURE 8.15 b

Moving Average Confluence Method Strategy Applied to Futures.

Trading Strategy Evaluation (Stocks)

Strategy Name: Moving average confluence method
Parameters: 1 day/4 day, 2 day/8 day, ..., to 20 day/80 day
Description: Enter long when MACS > 60, enter short when MACD < 40
Run Dates: 1/1/1990 – 12/31/2001

	Market	Net Profit	K-ratio	Sharpe Ratio	Max DD	# of Trades	% Win	Avg. hrs (000)	Avg. Profit Per Con.	Avg. Win	Avg. Loss	Avg. Bars Win	Avg. Bars Loss
Energy	SLB	−299,550	−0.03	−0.16	−538,638	70	33	16.77	−274	62,541	−37,448	86	22
	XOM	−322,433	−0.03	−0.19	−382,750	61	26	40.60	−130	63,697	−29,805	95	33
Materials	AA	−488,370	−0.03	−0.26	−633,194	64	38	49.74	−157	49,173	−41,963	78	28
	DD	−481,804	0.00	−0.25	−584,969	72	25	21.11	−321	70,925	−32,679	85	27
	IP	−1,284,632	−0.33	−0.65	−1,334,292	74	23	16.79	−1,064	44,722	−36,526	76	30
Industrials	BA	21,154	−0.05	0.01	−495,496	60	33	19.90	−4	68,349	−34,282	92	29
	GE	397,460	0.11	0.20	−244,852	56	38	77.56	92	84,200	−39,044	101	26
	MMM	−649,652	−0.10	−0.36	−783,544	70	30	13.65	−740	43,558	−33,090	74	29
Consumer Discretionary	DIS	−39,653	−0.01	−0.02	−687,370	73	27	39.12	−11	87,676	−33,675	86	24
	GM	662,256	0.12	0.37	−252,199	51	49	12.48	1,033	63,114	−35,403	91	28
	HD	977,820	0.08	0.43	−587,847	57	25	53.79	303	161,195	−30,860	124	29
	WMT	190,632	0.01	0.10	−590,117	52	37	39.72	67	79,221	−41,402	99	33
Consumer Staples	G	−41,842	−0.04	−0.02	−459,940	58	38	34.76	−43	65,184	−42,219	94	24
	KO	−574,376	−0.11	−0.25	−946,480	69	29	26.40	−307	76,793	−42,763	89	25
	MO	972,236	0.21	0.48	−247,281	50	36	23.33	826	106,953	−30,049	108	33
	PG	−118,174	−0.01	−0.06	−330,462	68	26	20.93	−102	78,277	−31,090	85	29
Healthcare	AMGN	802,597	0.09	0.31	−375,239	60	32	54.25	242	120,627	−36,694	94	30
	BMY	475,952	0.11	0.24	−331,071	53	40	35.00	241	76,531	−36,256	98	29
	JNJ	365,694	0.05	0.18	−693,068	55	36	38.32	192	86,865	−38,060	97	31
	PFE	568,910	0.13	0.26	−458,046	58	31	70.93	139	109,264	−34,853	103	29
Financials	AIG	666,218	0.16	0.41	−229,454	52	40	41.83	306	83,861	−35,365	103	27
	FNM	−267,295	−0.05	−0.14	−592,285	72	21	23.18	−152	98,847	−30,473	99	27
	MER	125,573	0.03	0.06	−417,939	63	35	50.64	31	83,984	−42,678	93	23
Information Technology	AAPL	611,337	0.10	0.28	−325,234	59	49	18.12	530	67,045	−45,931	78	24
	DELL	2,878,617	0.18	0.65	−357,704	49	39	596.46	98	204,924	−34,783	110	30
	IBM	494,553	0.12	0.23	−407,155	65	32	18.92	328	87,931	−32,801	84	27
	INTC	1,352,515	0.26	0.57	−277,522	60	35	90.64	239	124,720	−33,803	90	28
	MSFT	433,233	0.05	0.18	−699,753	68	32	61.86	97	101,309	−39,547	85	24
	SUNW	1,490,155	0.18	0.65	−249,006	52	50	217.64	133	128,513	−41,406	109	28
	TXN	525,697	0.15	0.22	−482,004	57	30	93.83	99	128,513	−41,406	109	29
Telecom	VZ	−50,943	0.06	−0.03	−467,186	59	37	19.57	−69	47,768	−30,555	91	26
Indices	SPX	194,910	0.08	0.11	−477,118	58	29	2246.08	1	100,979	−37,604	107	29
	NDX	1,154,305	0.28	0.55	−181,621	51	41	1695.65	13	107,114	−37,519	104	27
	RUT	1,821,462	0.30	0.65	−243,548	51	45	5278.06	6	126,067	−41,092	92	32
	Average	369,546	0.06	0.14	−481,306	60	34	328.17	48	89,868	−36,400	94	28

Portfolio Statistics

Net Profit:	12,564,561	Sharpe ratio:	0.51
Drawdown:	−4,434,865	Correlation to breakout:	0.91
K-ratio:	0.19	Correlation to 10-40 MA:	0.89

© 2002 Lars Kestner – All Rights Reserved

FIGURE 8.16a

Moving Average Confluence Method Strategy Applied to Stocks.

Breakdown Statistics (Stocks)

System Name: Moving average confluence method
Parameters: 1 day/4 day, 2 day/8 day, ..., to 20 day/80 day
Description: Enter long when MACS > 60, enter short when MACD < 40
Run Dates: 1/1/1990 – 12/31/2001

Breakdown by Market Sector

Market Sector	Average Net Profit	Average K-ratio	Average Sharpe Ratio	Average Max DD	Average Num Trades	Average % Win	Avg. Profit Per Contract	Average Win	Average Loss	Avg. Bars Win	Avg. Bars Loss
Energy	-310,992	-0.03	-0.18	-460,694	66	30	-202	63,119	-33,627	91	27
Materials	-751,602	-0.12	-0.39	-850,818	70	28	-514	54,940	-37,056	80	28
Industrials	-77,013	-0.01	-0.05	-507,964	62	34	-217	65,369	-35,472	89	28
Discretionary	447,764	0.05	0.22	-529,383	58	34	348	97,802	-35,335	100	29
Staples	59,461	0.01	0.04	-496,041	61	32	93	81,802	-36,530	94	28
Healthcare	553,288	0.10	0.25	-464,356	57	35	204	98,322	-36,466	98	30
Financials	174,832	0.05	0.11	-413,237	62	32	61	88,897	-36,172	98	26
Info. Tech.	1,112,301	0.15	0.40	-399,768	59	38	218	115,430	-37,735	92	27
Telecom	-50,943	0.06	-0.03	-467,186	59	37	-69	47,768	-30,555	91	26
Indices	1,056,892	0.22	0.44	-300,763	53	39	7	111,386	-38,738	101	29

Performance Breakdown by Year

Year	Net Profit	K-ratio	Sharpe Ratio	Year	Net Profit	K-ratio	Sharpe Ratio
1990	1,889,846	0.56	1.25	1996	825,690	0.02	0.34
1991	3,164,339	0.19	1.49	1997	2,678,434	0.25	0.80
1992	388,988	0.02	0.40	1998	2,374,958	0.31	1.29
1993	-761,218	-0.38	-0.80	1999	257,827	-0.23	0.07
1994	-1,384,984	-0.38	-1.25	2000	-797,707	-0.24	-0.31
1995	6,424,465	0.86	2.96	2001	-2,514,841	-0.33	-1.40

Profitability Windows

Length	Number of Windows	Num. of Profitable Windows	Percent Profitable
1 Month	144	78	54.17%
3 Months	142	70	49.30%
6 Months	139	81	58.27%
12 Months	133	75	56.39%
18 Months	127	80	62.99%
24 Months	121	78	64.46%

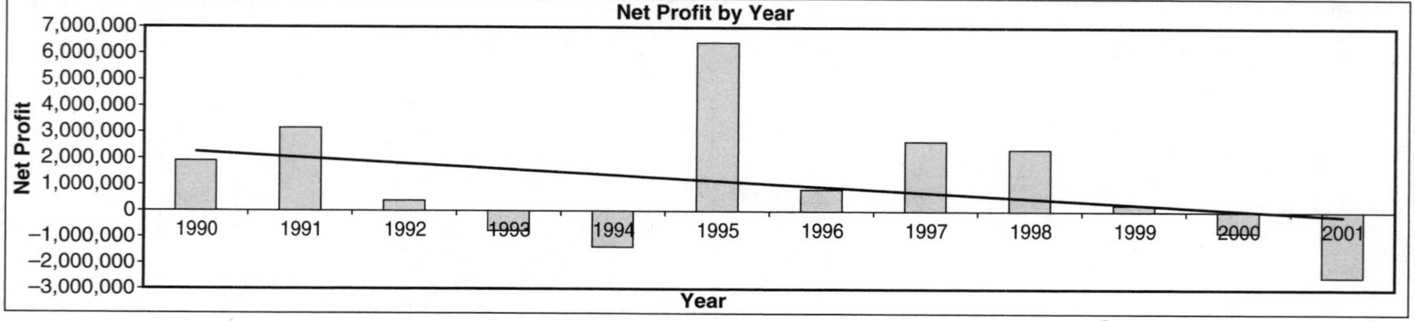

Net Profit by Year

© 2002 Lars Kestner – All Rights Reserved

FIGURE 8.16b

Moving Average Confluence Method Strategy Applied to Stocks.

NEI = (Close – Average of Past 50 Closes)/Standard Deviation of Past 50
Price Changes

Sort the NEI of the past 50 days. Then:

Upper NEI band = Today's 50-day moving average + value of 10th-ranked NEI
Lower NEI band = Today's 50-day moving average + value of 40th-ranked NEI

To calculate the NEI we first compare today's close to today's 50-day moving average of closes. We divide this difference by the standard deviation of past 50 price changes to arrive at today's NEI value. This NEI value gives us a normalized measurement of where today's price is in comparison to the past 50 days. Next, we compare yesterday's close to yesterday's 50-day moving average of closes. Again, we divide this difference by today's standard deviation of past 50 price changes to arrive at yesterday's NEI value. We continue this process until we have 50 NEI values calculated from today's price data and the 49 days prior.

Once we have the 50 NEI values, we sort these in order, where the first value is the greatest value and the 50th-ranked value is the smallest value. Next we create the upper NEI band by adding the 10th-sorted NEI value to today's 50-day moving average. We create the lower NEI band by adding the 40th-sorted NEI value to today's 50-day moving average.

I enter short when prices rise above and then fall below the upper NEI band. Long entries are initiated when prices fall below and then rise above the lower NEI band. Sample NEI signals are displayed in Figure 8.17 for ExxonMobil (XOM). The NEI seems to do well at predicting exhaustion points during trendless markets. As prices rise above the lower NEI band in mid-August, we enter long. Profits are taken and shorts entered when prices fall below the upper NEI band just one week later.

The NEI strategy generates some interesting performance quirks. Looking at the futures data (Figures 8.18a and 8.18b), the NEI strategy produces a Sharpe ratio of –0.45 and a K-ratio of –0.04. At first glance, we would dismiss this performance due to a lack of profitability. But when we delve further, we see that when tested on futures data, the NEI has produced profits five of the past six years. Note how the equity curve rises consistently from 1996 to the present. This characteristic suggests that perhaps performance has turned the corner and will be profitable in the future.

Stock performance is not as optimistic (Figures 8.19a and 8.19b). The NEI produced profits when tested on stocks in just 3 of 12 years tested. Similar to the futures performance, most of the positive performance has been recent. Three of the past five years were profitable.

Multiple Entry Oscillator System

Overbought/oversold indicators such as the Relative Strength Index (RSI) and stochastics are typically used to identify market tops and bottoms during exhaustion

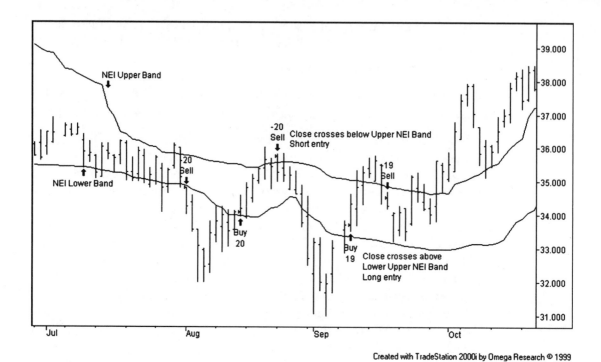

Created with TradeStation 2000i by Omega Research © 1999

FIGURE 8.17

Normalized Envelope Indicator Strategy Applied to ExxonMobil.

phases of trends. I use the Multiple Entry Oscillator System in an entirely different manner. Using any oscillator, I add to longs as the trend becomes stronger, while I exit longs and enter shorts as the trend becomes weaker. The unique property of this strategy is that the strength of the trend determines the strength of our signal. One sample of this method is:

Oscillator crosses above 55: long one unit
Oscillator crosses above 70: long two units
Oscillator crosses above 85: long three units
Oscillator crosses below 45: short one unit
Oscillator crosses below 30: short two units
Oscillator crosses below 15: short three units

We utilize a 20-day Slow %K stochastic as the base oscillator for our trading signals. Our strategy can be long or short anywhere between one and three units depending on the value of the 20-day Slow %K stochastic.

The graph in Figure 8.20 details signals applied to International Paper (IP). As the market declines in the beginning of the test period, we see that longs are

Trading Strategy Evaluation (Futures)

Strategy Name: Normalized envelope indicator
Parameters: 50 days compared to 50 day average, NEI uses #10 and #40 ranks
Description: Enter long when close < lower NEI band, enter short when close > upper NEI band
Run Dates: 1/1/1990 – 12/31/2001

	Market	Net Profit	K-ratio	Sharpe Ratio	Max DD	# of Trades	% Win	Avg. Contracts	Avg. Profit Per Con.	Avg. Win	Avg. Loss	Avg. Bars Win	Avg. Bars Loss
FX	AD	−642,110	−0.18	−0.34	−1,086,750	77	55	24.85	−335	32,734	−57,592	28	53
	BP	425,163	0.15	0.22	−458,888	82	59	18.28	301	41,151	−44,842	29	48
	CD	−900,140	−0.07	−0.41	−1,198,100	78	56	48.61	−241	29,995	−65,720	24	57
	JY	−1,237,250	−0.24	−0.56	−1,549,738	77	55	14.19	−1,001	36,681	−75,269	29	50
	SF	−386,775	−0.08	−0.19	−779,238	83	53	16.12	−297	40,876	−56,290	29	45
Rates	ED	741,925	0.04	0.32	−875,550	91	56	82.41	99	55,148	−51,765	29	38
	TY	−674,094	−0.08	−0.31	−1,236,891	85	56	30.21	−247	38,696	−67,321	26	47
	US	−953,719	−0.20	−0.48	−1,361,031	89	54	20.56	−525	34,624	−63,952	25	45
Stock	SP	838,988	0.23	0.48	−278,988	100	71	8.95	997	31,533	−46,437	26	38
Metals	GC	−374,470	−0.03	−0.17	−646,320	82	49	46.04	−97	39,446	−46,264	28	45
	HG	150,650	−0.04	0.07	−706,925	70	59	33.25	42	43,404	−57,963	35	53
	PL	−145,350	0.02	−0.07	−790,935	96	59	50.01	−10	29,120	−43,837	25	39
	SL	258,435	0.04	0.14	−465,810	91	64	34.17	57	30,024	−47,382	25	46
Energy	CL	27,680	−0.02	0.01	−837,950	83	57	27.99	18	48,811	−62,564	29	46
	HO	509,094	0.14	0.23	−400,155	86	51	23.62	254	54,562	−44,852	31	38
	HU	−219,744	0.04	−0.09	−774,803	89	60	22.58	−96	34,979	−56,867	27	44
Grains	C	−576,850	0.00	−0.25	−771,575	76	53	80.62	−98	43,092	−64,592	29	51
	S	825	0.02	0.00	−804,750	80	55	31.95	−8	38,366	−47,432	29	48
	W	−582,550	−0.14	−0.27	−915,900	85	59	51.08	−138	32,730	−63,841	25	50
Meats	FC	364,890	0.11	0.19	−431,070	91	54	41.09	82	40,878	−40,412	28	39
	LC	344,580	0.11	0.18	−431,184	92	63	50.54	82	36,096	−50,359	27	42
	LH	−44,256	0.04	−0.02	−629,728	78	58	32.11	2	38,383	−52,193	34	45
	PB	−506,232	−0.06	−0.24	−913,100	94	62	20.98	−229	29,704	−60,386	24	45
Softs	CC	276,690	0.01	0.14	−483,540	100	64	51.13	58	30,617	−46,218	23	41
	CT	−602,200	−0.04	−0.31	−1,237,920	78	62	25.24	−305	35,331	−76,561	30	52
	JO	−243,420	0.01	−0.11	−668,325	89	57	35.78	−72	29,007	−44,936	26	43
	KC	−808,403	−0.17	−0.34	−1,081,328	82	54	14.16	−696	38,604	−65,951	26	48
	LB	−102,528	0.03	−0.03	−1,233,944	75	63	33.07	−63	46,095	−82,967	31	54
	SB	−490,090	−0.07	−0.25	−808,797	92	59	54.49	−89	30,594	−55,250	24	44
	Average	−185,042	−0.01	−0.08	−795,308	82	56	34.14	−85	36,376	−54,667	27	45

Portfolio Statistics

Net Profit:	−5,551,261	Sharpe ratio:	−0.45
Drawdown:	−9,908,916	Correlation to breakout:	−0.28
K-ratio:	−0.04	Correlation to 10-40 MA:	−0.32

© 2002 Lars Kestner – All Rights Reserved

FIGURE 8.18a

Normalized Envelope Indicator Strategy Applied to Futures.

Breakdown Statistics (Futures)

System Name: Normalized envelope indicator
Parameters: 50 days compared to 50 day average, NEI uses #10 and #40 ranks
Description: Enter long when close < lower NEI band, enter short when close > upper NEI band
Run Dates: 1/1/1990 – 12/31/2001

Breakdown by Market Sector

Market Sector	Average Net Profit	Average K-ratio	Average Sharpe Ratio	Average Max DD	Average Num Trades	Average % Win	Avg. Profit Per Contract	Average Win	Average Loss	Avg. Bars Win	Avg. Bars Loss
FX	-548,223	-0.08	-0.26	-1,014,543	79	55	-315	36,287	-59,943	28	51
Rates	-221,472	-0.06	-0.12	-868,368	66	42	-168	32,117	-45,760	20	33
Stock	838,988	0.23	0.48	-278,988	100	71	997	31,533	-46,437	26	38
Metals	-27,684	0.00	-0.01	-652,498	85	58	-2	35,499	-48,861	29	46
Energy	105,677	0.05	0.05	-670,969	86	56	59	46,118	-54,761	29	43
Grains	-386,192	-0.04	-0.17	-830,742	80	55	-81	38,063	-58,622	28	49
Meats	39,746	0.05	0.03	-601,271	89	59	-16	36,265	-50,838	28	43
Softs	-328,325	-0.04	-0.15	-918,976	86	60	-195	35,041	-61,981	27	47

Performance Breakdown by Year

Year	Net Profit	K-ratio	Sharpe Ratio
1990	-3,285,612	-0.94	-3.15
1991	-651,258	-0.21	-0.79
1992	-2,427,188	-1.43	-2.87
1993	-2,175,495	-0.26	-1.47
1994	453,143	0.32	-0.45
1995	-816,567	-0.21	-0.65

Year	Net Profit	K-ratio	Sharpe Ratio
1996	1,813,816	0.64	1.94
1997	-694,151	-0.04	-0.72
1998	331,462	0.10	0.55
1999	715,566	0.23	1.00
2000	290,649	0.25	0.29
2001	604,543	0.03	0.51

Length	Number of Windows	Num. of Profitable Windows	Percent Profitable
1 Month	144	66	45.83%
3 Months	142	65	45.77%
6 Months	139	65	46.76%
12 Months	133	62	46.62%
18 Months	127	67	52.76%
24 Months	121	69	57.02%

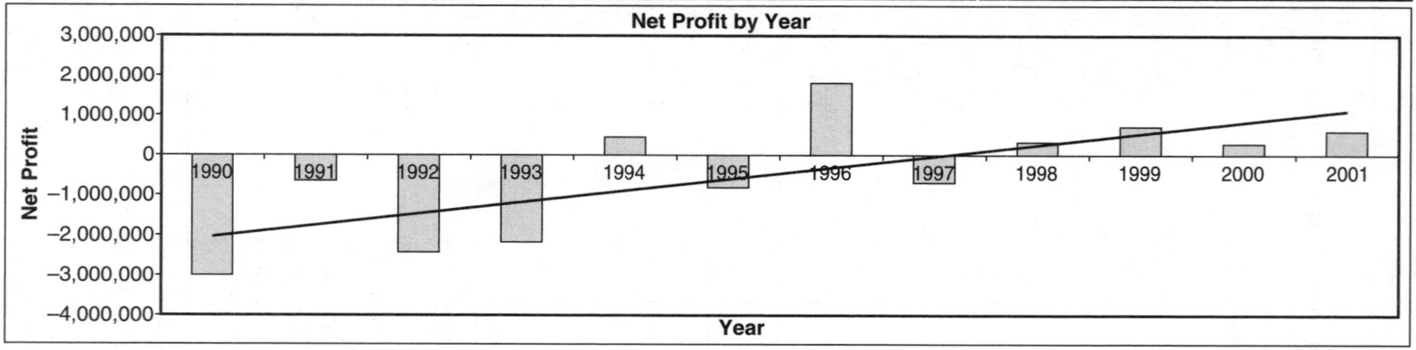

Net Profit by Year

© 2002 Lars Kestner – All Rights Reserved

FIGURE 8.18b

Normalized Envelope Indicator Strategy Applied to Futures.

Trading Strategy Evaluation (Stocks)

Strategy Name: Normalized envelope indicator
Parameters: 50 days compared to 50 day average, NEI uses #10 and #40 ranks
Description: Enter long when close < lower NEI band, enter short when close > upper NEI band
Run Dates: 1/1/1990 – 12/31/2001

	Market	Net Profit	K–ratio	Sharpe Ratio	Max DD	# of Trades	% Win	Avg. hrs (000)	Avg. Profit Per Con.	Avg. Win	Avg. Loss	Avg. Bars Win	Avg. Bars Loss
Energy	SLB	−114,139	−0.01	−0.06	−544,369	98	62	16.14	−31	28,810	−48,842	22	44
	XOM	−687,879	−0.22	−0.45	−905,068	99	58	43.12	−165	19,259	−42,872	21	43
Materials	AA	−1,455,002	−0.12	−0.13	−4,844,244	2293	35	12.37	−56	24,012	−14,000	12	4
	DD	−103,561	−0.08	−0.06	−784,458	88	65	20.45	−39	30,923	−59,147	24	51
	IP	141,281	0.03	0.07	−383,525	98	64	16.39	110	26,330	−42,355	21	48
Industrials	BA	305,088	0.06	0.18	−493,964	94	61	21.37	170	37,387	−48,380	26	40
	GE	670,171	0.14	0.35	−358,230	103	58	77.22	80	37,247	−37,138	25	36
	MMM	−444,449	−0.09	−0.24	−691,453	86	55	13.71	−319	28,791	−44,352	28	43
Consumer Discretionary	DIS	329,446	0.01	0.17	−361,687	94	59	36.11	100	37,001	−43,495	23	45
	GM	−892,065	−0.25	−0.48	−1,004,652	86	53	13.64	−763	30,373	−57,309	26	46
	HD	139,237	−0.02	0.07	−440,269	102	62	76.32	21	34,271	−51,174	25	37
	WMT	−4,441	0.05	0.00	−635,953	83	61	37.79	−7	33,391	−53,920	28	50
Consumer Staples	G	−281,908	−0.04	−0.16	−518,222	94	56	36.15	−71	29,128	−43,529	23	43
	KO	−221,412	−0.03	−0.12	−656,138	85	60	28.08	−102	32,530	−55,925	27	47
	MO	−693,692	−0.18	−0.34	−936,624	79	52	25.11	−341	40,322	−61,285	26	51
	PG	−310,136	0.00	−0.16	−497,059	80	58	19.96	−179	30,870	−50,165	29	48
Healthcare	AMGN	235,565	−0.02	0.10	−658,798	89	62	75.39	37	43,215	−62,631	26	47
	BMY	−407,594	−0.02	−0.25	−728,390	99	58	32.55	−108	28,456	−46,869	23	39
	JNJ	−83,555	0.01	−0.05	−629,002	95	62	36.50	−29	29,402	−50,982	22	48
	PFE	−767,515	−0.27	−0.43	−968,131	88	57	69.16	−127	30,845	−60,972	25	45
Financials	AIG	−610,897	−0.21	−0.34	−868,551	98	55	37.85	−159	29,574	−49,657	22	41
	FNM	−169,531	−0.10	−0.10	−644,898	115	60	22.97	−69	25,666	−42,478	18	38
	MER	67,581	0.05	0.04	−479,612	94	63	55.84	17	36,895	−59,622	24	45
Information Technology	AAPL	−199,920	−0.05	−0.10	−654,078	78	54	17.08	−106	45,073	−53,761	28	49
	DELL	−616,552	−0.01	−0.26	−1,142,010	88	55	589.36	−11	46,662	−70,242	22	48
	IBM	−485,297	−0.03	−0.24	−717,493	79	57	20.20	−295	41,837	−69,198	31	48
	INTC	−808,817	−0.14	−0.36	−1,235,849	92	55	129.06	−62	42,826	−71,319	23	45
	MSFT	−378,754	0.01	−0.18	−730,517	88	58	77.94	−44	41,577	−65,493	27	43
	SUNW	−1,070,027	−0.15	−0.52	−1,314,211	84	54	236.18	−54	37,426	−70,760	24	50
	TXN	128,117	−0.01	0.07	−731,439	98	59	84.40	16	38,169	−52,052	23	41
Telecom	VZ	−282,375	0.02	−0.16	−1,034,674	95	61	22.55	−118	27,912	−50,562	21	47
Indices	SPX	1,099,655	0.26	0.57	−297,996	98	66	2337.27	5	39,180	−42,651	25	41
	NDX	−301,906	−0.12	−0.14	−958,990	90	54	1448.44	−2	42,498	−58,110	24	44
	RUT	241,090	0.07	0.08	−735,468	84	60	5799.64	1	67,746	−89,788	26	49
	Average	−236,300	−0.04	−0.11	−840,765	156	58	340.77	−79	35,165	−53,560	24	44

Portfolio Statistics

Net Profit:	−8,034,193	Sharpe ratio:	−0.38
Drawdown:	−10,324,072	Correlation to breakout:	−0.23
K–ratio:	−0.22	Correlation to 10–40 MA:	−0.24

© 2002 Lars Kestner – All Rights Reserved

FIGURE 8.19a

Normalized Envelope Indicator Strategy Applied to Stocks.

Breakdown Statistics Stocks)

System Name: Normalized envelope indicator
Parameters: 50 days compared to 50 day average, NEI uses #10 and #40 ranks
Description: Enter long when close < lower NEI band, enter short when close > upper NEI band
Run Dates: 1/1/1990 – 12/31/2001

Breakdown by Market Sector

Market Sector	Average Net Profit	Average K-ratio	Average Sharpe Ratio	Average Max DD	Average Num Trades	Average % Win	Avg. Profit Per Contract	Average Win	Average Loss	Avg. Bars Win	Avg. Bars Loss
Energy	-401,009	-0.12	-0.26	-724,719	99	60	-98	24,034	-45,857	22	43
Materials	-472,427	-0.06	-0.04	-2,004,076	826	55	5	27,088	-38,501	19	34
Industrials	176,937	0.04	0.09	-514,549	94	58	-23	34,475	-43,290	26	40
Discretionary	-106,956	-0.05	-0.06	-610,640	91	59	-162	33,759	-51,474	25	44
Staples	-376,787	-0.06	-0.19	-652,011	85	56	-173	33,213	-52,726	26	47
Healthcare	-255,775	-0.08	-0.15	-746,080	93	60	-57	32,980	-55,363	24	45
Financials	-237,616	-0.09	-0.13	-664,354	102	59	-70	30,712	-50,586	21	41
Info. Tech.	-490,179	-0.05	-0.23	-932,228	87	56	-79	41,939	-64,689	25	46
Telecom	-282,375	0.02	-0.16	-1,034,674	95	61	-118	27,912	-50,562	21	47
Indices	346,280	0.07	0.17	-664,151	91	60	1	49,808	-63,516	25	44

Performance Breakdown by Year

Year	Net Profit	K-ratio	Sharpe Ratio	Year	Net Profit	K-ratio	Sharpe Ratio
1990	-1,196,397	-0.26	-0.63	1996	-642,849	0.02	-0.36
1991	-373,994	-0.26	-0.21	1997	524,114	0.02	0.23
1992	-1,829,761	-0.46	-1.22	1998	-1,594,650	-0.34	-0.81
1993	-471,818	-0.02	-0.34	1999	1,894,966	0.51	2.95
1994	-1,196,252	-0.25	-0.72	2000	-2,527,312	-0.53	-1.56
1995	-1,347,115	-0.27	-0.72	2001	971,527	0.26	0.99

Profitability Windows

Length	Number of Windows	Num. of Profitable Windows	Percent Profitable
1 Month	144	68	47.22%
3 Months	142	58	40.85%
6 Months	139	40	28.78%
12 Months	133	25	18.80%
18 Months	127	25	19.69%
24 Months	121	15	12.40%

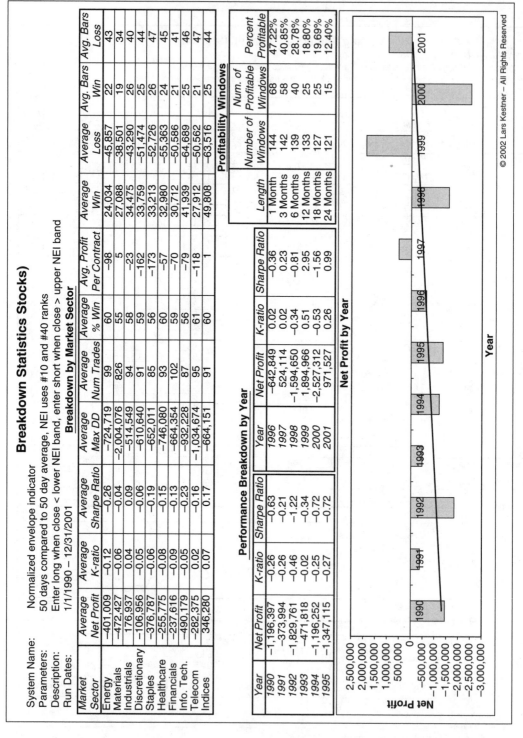

Net Profit by Year

© 2002 Lars Kestner – All Rights Reserved

FIGURE 8.19 b

Normalized Envelope Indicator Strategy Applied to Stocks.

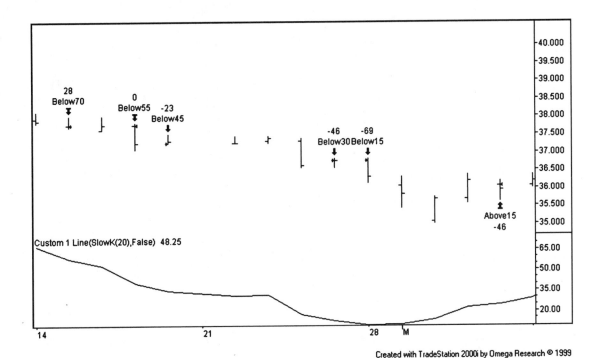

Created with TradeStation 2000i by Omega Research © 1999

FIGURE 8.20

Multiple Entry Oscillator Strategy Applied to International Paper.

exited. Our first short position is entered as the oscillator drops below 45. The second is entered as the oscillator falls below 30, and the third and final short entry is established as the oscillator drops below 15. The last signal on the chart is a short cover of one unit as the oscillator rises back above 15.

Figure 8.21 illustrates the equity curve of the Multiple Entry Oscillator System applied to our futures markets. Performance is good, earning just over $12,500,000 with a Sharpe ratio of 0.34 and a K-ratio of 0.23. However, the Multiple Entry Oscillator System leaves much to be desired, as performance does not approach the profitability of other trend-following strategies. Applied to stocks, profitability of the strategy truly deteriorates (Figure 8.22). With a loss of over $21,000,000, a Sharpe ratio of –0.39 and a K-ratio of –0.18, stocks produce profits in only 5 out of 12 years.

Adjusted Stochastic

In the March 1998 issue of *Futures* magazine, Mark Etzkorn and George Pruitt introduced a channel breakout system that adjusts its length based on changes in market volatility. In their system, as the standard deviation of closes increased,

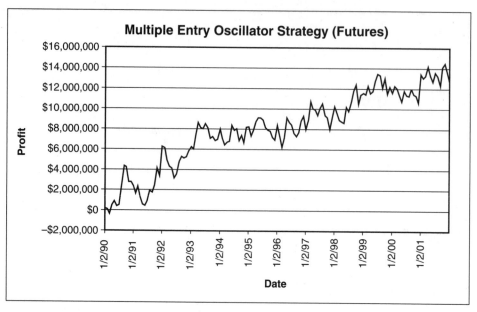

FIGURE 8.21

Multiple Entry Oscillator Strategy Applied to Futures.

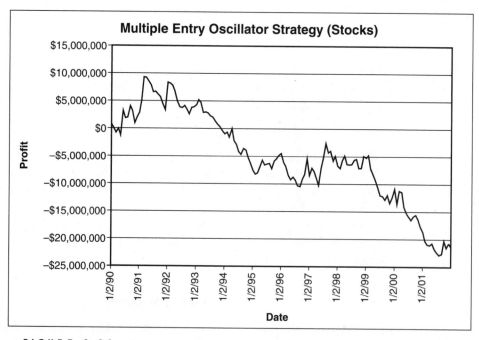

FIGURE 8.22

Multiple Entry Oscillator Strategy Applied to Stocks.

they also increased the look-back range of their breakout entries. More volatile markets would require as much as a 60-day channel breakout to initiate longs or shorts, while less volatile markets could require as small as a 20-day channel breakout to initiate trades.

This thinking sparked me to apply the idea and create a new oscillator that would also adjust based on market volatility. While my procedure and definition of market volatility is different than Etzkorn and Pruitt's, the rationale is similar. Oscillators are wonderful tools for calculating the relative price ranges over the short term. The problem, however, is that in times when prices are less volatile and not moving, small price changes can cause oscillator readings to exhibit overbought and oversold conditions. As prices become more volatile, indicated by a large 14-day range, then recent price moves should have more weight than during periods of low volatility accompanied by small 14-day price ranges. For that reason, I introduce a new adjusted stochastic that adjusts a 14-day Slow %K stochastic using a combination of the high-to-low range of the past 14 days and the high-to-low range of the past 100 days.

New Stochastic = (14-day Slow %K stochastic − 50) · (highest high of past 14 days − lowest low of past 14 days)/(highest high of past 100 days − lowest low of past 100 days) + 50

Essentially, we rescale the 14-day stochastic based on the relative volatility of the past 14 days to the volatility of the past 100 days.

As expected, we see that the new stochastic measure is muted compared to a typical 14-day %K stochastic. Values of our new oscillator typically range between 35 and 65, compared to more typical ranges of 20 and 80 seen by short-term oscillators. As such, we need to adjust our extreme values that generate trading signals. We will take countertrend short positions when the adjusted stochastic rises above 65 and then falls back below 65. Countertrend long positions are entered when the adjusted stochastic declines below and then rises back above 35.

Signals for our adjusted stochastic are applied to Texas Instruments (TXN) in the Figure 8.23 chart. The strength of the September rally causes our adjusted stochastic to rise above 80—a powerful move indeed. As prices retrace, we enter short in early October as the adjusted stochastic falls below 65. The subsequent decline takes the adjusted stochastic below 35 in late October. We enter long on a rise of the adjusted stochastic above 35 at the beginning of November.

On futures markets (Figures 8.24a and 8.24b), our adjusted stochastic generates a Sharpe ratio of −1.08 and a K-ratio of −0.43. On stocks (Figures 8.25a and 8.25b), our adjusted stochastic generates a Sharpe ratio of −0.97 and a K-ratio of −0.32. Among the worst performing futures sectors are interest rates, currencies, and petroleum. Among the worst performing stock sectors are health care, financials, and technology.

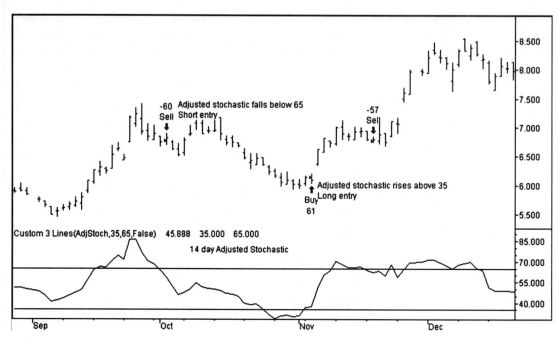

Created with TradeStation 2000i by Omega Research © 1999

FIGURE 8.23

Adjusted Stochastic Strategy Applied to Texas Instruments.

Many traders might quickly write off this performance and move on to something profitable. Remember that some of the worst performing strategies are actually diamonds in the rough. Performance of the adjusted stochastic strategy is so bad that I would consider using the exact opposite of the rules as the basis of a profitable strategy.

Three in a Row

You might be surprised at how well very simple ideas work. The principle of three in a row sounds simple, yet the results are very powerful. We buy when three conditions are met:

1. Today's close is greater than the close five days ago.

2. The close 5 days ago is greater than the close 10 days ago.

3. The close 10 days ago is greater than the close 15 days ago.

Short entries are similar, also requiring three conditions:

Trading Strategy Evaluation (Futures)

Strategy Name: Adjusted stochastic
Parameters: 14 day Slow %K adjusted by 100 day range
Description: Enter long when adjusted Stochastic < 35, enter short when adjusted Stochastic > 65
Run Dates: 1/1/1990 – 12/31/2001

	Market	Net Profit	K-ratio	Sharpe Ratio	Max DD	# of Trades	% Win	Avg. Contracts	Avg. Profit Per Con.	Avg. Win	Avg. Loss	Avg. Bars Win	Avg. Bars Loss
FX	AD	−691,280	−0.21	−0.38	−858,900	49	53	25.58	−543	32,879	−66,736	41	83
	BP	−357,925	0.00	−0.20	−571,325	57	60	18.05	−323	27,727	−55,443	34	81
	CD	−95,700	0.02	−0.04	−623,470	60	62	46.54	−33	37,798	−64,774	32	80
	JY	−1,309,588	−0.15	−0.67	−1,312,188	36	44	13.54	−2,398	42,937	−92,789	37	119
	SF	−895,550	−0.19	−0.46	−1,037,525	39	51	15.75	−1,470	34,059	−83,367	35	109
Rates	ED	−2,579,300	−0.18	−1.12	−2,605,975	35	54	90.25	−424	43,863	−135,845	33	125
	TY	−1,438,625	−0.21	−0.75	−1,631,141	40	45	29.17	−1,204	36,478	−93,704	34	109
	US	−1,484,750	−0.21	−0.78	−1,586,344	44	48	20.69	−1,591	33,263	−93,327	32	101
Stock	SP	−115,538	−0.11	−0.07	−1,172,938	53	74	8.26	−253	37,245	−111,663	30	130
Metals	GC	53,110	−0.05	0.02	−896,450	46	59	43.28	32	55,024	−74,788	37	104
	HG	−827,200	−0.14	−0.43	−1,306,725	40	55	32.68	−608	39,619	−92,612	33	126
	PL	−429,475	−0.07	−0.25	−693,145	46	61	49.32	−144	29,630	−64,288	43	93
	SL	486,060	0.12	0.25	−397,500	51	73	30.77	332	41,135	−71,459	38	115
Energy	CL	−1,587,500	−0.39	−0.66	−1,752,940	38	50	28.77	−1,399	37,771	−118,260	45	111
	HO	−591,641	−0.15	−0.26	−994,157	52	60	25.49	−397	44,069	−90,136	33	91
	HU	363,439	0.08	0.14	−607,345	60	63	23.10	281	42,242	−55,283	29	84
Grains	C	−969,950	−0.17	−0.41	−1,265,750	40	50	77.61	−293	47,995	−93,484	38	110
	S	113,288	0.02	0.06	−591,238	58	59	30.05	77	38,428	−48,811	37	72
	W	−811,213	−0.12	−0.40	−1,046,488	43	60	50.59	−377	42,984	−113,965	33	125
Meats	FC	−475,865	−0.03	−0.23	−1,131,840	55	58	39.36	−212	39,616	−75,087	41	73
	LC	−35,788	0.07	−0.02	−585,176	56	66	50.95	48	37,695	−66,271	32	92
	LH	41,396	−0.04	0.02	−584,988	51	71	32.92	34	37,186	−85,493	40	103
	PB	69,460	−0.03	0.03	−596,324	59	61	20.63	110	41,777	−59,561	31	82
Softs	CC	352,380	0.07	0.18	−744,000	65	72	49.85	111	33,826	−68,306	26	98
	CT	−1,130,720	−0.10	−0.55	−1,219,170	49	65	24.48	−943	31,439	−125,743	29	120
	JO	604,988	0.08	0.28	−506,850	56	68	36.40	302	41,251	−52,846	36	90
	KC	−774,656	−0.07	−0.27	−1,763,156	50	62	11.73	−1,057	42,592	−102,093	37	90
	LB	221,864	0.06	0.07	−1,225,360	65	74	33.65	86	42,963	−110,214	32	87
	SB	−407,613	−0.05	−0.21	−666,557	50	64	52.82	−147	31,382	−77,420	33	103
	Average	−490,130	−0.07	−0.24	−999,165	48	58	33.74	−413	37,496	−81,459	34	97

Portfolio Statistics

Net Profit:	−14,703,893	Sharpe ratio:	−1.08
Drawdown:	−15,093,668	Correlation to breakout:	−0.75
K-ratio:	−0.43	Correlation to 10-40 MA:	−0.74

© 2002 Lars Kestner – All Rights Reserved

FIGURE 8.24a

Adjusted Stochastic Strategy Applied to Futures.

Breakdown Statistics (Futures)

System Name: Adjusted stochastic
Parameters: 14 day Slow %K adjusted by 100 day range
Description: Enter long when adjusted Stochastic < 35, enter short when adjusted Stochastic > 65
Run Dates: 1/1/1990 – 12/31/2001

Breakdown by Market Sector

Market Sector	Average Net Profit	Average K-ratio	Average Sharpe Ratio	Average Max DD	Average Num. Trades	Average % Win	Avg. Profit Per Contract	Average Win	Average Loss	Avg. Bars Win	Avg. Bars Loss
FX	-670,009	-0.10	-0.35	-880,682	48	54	-953	35,080	-72,622	36	94
Rates	-1,375,669	-0.15	-0.66	-1,455,865	30	37	-805	28,401	-80,719	25	84
Stock	-115,538	-0.11	-0.07	-1,172,938	53	74	-253	37,245	-111,663	30	130
Metals	-179,376	-0.04	-0.10	-823,455	46	62	-97	41,352	-75,787	38	109
Energy	-605,234	-0.15	-0.26	-1,118,147	50	58	-505	41,360	-87,893	36	95
Grains	-555,958	-0.09	-0.25	-967,825	47	56	-197	43,136	-85,420	36	102
Meats	-100,199	-0.01	-0.05	-724,582	55	64	-5	39,069	-71,603	36	88
Softs	-188,960	0.00	-0.08	-1,020,849	56	68	-275	37,242	-89,437	32	98

Performance Breakdown by Year

Year	Net Profit	K-ratio	Sharpe Ratio
1990	-3,339,489	-1.03	-3.11
1991	-718,754	-0.09	-0.58
1992	-1,069,354	-0.23	-0.85
1993	-1,677,855	-0.22	-1.62
1994	-1,730,938	-0.56	-1.37
1995	-729,491	-0.11	-0.71

Year	Net Profit	K-ratio	Sharpe Ratio
1996	-948,425	-0.33	-0.87
1997	-215,489	0.14	-0.20
1998	-2,212,869	-0.89	-2.42
1999	899,645	0.30	0.37
2000	-1,928,156	-0.62	-1.75
2001	-976,494	-0.24	-0.74

Length	Number of Windows	Num. of Profitable Windows	Percent Profitable
1 Month	144	58	40.28%
3 Months	142	48	33.80%
6 Months	139	35	25.18%
12 Months	133	14	10.53%
18 Months	127	2	1.57%
24 Months	121	0	0.00%

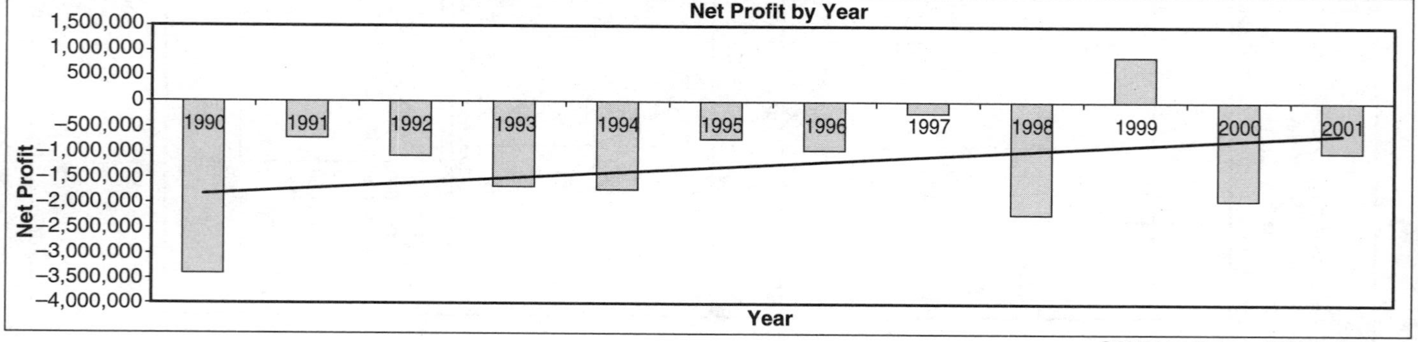

Net Profit by Year

© 2002 Lars Kestner – All Rights Reserved

FIGURE 8.24b

Adjusted Stochastic Strategy Applied to Futures.

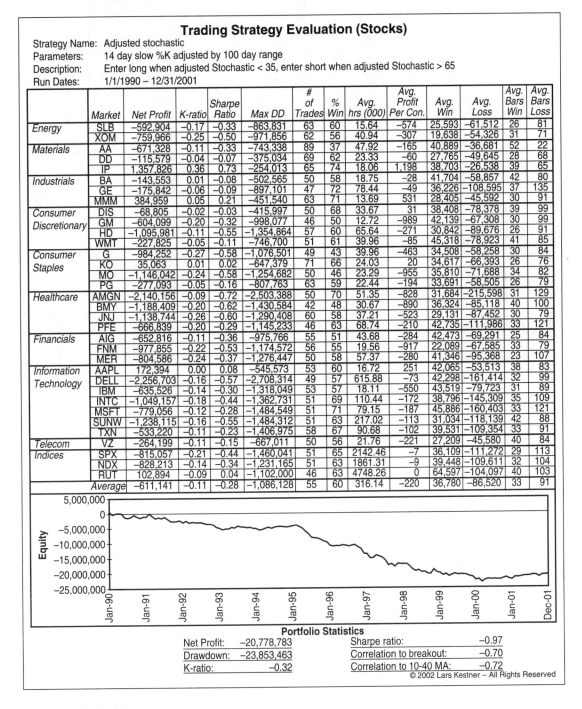

Trading Strategy Evaluation (Stocks)

Strategy Name: Adjusted stochastic
Parameters: 14 day slow %K adjusted by 100 day range
Description: Enter long when adjusted Stochastic < 35, enter short when adjusted Stochastic > 65
Run Dates: 1/1/1990 – 12/31/2001

	Market	Net Profit	K-ratio	Sharpe Ratio	Max DD	# of Trades	% Win	Avg. hrs (000)	Avg. Profit Per Con.	Avg. Win	Avg. Loss	Avg. Bars Win	Avg. Bars Loss
Energy	SLB	−592,904	−0.17	−0.33	−863,831	63	60	15.64	−574	25,593	−61,512	26	81
	XOM	−759,966	−0.25	−0.50	−971,856	62	56	40.94	−307	19,638	−54,326	31	71
Materials	AA	−671,328	−0.11	−0.33	−743,338	89	37	47.92	−165	40,889	−36,681	52	22
	DD	−115,579	−0.04	−0.07	−375,034	69	62	23.33	−60	27,765	−49,645	28	68
	IP	1,357,826	0.36	0.73	−254,013	65	74	18.06	1,198	38,703	−26,538	39	65
Industrials	BA	−143,553	0.01	−0.08	−502,565	50	58	18.75	−28	41,704	−58,857	42	80
	GE	−175,842	−0.06	−0.09	−897,101	47	72	78.44	−49	36,226	−108,595	37	135
	MMM	384,959	0.05	0.21	−451,540	63	71	13.69	531	28,405	−45,592	30	91
Consumer Discretionary	DIS	−68,805	−0.02	−0.03	−415,997	50	68	33.67	31	38,408	−78,378	39	99
	GM	−604,099	−0.20	−0.32	−998,077	46	50	12.72	−989	42,139	−67,308	30	99
	HD	−1,095,981	−0.11	−0.55	−1,354,864	57	60	65.64	−271	30,842	−89,676	26	91
	WMT	−227,825	−0.05	−0.11	−746,700	51	61	39.96	−85	45,318	−78,923	41	85
Consumer Staples	G	−984,252	−0.27	−0.58	−1,076,501	49	43	39.96	−463	34,508	−58,258	30	84
	KO	35,063	0.01	0.02	−647,379	71	66	24.03	20	34,617	−66,393	26	76
	MO	−1,146,042	−0.24	−0.58	−1,254,682	50	46	23.29	−955	35,810	−71,688	34	82
	PG	−277,093	−0.05	−0.16	−807,763	63	59	22.44	−194	33,691	−58,505	26	79
Healthcare	AMGN	−2,140,156	−0.09	−0.72	−2,503,388	50	70	51.35	−828	31,684	−215,598	31	129
	BMY	−1,188,409	−0.20	−0.62	−1,430,584	42	48	30.67	−890	36,324	−85,118	40	100
	JNJ	−1,138,744	−0.26	−0.60	−1,290,408	60	58	37.21	−523	29,131	−87,452	30	79
	PFE	−666,839	−0.20	−0.29	−1,145,233	46	63	68.74	−210	42,735	−111,986	33	121
Financials	AIG	−652,816	−0.11	−0.36	−975,766	55	51	43.68	−284	42,473	−69,291	25	84
	FNM	−977,855	−0.22	−0.53	−1,174,572	56	55	19.56	−917	22,089	−67,585	33	79
	MER	−804,586	−0.24	−0.37	−1,276,447	50	58	57.37	−280	41,346	−95,368	23	107
Information Technology	AAPL	172,394	0.00	0.08	−545,573	53	60	16.72	251	42,065	−53,513	38	83
	DELL	−2,256,703	−0.16	−0.57	−2,708,314	49	57	615.88	−73	42,298	−161,414	32	99
	IBM	−635,526	−0.14	−0.30	−1,318,049	53	57	18.11	−550	43,519	−79,723	31	89
	INTC	−1,049,157	−0.18	−0.44	−1,362,731	51	69	110.44	−172	38,796	−145,309	35	109
	MSFT	−779,056	−0.12	−0.28	−1,484,549	51	71	79.15	−187	45,886	−160,403	33	121
	SUNW	−1,238,115	−0.16	−0.55	−1,484,312	51	63	217.02	−113	31,034	−118,139	42	88
	TXN	−533,220	−0.11	−0.23	−1,406,975	58	67	90.68	−102	39,531	−109,354	33	91
Telecom	VZ	−264,199	−0.11	−0.15	−667,011	50	56	21.76	−221	27,209	−45,580	40	84
Indices	SPX	−815,057	−0.21	−0.44	−1,460,041	51	65	2142.46	−7	36,109	−111,272	29	113
	NDX	−828,213	−0.14	−0.34	−1,231,165	51	63	1861.31	−9	39,448	−109,611	32	104
	RUT	102,894	−0.09	0.04	−1,102,000	46	63	4748.26	0	64,597	−104,097	40	103
	Average	−611,141	−0.11	−0.28	−1,086,128	55	60	316.14	−220	36,780	−86,520	33	91

Portfolio Statistics

Net Profit: −20,778,783   Sharpe ratio: −0.97
Drawdown: −23,853,463   Correlation to breakout: −0.70
K-ratio: −0.32   Correlation to 10-40 MA: −0.72

© 2002 Lars Kestner – All Rights Reserved

FIGURE 8.25a

Adjusted Stochastic Strategy Applied to Stocks.

Breakdown Statistics (Stocks)

System Name: Adjusted stochastic
Parameters: 14 day slow %K adjusted by 100 day range
Description: Enter long when adjusted by Stochastic < 35, enter short when adjusted Stochastic > 65
Run Dates: 1/1/1990 – 12/31/2001

Breakdown by Market Sector

Market Sector	Average Net Profit	Average K-ratio	Average Sharpe Ratio	Average Max DD	Average Num. Trades	Average % Win	Avg. Profit Per Con.	Average Win	Average Loss	Avg. Bars Win	Avg. Bars Loss
Energy	-676,435	-0.21	-0.41	-917,844	63	58	-440	22,616	-57,919	29	76
Materials	190,306	0.07	0.11	-457,462	74	58	324	35,786	-37,621	40	52
Industrials	21,855	0.00	0.02	-617,069	53	67	151	35,445	-71,015	36	102
Discretionary	-499,178	-0.09	-0.26	-878,910	51	60	-329	39,177	-78,571	34	93
Staples	-593,081	-0.14	-0.32	-946,581	58	53	-398	34,656	-63,711	29	80
Healthcare	-1,283,537	-0.19	-0.56	-1,592,403	50	60	-612	34,969	-125,038	34	107
Financials	-811,752	-0.19	-0.42	-1,142,262	54	55	-494	35,303	-77,415	27	90
Info. Tech.	-902,769	-0.13	-0.33	-1,472,929	52	63	-135	40,447	-118,265	35	97
Telecom	-264,199	-0.11	-0.15	-667,011	50	56	-221	27,209	-45,580	40	84
Indices	-513,458	-0.15	-0.25	-1,264,402	49	63	-5	46,718	-108,326	34	107

Performance Breakdown by Year

Year	Net Profit	K-ratio	Sharpe Ratio	Year	Net Profit	K-ratio	Sharpe Ratio
1990	-1,675,515	-0.30	-0.84	1996	-2,791,438	-0.26	-1.46
1991	-1,973,857	-0.51	-0.96	1997	-3,426,750	-0.43	-1.19
1992	-1,944,597	-0.45	-1.53	1998	-3,006,616	-0.36	-1.27
1993	-87,637	0.10	-0.08	1999	-2,371,004	-0.23	-0.85
1994	824,850	0.41	0.81	2000	72,879	0.15	0.05
1995	-6,655,683	-1.40	-4.31	2001	1,653,293	0.36	1.33

Profitability Windows

Length	Number of Windows	Num. of Profitable Windows	Percent Profitable
1 Month	144	56	38.89%
3 Months	142	55	38.73%
6 Months	139	40	28.78%
12 Months	133	25	18.80%
18 Months	127	17	13.39%
24 Months	121	8	6.61%

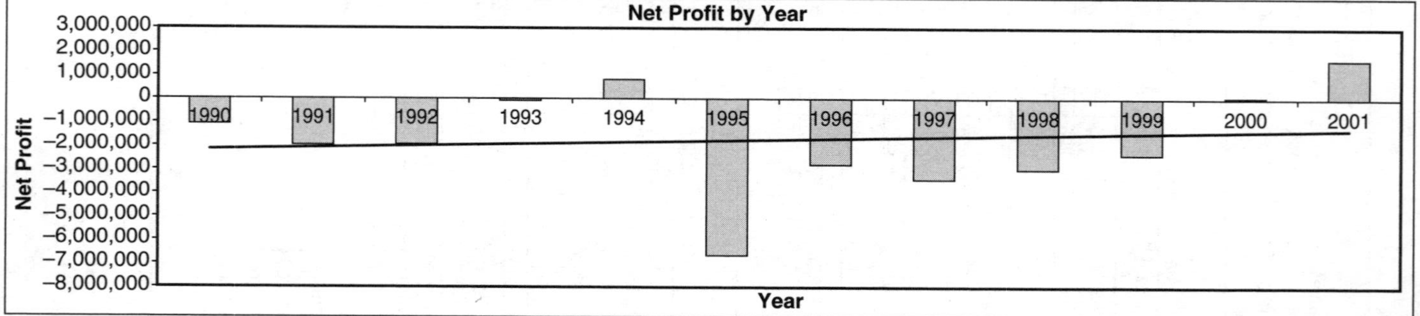

Net Profit by Year

© 2002 Lars Kestner – All Rights Reserved

FIGURE 8.25b

Adjusted Stochastic Strategy Applied to Stocks.

1. Today's close is less than the close five days ago.
2. The close 5 days ago is less than the close 10 days ago.
3. The close 10 days ago is less than the close 15 days ago.

The chart in Figure 8.26 applies the three in a row strategy to the Nasdaq 100. While there is only one signal, it would appear that the three in a row strategy enters early in the trend.

Who says simple cannot work? The three in a row strategy produces strong performance on both futures and stocks (Figures 8.27a through 8.28b). Futures tests generate profits in 10 out of 12 years. Stocks produce profits in 8 out of 12 years. Strong sectors include currencies, interest rates, petroleum, technology stocks, telecom stocks, and stock indices.

While I do not advocate using this idea alone as a trading strategy, the results do demonstrate the value of the trading signals. The strategy can be incorporated with more complex techniques to produce a very profitable trading strategy.

Volume Reversal Strategy

Academics, long proponents of the efficient markets hypothesis, have begun to back-test trading ideas to either verify the hypothesis or attempt to poke holes in

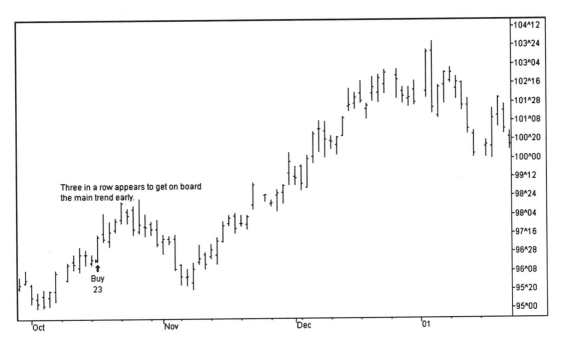

FIGURE 8.26

Three in a Row Strategy Applied to T-bonds.

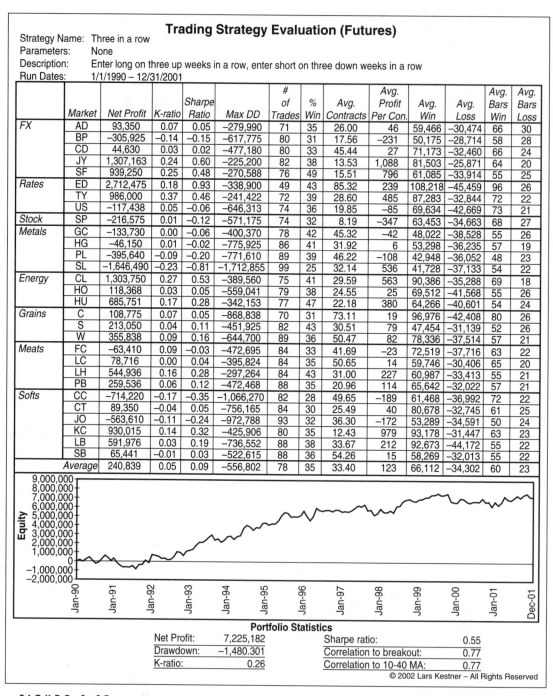

Trading Strategy Evaluation (Futures)

Strategy Name: Three in a row
Parameters: None
Description: Enter long on three up weeks in a row, enter short on three down weeks in a row
Run Dates: 1/1/1990 – 12/31/2001

	Market	Net Profit	K-ratio	Sharpe Ratio	Max DD	# of Trades	% Win	Avg. Contracts	Avg. Profit Per Con.	Avg. Win	Avg. Loss	Avg. Bars Win	Avg. Bars Loss
FX	AD	93,350	0.07	0.05	−279,990	71	35	26.00	46	59,466	−30,474	66	30
	BP	−305,925	−0.14	−0.15	−617,775	80	31	17.56	−231	50,175	−28,714	58	28
	CD	44,630	0.03	0.02	−477,180	80	33	45.44	27	71,173	−32,460	66	24
	JY	1,307,163	0.24	0.60	−225,200	82	38	13.53	1,088	81,503	−25,871	64	20
	SF	939,250	0.25	0.48	−270,588	76	49	15.51	796	61,085	−33,914	55	25
Rates	ED	2,712,475	0.18	0.93	−338,900	49	43	85.32	239	108,218	−45,459	96	26
	TY	986,000	0.37	0.46	−241,422	72	39	28.60	485	87,283	−32,844	72	22
	US	−117,438	0.05	−0.06	−646,313	74	36	19.85	−85	69,634	−42,669	73	21
Stock	SP	−216,575	0.01	−0.12	−571,175	74	32	8.19	−347	63,453	−34,663	68	27
Metals	GC	−133,730	0.00	−0.06	−400,370	78	42	45.32	−42	48,022	−38,528	55	26
	HG	−46,150	0.01	−0.02	−775,925	86	41	31.92	6	53,298	−36,235	57	19
	PL	−395,640	−0.09	−0.20	−771,610	89	39	46.22	−108	42,948	−36,052	48	23
	SL	−1,646,490	−0.23	−0.81	−1,712,855	99	25	32.14	536	41,728	−37,133	54	22
Energy	CL	1,303,750	0.27	0.53	−389,560	75	41	29.59	563	90,386	−35,288	69	18
	HO	118,368	0.03	0.05	−559,041	79	38	24.55	25	69,512	−41,568	55	26
	HU	685,751	0.17	0.28	−342,153	77	47	22.18	380	64,266	−40,601	54	24
Grains	C	108,775	0.07	0.05	−868,838	70	31	73.11	19	96,976	−42,408	80	26
	S	213,050	0.04	0.11	−451,925	82	43	30.51	79	47,454	−31,139	52	26
	W	355,838	0.09	0.16	−644,700	89	36	50.47	82	78,336	−37,514	57	21
Meats	FC	−63,410	0.09	−0.03	−472,695	84	33	41.69	−23	72,519	−37,716	63	22
	LC	78,716	0.00	0.04	−395,824	84	35	50.65	14	59,746	−30,406	65	20
	LH	544,936	0.16	0.28	−297,264	84	43	31.00	227	60,987	−33,413	55	21
	PB	259,536	0.06	0.12	−472,468	88	35	20.96	114	65,642	−32,022	57	21
Softs	CC	−714,220	−0.17	−0.35	−1,066,270	82	28	49.65	−189	61,468	−36,992	72	22
	CT	89,350	−0.04	0.05	−756,165	84	30	25.49	40	80,678	−32,745	61	25
	JO	−563,610	−0.11	−0.24	−972,788	93	32	36.30	−172	53,289	−34,591	50	24
	KC	930,015	0.14	0.32	−425,906	80	35	12.43	979	93,178	−31,447	63	23
	LB	591,976	0.03	0.19	−736,552	88	38	33.67	212	92,673	−44,172	55	22
	SB	65,441	−0.01	0.03	−522,615	88	36	54.26	15	58,269	−32,013	55	22
	Average	240,839	0.05	0.09	−556,802	78	35	33.40	123	66,112	−34,302	60	23

Portfolio Statistics

Net Profit:	7,225,182	Sharpe ratio:	0.55
Drawdown:	−1,480.301	Correlation to breakout:	0.77
K-ratio:	0.26	Correlation to 10-40 MA:	0.77

© 2002 Lars Kestner – All Rights Reserved

FIGURE 8.27a

Three in a Row Strategy Applied to Futures.

Breakdown Statistics (Futures)

System Name: Three in a row
Parameters: None
Description: Enter long on three up weeks in a row, enter short on three down weeks in a row
Run Dates: 1/1/1990 – 12/31/2001

Breakdown by Market Sector

Market Sector	Average Net Profit	Average K-ratio	Average Sharpe Ratio	Average Max DD	Average Num Trades	Average % Win	Avg. Profit Per Contract	Average Win	Average Loss	Avg. Bars Win	Avg. Bars Loss
FX	415,694	0.09	0.20	-374,147	78	37	345	64,681	-30,287	62	25
Rates	895,259	0.15	0.33	-306,659	49	30	160	66,284	-30,243	60	17
Stock	-216,575	0.01	-0.12	-571,175	74	32	-347	63,453	-34,663	68	27
Metals	-555,503	-0.08	-0.27	-915,190	88	37	-170	46,499	-36,987	53	23
Energy	702,623	0.16	0.29	-430,251	77	42	323	74,722	-39,153	59	23
Grains	225,888	0.07	0.10	-655,154	80	37	60	74,255	-37,020	63	24
Meats	204,945	0.08	0.10	-409,563	85	36	83	64,723	-33,389	60	21
Softs	66,492	-0.03	0.00	-746,716	86	33	148	73,259	-35,326	59	23

Performance Breakdown by Year

Year	Net Profit	K-ratio	Sharpe Ratio	Year	Net Profit	K-ratio	Sharpe Ratio
1990	306,767	0.09	0.30	1996	-73,960	0.15	-0.05
1991	425,295	0.08	0.31	1997	334,270	-0.01	0.29
1992	489,823	0.18	0.51	1998	1,030,926	0.48	1.01
1993	1,526,658	0.30	1.45	1999	-315,673	-0.07	-0.92
1994	1,552,373	0.48	1.28	2000	101,435	-0.10	0.09
1995	1,321,623	0.35	1.28	2001	503,124	0.30	0.44

Length	Number of Windows	Num. of Profitable Windows	Percent Profitable
1 Month	144	83	57.64%
3 Months	142	89	62.68%
6 Months	139	99	71.22%
12 Months	133	98	73.68%
18 Months	127	100	78.74%
24 Months	121	107	88.43%

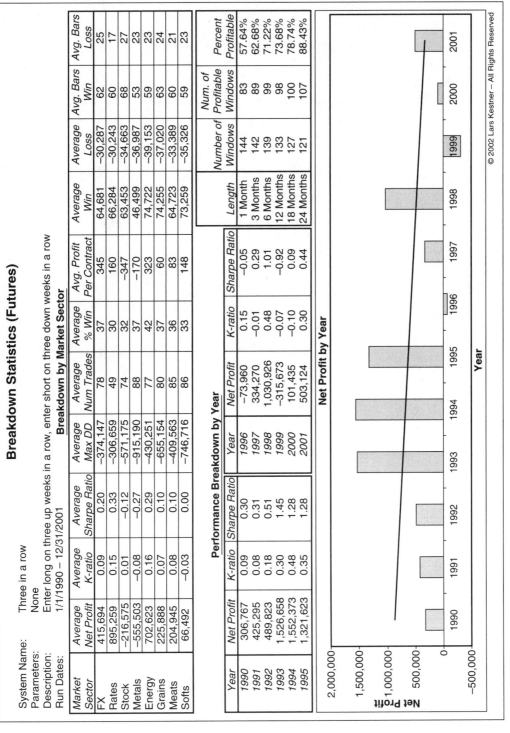

Net Profit by Year

© 2002 Lars Kestner – All Rights Reserved

FIGURE 8.27b

Three in a Row Strategy Applied to Futures.

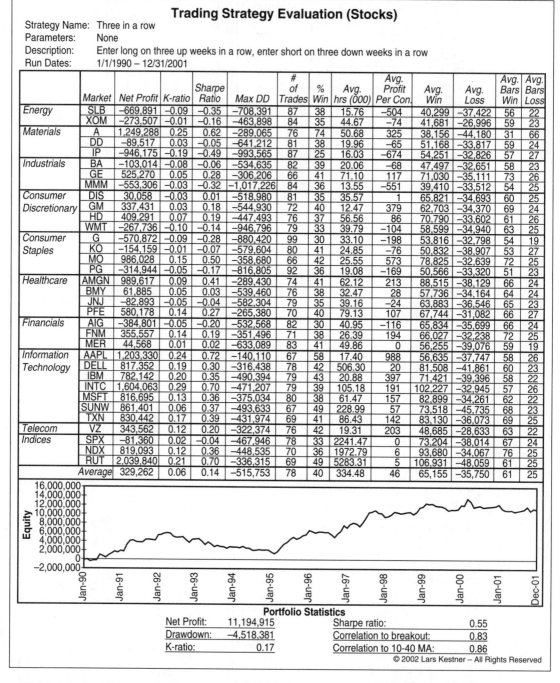

Trading Strategy Evaluation (Stocks)

Strategy Name: Three in a row
Parameters: None
Description: Enter long on three up weeks in a row, enter short on three down weeks in a row
Run Dates: 1/1/1990 – 12/31/2001

	Market	Net Profit	K-ratio	Sharpe Ratio	Max DD	# of Trades	% Win	Avg. hrs (000)	Avg. Profit Per Con.	Avg. Win	Avg. Loss	Avg. Bars Win	Avg. Bars Loss
Energy	SLB	−669,891	−0.09	−0.35	−708,391	87	38	15.76	−504	40,299	−37,422	56	22
	XOM	−273,507	−0.01	−0.16	−463,898	84	35	44.67	−74	41,681	−26,996	59	23
Materials	A	1,249,288	0.25	0.62	−289,065	76	74	50.68	325	38,156	−44,180	31	66
	DD	−89,517	0.03	−0.05	−641,212	81	38	19.96	−65	51,168	−33,817	59	24
	IP	−946,175	−0.19	−0.49	−993,565	87	25	16.03	−674	54,251	−32,826	57	27
Industrials	BA	−103,014	−0.08	−0.06	−534,635	82	39	20.06	−68	47,497	−32,651	58	23
	GE	525,270	0.05	0.28	−306,206	66	41	71.10	117	71,030	−35,111	73	26
	MMM	−553,306	−0.03	−0.32	−1,017,226	84	36	13.55	−551	39,410	−33,512	54	25
Consumer	DIS	30,058	−0.03	0.01	−518,980	81	35	35.57	1	65,821	−34,693	60	25
Discretionary	GM	337,431	0.03	0.18	−544,930	72	40	12.47	379	62,703	−34,370	69	24
	HD	409,291	0.07	0.19	−447,493	76	37	56.56	86	70,790	−33,602	61	26
	WMT	−267,736	−0.10	−0.14	−946,796	79	33	39.79	−104	58,599	−34,940	63	25
Consumer	G	−570,872	−0.09	−0.28	−880,420	99	30	33.10	−198	53,816	−32,798	54	19
Staples	KO	−154,159	−0.01	−0.07	−579,604	80	41	24.85	−76	50,832	−38,907	53	27
	MO	986,028	0.15	0.50	−358,680	66	42	25.55	573	78,825	−32,639	72	25
	PG	−314,944	−0.05	−0.17	−816,805	92	36	19.08	−169	50,566	−33,320	51	23
Healthcare	AMGN	989,617	0.09	0.41	−289,430	74	41	62.12	213	88,515	−38,129	66	24
	BMY	61,885	0.05	0.03	−539,460	76	38	32.47	28	57,736	−34,164	64	24
	JNJ	−82,893	−0.05	−0.04	−582,304	79	35	39.16	−24	63,883	−36,546	65	23
	PFE	580,178	0.14	0.27	−265,380	70	40	79.13	107	67,744	−31,082	66	27
Financials	AIG	−384,801	−0.05	−0.20	−532,568	82	30	40.95	−116	65,834	−35,699	66	24
	FNM	355,557	0.14	0.19	−351,496	71	38	26.39	194	66,027	−32,238	72	25
	MER	44,568	0.01	0.02	−633,089	83	41	49.86	0	56,255	−39,076	59	19
Information	AAPL	1,203,330	0.24	0.72	−140,110	67	58	17.40	988	56,635	−37,747	58	26
Technology	DELL	817,352	0.19	0.30	−316,438	78	42	506.30	20	81,508	−41,861	60	23
	IBM	782,142	0.20	0.35	−490,394	79	43	20.88	397	71,421	−39,396	58	22
	INTC	1,604,063	0.29	0.70	−471,207	79	39	105.18	191	102,227	−32,945	57	26
	MSFT	816,695	0.13	0.36	−375,034	80	38	61.47	157	82,899	−34,261	62	22
	SUNW	861,401	0.06	0.37	−493,633	67	49	228.99	57	73,518	−45,735	68	23
	TXN	830,442	0.17	0.39	−431,974	69	41	86.43	142	83,130	−36,073	69	25
Telecom	VZ	343,562	0.12	0.20	−322,374	76	42	19.31	203	48,685	−28,633	63	22
Indices	SPX	−81,360	0.02	−0.04	−467,946	78	33	2241.47	0	73,204	−38,014	67	24
	NDX	819,093	0.12	0.36	−448,535	70	36	1972.79	6	93,680	−34,067	76	25
	RUT	2,039,840	0.21	0.70	−336,315	69	49	5283.31	5	106,931	−48,059	61	25
	Average	329,262	0.06	0.14	−515,753	78	40	334.48	46	65,155	−35,750	61	25

Portfolio Statistics

Net Profit:	11,194,915	Sharpe ratio:	0.55
Drawdown:	−4,518,381	Correlation to breakout:	0.83
K-ratio:	0.17	Correlation to 10-40 MA:	0.86

© 2002 Lars Kestner – All Rights Reserved

FIGURE 8.28a

Three in a Row Strategy Applied to Stocks.

Breakdown Statistics (Stocks)

System Name: Three in a row
Parameters: None
Description: Enter long on three up weeks in a row, enter short on three down weeks in a row
Run Dates: 1/1/1990 – 12/31/2001

Breakdown by Market Sector

Market Sector	Average Net Profit	Average K-ratio	Average Sharpe Ratio	Average Max DD	Average Num Trades	Average % Win	Avg. Profit Per Contract	Average Win	Average Loss	Avg. Bars Win	Avg. Bars Loss
Energy	-471,699	-0.05	-0.26	-586,145	86	36	-289	40,990	-32,209	57	22
Materials	71,199	0.03	0.03	-641,281	81	46	-138	47,858	-36,941	49	39
Industrials	-43,683	-0.02	-0.03	-619,356	77	39	-168	52,646	-33,758	62	25
Discretionary	127,261	-0.01	0.06	-614,550	77	36	91	64,478	-34,401	63	25
Staples	-13,487	0.00	0.00	-658,877	84	37	32	58,510	-34,416	58	23
Healthcare	387,197	0.06	0.17	-419,144	75	39	81	69,470	-34,980	65	25
Financials	5,108	0.03	0.00	-505,718	79	36	26	62,706	-35,671	66	23
Info. Tech.	987,918	0.18	0.46	-388,399	74	44	279	78,763	-38,288	62	24
Telecom	343,562	0.12	0.20	-322,374	76	42	203	48,685	-28,633	63	22
Indices	925,857	0.12	0.34	-417,598	72	39	4	91,272	-40,047	68	25

Performance Breakdown by Year

Year	Net Profit	K-ratio	Sharpe Ratio	Year	Net Profit	K-ratio	Sharpe Ratio
1990	2,064,410	0.58	1.27	1996	565,076	0.07	0.28
1991	3,427,289	0.38	1.68	1997	2,431,270	1.04	1.04
1992	-876,591	-0.38	-0.62	1998	2,306,713	0.36	1.66
1993	-1,753,084	-0.53	-1.26	1999	350,420	-0.21	0.16
1994	-1,034,538	-0.51	-1.31	2000	165,025	-0.11	0.07
1995	4,751,283	1.00	3.19	2001	-1,072,439	-0.05	-0.65

Profitability Windows

Length	Number of Windows	Num. of Profitable Windows	Percent Profitable
1 Month	144	80	55.56%
3 Months	142	72	50.70%
6 Months	139	83	59.71%
12 Months	133	85	63.91%
18 Months	127	85	66.93%
24 Months	121	86	71.07%

Net Profit by Year

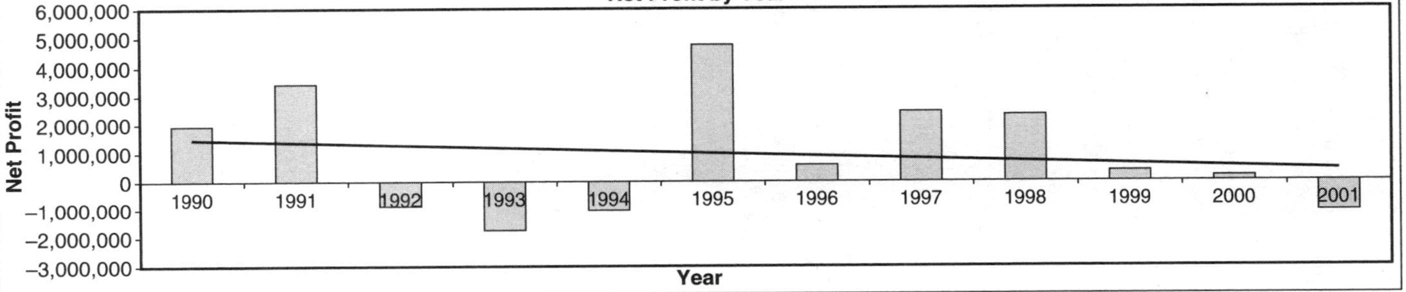

© 2002 Lars Kestner – All Rights Reserved

FIGURE 8.28b

Three in a Row Strategy Applied to Stocks.

its foundation. Whereas the 1980s saw a plethora of unsuccessful academic ideas, more recent research has uncovered potentially valuable strategies. One such example is the work done by Michael Cooper, a professor of finance at Purdue University. Cooper studied stock returns from 1962 to 1993. His research found that one-week returns accompanied by a decrease in trading volume tend to reverse the following week.

Using this idea, we test the theory on stock data. For entries, we require that the five-day absolute price change be greater than the 100-day standard deviation of price changes and the five-day average volume be less than 75 percent of the five-day average volume beginning 10 days prior. These conditions identify significant price movement accompanied with a decrease in trading volume. We enter long if the most recent five-day price change is negative while we enter short if the five-day price change is positive. All entries are exited on the fifth day of the trade.

We apply the volume reversal strategy to Johnson & Johnson (JNJ) in the chart below (Figure 8.29). Based on these signals, it appears that the volume reversal strategy does well to pick short-term tops and bottoms. This is the first and only strategy within this text to use data other than price to generate trading signals.

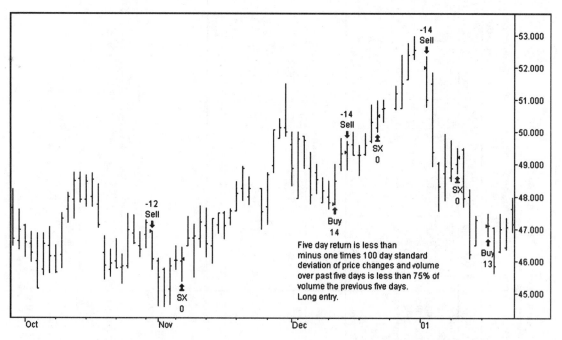

Created with TradeStation 2000i by Omega Research © 1999

FIGURE 8.29

Volume Reversal Strategy Applied to Johnson & Johnson.

Results from the volume reversal strategy are spectacular (Figures 8.30a and 8.30b). Stocks produce a Sharpe ratio of 1.15 and a K-ratio of 0.49. The strategy is profitable in 9 out of 12 years. Best performing sectors are energy, industrials, and financials.

Saitta's Support and Resistance Strategy

My favorite technical analyst on Wall Street, Alex Saitta, may not be the best known, but I believe he is one of only a handful that puts his predictions on the line day in and day out without the typical hedging jargon associated with this type of analysis. Saitta is known for writing a daily piece at Salomon Smith Barney during the 1990s which focused on short-term market trends in the stock and bond markets. Contrary to the typical technical analyst at an investment bank, Saitta was very involved in research and has created a number of quantitative techniques for trading. One of my favorite techniques is his method of defining market tops and bottoms.

Saitta begins with a 20-day simple moving average of highs and lows. When prices rise above the average of highs, the market has ended a negative phase and entered into a positive phase. When the market falls below the average of lows, a positive trend has ended and a negative trend has started. The beauty here is not of trend definition; rather, it is the method to determine previous important tops and bottoms. At the time a new uptrend has started, Saitta looks for the lowest closing price (or low) over the prior downtrend. This point defines a market bottom. At the time a new downtrend has started, the highest close of the previous uptrend denotes a market top.

My strategy uses Saitta's tops and bottoms, defined from the method above, to define support and resistance points.

The old saying in market lore is that old resistance becomes new support and old support becomes new resistance. The idea is that once a previous top has been formed, investors and traders will likely clump sell orders near the previous top. After all, market participants who did not sell at the previous high will not want to make the same mistake twice. Once prices punch through the old top, sellers have exhausted their ammunition and buyers will typically take the market higher.

The same principles apply to market bottoms. Buyers who missed buying the last bottom will clump orders near old lows. If enough sellers are able to push prices through this band of support, buyers will be sparse and lower prices are likely.

We will use the Saitta support and resistance points to determine where these clumps of buy and sell orders are located in the market. Long positions for the Saitta support and resistance strategy are entered when prices rise above a previous market top, while short positions are entered when prices fall below a previous market bottom.

The chart below (Figure 8.31) applies signals to the Japanese yen. The solid lines represent previous Saitta tops and bottoms. Because tops (bottoms) reset

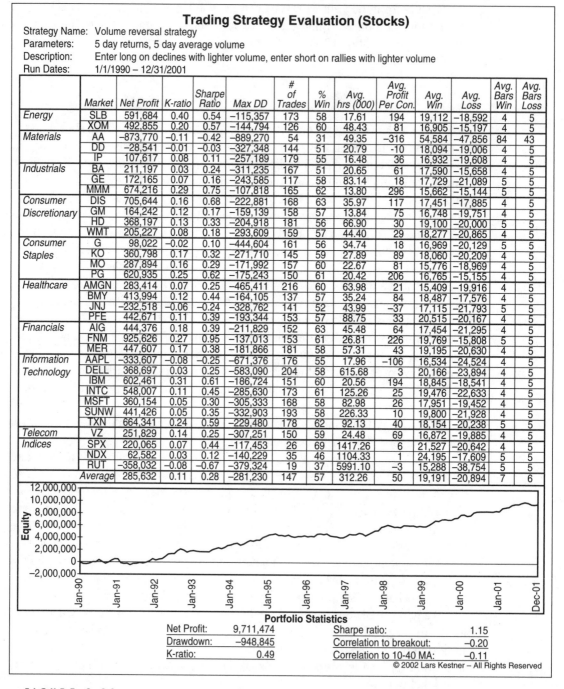

Trading Strategy Evaluation (Stocks)

Strategy Name: Volume reversal strategy
Parameters: 5 day returns, 5 day average volume
Description: Enter long on declines with lighter volume, enter short on rallies with lighter volume
Run Dates: 1/1/1990 – 12/31/2001

	Market	Net Profit	K-ratio	Sharpe Ratio	Max DD	# of Trades	% Win	Avg. hrs (000)	Avg. Profit Per Con.	Avg. Win	Avg. Loss	Avg. Bars Win	Avg. Bars Loss
Energy	SLB	591,684	0.40	0.54	−115,357	173	58	17.61	194	19,112	−18,592	4	5
	XOM	492,855	0.20	0.57	−144,794	126	60	48.43	81	16,905	−15,197	4	5
Materials	AA	−873,770	−0.11	−0.42	−889,270	54	31	49.35	−316	54,584	−47,856	84	43
	DD	−28,541	−0.01	−0.03	−327,348	144	51	20.79	−10	18,094	−19,006	4	5
	IP	107,617	0.08	0.11	−257,189	179	55	16.48	36	16,932	−19,608	4	5
Industrials	BA	211,197	0.03	0.24	−311,235	167	51	20.65	61	17,590	−15,658	4	5
	GE	172,165	0.07	0.16	−243,585	117	58	83.14	18	17,729	−21,089	5	5
	MMM	674,216	0.29	0.75	−107,818	165	62	13.80	296	15,662	−15,144	5	5
Consumer Discretionary	DIS	705,644	0.16	0.68	−222,881	168	63	35.97	117	17,451	−17,885	4	5
	GM	164,242	0.12	0.17	−159,139	158	57	13.84	75	16,748	−19,751	4	5
	HD	368,197	0.13	0.33	−204,918	181	56	66.90	30	19,100	−20,000	5	5
	WMT	205,227	0.08	0.18	−293,609	159	57	44.40	29	18,277	−20,865	4	5
Consumer Staples	G	98,022	−0.02	0.10	−444,604	161	56	34.74	18	16,969	−20,129	5	5
	KO	360,798	0.17	0.32	−271,710	145	59	27.89	89	18,060	−20,209	4	5
	MO	287,894	0.16	0.29	−171,992	157	60	22.67	81	15,776	−18,969	4	5
	PG	620,935	0.25	0.62	−175,243	150	61	20.42	206	16,765	−15,155	4	5
Healthcare	AMGN	283,414	0.07	0.25	−465,411	216	60	63.98	21	15,409	−19,916	4	5
	BMY	413,994	0.12	0.44	−164,105	137	57	35.24	84	18,487	−17,576	4	5
	JNJ	−232,518	−0.06	−0.24	−328,762	141	52	43.99	−37	17,115	−21,793	5	5
	PFE	442,671	0.11	0.39	−193,344	153	57	88.75	33	20,515	−20,167	4	5
Financials	AIG	444,376	0.18	0.39	−211,829	152	63	45.48	64	17,454	−21,295	4	5
	FNM	925,626	0.27	0.95	−137,013	153	61	26.81	226	19,769	−15,808	5	5
	MER	447,607	0.17	0.38	−181,866	181	58	57.31	43	19,195	−20,630	4	5
Information Technology	AAPL	−333,607	−0.08	−0.25	−671,376	176	55	17.96	−106	16,534	−24,524	4	5
	DELL	368,697	0.03	0.25	−583,090	204	58	615.68	3	20,166	−23,894	4	5
	IBM	602,461	0.31	0.61	−186,724	151	60	20.56	194	18,845	−18,541	4	5
	INTC	548,007	0.11	0.45	−285,630	173	61	125.26	25	19,476	−22,633	4	5
	MSFT	360,154	0.05	0.30	−305,333	168	58	82.98	26	17,951	−19,452	4	5
	SUNW	441,426	0.05	0.35	−332,903	193	58	226.33	10	19,800	−21,928	4	5
	TXN	664,341	0.24	0.59	−229,480	178	62	92.13	40	18,154	−20,238	5	5
Telecom	VZ	251,829	0.14	0.25	−307,251	150	59	24.48	69	16,872	−19,885	4	5
Indices	SPX	220,065	0.07	0.44	−117,453	26	69	1417.26	6	21,527	−20,642	4	5
	NDX	62,582	0.03	0.12	−140,229	35	46	1104.33	1	24,195	−17,609	5	5
	RUT	−358,032	−0.08	−0.67	−379,324	19	37	5991.10	−3	15,288	−38,754	5	5
	Average	285,632	0.11	0.28	−281,230	147	57	312.26	50	19,191	−20,894	7	6

Portfolio Statistics

Net Profit:	9,711,474	Sharpe ratio:	1.15
Drawdown:	−948,845	Correlation to breakout:	−0.20
K-ratio:	0.49	Correlation to 10-40 MA:	−0.11

© 2002 Lars Kestner – All Rights Reserved

FIGURE 8.30a

Volume Reversal Strategy Applied to Stocks.

Breakdown Statistics (Stocks)

System Name: Volume reversal strategy
Parameters: 5 day returns, 5 day average volume
Description: Enter long on declines with lighter volume, enter short on rallies with lighter volume
Run Dates: 1/1/1990 – 12/31/2001

Breakdown by Market Sector

Market Sector	Average Net Profit	Average K-ratio	Average Sharpe Ratio	Average Max DD	Average Num Trades	Average % Win	Avg. Profit Per Contract	Average Win	Average Loss	Avg. Bars Win	Avg. Bars Loss
Energy	542,270	0.30	0.56	-130,076	150	59	137	18,009	-16,894	4	5
Materials	-264,898	-0.01	-0.11	-491,269	126	46	-96	29,870	-28,823	31	18
Industrials	352,526	0.13	0.38	-220,879	150	57	125	16,993	-17,297	4	5
Discretionary	360,828	0.12	0.34	-220,137	167	58	63	17,894	-19,625	4	5
Staples	341,912	0.14	0.33	-265,887	153	59	98	16,892	-18,616	4	5
Healthcare	226,890	0.06	0.21	-287,906	162	56	25	17,881	-19,863	4	5
Financials	605,870	0.21	0.58	-176,903	162	61	111	18,806	-19,244	4	5
Info. Tech.	378,783	0.10	0.33	-370,648	178	59	28	18,704	-21,602	4	5
Telecom	251,829	0.14	0.25	-307,251	150	59	69	16,872	-19,885	4	5
Indices	-25,129	0.01	-0.04	-212,335	27	51	1	20,337	-25,668	5	5

Performance Breakdown by Year

Year	Net Profit	K-ratio	Sharpe Ratio	Year	Net Profit	K-ratio	Sharpe Ratio
1990	562,257	0.28	0.71	1996	115,403	-0.09	0.18
1991	-171,198	0.10	-0.18	1997	1,663,250	0.42	1.98
1992	1,575,264	0.52	1.90	1998	-20,064	0.01	-0.04
1993	935,924	0.49	1.66	1999	1,938,768	0.77	3.08
1994	1,677,098	0.73	2.48	2000	578,401	0.38	0.96
1995	-272,202	-0.28	-0.52	2001	1,187,648	0.31	1.69

Profitability Windows

Length	Number of Windows	Num. of Profitable Windows	Percent Profitable
1 Month	144	91	63.19%
3 Months	142	97	68.31%
6 Months	139	115	82.73%
12 Months	133	116	87.22%
18 Months	127	119	93.70%
24 Months	121	117	96.69%

Net Profit by Year

© 2002 Lars Kestner – All Rights Reserved

FIGURE 8.30b

Volume Reversal Strategy Applied to Stocks.

235

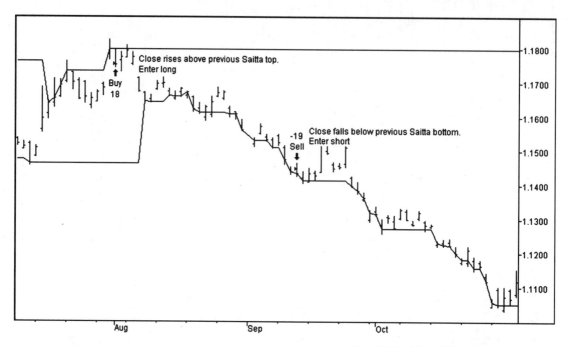

Created with TradeStation 2000i by Omega Research © 1999

FIGURE 8.31

Saitta Support and Resistance Strategy Applied to Japanese Yen.

each time prices close below (above) the 20-day moving average of lows (highs), the solid lines are discontinuous and can jerk around often. Long entries are established as prices rise above the solid upper line, while shorts are entered as prices fall below the solid lower line.

Performance of the Saitta support and resistance strategy is strong over both futures and stocks (Figures 8.32a through 8.33b). Over futures markets, the strategy produces a Sharpe ratio of 0.66 and a K-ratio of 0.30. Especially strong sectors are the typical trending markets: interest rates, currencies, and petroleum. When tested on stocks, the strategy produces a Sharpe ratio of 0.51 and a K-ratio of 0.19 and is profitable in 7 out of 12 years. Top performing sectors are consumer discretionary, health care, technology, and stock indices.

THE VALUE OF STOP LOSS EXITS

One popular idea is to trade a 40-day entry/20-day exit channel breakout with a stop that is two times the 20-day average true range away from the entry. This stop is used to minimize losses much quicker than the 20-day extreme built into

Trading Strategy Evaluation (Futures)

Strategy Name: Alex Saitta's support and resistance strategy
Parameters: 20 day average of highs and lows to determine entry points
Description: Enter long when closes rises above last high, enter short when prices fall below last low
Run Dates: 1/1/1990 – 12/31/2001

	Market	Net Profit	K-ratio	Sharpe Ratio	Max DD	# of Trades	% Win	Avg. Contracts	Avg. Profit Per Con.	Avg. Win	Avg. Loss	Avg. Bars Win	Avg. Bars Loss
FX	AD	−556,990	−0.12	−0.31	−822,670	57	32	25.19	−371	62,911	−42,696	95	32
	BP	162,650	−0.02	0.09	−495,600	51	33	18.08	229	69,953	−28,766	104	35
	CD	430,520	0.05	0.20	−531,360	43	37	46.11	179	85,464	−37,471	112	42
	JY	1,808,000	0.52	0.89	−155,963	45	53	13.87	2,685	104,029	−39,081	101	26
	SF	1,021,900	0.27	0.56	−235,588	51	51	15.71	1,306	73,042	−34,091	90	27
Rates	ED	2,755,450	0.34	1.27	−144,225	24	50	83.72	779	169,844	−39,429	172	50
	TY	1,145,875	0.43	0.56	−262,266	39	51	29.13	1,024	100,450	−44,490	117	35
	US	895,938	0.36	0.47	−311,594	41	54	20.40	1,070	81,594	−47,365	105	36
Stock	SP	−451,838	−0.15	−0.25	−827,813	62	27	9.35	−840	79,370	−40,807	92	32
Metals	GC	−229,600	−0.01	−0.09	−577,820	51	37	44.56	−93	68,505	−47,280	97	36
	HG	−572,225	−0.08	−0.29	−854,575	58	36	32.25	−266	58,291	−46,508	84	33
	PL	−1,172,675	−0.18	−0.55	−1,252,625	60	27	49.21	−413	47,870	−45,139	110	28
	SL	−627,845	−0.11	−0.32	−688,930	51	25	33.25	−319	59,956	−34,755	108	41
Energy	CL	1,490,920	0.21	0.58	−428,040	45	33	30.39	990	168,165	−38,933	128	34
	HO	1,160,195	0.24	0.44	−249,039	45	38	22.78	1,041	132,918	−42,576	113	36
	HU	428,341	0.08	0.17	−553,606	55	31	19.14	418	113,768	−39,304	106	32
Grains	C	1,400,175	0.12	0.45	−752,850	53	38	75.69	349	141,211	−43,153	97	33
	S	95,400	−0.03	0.04	−619,800	49	39	31.02	7	68,782	−43,228	105	31
	W	93,638	0.08	0.04	−411,613	50	30	53.16	50	115,564	−45,698	132	29
Meats	FC	18,735	0.01	0.01	−677,020	54	24	41.67	1	110,932	−35,140	113	38
	LC	152,300	−0.04	0.08	−325,284	52	33	49.92	60	81,797	−35,294	110	33
	LH	−552,644	−0.11	−0.25	−675,824	54	33	32.44	−321	66,621	−48,907	102	33
	PB	842,184	0.18	0.39	−228,188	44	34	20.60	909	112,310	−29,679	118	43
Softs	CC	−472,650	−0.09	−0.25	−818,580	52	29	50.00	−211	79,845	−47,197	118	32
	CT	377,410	0.00	0.18	−717,445	47	36	24.81	−70	83,936	−50,297	101	34
	JO	−787,103	−0.11	−0.32	−1,180,568	52	27	34.53	−440	71,171	−47,025	117	34
	KC	898,125	0.09	0.26	−695,531	39	38	12.38	1,570	138,621	−46,177	118	39
	LB	449,896	0.03	0.14	−436,264	46	37	31.28	306	104,684	−46,177	122	32
	SB	180,622	0.05	0.10	−345,990	45	33	53.89	66	94,986	−42,139	119	37
	Average	346,157	0.07	0.14	−542,556	47	35	33.48	323	91,553	−40,589	107	33

Portfolio Statistics

Net Profit:	10,384,705	Sharpe ratio:	0.66
Drawdown:	−1,464,797	Correlation to breakout:	0.83
K-ratio:	0.30	Correlation to 10-40 MA:	0.78

© 2002 Lars Kestner – All Rights Reserved

FIGURE 8.32a

Saitta Support and Resistance Strategy Applied to Futures.

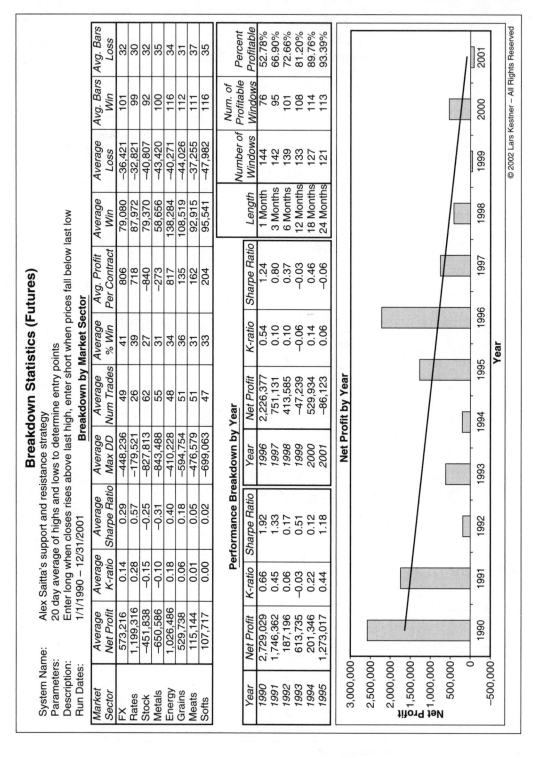

FIGURE 8.32b

Saitta Support and Resistance Strategy Applied to Futures.

Trading Strategy Evaluation (Stocks)

Strategy Name: Alex Saitta's support and resistance strategy
Parameters: 20 day average of highs and lows to determine entry points
Description: Enter long when closes rises above last high, enter short when prices fall below last low
Run Dates: 1/1/1990 – 12/31/2001

	Market	Net Profit	K-ratio	Sharpe Ratio	Max DD	# of Trades	% Win	Avg. hrs (000)	Avg. Profit Per Con.	Avg. Win	Avg. Loss	Avg. Bars Win	Avg. Bars Loss
Energy	SLB	−770,951	−0.27	−0.37	−1,103,066	70	30	16.46	−688	71,074	−46,644	95	21
	XOM	−919,682	−0.21	−0.52	−926,412	66	26	41.82	−334	57,403	−38,730	88	31
Materials	AA	−125,986	−0.03	−0.12	−309,983	182	53	48.38	−15	16,184	−20,035	4	5
	DD	−1,069,630	−0.19	−0.52	−1,105,120	60	25	21.13	−841	64,730	−45,277	89	37
	IP	−1,147,329	−0.21	−0.57	−1,182,684	60	20	16.92	−1,152	56,435	−38,472	98	38
Industrials	BA	−109,846	−0.02	−0.05	−743,222	50	30	20.84	−124	88,237	−41,510	108	40
	GE	384,595	0.08	0.21	−443,393	56	39	81.07	84	80,336	−40,797	95	26
	MMM	−731,360	−0.10	−0.36	−801,993	56	30	12.21	−1,068	41,197	−36,686	89	39
Consumer Discretionary	DIS	−107,817	−0.08	−0.05	−643,793	54	30	37.15	−55	91,495	−41,448	93	40
	GM	1,333,680	0.61	0.74	−169,974	40	58	13.39	2,462	80,329	−31,115	103	37
	HD	789,199	0.02	0.38	−483,021	52	37	46.51	306	105,096	−38,052	111	27
	WMT	441,697	0.07	0.24	−457,395	48	38	37.14	228	94,567	−43,184	115	30
Consumer Staples	G	201,646	0.02	0.10	−340,300	50	38	35.29	88	71,513	−38,842	112	26
	KO	254,174	0.07	0.11	−513,218	48	38	27.20	200	84,096	−41,770	105	35
	MO	1,008,304	0.23	0.49	−330,856	45	40	25.96	846	115,989	−40,715	121	30
	PG	−53,104	−0.06	−0.03	−495,596	58	34	19.34	−96	67,276	−38,255	90	31
Healthcare	AMGN	2,728,074	0.16	0.74	−349,765	39	41	46.38	1,512	231,895	−42,396	128	42
	BMY	276,366	0.06	0.13	−727,730	55	27	33.96	130	117,146	−37,873	116	30
	JNJ	723,120	0.12	0.33	−409,396	42	33	31.00	545	130,164	−39,728	132	41
	PFE	1,228,493	0.22	0.57	−375,697	44	36	72.71	391	141,733	−36,349	117	39
Financials	AIG	84,882	0.03	0.04	−485,375	51	33	44.85	38	103,422	−49,171	104	34
	FNM	61,365	−0.02	0.03	−561,895	55	31	21.21	57	77,784	−33,039	98	35
	MER	158,699	0.03	0.07	−473,476	52	31	50.42	64	113,997	−45,975	113	33
Information Technology	AAPL	310,417	0.09	0.14	−218,125	43	37	18.59	397	87,668	−40,206	108	44
	DELL	1,113,312	0.14	0.36	−789,905	48	27	457.61	52	218,525	−48,521	141	34
	IBM	696,669	0.12	0.35	−432,425	44	34	15.80	891	114,666	−37,958	124	39
	INTC	1,870,480	0.32	0.69	−338,165	48	35	110.94	350	177,521	−37,236	112	35
	MSFT	912,750	0.12	0.36	−506,060	50	36	75.82	241	143,165	−51,962	129	21
	SUNW	1,092,793	0.05	0.45	−565,575	45	49	214.57	111	96,673	−45,785	100	33
	TXN	624,834	0.21	0.30	−212,574	57	42	75.43	141	78,795	−38,904	88	28
Telecom	VZ	−847,372	−0.07	−0.44	−932,672	57	32	20.17	−789	47,839	−45,356	87	35
Indices	SPX	112,353	0.03	0.06	−401,672	62	34	2246.64	1	77,308	−37,345	85	29
	NDX	1,019,045	0.15	0.45	−403,300	69	39	1560.51	9	95,459	−37,758	72	22
	RUT	2,027,382	0.24	0.67	−234,837	50	44	5289.71	8	141,787	−38,903	95	34
	Average	399,154	0.06	0.15	−543,196	56	36	320.21	117	99,456	−40,176	102	32

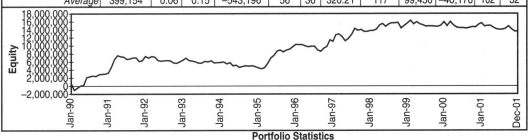

Portfolio Statistics

Net Profit:	13,571,252	Sharpe ratio:	0.51
Drawdown:	−3,277,213	Correlation to breakout:	0.88
K-ratio:	0.19	Correlation to 10-40 MA:	0.77

© 2002 Lars Kestner – All Rights Reserved

FIGURE 8.33a

Saitta Support and Resistance Strategy Applied to Stocks.

Breakdown Statistics (Stocks)

System Name: Alex Saitta's support and resistance strategy
Parameters: 20 day average of highs and lows to determine entry points
Description: Enter long when closes rises above last high, enter short when prices fall below last low
Run Dates: 1/1/1990– 12/31/2001

Breakdown by Market Sector

Market Sector	Average Net Profit	Average K-ratio	Average Sharpe Ratio	Average Max DD	Average Num Trades	Average % Win	Avg. Profit Per Contract	Average Win	Average Loss	Avg. Bars Win	Avg. Bars Loss
Energy	-845,317	-0.24	-0.45	-1,014,739	68	28	-511	64,239	-42,687	92	26
Materials	-780,982	-0.15	-0.40	-865,929	101	33	-669	45,783	-34,594	64	27
Industrials	-152,204	-0.02	-0.07	-662,869	54	33	-369	69,923	-39,664	97	35
Discretionary	614,190	0.15	0.33	-438,546	49	40	735	92,872	-38,450	106	33
Staples	352,755	0.07	0.17	-419,993	50	37	259	84,718	-39,895	107	31
Healthcare	1,239,013	0.14	0.44	-465,647	45	34	644	155,235	-39,087	123	38
Financials	101,649	0.01	0.05	-506,915	53	32	53	98,401	-42,728	105	34
Info. Tech.	945,894	0.15	0.38	-437,547	48	37	312	131,002	-42,939	115	33
Telecom	-847,372	-0.07	-0.44	-932,672	57	32	-789	47,839	-45,356	87	35
Indices	1,052,927	0.14	0.39	-346,603	60	39	6	104,852	-38,002	84	28

Performance Breakdown by Year

Year	Net Profit	K-ratio	Sharpe Ratio	Year	Net Profit	K-ratio	Sharpe Ratio
1990	2,650,429	0.52	0.96	1996	744,657	0.03	0.32
1991	4,088,293	0.14	1.41	1997	2,758,889	0.26	0.92
1992	-936,929	-0.35	-0.71	1998	1,839,746	0.20	0.82
1993	-578,383	-0.22	-0.49	1999	302,885	-0.14	0.08
1994	-1,375,570	-0.40	-1.11	2000	-262,378	-0.06	-0.13
1995	5,807,902	0.84	3.22	2001	-2,113,636	-0.37	-1.45

Profitability Windows

Length	Number of Windows	Num. of Profitable Windows	Percent Profitable
1 Month	144	80	55.56%
3 Months	142	76	53.52%
6 Months	139	83	59.71%
12 Months	133	71	53.38%
18 Months	127	77	60.63%
24 Months	121	77	63.64%

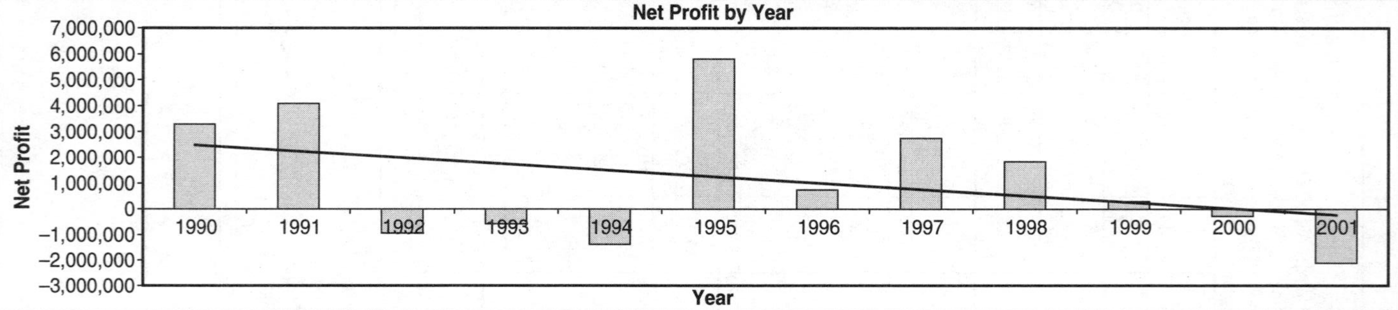

Net Profit by Year

© 2002 Lars Kestner – All Rights Reserved

FIGURE 8.33b

Saitta Support and Resistance Strategy Applied to Stocks.

the strategy. For example, suppose IBM makes a 40 day high and we buy stock the next day at $100. At the time of entry, the lowest close of the past 20 days is $90 and the average true range over the past 20 days is $2.50. In our traditional channel breakout where we buy at 40-day highs and exit longs at 20-day lows, our risk would be $10 (the difference between the entry and 20-day low). Instead of taking the $10 risk between our entry and exit points, we may choose to exit longs if IBM falls more than twice the 20-day average true range below our entry. Using this tighter "stop loss" strategy, we reduce our initial risk from $10 to $5.

On paper, the idea of minimizing losses sounds great, but does it really add to the bottom line?

If we research the channel breakout signals of INTC between 1990 and 2001, the average distance between entries of a 40-day channel breakout and exits at the time of entry (dictated by the 20-day high or low) is 15 percent. Twice the average true range at the time of each entry averages 7 percent over the life of the test. This confirms that using the average true range exit will provide the strategy with a quicker exit should the trade become immediately unprofitable. Popular wisdom suggests that cutting losses by using this tighter exit will help performance. We will test the channel breakout with and without the average true range exit to determine if performance actually improves.

To determine the usefulness of the stop loss, I test two strategies. One strategy utilizes the 40-day/20-day channel breakout, where we enter on 40-day highs and lows and exit if an opposite 20-day extreme occurs. That is, if we're long, we will exit if today's close is the lowest close of the past 20 days. The other strategy, in addition to exiting on an opposite 20-day extreme, exits longs if prices fall below two times the 20-day average true range from the entry price. Short positions are exited if prices rise more than two times the 20-day average true range above the entry point. Which performs better?

The performance numbers in Figure 8.34 speak for themselves. Coinciding with popular belief, the strategy with a stop loss calculated from the entry point yields a higher net profit, Sharpe ratio, and K-ratio than the strategy without the "risk minimizing" stop loss. For futures markets, the strategy utilizing the tighter two average true range stop loss produces a net profit of $10,580,769, a Sharpe ratio of 0.66, and a K-ratio of 0.21, all greater than the standard channel breakout, which produces a net profit of $5,971,279, a Sharpe ratio of 0.41, and a K-ratio of 0.12.

Performance tests on stocks also favor using the tighter true average true range stop loss. The channel breakout using the stop loss produces a net profit of $9,486,543, a Sharpe ratio of 0.36, and a K-ratio of 0.15, all greater than the standard channel breakout, which produces a net profit of $3,511,542, a Sharpe ratio of 0.16, and a K-ratio of 0.06.

Futures	Plain vanilla	With 2 ATR stop loss
Profit	$5,971,279	$10,580,769
Sharpe Ratio	0.41	0.66
K-ratio	0.12	0.21

Stocks	Plain vanilla	With 2 ATR stop loss
Profit	$3,511,542	$9,486,543
Sharpe Ratio	0.16	0.36
K-ratio	0.06	0.15

FIGURE 8.34

Profit, Sharpe Ratios, and K-ratios of Channel Breakout Strategy with Stop Loss. In fact, adding a tighter stop loss than our natural 20-day exit does improve performance.

PYRAMIDING VS. PROFIT TAKING

Pyramiding and profit taking are very different concepts. Pyramiding involves adding to winning positions during the trade. For example, after buying IBM at $100, we could pyramid the position by buying more shares if IBM rises to $105, and still more if it reaches $110. Profit taking entails just the opposite. After buying IBM at $100, we would sell the stock at $105, regardless of whether our trading model is still flashing a long signal. Similar to the debate on the value of optimization, the argument over whether to add to winning positions or take money off the table by taking profits leads to a heated discussion. We will look at the numbers behind the debate and develop our own conclusions about pyramiding versus profit taking.

Using the 40-day entry/20-day exit channel breakout, we test three exit strategies:

Strategy 1: Ordinary channel breakout. Enter long when today's close is the highest of the past 40 closes. Enter short when today's close is the lowest close of the past 40 closes. Exit long if today's close is the lowest close of the past 20 days. Exit short if today's close is the highest close of the past 20 days.

Strategy 2: In addition to the ordinary channel breakout entry and exit rules, we will also exit if open profit is greater than three times the average true range of the past 20 days. No new long entries are allowed unless five days have passed since the last 40-day high. No new short entries are allowed unless five days have passed since the last 40-day low.

Strategy 3: In addition to the ordinary channel breakout entry and exit rules, we add another unit long if today is a 40-day high and there have been no new 40-day highs over the five previous days. We add another unit short if today is a 40-day low and there have been no new 40-day lows over the five previous days.

Strategy 2 is an example of profit taking, while Strategy 3 pyramids extra risk as profits accrue from a specific trade.

Surprisingly, neither the profit taking (Strategy 2) nor the pyramiding versions (Strategy 3) of the channel breakout outperform a standard (plain vanilla) channel breakout (Strategy 1). In both futures markets and stocks (Figure 8.35), the standard channel breakout generates better reward-to-risk measure than either of the two versions. These results suggest that neither pyramiding as profits accrue nor profit taking as trades generate profits is superior to following standard channel breakout rules.

NEW TREND FILTERS

In addition to the trend filters mentioned in earlier chapters, I will introduce three more. We might only want to make trades if we can confirm the overall direction of the market's trend. One possibility is to take long entries only if a 40-day high was made more recently than a 40-day low. We might combine this filter with a moving average crossover for a dual trend trading system.

Another new trend filter involves using recent high-to-low ranges. We make trades only when recent price action is volatile enough to signal that important information is entering the marketplace. This can be accomplished by filtering trades and taking positions only when the high-to-low range of the past 10 days is greater than the high-to-low range of the 10 days beginning 20 days ago.

There is also room for another trend filter, one calculated differently than the popular ADX and VHF filters. One method to determine if a market is trending is to gauge the overlap of today's price action compared with previous action. If today's price range overlaps with a majority of the previous 20 days, then a market can be said to be trendless. Less overlap indicates that a trend is present.

We compare today's close to the high-to-low ranges over the past 100 days. If today's close is contained in a prior day's high-to-low range, we can consider today not to be trending. As more of the past 20 days overlaps with today's close, the more rangebound the market is. We calculate the percentage of days with over-

Futures	Plain vanilla	Pyramiding	Profit taking
Sharpe Ratio	0.41	0.16	0.24
K-ratio	0.12	0.06	0.1
Stocks	**Plain vanilla**	**Pyramiding**	**Profit taking**
Sharpe Ratio	0.16	0.15	−0.08
K-ratio	0.06	0.08	−0.02

F I G U R E   8 . 3 5

Sharpe Ratio and K-ratio of Pyramiding and Profit-Taking Versions of Channel Breakout Strategy. Our plain vanilla channel breakout outperforms both the pyramiding and profit-taking versions.

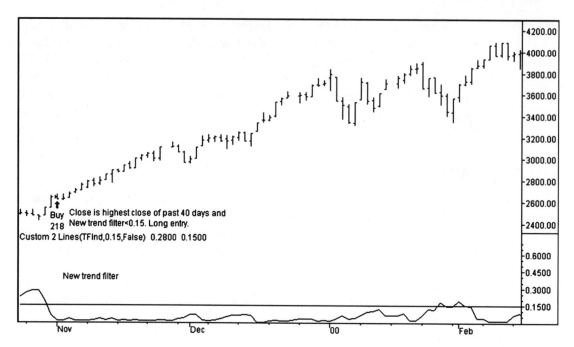

Created with TradeStation 2000i by Omega Research © 1999

FIGURE 8.36

Channel Breakout with Trend Filter Applied to Nasdaq 100. Low values of our trend filter suggest that a major trend is underway.

lap and plot this value as a trend statistic. Low values of the trend statistic indicate there's little overlap of price and the market is trending. High values of the trend statistic indicate there's much overlap of price and the market is congested.

We can apply our new trend filter to channel breakout signals. Ideally, our filter will keep us on the sidelines when the market is flat and not trending, and in the market when trends are developing. Long positions are established if today's close is the highest close of the past 40 days and the trend statistic is less than 0.15. Long positions are exited if today's close is the lowest close of the past 20 days. Short positions are established if today's close is the lowest close of the past 40 days and the trend statistic is less than 0.15. Short positions are exited if today's close is the highest close of the past 20 days.

Figure 8.36 details signals applied to the Nasdaq 100. In early November a 40-day high is accompanied with a trend statistic below 0.15. This led to a profitable long entry.

It appears that our trend filter aids performance on both futures and stocks (Figure 8.37). Our new channel breakout strategy improves net profit, Sharpe ratios, and K-ratios for both stock and futures data when compared to a standard channel breakout strategy.

Futures	Plain vanilla	with trend filter
Profit	$5,971,279	$7,434,945
Sharpe Ratio	0.41	0.52
K-ratio	0.12	0.18
Stocks	**Plain vanilla**	**with trend filter**
Profit	$3,511,542	$4,468,153
Sharpe Ratio	0.16	0.22
K-ratio	0.06	0.07

FIGURE 8.37

Profit, Sharpe Ratios, and K-ratios of Filtered and Nonfiltered Channel Breakout Strategies. Adding a trend filter appears to improve performance.

On futures, the trend filter channel breakout generates net profit of $7,434,945, a Sharpe ratio of 0.52, and a K-ratio of 0.18, compared to the standard (plain vanilla) channel breakout, which generates net profit of $5,971,279, a Sharpe ratio of 0.41, and K-ratio of 0.12.

On stocks, the trend filter channel breakout generates net profit of $4,468,153, a Sharpe ratio of 0.22, and a K-ratio of 0.07, compared to the standard channel breakout, which generates net profit of $3,511,542, a Sharpe ratio of 0.16, and K-ratio of 0.06. These results suggest that adding a new and improved trend filter can indeed improve profitability of standard trend following strategies.

CHAPTER 9

New Ideas of Markets

Trading Doesn't End with Stocks and Futures

As investors, we think of markets as stocks, bonds, and real estate. While shorter term traders might add futures and options to the list of tradable assets, this is usually where the list ends. But there's an entire spectrum of other markets traded by banks and hedge funds that many market participants may not be familiar with. While credit spreads, swap spreads, volatility swaps, and stock pairs may not be well known to the average trader, these markets are a mainstay in the equity and fixed-income arbitrage world.

Because the profitability of true arbitrage has declined over the years, hedge funds and proprietary trading desks have begun to trade riskier strategies that often involve buying one security while selling another. Arbitrage trading in today's marketplace involves taking risk, whether that risk is being long the 10-year note and short the two-year note, long General Motors and short Ford, or trading products such as option volatility or fixed income credit spreads. Despite designations like fixed-income arbitrage, statistical arbitrage, or volatility arbitrage, trading activity in these products can better be classified as relative value trading.

THE WORLD OF RELATIVE VALUE TRADING

In this chapter we'll introduce readers to the wonderful world outside of CNBC. Like many Wall Street professionals, I'm tuned into CNBC throughout the trading day and subject to the same endless "buy, sell, or hold" discussions with the portfolio manager du jour. Contrary to what's shown on CNBC, there is an entire world of markets outside of equities. These markets include corporate bonds, other interest rate products, and derivatives based on market volatility. Although it is atypical and probably inappropriate for the individual investor to trade most of these markets, there are hundreds of hedge funds and Wall Street trading desks actively pursuing this relative value trading.

Hedge funds and proprietary desks are the largest traders of relative value trading. Usually structured as limited partnerships, hedge funds are private investment vehicles used by wealthy individuals and institutions to take advantage of more flexible investment strategies than typical mutual funds. Unlike most mutual funds, which are not allowed to sell short or borrow to create leveraged positions, hedge funds very commonly use leverage and derivatives to create portfolios designed to profit in both rising and falling stock and bond markets.

The trading desks of Wall Street's largest firms also trade relative value strategies. Goldman Sachs, Morgan Stanley, and Salomon Smith Barney have hundreds of millions of dollars devoted to trading the yield curve, credit spreads, volatility, and stock pairs. This trading is instrumental in their daily business and contributes heavily to their bottom line.

While there are thousands of relative value strategies employed by proprietary trading desks and hedge funds, I believe that each strategy can be grouped into four subsets:

- Pure arbitrage
- Bottom-up relative value
- Top-down relative value
- Macro trading

Pure Arbitrage

Pure arbitrage exists when there is a specific relationship between one or more assets. Arbitraging the same stock trading on two exchanges or trading the underlying index versus its corresponding futures market are two examples. The expected profit in these activities has become virtually negligible, and often only low cost trading desks even attempt to execute these strategies.

The term *arbitrage* has been incorrectly used to describe virtually all types of trading. Historically, arbitrage has referred to creating risk-free returns by trading two like markets and profiting from the difference in price. For example, a stock trader might trade local shares of cellular giant Nokia in Finland versus the American Depository Receipts (ADRs) that trade in New York. Consider the following prices:

Nokia trading in Finland at €14 per share
Nokia ADRs trading in New York at $15 per share
USD/€ exchange rate trading at 1.00$/€

In this example, a trader buys the local shares trading in Finland at 14 euros per share, sells ADRs trading in New York at $15, and exchanges the U.S. dollar proceeds, or $15, for €15. The trade then converts the local shares to ADRs in order to zero out the position. In the process, the trader profited between the difference of the price of the local shares and the ADRs.

Another example of true arbitrage is stock index arbitrage, in which traders exploit the difference between the current prices of individual stocks traded on exchanges and the current price of stock index futures traded on the Chicago Mercantile Exchange. Because the price of stock index futures is based on a basket of the individual stocks, a strict pricing relationship must exist between the stocks and futures. The futures will be priced based on the current level of the stocks, the dividends paid until maturity, and interest rates. If the futures trade too high versus the underlying stocks, traders would do the following:

1. Borrow $1 million at the current interest rate
2. Use the borrowed money to buy $1 million of stocks based on current weights within the index
3. Sell futures contracts of the stock index worth $1 million
4. Pay daily interest on the loan
5. Receive any dividend payouts from the stocks held in the position
6. Unwind the stocks at futures expiration (morning of the third Friday of March, June, September, and December)

The stock index arbitrage strategy above is another type of true arbitrage that was once practiced widely among proprietary trading desks. The profitability of both the local/ADR and stock index arbitrage has become virtually zero with advances in technology and as more firms engage in the trading strategy.

Bottom-Up Relative Value

Bottom-up relative value strategies are less common than the other three components of the relative value umbrella. In bottom-up strategies, the trader starts with a pool of potential assets, such as stocks within the S&P 500. Based on set criteria, the trader may pick 10 stocks to buy and 10 stocks to short, subject to risk-minimizing criteria.

An example is the study reviewed in Chapter 1 where we bought a portfolio of stocks that underperformed the index and shorted a portfolio of stock that outperformed. Each stock was picked so the net characteristics of the portfolio minimized a specified risk profile. In bottom-up models, strategies could pick assets from the world of corporate bonds, mortgages, global currencies, or technology stocks.

Another possibility of a bottom-up relative value strategy would be a currency trader focusing on one region of the world. A trader might have 10 currencies from the Asia-Pacific region to buy or sell, and he or she may choose two currencies to be long, and two to be short, based on economic factors and price models. By being both long and short, this strategy would create a reasonably hedged portfolio.

In each example, the key to defining a bottom-up trading strategy is that the trader begins with a pool of possible assets, and his models then select which assets to trade.

Top-Down Relative Value

Top-down relative value models are the most commonly used. In contrast to the bottom-up strategy, these top-down models preselect pairs of securities to trade, often based on factors such as similarity of industry, time to maturity of bonds, or correlations of currencies.

Short-term stock pair trading has become widespread in the past five years. In one example, one correlated stock is traded against another when price patterns emerge. The trades are typically short-term in nature, lasting anywhere from five minutes to five days before positions are unwound. By comparing two similar companies, such as General Motors and Ford, traders might make assumptions regarding the relative performance of the two stocks. If General Motors outperforms Ford by a large amount, traders may short General Motors and buy Ford as a hedge, expecting the performance gap to close in the future.

Another example of a top-down model is yield curve trading. In addition to trading interest rates by buying and selling bonds, we can trade the relative pricing among bonds. We might make assumptions regarding the pricing of a long-term instrument, such as the 30-year Treasury bond, and a shorter-term instrument, such as the two-year Treasury note. Similar to the stock pairs, if one asset outperforms the other, we may sell the strongest performing asset and buy the weaker asset, on the premise that performance will revert in the near future.

Yet another possibility is to trade natural substitutes, such as the relative pricing of natural gas versus heating oil. Residential and commercial property is typically heated by two sources: natural gas and heating oil. If one fuel becomes more expensive relative to the other, the market will adjust as people switch heating choices. While this process may take some time, eventually the market prices will adjust.

Another top-down relationship is the connection between the price of underlying commodities and the share prices of companies that produce, mine, or manufacture the underlying products. We might trade an index of gold stocks against the metal itself, buying one and selling the other when prices move in a specific manner. The common thread among top-down relative value models is that the securities traded are constant and are usually selected based on some inherent relationship.

Macro Trading

In pure arbitrage, bottom-up, and top-down models, two securities are traded by comparing their values to each other. In macro relative value trades, we take long and short positions in securities regardless of the overall portfolio. To this point, most of the book has been dedicated to this style of macro trading. In earlier chapters, we looked at trading futures and stocks from a long and short perspective without regard for where other stocks, futures, or indices are priced. These same strategies can be applied to more esoteric markets.

INTRODUCING RELATIVE VALUE MARKETS

Our focus will now shift to applying quantitative strategies to top-down relative value trading. To trade these new strategies, we need to define certain relative value markets. We're looking to trade the relative value of one security against the other. In relative value trading, we are usually indifferent to general market moves. Our positions are structured by buying one bond and shorting another, or by buying one stock and shorting another in a similar industry.

The possibilities in relative value trading are endless, and new products are being created every day. Whether it is weather derivatives, pollution credits, or cheddar cheese futures, our quantitative trading methods will prepare us for the day when these new products begin trading. We'll focus on seven general markets for our relative value trading strategies:

- Yield curve markets
- Credit spreads
- Equity volatility
- Relative performance of stock indices
- Single stock pairs
- Commodity substitutes
- Stock and commodity relationships

Yield Curve Markets

Most individual investors are familiar with fixed income products such as bonds and mortgages. After all, many readers have home mortgages or investments in government securities. When faced with investment decisions within the fixed income world, the most important factor is often determining which maturity bond to buy. Interest rates vary over differing maturities, and these differences can be very volatile over time.

As we see in Figure 9.1, bonds with different maturities have different yields. This occurs because of a number of factors, such as future inflationary expectations, expected changes in government borrowing, and future expectations of Federal Reserve interest rate policy. The difference in yields can lead to preferences in investments.

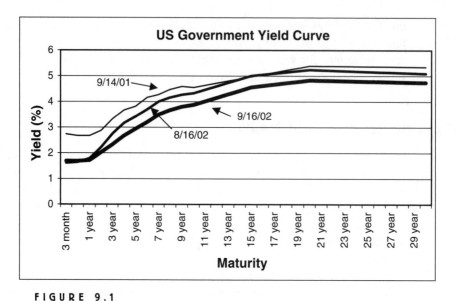

FIGURE 9.1

U.S. Government Yield Curve. Differing maturity bonds pay varying interest rates.

Currently, the two-year Treasury note yields 2 percent, while the 10-year Treasury note yields 4 percent. As an investor, I may prefer to buy the higher yielding 10-year note instead of the lower yielding two-year Note. Relative value players would take the trade one step further by buying the 10-year note and shorting the two-year note, expecting the yield differentials to return to more normal levels.

The difference in yields between maturities can be very volatile. Figure 9.2 graphs the difference between the 10-year note and the two-year note between 1990 and 2001.

Another interest rate play is to value the curvature of the yield curve over time. Note that in the yield curve graph above, the yield does not follow a straight line compared with maturity. The curve actually bends as time to maturity increases. This degree of this curvature changes over time and can be measured by comparing the yields of three maturities. If we want to measure the bend between the two-year note, 10-year note, and 30-year bond, we create the following series:

Butterfly = 10-year yield – 0.5 · two-year yield – 0.5 · 30-year yield

The combination of three yields in this manner is often referred to as a butterfly trade, as shown in Figure 9.3. When the butterfly trades high in yield, we will buy the 10-year note and sell the two-year note and 30-year bond. When the butterfly trades low, we buy the two-year note and 30-year bond while selling the 10-year note.

For the purpose of trading the yield curve using quantitative trading methods, we create four yield curve series using constant maturity yields of U.S. Treasury products:

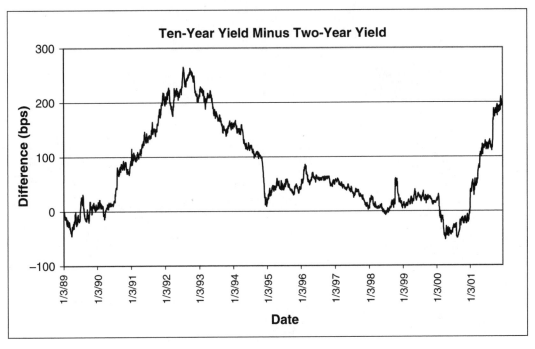

FIGURE 9.2

10-Year Yield minus Two-Year Yield. By purchasing one bond and shorting another, we can gain exposure to the difference between yields of different maturity bonds.

2's–10's: Yield of 10-year Treasury note minus yield of two-year Treasury note

2's–5's: Yield of five-year Treasury note minus yield of five-year Treasury note

10's–30's: Yield of 30-year Treasury bond minus yield of 10-year Treasury note

2–10–30 Fly: Yield of 10-year Treasury note minus 50 percent of two-year
   Treasury note and 50 percent of 30-year Treasury bond

Using these yield curve data series, we will test our trading methodologies to determine if we can predict movement in the U.S. Treasury yield curve. If our strategies are profitable, we can trade either futures or the actual government bonds to establish positions.

Credit Spreads

While the debt of the U.S. government is safe (after all, the government can always print money), debt of individual corporations or municipalities carries no such guarantee. As a result, nongovernment debt trades at higher yields than corresponding government Treasuries to compensate investors for taking this risk. *Credit spreads* are the excess yields required by investors to accept the added risks of investing in these non-Treasury investments.

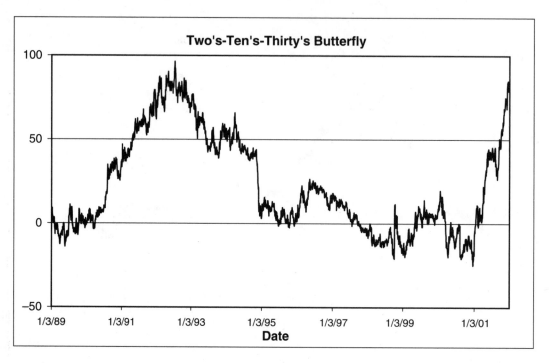

FIGURE   9.3

Two's-10's-30's Butterfly. By purchasing two bonds and shorting another bond, we can gain exposure to the curvature of the yield curve.

The recent demise of Enron and WorldCom explain how important it is to measure the credit of these securities. Once rated investment grade, the bonds of Enron and WorldCom (which once traded near 100) now trade for pennies on the dollar after each companies' problems were brought to light. When a company is not able to make an interest payment, their bonds are said to be in default. Bondholders, banks, and shareholders then begin to restructure the company in whatever way possible to return money to each class of owners. Once banks are paid in full, bondholders begin to receive money. Only after all creditors have been paid in full do shareholders receive any remaining value. In many default situations, bondholders may only receive pennies on the dollar if the financial health of the company is truly troubled.

The risk of default creates a premium in yields of corporate bonds versus corresponding Treasuries. This difference, or credit spread, tends to narrow during a growing economy as business prospects improve and the likelihood of bond defaults diminishes. Conversely, credit spreads widen during weak economies, as troubling business prospects hurt the potential for repayment of corporate debt.

There are two widely watched market measures of credit riskiness: swap spreads and high yield spreads. Swap spreads are vehicles used to trade the yield difference between the London Interbank Offered Rate (LIBOR) and U.S. Treasuries. LIBOR is the predominant business lending index in the United States. It is an international average of offered rates for dollar deposits based on quotes at eight major banks. Being an overseas deposit, it does not carry FDIC depositor insurance, and therefore carries the credit risk of the bank that holds the deposit. As a result, these deposits carry risk and trade at higher yields than U.S. Treasuries.

The spread that LIBOR trades over comparable U.S. Treasury yields can be traded by means of a swap spread with maturities between one year and 30 years. (See Figure 9.4 for a history of five-year swap spreads.) The swap spread product was utilized heavily by Long Term Capital Management. In *When Genius Failed*, author Roger Lowenstein reported that LTCM lost approximately $1.6 billion by shorting swap spreads.

Swap spreads = Five-year swap spread yields

High yield spreads are calculated by taking an average yield-to-maturity of high yield bonds and subtracting the interest rate of a corresponding U.S. Treasury.

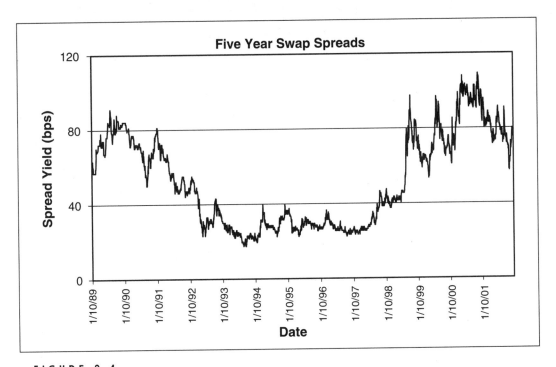

FIGURE   9.4

Five-Year Swap Spreads. Swap spreads measure the difference between government debt and highly rated corporate debt.

High yield bonds are by definition rated lower than BBB by major debt-rating agencies. Companies with such low credit ratings have significant risk of discontinuing interest payments on outstanding debt.

If a company is forced into bankruptcy due to a default on its interest payments, bondholders face much uncertainty whether they will receive any payment on their claims to the company's assets. Due to this uncertainty, investors require higher yields to compensate for the added risk. The yield spread between high yield bonds and Treasury notes signifies the market's perceived riskiness of this lower quality corporate credit. Our values of high yield credit spreads are derived from subtracting a five-year Treasury note yield from the average yield to maturity on the Merrill Lynch Master II index (see Figure 9.5).

High yield = Yield to Maturity on Merrill Lynch Master II Index – five-year
Treasury yield

We'll test our trading strategies on these two series to determine if credit spreads are predictable and follow historical patterns. Swap spreads are readily traded as Over-the-Counter derivatives products, while high yield spreads can be

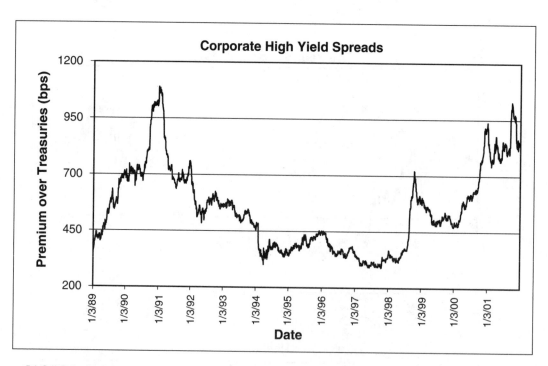

FIGURE 9.5

Corporate High Yield Spreads. High yield spreads measure the extra payment that companies with weak balance sheets must pay in order to finance their debt.

traded by buying high yield bonds and shorting an equal amount of Treasury notes or futures to remove their exposure to interest rates.

Equity Volatility

Volatility is slowly becoming a better understood market phenomenon. Many trading desks on Wall Street focus solely on trading and managing the volatility risk associated with stocks, stock indices, and bonds. Some hedge funds that trade volatility view their exposure to it as an asset class similar to stocks, bonds, or real estate.

Investors can trade volatility through options such as calls and puts. A trader who buys a call option has the right, but not the obligation, to buy a security at a fixed price at a specific date in the future. If I buy a one-month $100 strike call option on IBM, I have the right to buy IBM at $100 per share for the next month. If, at the end of the month, IBM is below $100, I allow my option to expire and I walk away. If IBM is above $100, I exercise my right and buy IBM at $100. At that point I can sell the shares or hold on to them in anticipation of further advance. A call option has a payoff structure similar to a hockey stick (Figure 9.6).

A trader who buys a put option has the right, but not the obligation, to sell a security. If I buy a one-month $100 strike put option on IBM, I have the right to sell IBM at $100 per share for the next month. If, at the end of the month, IBM is above $100, I allow my option to expire and I walk away. If IBM is below $100, I exercise my right and sell IBM at $100. Similar to the call option, at that point I can buy the shares or hold on to the short in anticipation of further declines. A put option also has a payoff structure similar to a hockey stick (Figure 9.7).

Here's where the volatility component gets interesting. If I simultaneously buy both a call and put option of the same strike—called a "straddle" in popular terminology—my payoff diagram looks like the graph in Figure 9.8.

It becomes clear that when I buy the call and put combination, I am indifferent to whether the stock rises or falls. However, I make more money if the stock is more volatile and moves far away from $100. In essence, this is what volatility traders are trying to accomplish. They buy cheap options and sell rich options that appear to be mispriced by the market. Volatility traders constantly trade stock or futures on the underlying asset in order to immunize the directional bet embedded in calls and puts, leaving them with a pure play on volatility.

The most popular measure of stock market volatility is derived from option prices on broad market indices. The Chicago Board Options Exchange has maintained a daily record of the volatility implied by options prices since 1986. The CBOE's Volatility Index (VIX) measures at-the-money option volatility on the S&P 100 (OEX). The VIX was developed by Robert Whaley to track implied volatility on the S&P 100. Using four options from the nearest contract month and four options from the second nearest option month, the VIX interpolates the implied volatility of a hypothetical at-the-money option with 30 calendar days to expiration.

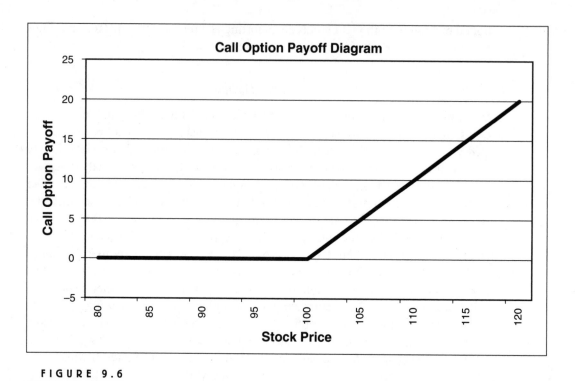

FIGURE 9.6

Call Option Payoff Diagram. Call options give the purchaser the right, but not the obligation, to buy the underlying asset.

Large discrepancies exist between the VIX and actual levels of implied volatility. A computational error in the VIX flaws its representation of implied volatility. Salomon Smith Barney's Leon Gross (February 2001) was the first to publish the bias in the VIX calculation methodology. As we see in Figure 9.9, the VIX and actual implied volatility of OEX options track each other very closely. In fact, the ratio of the two measures seems to be constant, with the VIX always roughly 1.20 times the level of actual implied volatility.

Whaley, in his attempts to correct for a weekend effect present in options, incorrectly adjusted for the difference between calendar days in a year (365) and trading days in a year (roughly 252). As a result, if we multiply the VIX by SQRT (252/365), we arrive at an unbiased estimate of one month implied volatility on the S&P 100.

Despite its bias, the VIX does measure the relative value of stock market implied volatility. Its most common use is for market-timing the S&P 500—a use that has received much notoriety over the past couple of years. Increases in the VIX are a result of higher option prices—often a sign of market worry. This worry can lead to good buying opportunities for stocks. Lower VIX levels are a result of falling option prices—often a sign of market complacency and a good selling opportunity for stocks. In this chapter, however, we will focus on trading the actu-

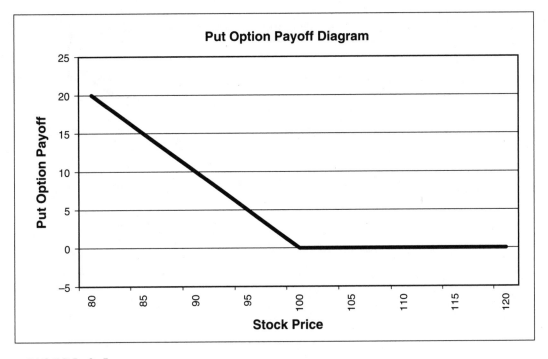

FIGURE 9.7

Put Option Payoff Diagram. Put options give the purchaser the right, but not the obligation, to sell the underlying asset.

al levels of the VIX and view it as a bona fide stand-alone market that we can trade within our relative value umbrella.

The VIX measures implied volatility, which can be traded in the form of straddles, strangles, or more esoteric products such as volatility swaps. (For more information and detail on trading volatility, see Demeterfi et al., "More Than You Ever Wanted to Know About Volatility Swaps," Goldman Sachs Quantitative Strategy Research Notes, March 1999; and Leon Gross, "Introducing Volatility Swaps," Salomon Smith Barney, January 1998.) When our models generate buy signals, we can gain exposure to volatility by purchasing straddles, strangles, and volatility swaps. When our models generate sell signals on the VIX, we can sell straddles, strangles, and volatility swaps in order to gain exposure to volatility.

VIX = closing VIX price

Relative Performance of Stock Indices

We will also study the relative performance of U.S. stock indices, utilizing the S&P 500, the Nasdaq 100, and the Russell 2000. The S&P 500 is a capitalization-weight-

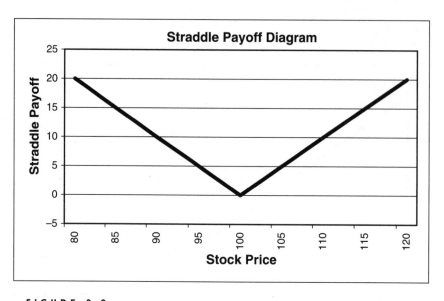

FIGURE 9.8

Straddle Payoff Diagram. By purchasing a call and a put, we create a strategy that gains exposure to an asset's volatility.

ed index of large cap U.S. equities. The Nasdaq 100 (sometimes referred to as the NDX) is a modified capitalization-weighted index of the largest 100 nonfinancial stocks trading on the Nasdaq marketplace. The Nasdaq 100 is highly weighted toward information technology, telecommunication service, and biotechnology companies. The Frank Russell Company created the Russell 2000 as a benchmark for small cap performance. The Russell 2000 is comprised of U.S. stocks whose market cap ranks between 1001 and 3000 in the universe of all U.S. equities.

Each index has periods of outperformance. In the 1980s, small cap stocks, as measured by the Russell 2000, outperformed large caps for many years. In the mid-1990s, the nifty-fifty theme of large multinational corporations was very prominent and the S&P 500 outperformed other indices. In the late 1990s, the technology bubble led to stellar returns for technology stocks. As a result, the Nasdaq 100 outperformed other stock index benchmarks (Figure 9.10).

Our goal will be to trade the relative performance of one stock index versus another. We will study past data and test models to determine if we can predict periods of outperformance. Positions can be instituted by trading stock index futures listed on the Chicago Mercantile Exchange, or Exchange Traded Funds such as the SPY for the S&P 500, the QQQ for the Nasdaq 100, and the IWM for the Russell 2000.

We create two series to test long/short strategies for trading the S&P 500 against the NDX and for trading the S&P 500 against the Russell 2000. Each series is calculated by taking the natural log of one index divided by another. Logarithms are mathematical functions used to simplify and manipulate equations

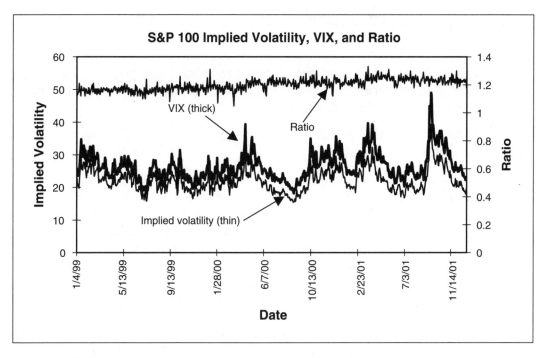

FIGURE 9.9

S&P 100 Implied Volatility, VIX, and Ratio. The VIX constantly gives readings about 1.2 times the value of at-the-money implied volatility of the S&P 100.

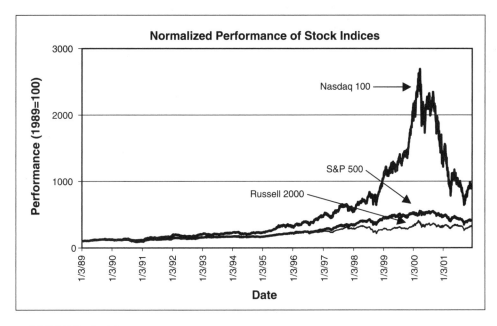

FIGURE 9.10

Normalized Performance of Stock Indices. The S&P 500, Nasdaq 100, and Russell 2000 have had periods of outperformance and underperformance.

that involve exponents. One special case, the natural log, is primarily used within the physical sciences. The natural log function is included in most software packages, such as Excel and TradeStation:

SPX/NDX = ln(SPX/NDX)
SPX/RUY = ln(SPX/RUY)

Each of the two time series represents the normalized performance of one index versus another (Figure 9.11). When the new series increases, the S&P 500 is outperforming the other index on a percentage basis. When the new series is falling, the S&P 500 is underperforming on a percentage basis. We will use this natural log method for many of the price relationships we study.

By utilizing a natural log of the price ratio, we are indifferent as to the securities chosen in the numerator or denominator of the ratio. These ratios will be symmetrical using the log method, while if only price ratios are used, the market selected for the numerator or denominator will affect trading results. Figure 9.12 also plots two series: the natural log of the S&P 500 divided by the Nasdaq 100, and then the natural log of the Nasdaq 100 divided by the S&P 500.

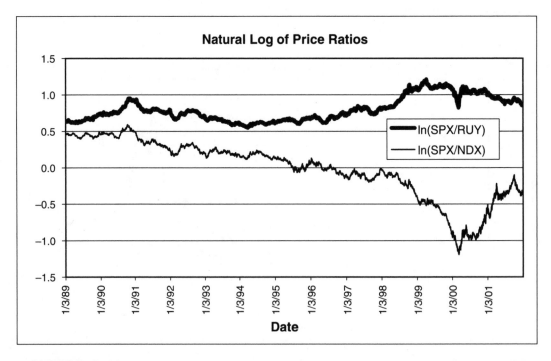

FIGURE 9.11

Natural Log of Price Ratios. In each case, the S&P 500 is outperforming when the series rises and underperforming when the series falls.

In Figure 9.12 not only are the two series mirror images of each other, but their scales are identical. That is, if one series rises by 0.20, the other series will decline by 0.20, and vice versa.

Single Stock Pairs

Stock pairs will be used frequently in our market-neutral relative value tests. *Pairs trading*, as it is known on Wall Street, is used extensively by proprietary trading desks and hedge funds. Typically, pairs are identified using correlation analysis. Once they are identified, deviations from an expected value generate trading signals. I have arbitrarily picked 15 pairs of stocks from the U.S. market based on similarities in businesses. In each case, price series are calculated by taking the natural log of the ratio of stock prices.

Two of the pairs, UN/UL and RD/SC, have a particularly unique relationship (see Figures 9.13 and 9.14). Unilever PLC (UL) and Unilever NV (UN) are holding companies that have a defined economic interest in their parent company, the Dutch and English based Unilever Company. However, both shares trade independently and are not fungible, meaning that one share cannot be exchanged equally for another.

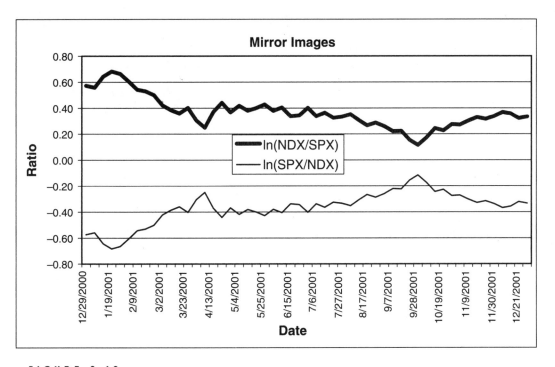

FIGURE 9.12

Mirror Images. Due to the principles of natural logs, the ln(NDX/SPX) always equals negative value of ln(SPX/NDX).

Since this is the case, no perfect arbitrage exists in the markets. The relative prices of UN and UL should move in tandem based on their claim on the assets of their parent—the Unilever Company. However, we find that these price ratios are not constant. As a result, the relative value of the two shares float, often reaching extremes where it is profitable to buy one stock and short the other stock.

A similar case exists for Royal Dutch NV and Shell Transportation and Trading PLC (Figure 9.13). Both companies' sole assets are fixed interests in the Dutch-based Royal Dutch Shell. Royal Dutch owns 60 percent of the combined firm, while Shell owns 40 percent. Despite the fact that each companies' net worth is tied to the same asset (the parent company, Royal Dutch Shell), the value of Royal Dutch shares fluctuate over time compared with Shell share prices. The inherent relative value of the Unilever NV/Unilever PLC and Royal Dutch/Shell pairs make these markets ideally suited for our relative value trading.

Commodity Substitutes

Commodity markets lend themselves well to relative value trading due to the substitution effect among related markets. If natural gas becomes too expensive for heating homes in the winter, heating oil is a substitute. Prices of soybeans will

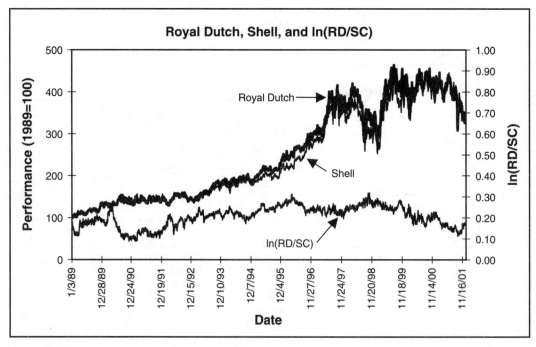

FIGURE 9.13

Royal Dutch, Shell, and ln(RD/SC). Royal Dutch and Shell are linked through their shared ownership of Royal Dutch Shell.

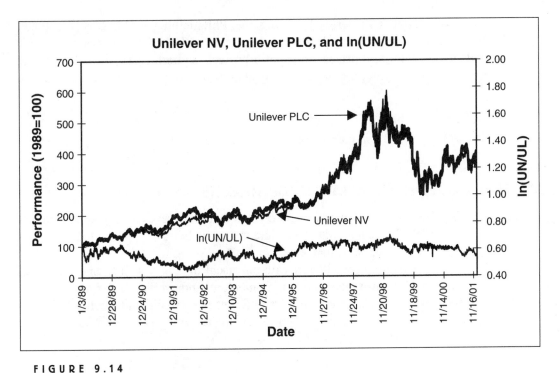

FIGURE 9.14

Unilever NV, Unilever PLC, and ln(UN/UL). Unilever NV and Unilever PLC are linked through their shared ownership of Unilever.

affect the prices of end products such as soybean oil and soybean meal. Gold and silver often trade in tandem with each other. To study these and other commodity price relationships, we create the ratios of natural log spot prices from four commodity pairs. Using spot (or cash) market prices instead of futures eliminates the need to adjust differing futures contract cycles.

Stock and Commodity Relationships

Finally, we will look at the relationship between commodity related stocks and the fluctuations of the underlying commodities that drive their earnings.

Gold producers, for example, are exposed to the absolute levels of gold prices. The producers have reasonably fixed production costs and typically do not hedge their entire production by selling gold futures or forwards. As a result, increases in gold lead to higher prices for gold stocks, and lower gold prices lead to decreases in gold stocks (Figure 9.15).

A similar relationship exists between oil refiners and the price of oil (Figure 9.16). The refiners' margins increase as oil prices rise and contract when oil prices fall. As a result, there is a material link between oil stock prices and the price of crude oil.

We create two series by using the Philadelphia Gold & Silver Index (XAU) as our proxy for gold stocks, the Amex Oil Index (XOI) as our proxy for oil stocks, spot gold prices, and spot oil prices. In both cases, we calculate the new series by taking the natural log of the ratio of the stocks to the commodity prices.

XAU/Gold = ln(XAU/Spot gold prices)

XOI/Oil = ln(XOI/Spot crude prices)

DEVELOPING STRATEGIES FOR RELATIVE VALUE MARKETS

Having defined 30 new markets and divided them into seven asset classes (see listing, Figure 9.17), we now want to explore the profitability of applying trading strategies to these relative value markets.

As in Chapter 7, we'll start with our usual trading systems: channel breakout, dual moving average crossover, momentum, and oscillators. Expected results for these new markets might be a bit different from traditional stock and futures markets. In earlier chapters, I introduced behavioral evidence concerning the

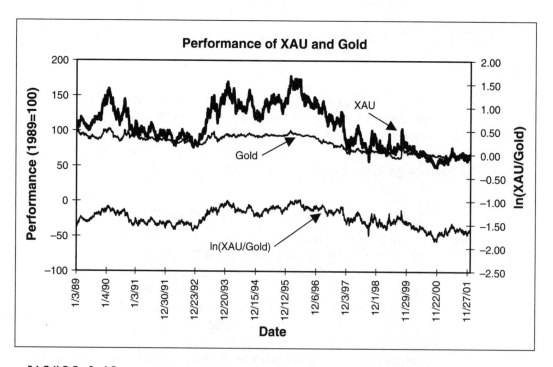

FIGURE 9.15

Performance of XAU and Gold. Gold and gold mining stocks tend to move in similar directions.

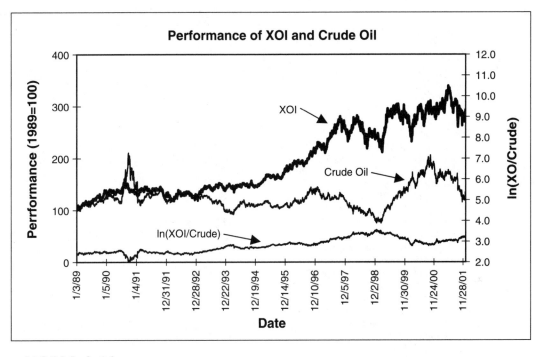

FIGURE 9.16

Performance of XOI and Crude Oil. Crude oil and oil refining stocks tend to move in similar directions.

human tendency to fight trends. This tendency might explain why trends occur in stocks and futures. But the relative value spread markets we are studying in this chapter may not follow similar patterns since these markets are typically not in the public eye and only small pockets of traders track their movement. As a result, typical trend-following techniques may prove ineffective. In addition, the substitution effect might even suggest that movement away from a mean will quickly be corrected with a move back toward the mean.

For example, when natural gas rises compared to heating oil, market prices will cause changes in demand for each product. Natural gas will be replaced by heating oil and the relative prices will converge. If the Nasdaq 100 rallies versus the S&P 500, rational valuations may cause investors to sell the overvalued Nasdaq 100 and buy the undervalued S&P 500. Countertrend and mean reversion strategies could prove profitable when applied to these relative value markets.

APPLYING QUANTITATIVE TRADING STRATEGIES TO RELATIVE VALUE MARKETS

Similar to both the stock and futures tests, position sizes for our relative value trades are a function of the 100-day standard deviation of price changes.

Market	Sector	Symbol
10 year yield minus 2 year yield	Yield Curve	2's-10's
5 year yield minus 2 year yield		2's-5's
30 year yield minus 10 year yield		10's-30's
10 year yield minus 0.5 2 year yield minus 0.5 30 year yield		2-10-30 Fly
5 year swap spreads	Credit Spreads	Swap spreads
Yield to maturity of Merrill Lynch Master II Index minus 5 year Treasury yields		High yield
CBOE Volatility Index	Volatility	VIX
Natural log of corn/wheat	Commodity	C/W
Natural log of soybeans/soybean oil		S/BO
Natural log of soybeans/soybean meal		S/SM
Natural log of gold/silver		GC/SL
Natural log of S&P 500/Nasdaq 100	Stock indices	SPX/NDX
Natural log of S&P 500/Russell 2000		SPX/RUT
Natural log of Bear Stearns/Merrill Lynch	Stock Pairs	BSC/MER
Natural log of CVS/Walgreen		CVS/WAG
Natural log of Delta/AMR Corporation		DAL/AMR
Natural log of Dupont/Dow Chemical		DD/DOW
Natural log of Fannie Mae/Freddie Mac		FNM/FRE
Natural log of General Motors/Ford		GM/F
Natural log of Coca Cola/Pepsi		KO/PEP
Natural log of Motorola/Texas Instruments		MOT/TXN
Natural log of Microsoft/Intel		MSFT/INTC
Natural log of Pfizer/Merck		PFE/MRK
Natural log of Verizon/SBC Communications		VZ/SBC
Natural log of Wal-Mart/Home Depot		WMT/HD
Natural log of Exxon Mobil/British Petroleum		XOM/BP
Natural log of Royal Dutch/Shell		RD/SC
Natural log of Unilever NV/Unilever PLC		UN/UL
Natural log of PHLX Gold and Silver Index/Gold	Commodity vs. Stock	XAU/GC
Natural log of AMEX Oil Index/Crude oil		XOI/CL

FIGURE 9.17

Table of Relative Value Markets. Thirty relative value markets are tested in our performance evaluation.

Position size = $10,000/100-day standard deviation of price changes

We test our stable of relative value markets on seven strategies:

- Channel breakout
- Dual moving average crossover
- Relative Strength Index
- Stochastics
- Momentum
- Difference from 100-day moving average
- Difference between 10- and 40-day moving averages

The results are analyzed in a similar fashion to futures markets and stocks.

Channel Breakout

The channel breakout is the first strategy we test on relative value markets. Longs are entered when a market's close is the highest close of the past 40 days, and shorts entered when a market's close is the lowest close of the past 40 days. Longs are exited if today's close is the lowest of the past 20 days. Shorts are exited if today's close is the highest of the past 20 days.

The channel breakout produces profits in only 4 out of 12 years (Figures 9.18a and 9.18b). Generally a losing strategy, some bright spots occur within credit spreads and stock index pairs trading. Performance on stock pairs is terrible, with only 2 out of 15 stock pairs generating profits over the 12-year test.

Dual Moving Average Crossover

We use crosses of two moving averages for creating trading signals. A 10-day and 40-day simple moving average is calculated every day. Long entries are established if the 10-day average crosses above the 40-day average. Short entries are established if the 10-day average crosses below the 40-day average.

The chart in Figure 9.19 details moving average crossover signals applied to the yield spread between two-year and 10-year Treasury notes. We see that the price action is very choppy, and often our strategy buys at short-term highs and sells at short-term lows. Trend-following strategies such as this may not be ideal for relative value markets.

Although performance of the moving average crossover is better than the channel breakout, the results leave much to be desired (Figures 9.20a and 9.20b). The moving average crossover produces profits in only 3 of the 12 years tested. After making money in 1990 and 1991, the strategy has performed very poorly since.

Momentum

Testing a strategy utilizing 80-day momentum, long entries are established if today's close is greater than the close 80 days ago, and short entries are established if today's close is less than the close 80 days ago.

The characteristics of trend-following strategies applied to relative value markets is just what we would expect. Testing the 80-day momentum strategy, our third trend-following strategy, produces losses similar to the previous two strategies (Figures 9.21a and 9.21b). The 80-day momentum strategy generates profits in the first two years of the test, followed by 10 consecutive years of losses. Volatility and stock pairs perform especially poorly. Only 2 of the 15 stock pairs generate profits.

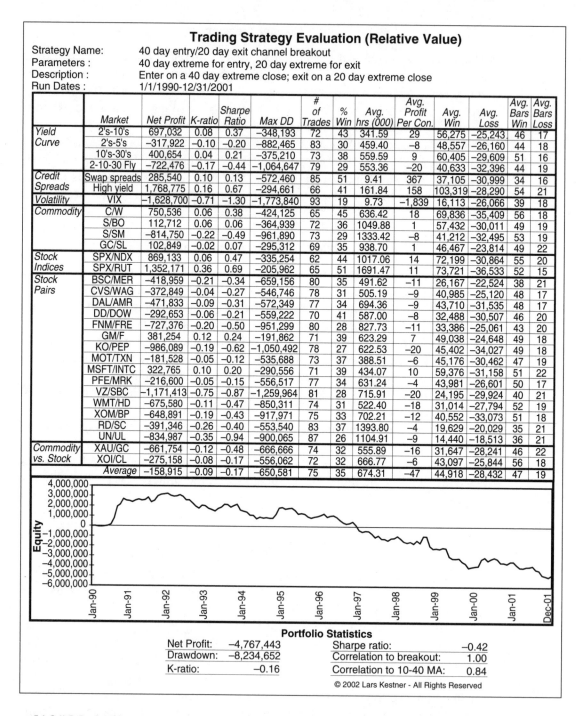

Trading Strategy Evaluation (Relative Value)

Strategy Name: 40 day entry/20 day exit channel breakout
Parameters : 40 day extreme for entry, 20 day extreme for exit
Description : Enter on a 40 day extreme close; exit on a 20 day extreme close
Run Dates : 1/1/1990-12/31/2001

	Market	Net Profit	K-ratio	Sharpe Ratio	Max DD	# of Trades	% Win	Avg. hrs (000)	Avg. Profit Per Con.	Avg. Win	Avg. Loss	Avg. Bars Win	Avg. Bars Loss
Yield Curve	2's-10's	697,032	0.08	0.37	−348,193	72	43	341.59	29	56,275	−25,243	46	17
	2's-5's	−317,922	−0.10	−0.20	−882,465	83	30	459.40	−8	48,557	−26,160	44	18
	10's-30's	400,654	0.04	0.21	−375,210	73	38	559.59	9	60,405	−29,609	51	16
	2-10-30 Fly	−722,476	−0.17	−0.44	−1,064,647	79	29	553.36	−20	40,633	−32,396	44	19
Credit Spreads	Swap spreads	285,540	0.10	0.13	−572,460	85	51	9.41	367	37,105	−30,999	34	16
	High yield	1,768,775	0.16	0.67	−294,661	66	41	161.84	158	103,319	−28,290	54	21
Volatility	VIX	−1,628,700	−0.71	−1.30	−1,773,840	93	19	9.73	−1,839	16,113	−26,066	39	18
Commodity	C/W	750,536	0.06	0.38	−424,125	65	45	636.42	18	69,836	−35,409	56	18
	S/BO	112,712	0.06	0.06	−364,939	72	36	1049.88	1	57,432	−30,011	49	19
	S/SM	−814,750	−0.22	−0.49	−961,890	73	29	1333.42	−8	41,212	−32,495	53	19
	GC/SL	102,849	−0.02	0.07	−295,312	69	35	938.70	1	46,467	−23,814	49	22
Stock Indices	SPX/NDX	869,133	0.06	0.47	−335,254	62	44	1017.06	14	72,199	−30,864	55	20
	SPX/RUT	1,352,171	0.36	0.69	−205,962	65	51	1691.47	11	73,721	−36,533	52	15
Stock Pairs	BSC/MER	−418,959	−0.21	−0.34	−659,156	80	35	491.62	−11	26,167	−22,524	38	21
	CVS/WAG	−372,849	−0.04	−0.27	−546,746	78	31	505.19	−9	40,985	−25,120	48	17
	DAL/AMR	−471,833	−0.09	−0.31	−572,349	77	34	694.36	−9	43,710	−31,535	48	17
	DD/DOW	−292,653	−0.06	−0.21	−559,222	70	41	587.00	−8	32,488	−30,507	46	20
	FNM/FRE	−727,376	−0.20	−0.50	−951,299	80	28	827.73	−11	33,386	−25,061	43	20
	GM/F	381,254	0.12	0.24	−191,862	71	39	623.29	7	49,038	−24,648	49	18
	KO/PEP	−986,089	−0.19	−0.62	−1,050,492	78	27	622.53	−20	45,402	−34,027	49	18
	MOT/TXN	−181,528	−0.05	−0.12	−535,688	73	37	388.51	−6	45,176	−30,462	47	19
	MSFT/INTC	322,765	0.10	0.20	−290,556	71	39	434.07	10	59,376	−31,158	51	22
	PFE/MRK	−216,600	−0.05	−0.15	−556,517	77	34	631.24	−4	43,981	−26,601	50	17
	VZ/SBC	−1,171,413	−0.75	−0.87	−1,259,964	81	28	715.91	−20	24,195	−29,924	40	21
	WMT/HD	−675,580	−0.11	−0.47	−850,311	74	31	522.40	−18	31,014	−27,794	52	19
	XOM/BP	−648,891	−0.19	−0.43	−917,971	75	33	702.21	−12	40,552	−33,073	51	18
	RD/SC	−391,346	−0.26	−0.40	−553,540	83	37	1393.80	−4	19,629	−20,029	35	21
	UN/UL	−834,987	−0.35	−0.94	−900,065	87	26	1104.91	−9	14,440	−18,513	36	21
Commodity vs. Stock	XAU/GC	−661,754	−0.12	−0.48	−666,666	74	32	555.89	−16	31,647	−28,241	46	22
	XOI/CL	−275,158	−0.08	−0.17	−556,062	72	32	666.77	−6	43,097	−25,844	56	18
	Average	−158,915	−0.09	−0.17	−650,581	75	35	674.31	−47	44,918	−28,432	47	19

Portfolio Statistics

Net Profit:	−4,767,443	Sharpe ratio:	−0.42
Drawdown:	−8,234,652	Correlation to breakout:	1.00
K-ratio:	−0.16	Correlation to 10-40 MA:	0.84

© 2002 Lars Kestner - All Rights Reserved

FIGURE 9.18a

Channel Breakout Strategy Applied to Relative Value Markets. The Channel Breakout Strategy does not generate profits on our relative value markets.

Breakdown Statistics (Relative Value)

System Name: 40 day entry/20 day exit channel breakout
Parameters: 40 day extreme for entry, 20 day extreme for exit
Description: Enter on a 40 day extreme close; exit on a 20 day extreme close
Run Dates: 1/1/1990-12/31/2001

Breakdown by Market Sector

Market Sector	Average Net Profit	Average K-ratio	Average Sharpe Ratio	Average Max DD	Average Num Trades	Average % Win	Avg. Profit Per Contract	Average Win	Average Loss	Avg. Bars Win	Avg. Bars Loss
Rates	14,322	-0.04	-0.02	-667,629	77	35	2	51,468	-28,352	46	17
Credit	1,027,158	0.13	0.40	-433,561	76	46	262	70,212	-29,645	44	19
Volatility	-1,628,700	-0.71	-1.30	-1,773,840	93	19	-1,839	16,113	-26,066	39	18
Commodity	37,837	-0.03	0.01	-511,567	70	36	3	53,737	-30,432	52	19
Stock Index	1,110,652	0.21	0.58	-270,608	64	47	13	72,960	-33,698	54	18
Stock Pairs	-445,739	-0.16	-0.35	-693,049	77	33	-8	36,636	-27,398	45	19
Stock/Comm.	-468,456	-0.10	-0.33	-611,364	73	32	-11	37,372	-27,043	51	20

Performance Breakdown by Year

Year	Net Profit	K-ratio	Sharpe Ratio	Year	Net Profit	K-ratio	Sharpe Ratio
1990	2,509,119	0.55	1.88	1996	-1,469,361	-0.63	-1.92
1991	744,226	0.34	0.94	1997	-579,241	-0.37	-0.84
1992	-1,210,463	-0.65	-1.80	1998	-1,217,603	-0.17	-0.87
1993	-537,939	0.01	-0.61	1999	-1,790,056	-0.85	-3.79
1994	396,370	0.06	0.42	2000	481,951	0.02	0.51
1995	-776,681	-0.54	-1.39	2001	-1,319,288	-0.58	-1.89

Profitability Windows

Length	Number of Windows	Num. of Profitable Windows	Percent Profitable
1 Month	144	64	44.44%
3 Months	142	51	35.92%
6 Months	139	42	30.22%
12 Months	133	40	30.08%
18 Months	127	23	18.11%
24 Months	121	13	10.74%

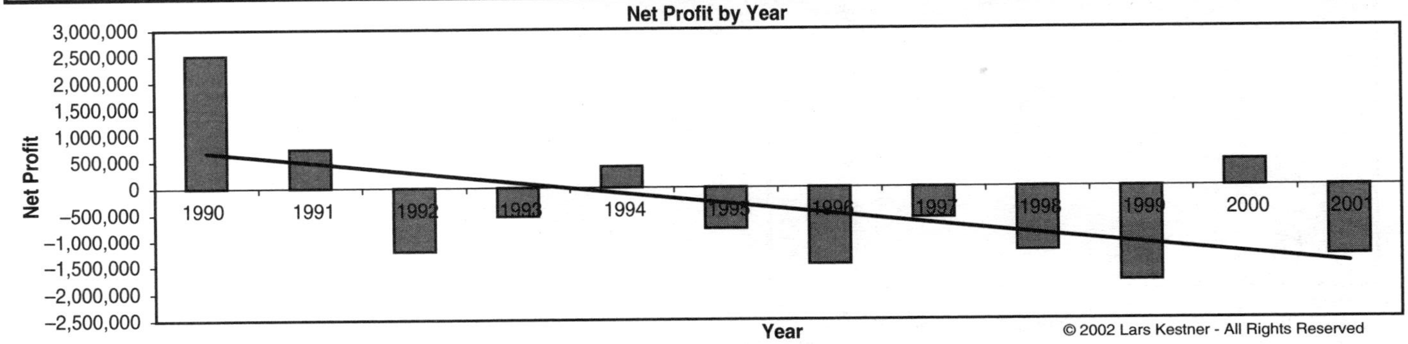

Net Profit by Year

© 2002 Lars Kestner - All Rights Reserved

FIGURE 9.18b

Channel Breakout Strategy Applied to Relative Value Markets. The Channel Breakout Strategy does not generate profits on our relative value markets.

271

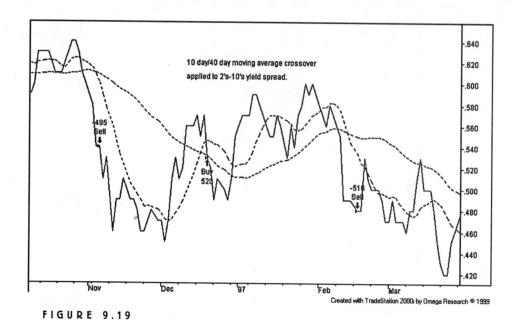

FIGURE 9.19

Moving Average Crossover Applied to Two's-10's Yield Difference. Our Moving Average Crossover tends to get whipsawed, buying at highs and selling at lows.

Stochastics

Two oscillators are tested on our relative value markets. The first uses a 14-day Slow %K stochastic to generate long and short entries. Long entries are established when today's 14-day Slow %K stochastic falls below and then rises back above 20. Short entries are established when today's 14-day Slow %K stochastic rises above and then falls below 80.

Our first countertrend trading strategy produces attractive profits when applied to our 30 relative value markets (Figures 9.22a and 9.22b). After losing money in 1990 and 1991, applying a 14-day Slow %K stochastic to trade has generated profits in 7 of the past 10 years. Especially strong are the results generated from trading volatility and stock pairs.

Relative Strength Index

In testing a 14-day Relative Strength Index, long entries are established if today's 14-day RSI falls below 35 and short entries are established if today's 14-day RSI rises above 65. There are no other rules and no rules for exiting positions, except for an entry in the opposite direction.

The chart in Figure 9.23 details signals applied to the yield spread between two-year and 10-year Treasury notes. As spreads rallied in late March, the 14-day

Trading Strategy Evaluation (Relative Value)

Strategy Name: 10 day/40 day Dual Moving Average Crossover
Parameters :   10 day average, 40 day average
Description :   Enter long when 10 day average crosses above 40 day average, short on cross below
Run Dates :   1/1/1990-12/31/2001

	Market	Net Profit	K-ratio	Sharpe Ratio	Max DD	# of Trades	% Win	Avg. hrs (000)	Avg. Profit Per Con.	Avg. Win	Avg. Loss	Avg. Bars Win	Avg. Bars Loss
Yield	2's-10's	235,256	0.02	0.11	−584,486	88	38	332.85	6	59,209	−32,410	51	22
Curve	2's-5's	−299,835	−0.11	−0.15	−1,029,865	112	42	461.21	−6	34,718	−30,051	36	20
	10's-30's	904,718	0.09	0.46	−428,450	92	36	566.74	15	61,407	−20,942	56	19
	2-10-30 Fly	−616,285	−0.17	−0.37	−932,295	106	33	560.29	−13	32,664	−26,604	43	20
Credit	Swap spreads	271,450	0.12	0.11	−292,000	97	51	9.21	284	33,485	−28,902	43	18
Spreads	High yield	1,237,047	0.12	0.44	−358,206	80	36	159.15	90	100,808	−34,916	66	20
Volatility	VIX	−1,209,060	−0.51	−0.85	−1,421,540	133	31	9.86	−957	15,644	−20,612	36	16
Commodity	C/W	958,174	0.07	0.44	−450,085	96	44	639.96	16	58,487	−27,044	48	19
	S/BO	482,926	0.14	0.24	−406,788	85	39	1056.71	5	60,645	−29,019	58	21
	S/SM	−603,895	−0.12	−0.30	−1,193,963	93	40	1345.46	−5	36,928	−35,690	51	19
	GC/SL	417,735	0.06	0.23	−288,898	76	34	917.04	5	63,237	−25,697	65	26
Stock	SPX/NDX	1,099,510	0.09	0.61	−350,194	82	44	1051.22	12	65,563	−28,419	59	17
Indices	SPX/RUT	1,149,401	0.25	0.53	−232,086	80	41	1713.06	8	82,016	−34,813	64	19
Stock	BSC/MER	−648,514	−0.17	−0.42	−870,916	104	30	482.20	−13	30,786	−22,318	47	20
Pairs	CVS/WAG	−639,632	−0.08	−0.38	−915,779	98	34	500.79	−13	39,031	−29,913	54	19
	DAL/AMR	−635,213	−0.07	−0.34	−764,648	116	35	723.75	−8	36,853	−28,616	41	17
	DD/DOW	2,122	0.01	0.00	−554,597	98	43	588.57	0	36,763	−27,766	45	20
	FNM/FRE	−520,110	−0.13	−0.34	−954,381	113	35	802.05	−6	27,629	−22,193	42	18
	GM/F	468,689	0.08	0.27	−310,006	91	41	617.00	7	52,745	−28,927	56	17
	KO/PEP	−1,054,047	−0.18	−0.56	−1,095,996	118	31	624.47	−14	36,329	−29,546	44	17
	MOT/TXN	−125,835	−0.04	−0.07	−669,719	101	37	391.00	−3	47,303	−29,500	51	17
	MSFT/INTC	820,567	0.13	0.42	−376,788	88	43	456.51	20	61,488	−30,945	56	17
	PFE/MRK	−420,003	−0.12	−0.24	−512,535	106	37	623.27	−6	37,001	−27,463	46	18
	VZ/SBC	−726,397	−0.31	−0.47	−886,050	113	41	742.97	−9	21,697	−26,148	36	20
	WMT/HD	−217,049	0.01	−0.13	−709,965	86	41	521.10	−5	30,033	−25,378	54	21
	XOM/BP	−335,730	−0.10	−0.19	−674,743	104	30	675.33	−5	46,867	−24,377	50	19
	RD/SC	−373,030	−0.13	−0.32	−684,225	118	37	1355.75	−3	21,058	−18,323	38	17
	UN/UL	−769,393	−0.26	−0.67	−1,093,412	118	36	1080.47	−6	17,025	−20,152	37	19
Commodity	XAU/GC	−619,005	−0.13	−0.38	−895,148	103	34	538.02	−11	32,110	−25,783	47	20
vs. Stock	XOI/CL	545,249	0.09	0.32	−354,964	88	42	701.80	9	52,168	−27,156	57	18
	Average	−40,673	−0.04	−0.07	−676,424	99	38	674.93	−20	44,390	−27,321	49	19

Portfolio Statistics

Net Profit :   −1,220,189   Sharpe ratio :   −0.10
Drawdown :   −5,606,897   Correlation to breakout :   0.84
K-ratio :   −0.10   Correlation to 10-40 MA :   1.00

© 2002 Lars Kestner - All Rights Reserved

FIGURE 9.20a

Moving Average Crossover Strategy Applied to Relative Value Markets. The Moving Average Crossover does not generate profits on our relative value markets.

Breakdown Statistics (Relative Value)

System Name : 10 day/40 day Dual Moving Average Crossover
Parameters : 10 day average, 40 day average
Description : Enter long when 10 day average crosses above 40 day average, short on cross below
Run Dates : 1/1/1990-12/31/2001

Breakdown by Market Sector

Market Sector	Average Net Profit	Average K-ratio	Average Sharpe Ratio	Average Max DD	Average Num Trades	Average % Win	Avg. Profit Per Contract	Average Win	Average Loss	Avg. Bars Win	Avg. Bars Loss
Rates	55,964	-0.04	0.01	-743,774	100	37	1	46,999	-27,502	47	20
Credit	754,249	0.12	0.28	-325,103	89	43	187	67,146	-31,909	54	19
Volatility	-1,209,060	-0.51	-0.85	-1,421,540	133	31	-957	15,644	-20,612	36	16
Commodity	313,735	0.04	0.15	-584,934	88	39	5	54,824	-29,363	55	21
Stock Index	1,124,456	0.17	0.57	-291,140	81	43	10	73,789	-31,616	61	18
Stock Pairs	-344,905	-0.09	-0.23	-738,251	105	37	-4	36,174	-26,104	47	18
Stock/Comm.	-36,878	-0.02	-0.03	-625,056	96	38	-1	42,139	-26,470	52	19

Performance Breakdown by Year

Year	Net Profit	K-ratio	Sharpe Ratio	Year	Net Profit	K-ratio	Sharpe Ratio
1990	2,905,026	0.72	2.24	1996	-1,254,119	-0.32	-1.12
1991	1,245,467	0.38	1.54	1997	-408,494	-0.36	-0.44
1992	-789,412	-0.42	-0.85	1998	-960,937	-0.07	-0.73
1993	-1,058,896	-0.29	-1.31	1999	-472,557	-0.37	-0.34
1994	528,364	0.11	0.57	2000	3,833	-0.10	0.00
1995	-267,371	-0.21	-0.38	2001	-690,205	-0.19	-0.57

Profitability Windows

Length	Number of Windows	Num. of Profitable Windows	Percent Profitable
1 Month	144	75	52.08%
3 Months	142	60	42.25%
6 Months	139	52	37.41%
12 Months	133	51	38.35%
18 Months	127	37	29.13%
24 Months	121	32	26.45%

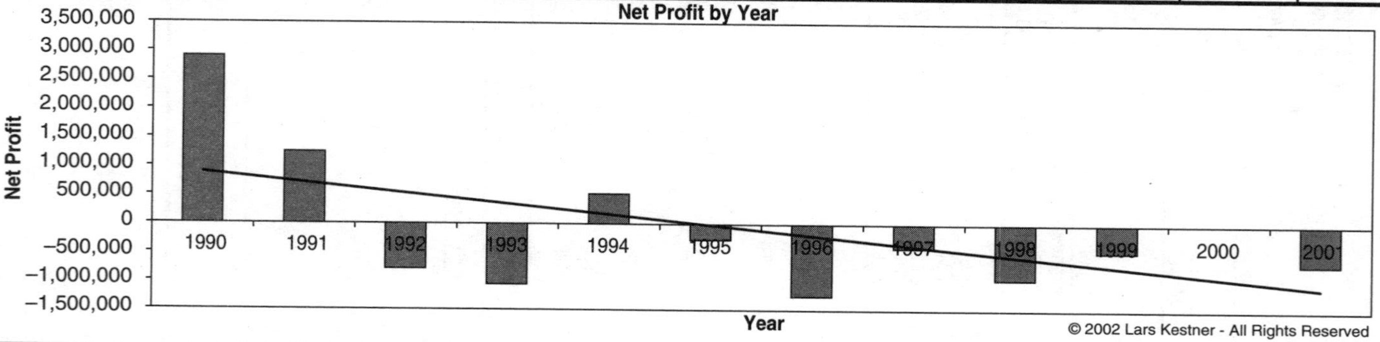

Net Profit by Year

© 2002 Lars Kestner - All Rights Reserved

FIGURE 9.20b

Moving Average Crossover Strategy Applied to Relative Value Markets. The Moving Average Crossover does not generate profits on our relative value markets.

274

Trading Strategy Evaluation (Relative Value)

Strategy Name :   80 day momentum
Parameters :   80 day momentum triggers entries and exits
Description :   Buy if today's close > close of 80 days ago; exit if today's close < close of 80 days ago
Run Dates :   1/1/1990–12/31/2001

	Market	Net Profit	K-ratio	Sharpe Ratio	Max DD	# of Trades	% Win	Avg. hrs (000)	Avg. Profit Per Con.	Avg. Win	Avg. Loss	Avg. Bars Win	Avg. Bars Loss
Yield Curve	2's-10's	1,598,921	0.22	0.74	−304,380	126	48	337.99	20	30,429	−15,267	34	9
	2's-5's	1,081,213	0.07	0.56	−505,268	150	49	452.04	5	23,513	−17,712	26	11
	10's-30's	154,568	0.02	0.07	−528,680	139	48	530.64	2	26,139	−22,141	31	12
	2-10-30 Fly	152,731	0.00	0.08	−602,579	162	44	531.36	0	26,083	−20,317	29	9
Credit Spreads	Swap spreads	182,470	0.05	0.08	−381,030	116	42	8.09	207	28,971	−18,285	40	16
	High yield	1,291,257	0.10	0.39	−327,797	132	37	177.15	56	56,061	−17,372	40	12
Volatility	VIX	−2,837,330	−0.68	−1.70	−2,868,450	338	33	9.55	−878	7,736	−16,368	9	9
Commodity	C/W	761,821	0.07	0.35	−467,571	153	43	632.10	8	34,167	−17,579	32	11
	S/BO	194,277	0.05	0.09	−417,228	130	42	1057.02	1	33,132	−21,153	36	15
	S/SM	−285,581	0.00	−0.15	−568,181	127	33	1317.94	−2	32,758	−19,613	47	12
	GC/SL	−155,902	−0.04	−0.09	−580,746	191	45	894.22	−1	17,204	−15,888	23	10
Stock Indices	SPX/NDX	397,073	0.05	0.18	−322,208	111	40	940.07	4	38,972	−19,116	52	11
	SPX/RUT	470,634	0.08	0.20	−420,990	93	38	1641.69	3	48,073	−22,318	59	17
Stock Pairs	BSC/MER	−607,555	−0.16	−0.38	−1,033,974	224	45	482.41	−6	13,234	−16,106	18	9
	CVS/WAG	−1,156,259	−0.28	−0.60	−1,490,565	194	35	519.41	−14	17,955	−20,379	20	12
	DAL/AMR	−1,948,703	−0.41	−0.97	−1,977,362	192	31	689.68	−15	15,337	−21,580	20	13
	DD/DOW	−1,116,598	−0.31	−0.68	−1,257,664	216	35	613.82	−9	16,836	−16,988	19	11
	FNM/FRE	−1,487,381	−0.50	−0.84	−1,512,468	273	40	803.15	−7	11,405	−16,595	13	9
	GM/F	56,101	−0.04	0.03	−623,073	160	43	603.77	0	23,377	−17,605	30	10
	KO/PEP	−722,894	−0.07	−0.41	−813,292	199	37	627.61	−6	20,310	−17,489	21	11
	MOT/TXN	−208,515	−0.01	−0.12	−638,139	173	39	372.52	−3	23,565	−16,785	32	8
	MSFT/INTC	331,365	0.08	0.17	−284,276	137	45	442.49	5	32,612	−22,227	36	11
	PFE/MRK	−596,030	−0.11	−0.29	−881,903	179	41	635.74	−6	16,926	−18,237	23	12
	VZ/SBC	−1,598,256	−0.25	−0.97	−1,686,266	203	32	735.05	−11	15,384	−18,828	21	12
	WMT/HD	−1,001,829	−0.22	−0.58	−1,066,840	242	41	505.46	−8	12,121	−15,603	16	10
	XOM/BP	−397,610	−0.07	−0.22	−804,598	166	34	712.02	−3	25,474	−16,583	31	11
	RD/SC	−1,170,134	−0.42	−0.78	−1,249,398	314	46	1335.60	−3	9,005	−14,965	12	8
	UN/UL	−1,635,764	−0.44	−1.16	−1,698,036	403	41	1079.29	−4	8,963	−12,940	9	6
Commodity vs. Stock	XAU/GC	−740,196	−0.14	−0.44	−923,104	191	41	536.62	−7	15,446	−17,333	23	11
	XOI/CL	−321,520	−0.09	−0.18	−510,848	171	37	686.32	−3	22,517	−17,221	30	10
	Average	−377,188	−0.12	−0.25	−891,564	187	40	663.69	−22	23,457	−18,020	28	11

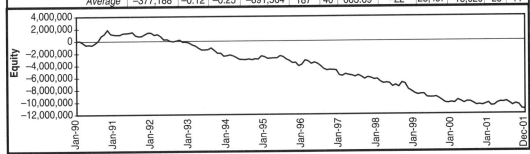

Portfolio Statistics

Net Profit :	−11,315,626	Sharpe ratio :	−0.92
Drawdown :	−13,187,360	Correlation to breakout :	0.64
K-ratio :	−0.39	Correlation to 10-40 MA :	0.57

© 2002 Lars Kestner - All Rights Reserved

FIGURE 9.21a

Momentum Strategy Applied to Relative Value Markets. Like other trend following strategies, the Momentum Strategy does not produce profits on relative value markets.

Breakdown Statistics (Relative Value)

System Name : 80 day momentum
Parameters : 80 day momentum trigger entries and exits
Description : Buy if today's close > close of 80 days ago; exit if today's close < close of 80 days ago
Run Dates : 1/1/1990-12/31/2001

Breakdown by Market Sector

Market Sector	Average Net Profit	Average K-ratio	Average Sharpe Ratio	Average Max DD	Average Num Trades	Average % Win	Avg. Profit Per Contract	Average Win	Average Loss	Avg. Bars Win	Avg. Bars Loss
Rates	746,858	0.08	0.36	-485,227	144	47	7	26,541	-18,859	30	11
Credit	736,864	0.07	0.24	-354,414	124	40	131	42,516	-17,829	40	14
Volatility	-2,837,330	-0.68	-1.70	-2,868,450	338	33	-878	7,736	-16,368	9	9
Commodity	128,654	0.02	0.05	-508,432	150	41	1	29,315	-18,558	34	12
Stock Index	433,854	0.07	0.19	-371,599	102	39	3	43,522	-20,717	55	14
Stock Pairs	-884,004	-0.21	-0.52	-1,134,524	218	39	-6	17,500	-17,527	21	10
Stock/Comm.	-530,858	-0.12	-0.31	-716,976	181	39	-5	18,982	-17,277	10	10

Performance Breakdown by Year

Year	Net Profit	Sharpe Ratio	K-ratio	Year	Net Profit	K-ratio	Sharpe Ratio
1990	1,072,852	0.72	0.30	1996	-1,815,839	-0.57	-1.36
1991	274,104	0.35	0.02	1997	-614,527	-0.45	-0.83
1992	-1,619,518	-2.06	-0.59	1998	-2,362,500	-0.40	-1.68
1993	-2,120,367	-2.42	-0.73	1999	-1,492,126	-0.83	-2.10
1994	-165,300	-0.22	-0.10	2000	-114,684	-0.22	-0.13
1995	-1,282,332	-1.35	-0.38	2001	-1,078,488	-0.16	-0.97

Profitability Windows

Length	Number of Windows	Num. of Profitable Windows	Percent Profitable
1 Month	144	59	40.97%
3 Months	142	39	27.46%
6 Months	139	31	22.30%
12 Months	133	19	14.29%
18 Months	127	13	10.24%
24 Months	121	7	5.79%

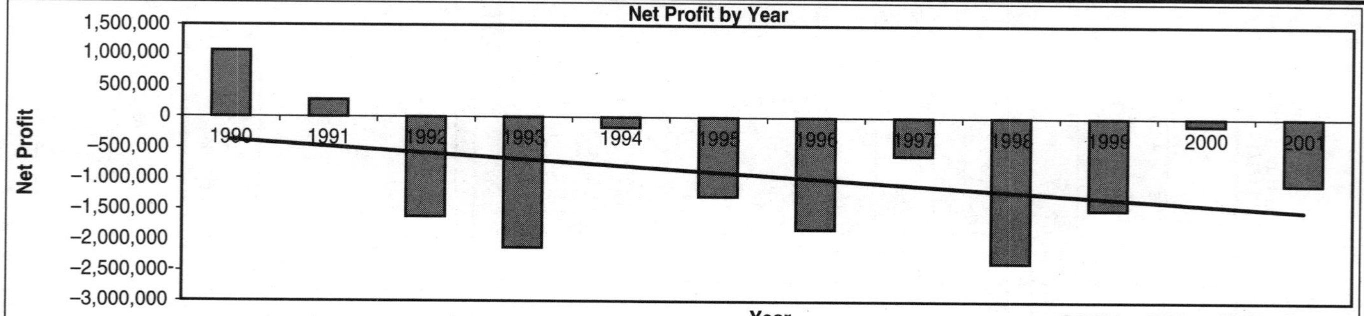

Net Profit by Year

© 2002 Lars Kestner - All Rights Reserved

FIGURE 9.21b

Momentum Strategy Applied to Relative Value Markets. Like other trend following strategies, the Momentum Strategy does not produce profits on relative value markets.

RSI rose above 65. Consequently, we entered short. In mid-July, after choppy price action, the spread market began to decline and the RSI fell below 35. At the point we closed our short position and entered long.

The performance of a 14-day RSI applied to our relative value markets (Figures 9.24a and 9.24b) is even better than the 14-day Slow %K stochastic. The 14-day RSI strategy is profitable in 8 of 12 years, generating a Sharpe ratio of 0.34 and a K-ratio of 0.16. Eleven out of 15 stock pairs are profitable.

Difference from 100-Day Moving Average

Using the traditional strategy above, the results show that most of our 30 relative value markets respond poorly to trend-following strategies, and all of which— channel breakout, moving average crossover, and momentum—lost money. The two countertrend strategies—Slow %K stochastics and RSI—made money. This feeds into our theory that using countertrend and trend exhaustion strategies will perform well when trading two or more markets that are natural substitutes.

Now we introduce the first of two new strategies designed to take advantage of this mean reversion in relative value markets. In countertrend trading strategies, we want to enter short positions when prices rise quickly. When prices fall quickly, we want to enter long positions. The first strategy we introduce normalizes the difference between today's close and today's 100-day moving average. First, we subtract the 100-day moving average from today's close. Next, we divide this value by the standard deviation of the past 100 price changes, to normalize this value across all markets. The result is a statistic that measures deviation from a long-term mean.

100-day Statistic = (Close minus 100-day moving average of closes) / 100-day standard deviation of price changes

Long entries are entered when the 100-day stat falls below –2.5, while short positions are established when this statistic rises above 2.5. Long entries are exited when the 100-day stat rises above zero, and short entries are exited when the 100-day stat falls below zero.

We apply this trading strategy to the VIX in the chart in Figure 9.25. As the VIX rises above its 100-day moving average in late October, the 100-day stat rises above 2.5 and we enter short. As the market retreats in late November, the 100-day stat falls below zero and we exit our short position. The decline continues through mid-February, when the 100-day stat falls below –2.5. At this point we enter long, exiting approximately one month later when the 100-day stat rises above zero.

Our creativity and thought process seems to pay off in this new strategy (Figures 9.26a and 9.26b). Our new strategy produces a Sharpe ratio of 0.49 and a K-ratio of 0.24, making money in 8 of the 12 years tested. Strongest performance

Trading Strategy Evaluation (Relative Value)

Strategy Name : 14 day Slow %K stochastics
Parameters : 14 days in stochastic calculation
Description : Enter long when %K crosses above 20, enter short when %K crosses below 80
Run Dates : 1/1/1990-12/31/2001

	Market	Net Profit	K-ratio	Sharpe Ratio	Max DD	# of Trades	% Win	Avg. hrs (000)	Avg. Profit Per Con.	Avg. Win	Avg. Loss	Avg. Bars Win	Avg. Bars Loss
Yield Curve	2's-10's	−431,043	−0.03	−0.19	−802,730	134	63	331.63	−5	25,580	−48,865	14	34
	2's-5's	12,939	0.02	0.01	−564,970	130	65	448.12	1	23,347	−43,260	15	38
	10's-30's	−243,842	0.01	−0.12	−584,754	140	60	562.62	−3	22,949	−39,003	13	34
	2-10-30 Fly	251,105	0.11	0.12	−436,515	138	67	550.23	6	22,692	−36,438	15	34
Credit Spreads	Swap spreads	−258,440	−0.08	−0.12	−952,000	156	69	9.20	−163	20,243	−48,989	13	33
	High yield	−2,227,816	−0.15	−0.71	−2,433,675	114	59	161.89	−115	28,550	−85,831	14	43
Volatility	VIX	1,630,490	0.35	1.04	−196,700	151	70	9.74	1,137	23,608	−18,472	14	33
Commodity	C/W	−1,436,564	−0.17	−0.68	−1,507,073	116	53	653.40	−19	25,006	−53,772	14	40
	S/BO	126,292	0.03	0.06	−919,659	140	65	1034.15	1	28,363	−50,229	12	38
	S/SM	1,308,262	0.34	0.67	−301,258	138	70	1351.50	7	29,461	−37,168	15	39
	GC/SL	−42,328	0.08	−0.02	−370,748	129	60	919.19	0	24,716	−37,096	14	39
Stock Indices	SPX/NDX	−848,315	−0.04	−0.43	−962,276	119	65	1039.21	−7	25,355	−66,630	14	46
	SPX/RUT	−1,570,349	−0.25	−0.73	−1,809,982	119	58	1762.10	−7	25,862	−65,263	13	42
Stock Pairs	BSCMER	762,514	0.14	0.52	−385,941	148	62	494.78	10	24,575	−26,843	13	32
	CVS/WAG	91,830	0.01	0.06	−507,461	133	64	502.50	2	23,449	−39,007	15	37
	DAL/AMR	−329,084	−0.08	−0.19	−691,774	141	61	716.94	−3	23,358	−42,409	14	33
	DD/DOW	−310,596	−0.03	−0.18	−787,042	132	55	581.90	−3	23,727	−33,680	15	33
	FNM/FRE	746,079	0.19	0.47	−486,780	146	67	813.01	6	21,864	−28,716	15	32
	GM/F	−435,620	−0.08	−0.24	−843,491	137	66	611.91	−5	21,885	−52,602	14	38
	KO/PEP	817,982	0.17	0.47	−362,845	148	70	616.67	9	22,351	−32,879	15	34
	MOT/TXN	−66,903	−0.02	−0.04	−648,838	133	65	392.91	−1	23,642	−44,858	15	38
	MSFT/INTC	−424,326	−0.06	−0.21	−896,248	131	65	435.00	−7	25,579	−56,471	13	41
	PFE/MRK	890,074	0.19	0.48	−419,406	142	68	631.87	10	26,599	−36,188	14	37
	VZ/SBC	1,670,054	0.59	1.12	−177,808	156	74	726.25	15	23,507	−26,419	14	33
	WMT/HD	843,196	0.14	0.48	−301,772	133	65	522.28	12	25,475	−28,710	15	37
	XOM/BP	1,176,590	0.26	0.68	−245,756	143	71	691.75	12	25,990	−34,894	15	36
	RD/SC	1,066,086	0.48	0.74	−249,644	135	69	1403.40	6	21,723	−22,387	16	35
	UN/UL	517,295	0.30	0.45	−185,845	142	63	1106.89	3	16,743	−19,030	15	32
Commodity vs. Stock	XAU/GC	970,459	0.28	0.52	−251,713	148	66	542.11	12	25,546	−30,612	13	34
	XOI/CL	666,767	0.24	0.34	−439,655	149	67	675.61	8	22,639	−30,340	13	33
	Average	164,093	0.10	0.14	−657,479	137	65	676.63	31	24,146	−40,569	14	36

Portfolio Statistics

Net Profit :	4,922,788	Sharpe ratio :	0.40
Drawdown :	−2,579,686	Correlation to breakout :	−0.69
K-ratio :	0.21	Correlation to 10-40 MA :	−0.61

© 2002 Lars Kestner - All Rights Reserved

FIGURE 9.22a

Stochastic Strategy Applied to Relative Value Markets. This countertrend strategy shows some promise.

Breakdown Statistics (Relative Value)

System Name : 14 day Slow %K stochastics
Parameters : 14 days in stochastic calculation
Description : Enter long when %K falls below 20, enter short when %K rises above 80
Run Dates : 1/1/1990-12/31/2001

Breakdown by Market Sector

Market Sector	Average Net Profit	Average K-ratio	Average Sharpe Ratio	Average Max DD	Average Num Trades	Average % Win	Avg. Profit Per Contract	Average Win	Average Loss	Avg. Bars Win	Avg. Bars Loss
Rates	-102,710	0.03	-0.05	-597,242	136	64	0	23,642	-41,892	14	35
Credit	-1,243,128	-0.12	-0.41	-1,692,838	135	64	-139	24,396	-67,410	14	38
Volatility	1,630,490	0.35	1.04	-196,700	151	70	1,137	23,608	-18,472	14	33
Commodity	-11,085	0.07	0.01	-774,685	131	62	-3	26,887	-44,566	14	39
Stock Index	-1,209,332	-0.15	-0.58	-1,386,129	119	61	-7	25,609	-65,946	14	44
Stock Pairs	467,678	0.15	0.31	-479,377	140	66	4	23,364	-35,006	14	35
Stock/Comm.	818,613	0.26	0.43	-345,684	149	67	10	24,092	-30,476	13	33

Performance Breakdown by Year

Year	Net Profit	K-ratio	Sharpe Ratio	Year	Net Profit	K-ratio	Sharpe Ratio
1990	-2,173,105	-0.47	-1.55	1996	1,786,731	0.50	1.50
1991	413,225	0.24	0.56	1997	864,950	0.68	1.63
1992	726,201	0.28	1.03	1998	2,002,389	0.34	1.19
1993	1,917,103	0.49	2.39	1999	866,062	0.36	0.66
1994	-1,152,919	-0.19	-1.26	2000	-283,086	-0.08	-0.25
1995	771,759	0.54	1.59	2001	-814,727	-0.24	-0.91

Profitability Windows

Length	Number of Windows	Num. of Profitable Windows	Percent Profitable
1 Month	144	83	57.64%
3 Months	142	89	62.68%
6 Months	139	93	66.91%
12 Months	133	90	67.67%
18 Months	127	88	69.29%
24 Months	121	96	79.34%

Net Profit by Year

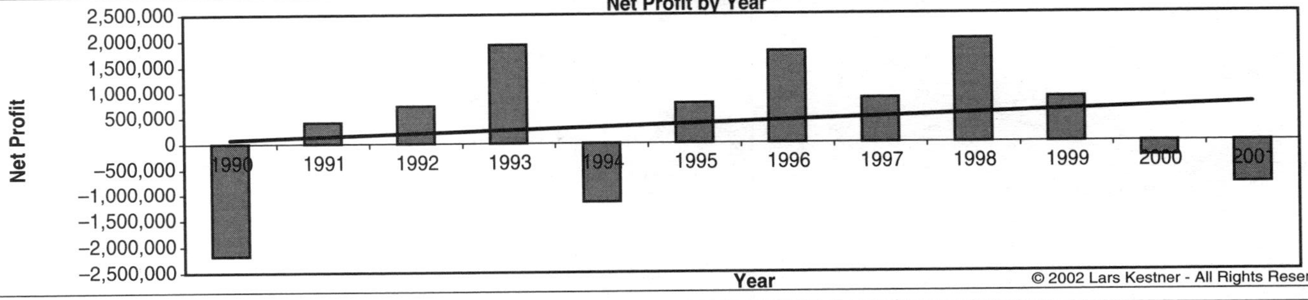

© 2002 Lars Kestner - All Rights Reserved

FIGURE 9.22b

Stochastic Strategy Applied to Relative Value Markets. This countertrend strategy shows some promise.

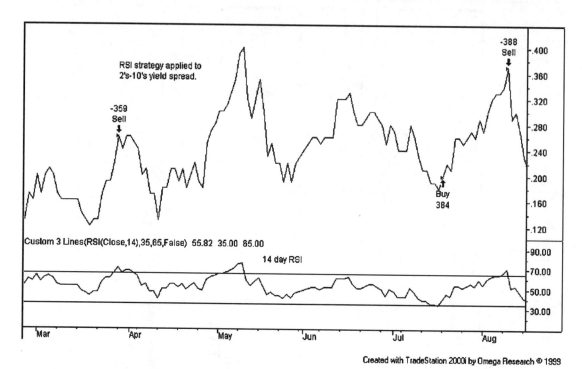

Created with TradeStation 2000i by Omega Research © 1999

FIGURE 9.23

RSI Strategy Applied to Two's-10's Yield Difference. Our RSI Strategy appears to identify tops and bottoms in the yield difference between two-year and ten-year notes.

is contributed from trading volatility, stock pairs, and the relative pricing between commodities and underlying stocks. Thirteen out of 15 stock pairs generate profits. Credit spreads and the relative performance of stock indices perform very poorly.

Difference Between 10- and 40-Day Moving Average

Our second method of determining price exhaustion compares the value of a 10-day moving average to the value of a 40-day moving average. When prices move too quickly, the 10-day moving average will separate from the 40-day moving average. This occurs because the 10-day moving average is more sensitive to recent price changes than the 40-day moving average.

$$10/40 \text{ stat} = (10\text{-day moving average} - 40\text{-day moving average}) / 100\text{-day standard deviation of price changes}$$

Long entries are established when the 10/40 stat falls below –2 and are exited if the 10/40 stat rises above zero. Short entries are established when the 10/40 stat rises above 2 and are exited if the 10/40 stat falls below zero.

Trading Strategy Evaluation (Relative Value)

Strategy Name : 14 day RSI
Parameters : 14 days in RSI calculation
Description : Enter long when %K falls below 35, enter short when %K rises above 65
Run Dates : 1/1/1990-12/31/2001

	Market	Net Profit	K-ratio	Sharpe Ratio	Max DD	# of Trades	% Win	Avg. hrs (000)	Avg. Profit Per Con.	Avg. Win	Avg. Loss	Avg. Bars Win	Avg. Bars Loss
Yield Curve	2's-10's	−609,085	−0.08	−0.28	−843,098	38	68	333.90	−43	47,456	−148,254	43	149
	2's-5's	−477,333	−0.02	−0.24	−772,165	22	77	466.09	3	60,508	−198,631	69	313
	10's-30's	−488,435	−0.05	−0.25	−623,410	36	64	549.78	−23	34,248	−95,138	46	145
	2-10-30 Fly	634,684	0.12	0.35	−379,502	38	79	521.51	40	58,090	−119,783	44	201
Credit Spreads	Swap spreads	−316,740	−0.10	−014	−824,000	46	52	8.51	−829	45,356	−64,240	33	101
	High yield	−1,604,259	−0.15	−0.58	−2,226,217	41	66	156.81	−245	40,340	−190,312	46	123
Volatility	VIX	1,281,900	0.27	0.74	−238,590	31	94	10.44	4,007	45,661	−13,855	79	350
Commodity	C/W	−648,977	−0.09	−0.31	−820,507	35	57	632.78	−29	42,901	−99,676	63	114
	S/BO	77,456	−0.02	0.04	−827,388	47	66	1050.48	2	45,854	−83,894	42	105
	S/SM	31,405	0.02	0.02	−419,270	42	64	1257.49	1	45,041	−78,663	44	121
	GC/SL	7,349	0.04	0.00	−474,796	35	57	918.92	2	42,601	−52,415	54	131
Stock Indices	SPX/NDX	−785,311	−0.06	−0.37	−903,505	37	41	1103.39	−19	64,145	−78,417	35	112
	SPX/RUT	−577,918	−0.08	−0.26	−861,609	39	56	1777.82	−7	50,396	−94,560	52	109
Stock Pairs	BSC/MER	786,386	0.21	0.49	−265,189	35	74	502.33	45	46,720	−47,983	60	161
	CVS/WAL	−57,232	0.01	−0.03	−533,965	30	63	529.84	−4	41,087	−76,889	78	138
	DAL/AMR	362,124	0.08	0.20	−354,597	40	65	679.98	13	42,784	−53,676	61	98
	DD/DOW	30,069	0.02	0.02	−364,066	31	52	618.47	2	48,084	−49,285	73	123
	FNM/FRE	1,068,405	0.30	0.67	−233,334	31	81	745.69	47	53,597	−40,551	83	97
	GM/F	−693,392	−0.18	−0.40	−782,531	32	47	600.24	−33	38,573	−70,821	52	124
	KO/PEP	760,037	0.06	0.43	−493,593	38	76	596.38	36	50,818	−72,948	47	160
	MOT/TXN	146,598	0.02	0.09	−473,052	34	62	396.97	13	49,556	−66,404	54	135
	MSFT/INTC	−118,065	−0.01	−0.06	−567,639	41	63	434.81	−6	48,153	−90,797	44	120
	PFE/MRK	674,809	0.13	0.38	−400,978	33	70	631.62	34	52,579	−50,791	66	142
	VZ/SBC	1,329,975	0.34	0.78	−250,472	39	82	771.65	43	50,356	−44,684	54	173
	WMT/HD	1,359,504	0.32	0.81	−167,166	44	80	560.87	55	46,967	−31,451	60	100
	XOM/BP	−348,082	−0.03	−0.20	−874,051	26	54	702.07	−19	53,295	−91,764	43	194
	RD/SC	1,108,010	0.37	0.92	−148,295	25	84	1506.77	29	60,528	−42,301	114	146
	UN/UL	528,807	0.13	0.55	−94,952	14	71	1215.80	32	62,957	−23,158	232	164
Commodity vs. Stock	XAU/GC	754,181	0.17	0.45	−270,368	42	76	554.42	33	39,826	−50,083	53	116
	XOI/CL	123,347	−0.01	0.07	−474,920	31	68	681.47	8	51,918	−91,572	58	175
	Average	144,674	0.06	0.13	−565,441	35	67	683.91	106	48,680	−77,100	63	148

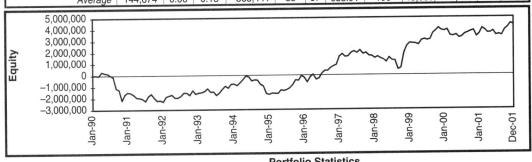

Portfolio Statistics

Net Profit :	4,340,217	Sharpe ratio :	0.34
Drawdown :	−2,599,481	Correlation to breakout :	−0.75
K-ratio	0.16	Correlation to 10-40 MA :	−0.69

© 2002 Lars Kestner - All Rights Reserved

FIGURE 9.24a

RSI Strategy Applied to Relative Value Markets. Similar to the Stochastic Strategy, the RSI Strategy also shows some promise when applied to relative value markets.

Breakdown Statistics (Relative Value)

System Name : 14 day RSI
Parameters : 14 days in RSI calculation
Description : Enter long when %K falls below 35, enter short when %K rises above 65
Run Dates : 1/1/1990-12/31/2001

Breakdown by Market Sector

Market Sector	Average Net Profit	Average K-ratio	Average Sharpe Ratio	Average Max DD	Average Num Trades	Average % Win	Avg. Profit Per Contract	Average Win	Average Loss	Avg. Bars Win	Avg. Bars Loss
Rates	−235,042	0.00	−0.11	−654,544	34	72	−6	50,076	−140,452	50	202
Credit	−960,500	−0.13	−0.36	−1,525,109	44	59	−537	42,848	−127,276	40	112
Volitility	1,281,900	0.27	0.74	−238,590	31	94	4,007	45,661	−13,855	79	350
Commodity	−133,192	−0.01	−0.06	−635,490	40	61	−6	44,099	−78,662	51	118
Stock Index	−681,615	−0.07	−0.32	−882,557	38	48	−13	57,270	−86,489	43	110
Stock Pairs	462,530	0.12	0.31	−400,259	33	68	19	49,737	−56,900	75	138
Stock/Comm.	438,764	0.08	0.26	−372,644	37	72	21	45,872	−70,828	56	145

Performance Breakdown by Year

Year	Net Profit	K-ratio	Sharpe Ratio	Year	Net Profit	K-ratio	Sharpe Ratio
1990	−1,475,248	−0.39	−0.96	1996	1,840,108	0.55	1.60
1991	−813,850	−0.27	−1.11	1997	−147,722	−0.01	−0.20
1992	757,832	0.29	0.91	1998	1,302,115	0.09	0.72
1993	763,636	0.26	0.95	1999	1,047,145	0.60	30.28
1994	−912,351	−0.16	−0.92	2000	−274,147	−0.02	−0.30
1995	1,455,162	0.82	2.20	2001	795,685	0.14	0.82

Profitability Windows

Length	Number of Windows	Num. of Profitable Windows	Percent Profitable
1 Month	144	78	54.17%
3 Months	142	82	57.75%
6 Months	139	85	61.15%
12 Months	133	91	68.42%
18 Months	127	91	71.65%
24 Months	121	102	84.30%

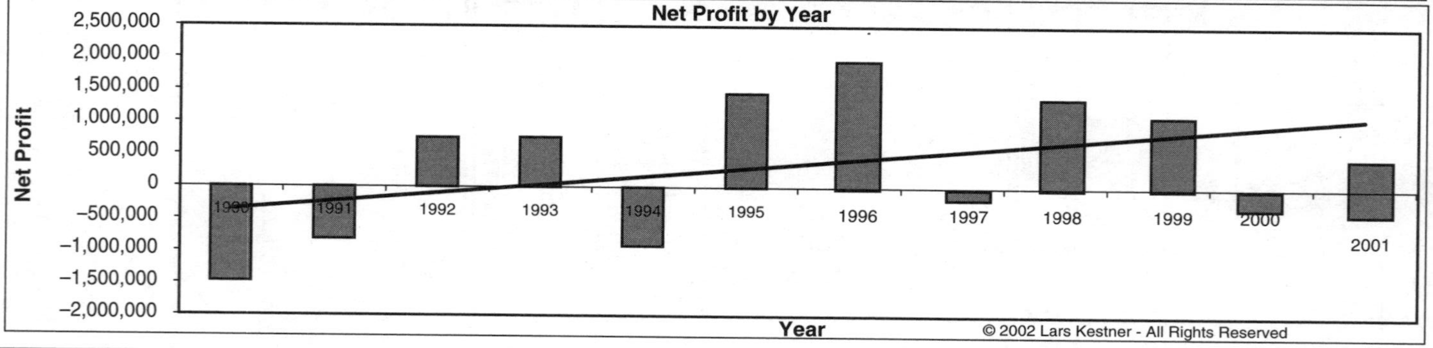

Net Profit by Year

© 2002 Lars Kestner - All Rights Reserved

FIGURE 9.24b

RSI Strategy Applied to Relative Value Markets. Similar to the Stochastic Strategy, the RSI Strategy also shows some promise when applied to relative value markets.

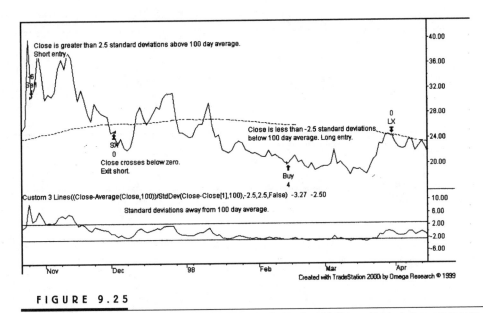

FIGURE 9.25

Difference from 100-day Moving Average Strategy Applied to the VIX. This oscillator strategy appears to correctly identify tops and bottoms in the VIX.

This strategy is applied to five-year swap spreads in Figure 9.27. We enter long in early August as the 10/40 stat falls below –2. Longs are exited as the 10/40 stat rises above zero in mid-September. A short position is established in late September as the 10/40 stat rises above 2. This short position is covered only a few days later as the 10/40 stat falls below zero.

Trading based on the difference between the 10-day and 40-day moving average does not produce strong results on relative value markets (Figures 9.28a and 9.28b). Among the strongest sectors are volatility and stock pairs. Trading in 11 of the 15 stock pairs is profitable. Most interesting is the fact that performance appears to be improving dramatically over time. After performing poorly in 1990 and 1991, the 10-day/40-day average strategy has produced profits in eight of the past ten years. In fact, the most profitable year was 2001. These results suggest that despite its overall mediocre performance, the 10-day/40-day average exhaustion strategy may perform superbly in the future.

NEW MARKETS, NEW OPPORTUNITIES

The strategies in this chapter mostly confirm our theory that the relative value markets introduced and studied are not prone to trends. Trend-following strategies were largely unsuccessful, especially when applied to stock pairs and volatility

Trading Strategy Evalution (Relative Value)

Strategy Name : Difference from 100 day moving average
Parameters : 100 day average
Description : Enter long when stat falls below –2.5, short when stat rises above 2.5, flat on crosses of zero
Run Dates : 1/1/1990–12/31/2001

	Market	Net Profit	K-ratio	Sharpe Ratio	Max DD	# of Trades	% Win	Avg. hrs (000)	Avg. Profit Per Con.	Avg Win	Avg Loss	Avg. Bars Win	Avg. Bars Loss
Yield Curve	2's-10's	–1,134,921	–0.11	–0.59	–1,204,453	42	64	344.28	–65	28,033	–113,011	20	116
	2's-5's	–594,457	0.00	–0.33	–753,424	52	77	473.11	5	29,564	–87,367	14	117
	10's-30's	–349,637	–0.03	–0.18	–510,610	51	69	553.25	–13	25,735	–78,490	21	94
	2-10-30 Fly	246,082	0.12	0.14	–298,542	55	71	563.96	13	34,932	–60,409	21	87
Credit Spreads	Swap spreads	–402,790	–0.14	–0.19	–935,543	47	64	8.88	–990	28,092	–73,855	24	98
	High yield	–1,284,717	–0.15	–0.42	–2,031,543	47	70	161.90	–167	32,905	–168,167	27	121
Volatility	VIX	1,714,990	0.50	1.35	–181,930	75	89	10.33	2,226	28,171	–20,388	20	39
Commodity	C/W	–613,350	–0.07	–0.30	–1,128,894	53	72	659.04	–17	27,501	–110,259	24	99
	S/BO	–75,430	–0.04	–0.04	–651,336	54	67	1074.36	–1	32,078	–67,646	21	94
	S/SM	303,967	0.05	0.20	–339,716	49	69	1328.22	4	34,305	–58,340	27	102
	GC/SL	155,061	0.05	0.09	–489,064	55	71	925.57	4	25,151	–49,903	29	69
Stock Indices	SPX/NDX	–855,891	–0.13	–0.44	–964,684	45	62	1046.11	–18	24,901	–91,741	28	101
	SPX/RUT	–1,001,906	–0.22	–0.46	–1,356,563	44	61	1759.93	–12	29,509	–100,600	27	110
Stock Pairs	BSC/MER	519,432	0.21	0.40	–254,041	59	75	474.88	19	24,346	–36,786	21	90
	CVS/WAG	208,054	0.07	0.14	–406,696	55	69	517.45	13	27,883	–41,296	27	70
	DAL/AMR	1,440,848	0.36	0.87	–211,296	64	83	717.52	31	34,060	–35,737	25	87
	DD/DOW	571,262	0.21	0.42	–282,302	62	71	607.79	16	27,185	–33,992	20	78
	FNM/FRE	1,129,884	0.44	0.80	–233,334	65	78	792.26	22	29,087	–25,255	18	77
	GM/F	–393,804	–0.13	–0.24	–496,060	47	55	604.50	–11	25,639	–47,256	21	86
	KO/PEP	896,749	0.18	0.56	–244,555	65	78	614.29	22	31,055	–49,075	20	87
	MOT/TXN	168,111	0.02	0.10	–416,846	58	69	389.25	7	26,558	–49,678	22	87
	MSFT/INTC	–419,078	–0.15	–0.25	–597,389	50	68	439.37	–19	31,522	–92,671	25	106
	PFE/MRK	609,396	0.14	0.36	–426,076	60	72	634.18	17	29,805	–37,977	19	85
	VZ/SBC	1,450,517	0.45	1.12	–197,344	78	85	747.73	25	29,028	–38,777	19	81
	WMT/HD	828,545	0.13	0.54	–284,742	62	76	528.08	25	28,955	–35,605	20	84
	XOM/BP	188,769	0.04	0.12	–467,208	51	69	720.35	5	32,697	–59,727	18	104
	RD/SC	895,407	0.59	0.88	–123,405	63	84	1381.72	10	22,318	–29,360	22	74
	UN/UL	843,961	0.50	1.04	–115,600	61	85	1154.13	12	19,518	–18,101	20	77
Commodity vs. Stock	XAU/GC	535,617	0.15	0.37	–250,630	53	70	537.65	19	26,429	–27,642	30	83
	XOI/CL	151,710	0.09	0.09	–397,009	55	76	681.63	6	28,408	–73,957	19	119
	Average	191,079	0.10	0.21	–541,693	56	72	681.72	40	28,512	–60,436	22	91

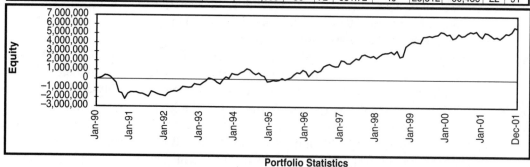

Portfolio Statistics

Net Profit :	5,732,381	Sharpe ratio :	0.49
Drawdown :	–2,620,449	Correlation to breakout :	–0.80
K-ratio :	0.24	Correlation to 10-40 MA :	–0.70

© 2002 Lars Kestner - All Rights Reserved

FIGURE 9.26a

Difference from 100-day Moving Average Strategy Applied to Relative Value Markets. This strategy produces very profitable trades.

Breakdown Statistics (Relative Value)

System Name :
Parameters : Difference from 100 day moving average
100 day average
Description : Enter long when stat falls below –2.5, short when stat rises above 2.5, flat on crosses of zero
Run Dates : 1/1/1990-12/31/2001

Breakdown by Market Sector

Market Sector	Average Net Profit	Average K-ratio	Average Sharpe Ratio	Average Max DD	Average Num Trades	Average % Win	Avg. Profit Per Contract	Average Win	Average Loss	Avg. Bars Win	Avg. Bars Loss
Rates	-458,233	-0.01	-0.24	-691,757	50	70	-15	29,566	-84,819	19	103
Credit	-843,754	-0.14	-0.31	-1,483,522	47	67	-578	30,498	-121,011	26	109
Volitility	1,714,990	0.50	1.35	-181,930	75	89	2,226	28,171	-20,388	20	39
Commodity	-57,438	0.00	-0.01	-652,253	53	70	-3	29,759	-71,537	25	91
Stock Index	-928,899	-0.18	-0.45	-1,160,624	45	62	-15	27,205	-96,171	28	106
Stock Pairs	595,870	0.20	0.46	-317,126	60	74	13	27,977	-42,086	21	85
Stock/Comm.	343,664	0.12	0.23	-323,820	54	73	12	27,419	-50,799	24	101

Performance Breakdown by Year

Year	Net Profit	K-ratio	Sharpe Ratio	Year	Net Profit	K-ratio	Sharpe Ratio
1990	-1,435,256	-0.41	-0.97	1996	1,242,797	0.46	1.11
1991	-416,993	-0.17	-0.61	1997	272,883	0.29	0.35
1992	1,230,722	0.77	2.10	1998	1,794,843	0.27	1.27
1993	1,151,305	0.27	1.20	1999	798,438	0.52	2.15
1994	-747,535	-0.21	-0.83	2000	-285,454	0.08	-0.30
1995	1,105,692	0.73	1.85	2001	1,013,733	0.20	1.05

Profitability Windows

Length	Number of Windows	Num. of Profitable Windows	Percent Profitable
1 Month	144	75	52.08%
3 Months	142	97	68.31%
6 Months	139	97	69.78%
12 Months	133	100	75.19%
18 Months	127	102	80.31%
24 Months	121	106	87.60%

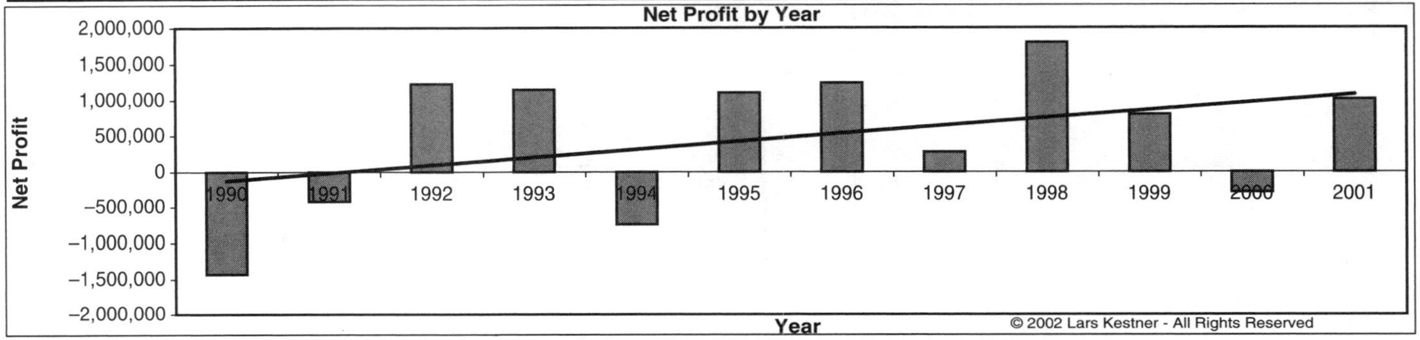

Net Profit by Year

© 2002 Lars Kestner - All Rights Reserved

FIGURE 9.26b

Difference from 100-day Moving Average Strategy Applied to Relative Value Markets. This strategy produces very profitable trades.

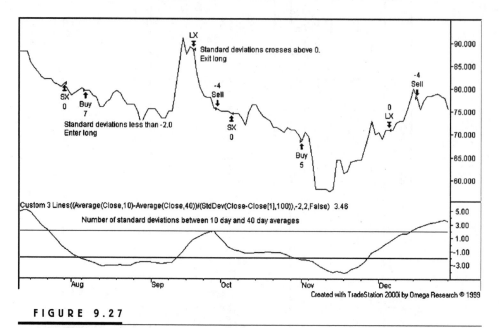

FIGURE 9.27

Difference Between 10-day and 40-day Average Strategy Applied to Five-Year Swap Spreads. This oscillator strategy appears to pinpoint short-term tops and bottoms.

markets. On the other hand, credit spreads and the relative performances of stock indices do seem to trend, as indicated by strong performance from channel break-out and moving average crossover strategies. Yield curve markets, commodity substitutes, and commodity/stock performance show mixed performance and no strong propensity to trend or mean revert.

By introducing new markets, we have stumbled upon a vast world of new opportunities. Unlike stock and futures markets, which have been studied ad nauseum for market inefficiencies, these new relative value markets are largely untapped and open to study using sound quantitative techniques. Although access to many of these new markets is limited only to well-capitalized institutions, new products may soon allow entry to smaller individual investors.

Trading Strategy Evaluation (Relative Value)

Strategy Name : Difference between 10 day and 40 day moving average
Parameters : 10 day and 40 day averages
Description : Enter long when stat falls below −2, short when stat rises above 2, flat on crosses of zero
Run Dates : 1/1/1990-12/31/2001

	Market	Net Profit	K-ratio	Sharpe Ratio	Max DD	# of Trades	% Win	Avg. hrs (000)	Avg. Profit Per Con.	Avg. Win	Avg. Loss	Avg. Bars Win	Avg. Bars Loss
Yield Curve	2's-10's	−386,244	−0.02	−0.21	−534,470	48	69	339.29	−21	33,629	−96,342	24	71
	2's-5's	93,182	0.06	0.06	−513,780	43	65	450.11	5	39,867	−67,433	24	60
	10's-30's	−696,499	−0.10	−0.43	−803,043	41	59	511.19	−31	26,735	−76,261	25	63
	2-10-30 Fly	593,941	0.27	0.42	−222,013	56	70	551.28	24	34,244	−35,267	22	52
Credit Spreads	Swap spreads	−67,190	−0.03	−0.03	−612,000	52	69	8.79	−169	30,364	−73,143	27	57
	High yield	−1,478,602	−0.15	−0.59	−2,046,757	46	54	161.00	−196	41,404	−118,316	26	73
Volatility	VIX	777,020	0.59	0.75	−143,660	38	76	9.59	2,195	33,253	−18,281	23	49
Commodity	C/W	−844,003	−0.10	−0.45	−1,029,945	48	65	636.43	−28	29,322	−104,021	25	68
	S/BO	−520,143	−0.13	−0.30	−931,199	51	55	1044.31	−10	36,075	−66,533	25	60
	S/SM	272,696	0.10	0.16	−346,848	52	56	1353.83	4	36,318	−33,970	27	54
	GC/SL	−21,406	−0.01	−0.01	−431,533	49	65	916.24	1	35,678	−65,813	28	67
Stock Indices	SPX/NDX	−857,526	−0.05	−0.51	−934,626	47	55	1097.94	−16	36,409	−84,851	24	67
	SPX/RUT	−1,289,499	−0.30	−0.68	−1,466,584	46	46	1776.70	−15	36,194	−79,393	24	67
Stock Pairs	BSC/MER	587,535	0.24	0.52	−211,321	52	71	500.91	22	28,278	−31,637	28	50
	CVS/WAG	109,795	−0.01	0.08	−430,219	52	69	508.58	4	28,195	−56,841	25	60
	DAL/AMR	373,636	0.05	0.24	−263,905	57	61	698.93	9	32,109	−34,100	25	47
	DD/DOW	138,417	0.07	0.11	−334,915	52	63	602.66	4	31,267	−47,022	23	57
	FNM/FRE	469,073	0.21	0.40	−291,088	43	74	787.80	14	29,959	−43,901	22	51
	GM/F	−551,075	−0.17	−0.38	−667,152	48	48	605.94	−17	30,348	−47,861	22	59
	KO/PEP	790,931	0.14	0.61	−228,820	53	72	604.02	25	35,575	−37,394	22	59
	MOT/TXN	−186,527	−0.07	−0.13	−347,539	49	57	390.38	−10	29,117	−47,705	25	55
	MSFT/INTC	−552,185	−0.13	−0.34	−823,572	50	60	439.76	−25	32,319	−75,682	28	67
	PFE/MRK	206,996	0.03	0.15	−392,520	51	63	633.77	6	31,519	−42,190	21	56
	VZ/SBC	374,054	0.22	0.35	−132,662	48	67	758.67	10	23,130	−23,043	29	46
	WMT/HD	415,701	004	0.28	−276,679	47	66	545.69	18	31,731	−33,202	24	57
	XOM/BP	−420,099	−0.07	−0.31	−688,730	46	50	716.13	−13	27,423	−45,688	25	54
	RD/SC	360,210	0.26	0.56	−207,524	36	78	1498.43	7	20,545	−27,258	26	47
	UN/UL	401,615	0.39	0.74	−81,302	25	80	1147.00	14	25,221	−19,265	26	45
Commodity vs. Stock	XAU/GC	687,765	0.24	0.53	−231,944	59	75	543.08	21	27,767	−35,600	25	53
	XOI/CL	−626,980	−0.16	−0.48	−747,108	37	41	697.32	−24	41,537	−56,820	21	62
	Average	−61,514	0.05	0.04	−545,782	47	63	684.53	60	31,851	−54,161	25	58

Portfolio Statistics

Net Profit :	−1,845,411	Sharpe ratio :	−0.18
Drawdown :	−4,402,173	Correlation to breakout :	−0.85
K-ratio :	−0.02	Correlation to 10-40 MA :	−0.86

© 2002 Lars Kestner - All Rights Reserved

FIGURE 9.28a

Difference Between 10-day and 40-day Strategy Applied to Relative Value Markets. Performance of this strategy is not as exciting as other counter-trend strategies.

Breakdown Statistics (Relative Value)

System Name :
Parameters :
Description : Difference between 10 day and 40 day moving average
10 day and 40 day averages
Enter long when stat falls below –2, short when stat rises above 2, flat on crosses of zero
Run Dates : 1/1/1990-12/31/2001

Breakdown by Market Sector

Market Sector	Average Net Profit	Average K-ratio	Average Sharpe Ratio	Average Max DD	Average Num Trades	Average % Win	Avg. Profit Per Contract	Average Win	Average Loss	Avg. Bars Win	Avg. Bars Loss
Rates	-98,905	0.05	-0.04	-518,327	47	66	-6	33,619	-68,826	24	61
Credit	-772,896	-0.09	-0.31	-1,329,379	49	62	-182	35,884	-95,730	26	65
Volatility	777,020	0.59	0.75	-143,660	38	76	2,195	33,253	-18,281	23	49
Commodity	-278,214	-0.03	-0.15	-684,881	50	60	-8	34,348	-67,584	26	62
Stock Index	-1,073,513	-0.18	-0.60	-1,200,605	47	50	-16	36,302	-82,122	24	67
Stock Pairs	167,872	0.08	0.19	-358,530	47	65	5	29,116	-40,853	25	54
Stock/Comm.	30,393	0.04	0.03	-489,526	48	58	-1	34,652	-46,210	23	58

Performance Breakdown by Year

Year	Net Profit	K-ratio	Sharpe Ratio	Year	Net Profit	K-ratio	Sharpe Ratio
1990	-2,241,580	-0.51	-1.73	1996	414,882	0.11	0.57
1991	-1,516,883	-0.95	-2.64	1997	311,460	0.28	0.41
1992	647,696	0.40	0.98	1998	100,234	-0.12	0.08
1993	20,588	-0.10	0.03	1999	395,401	0.32	1.34
1994	-933,100	-0.18	-1.31	2000	-702,768	-0.09	-0.76
1995	286,351	0.35	0.48	2001	1,377,482	0.34	1.49

Profitability Windows

Length	Number of Windows	Num. of Profitable Windows	Percent Profitable
1 Month	144	68	47.22%
3 Months	142	71	50.00%
6 Months	139	65	46.76%
12 Months	133	65	48.87%
18 Months	127	64	50.39%
24 Months	121	62	51.24%

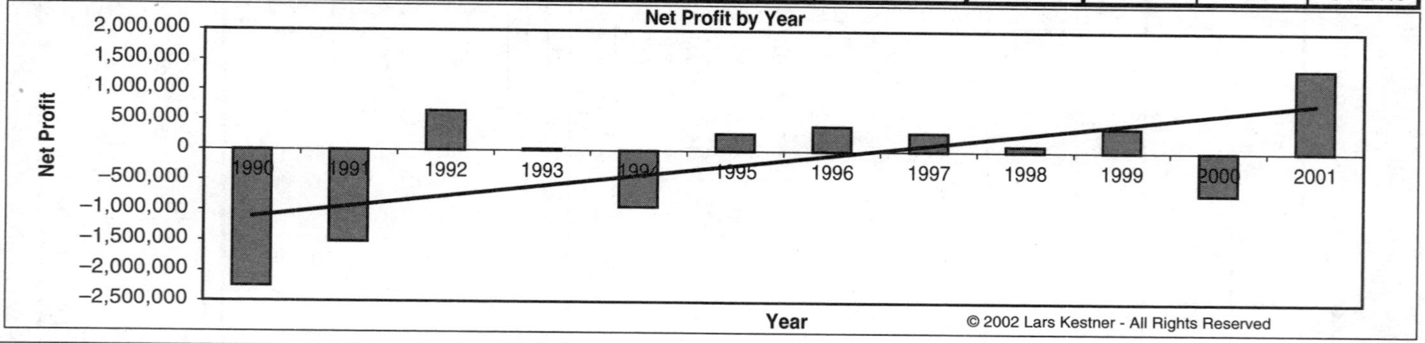

Net Profit by Year

© 2002 Lars Kestner - All Rights Reserved

FIGURE 9.28b

Difference Between 10-day and 40-day Strategy Applied to Relative Value Markets. Performance of this strategy is not as exciting as other counter-trend strategies.

CHAPTER 10

Investing in the S&P 500

Beating a Buy and Hold Return Using Quantitative Techniques

So far, we've focused on short- and medium-term trading for traders and market professionals. In addition to our professional duties of trading, market professionals have savings, 401(k)s, and other investments. Much of these investments are allocated to the equity markets. In this chapter we'll step back from complex strategies and employ quantitative techniques to analyze short- and long-term moves in the U.S. equity market. Using macroeconomic variables such as short-term and long-term interest rates, recent market performance, day-of-month effects, and the Volatility Index, we'll create trading strategies that generate signals to be either long the market or out of the market and invested in cash.

THE POPULARITY OF EQUITIES

There was no escaping the popularity of equities over the past five years. From the dot-com bubble to the bubbly personalities of CNBC, equities became the rage among every walk of life. Penny stocks even had their day in the sun, sometimes rising tenfold in a matter of days. Exchanges were quick to offer products to a public that had the trading itch. Exchange traded funds (ETFs) such as the SPDRs and the QQQs mimic popular stock indices and trade huge dollar volumes daily.

The subsequent sell-off of mid-2000 to the present has left some investors feeling battered, bruised, and in no mood to talk about the stock market. Whether we want to or not, however, we must make decisions about our investments and allocate between stocks, bonds, and other asset classes. The quantitative techniques we have studied throughout this book can help take the emotion out of the investing process and replace it with reliable time-tested strategies.

Anyone involved in the markets over the past five years was probably too involved to understand the euphoria associated with the unbelievable market moves. My guess is that when the dust settles and time begins to put 1998 through 2001 in historic perspective, we'll see unbelievable similarities to the end of the 1920s.

The historic market rise began with the proliferation of the Internet. Popular thinking had it that new industries would be created using the Internet as a means to reach customers. In fact, entire new industries sprouted to take advantage of this technological miracle. Online retailers would sell books, CDs, and even groceries to users over the Internet. Software companies would build these sites, monitoring millions of pieces of information, including buying habits of the consumers and inventory levels in warehouses. Networking companies became highly visible as the speed and reach of fiberoptic infrastructures needed to cross oceans and penetrate metropolitan areas. At the same time, "old economy" stocks not involved in the Internet suffered on perceptions that those not first to market in this brave new world would become corporate dinosaurs.

Anything involved with technology was awarded a hefty market capitalization. Internet portals, semiconductor equipment stocks, optical networking, business-to-business software, and PC stocks all saw shares rise to unbelievable heights. The key to most business models was market penetration. Losing money to achieve that market share was not an issue.

Perhaps the most amazing story was that of Juno, an Internet service provider. In December 1999, Juno's share price had been mired in a trading range between $15 and $20. On December 20, news from the company changed everything. Juno's management announced that it would no longer charge for its Internet access. Instead, it would give away the service, in the hope of gaining market share. Some might see this as a sign that the company had no pricing power or that the move was a desperate attempt to turn around a sliding business. Investors, however, did not react the same way. The stock rallied from $17 to a high of $87 over the three days following the announcement (Figure 10.1). It was an amazing time, with extraordinary reactions from investors.

Volatility in stocks during this time was also astonishing. I believe much of the reason for this volatility was the lack of experience with the prices where stocks were trading.

When prices trade in a range, traders have experience buying and selling. Over time, they learn that buyers step in at a price, say $40, and sellers offer stock at another price, say $60. If this pattern is repeated enough times, traders have great confidence to buy stock in the $40 to $45 area and offer stock around $55 to $60. This trading range eventually dampens volatility. On the other hand, consider a stock that runs from $50 to $200 with very few retracements. Now, traders are reluctant to step in and buy. After all, what's to keep a stock from falling back to

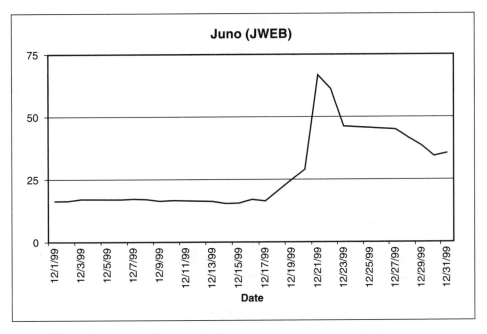

FIGURE 10.1

Juno (JWEB). Of all the strange things during the technology bubble, Juno's stock price increased by 400 percent when the company announced it would stop charging for its product.

old lows? Traders are equally reluctant to sell the stock at $200. If the stock ran from $50 to $200, what's to keep it from trading at $400? This inexperience with prices leads to a lack of liquidity and large percentage price moves. I believe the lack of a defined trading range caused increased market volatility, especially in technology stocks.

Day traders were another phenomenon that contributed to market volatility. Most of their trading involved momentum strategies where they would buy on strength and sell on weakness, specifically when they were able to spot large institutional orders. Day traders would buy or sell ahead of brokers executing those orders. This caused wild fluctuations in market prices on an intraday basis. Given the lack of overall liquidity in many technology names, day traders were able to move stocks by two to four points on very light volume.

Large option trades also affected daily volatility in the market. Many hedge funds that specialized in the technology sector ballooned in size from $25 to $50 million to well over $250 to $500 million due to performance and investor inflows. These hedge funds had enormous capital gains in many stocks that had risen five- or tenfold and were looking for methods to hedge these gains. By purchasing put options, hedge funds received the right to sell stocks if the stock declined, while keeping gains if stocks rallied. Market makers on the other side of these trades dynamically hedged the option risk by buying and selling the underlying stocks. These dynamic hedges required market makers to sell when markets declined and buy when they rallied—exacerbating large daily moves in technology names and contributing to excess market volatility.

While the popularity of equities has diminished over the past couple of years due to lagging returns, the stock market is still important both as an investment vehicle for individuals and as a means for companies to raise money from the capital markets and tweak their capital structure. In the remainder of this chapter, we'll explore methods to outperform buy and hold investment strategies.

THE IMPORTANCE OF INTEREST RATES IN PREDICTING EQUITY PRICES

The link between interest rates and returns in equities has been well documented and exists for a number of reasons. One of them can be summed up in the expression, "A Dollar Today Is Not Worth a Dollar Tomorrow." We'll go into this because many popular stock valuation models derive a company's worth by estimating the present value of future earnings.

Let's say I have $100 today and have to decide whether to loan it to my friend Joe or deposit the $100 in the bank and earn 5 percent interest.

Option 1	Option 2
Loan Joe $100 today	Deposit $100 in a bank at 5% interest
Receive $100 from Joe a year from now	Receive $105 from the bank a year from now

The fact that I can deposit my $100 today and receive $105 from the bank in a year is the principle of the time value of money. When we look at cash flows in the future, we need to adjust their value back by an interest rate to determine their present value. For example, the $100 loan to Joe may seem like a wash to most, but when we discount that repayment by the 5 percent we could be earning from the bank, the loan becomes a money-losing proposition. If all we care about is money, we're better off by putting our $100 in a bank and earning 5 percent.

Option 1	Option 2
Loan Joe $100 today	Deposit $100 in a bank at 5% interest
Receive $100 from Joe in 5 years	Receive $127 in 5 years

The concept becomes very important as the length of time increases. Suppose that Joe wishes to borrow the money for five years. Now the trade-off becomes whether to receive the original $100 from Joe after five years or to receive $127 back from the bank in five years. This example details the power of compounding. If I deposit $100 with the bank at 5 percent annual interest, at the end of year one, I will receive $105. At the beginning of year two, I deposit the $105 with the bank again at 5 percent annual interest. My $105 grows to $105 · (1 + 5%) = $110.25 at the end of year two. Again I deposit the $110.25 at the beginning of year three at 5 percent and receive $110.25 · (1 + 5%) = $115.76 at the end of year three. This process continues until the end of year five, where my original $100 becomes $127.

The same principle is applied when valuing companies.

From annual reports, we can determine a company's net profit. Suppose XYZ Inc. had $5 in profits during 2001 and is projecting this level of profitability for the foreseeable future. If we bought XYZ Inc. for $100 we would need to compare the trade-offs between paying $100 for annual cash intake of $5 and the alternative of depositing the $100 in the bank to earn interest.

	Alternatives	
Interest rate	Bank interest	XYZ returns
1%	$1	$5
5%	$5	$5
10%	$10	$5

As we see in the table above, the level of interest rates can dramatically change our preference from either buying XYZ Inc. or depositing our $100 in the bank and earning interest. Similar decisions are made in the trade-off between buying stocks and buying bonds. As a result, interest rates become very important when valuing a company's worth.

There are three theories why lower interest rates lead to higher stock prices. First, as yields fall, a company's cashflow looks more attractive versus bonds. This can raise the value of the company. Second, lower interest rates cause waves of home mortgage refinancing, and the extra cash from lower mortgage payments often finds its way into the stock market. A third potential link between interest rates and equities is that companies have greater ability to finance capital expenditure projects when interest rates are low. These expenditures modernize plants, raise productivity, and create new products through research and development. This spending often leads to improved profitability in the future.

Historical data support the theory that lower interest rates boost equity prices. If we look at monthly percentage returns of the S&P 500 versus the monthly percentage changes in the 10-year Treasury yield between 1970 and 2001 (Figure 10.2), we can see a distinct relationship. In Figure 10.2, as interest rates decline—measured by yields on the 10-year Treasury note—stocks are more likely to rise when interest rates rise. We can use this relationship to design strategies for timing the equity market.

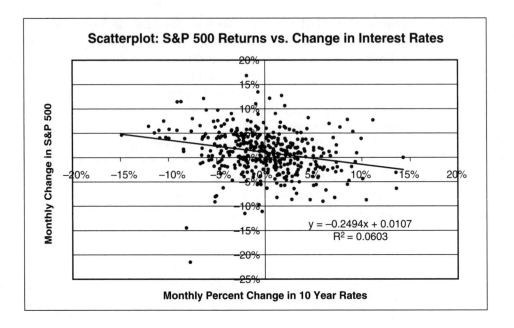

$$y = -0.2494x + 0.0107$$
$$R^2 = 0.0603$$

FIGURE 10.2

Scatterplot: S&P 500 Returns vs. Change in Interest Rates. Stock prices appear to increase when interest rates fall and fall when interest rates rise.

TESTING MEDIUM-TERM STRATEGIES

We test monthly returns of the S&P 500 using total returns—price changes plus dividends—from 1970 through the end of 2001. Positions can either be invested in the S&P 500 or cash. If invested in cash, the account receives the then going three-month T-bill rate. We will base investment decisions on past returns of the S&P 500, recent changes in 10-year Treasury note yields, and recent changes in one-year Treasury bill yields.

Most of these strategies can be considered simplistic—certainly when compared to other ideas tested previously in this book. Despite their simplicity, however, many of these strategies lead to outperformance of a buy and hold methodology, and with less risk.

When reporting results, we calculate the ending value of a $100 starting account balance. In order to better evaluate the performance of our trading methodologies, we'll calculate the ending account value of a contrary strategy, which invests exactly opposite our strategy, and compare it to our chosen strategy. When our strategy is invested in the S&P 500, the contrary account is in cash. When our strategy is in cash, the contrary strategy is invested in the S&P 500. I also report the percent of the time a strategy is invested in the market, which is a surrogate measure for risk: The less time we're in the market, the less risk we're taking with our money.

As listed in Figure 10.3, 25 strategies based on moving averages and momentum changes were tested on monthly data. The signals are generated using the monthly closing price of the S&P 500 total return index, a cumulative measure of the S&P 500 total return. For comparison purposes, the buy and hold account ends with $3661 in 2001, while the strategy always invested in cash finishes with only $944. Remember, each strategy starts with $100 in 1970.

What do these results tell us?

First, 54 percent of the strategies outperform the buy and hold case and take less risk in doing so. These performance numbers suggest that there may be an advantage to market timing.

The next important feature is that the best performing strategies were long the market when rates were falling. Buying stocks when the 10-year yield was less than its three-month average led to an ending account balance of $6819. This amounts to annual returns of 14.1 percent, compared with 11.9 percent annually for the buy and hold and 7.3 percent annually for the all cash strategy.

The other interesting performance detail is that buying the market during times of strong market returns produced some of the worst performance. The worst performing strategy bought the market when the S&P 500 was greater than its average over the past three months. This strategy turns $100 in 1970 into only $1310 in 2001—an annualized performance of only 8.4 percent—despite being invested roughly 63 percent of the time.

Perhaps the most interesting strategy is the one that invests in the market when both one year and 10-year interest rates are below their 12-month average and the stock market is above its 12-month average. Despite only being invested 38 percent of the time, this strategy produces annualized returns of 12.8 percent and handily beats a buy and hold return.

SHORT-TERM TRADING METHODOLOGIES

For those with shorter term trading horizons, we'll also develop a number of shorter term models and shed light on some market inefficiencies that are tradable using S&P 500 futures, exchange traded funds, or no-load index funds.

Index Funds and ETFs

Indexing and index funds grew tremendously during the 1990s, as equities rose in popularity with American households. Contrary to a typical mutual fund manager who picks stocks which he anticipates will beat the market, an index fund will buy all the stocks in an index and attempt only to match the performance of the index.

Index funds have the advantage of being low cost. Typical mutual funds charge 1.5 percent per year or more in expenses. This money is used to pay the portfolio manager and research analysts who pick the stocks held in the portfolio.

Strategy	Ending Account	Percent of Time Invested	Opposite Rules Ending Account
10 year yields<3 month average	6,819	50%	500
1 year yields<6 months ago	6,610	52%	523
1 year yields<12 month average	4,855	54%	712
SPX>12 month average and 1 year yields <12 month average and 10 year yields <12 month average	4,735	38%	730
1 year yields<12 months ago	4,442	53%	778
10 year yields<12 month average	4,379	54%	789
1 year yields<6 month average	4,337	51%	790
10 year yields<6 month average	4,290	51%	798
SPX>12 months ago	4,211	81%	821
1 year yields<3 months ago	4,202	48%	822
SPX>12 month average	4,123	76%	838
1 year yields<3 month average	4,089	50%	834
SPX>12 months ago and 1 year yield <12 months ago and 10 year yield <12 months ago	3,773	38%	904
Buy and Hold	3,661	100%	944
10 year yields<6 months ago	3,531	51%	979
10 year yields<12 months ago	3,165	49%	1,092
10 year yields<3 months ago	3,135	49%	1,102
SPX>6 months ago and 1 year yields <6 months ago and 10 year yields <6 months ago	2,732	33%	1,248
SPX>3 months ago and 1 year yields <3 months ago and 10 year yields <3 months ago	2,491	32%	1,369
SPX>6 month average and 1 year yields <6 month average and 10 year yields <6 month average	2,415	34%	1,418
SPX>6 months ago	2,132	72%	1,621
SPX>3 months ago	2,006	71%	1,722
SPX>6 month average	1,879	71%	1,823
SPX>3 month average and 1 year yields <3 month average and 10 year yields <3 month average	1,817	30%	1,876
SPX>3 month average	1,310	63%	2,603

FIGURE 10.3

Performance of Market Timing Strategies. Over 54 percent of the strategies beat the S&P 500 while taking less risk.

Because index funds simply match the holdings within a popular index, investment decisions are reasonably automatic and there is no need to pay for expensive stock research. Most index funds charge less than 0.3 percent in annual expenses. One of the largest mutual funds in the country is the Vanguard 500 Index Fund, which is designed to match the performance of the S&P 500. It has over $85 billion in assets.

Stock exchanges, quick to realize an opportunity, began to offer exchange traded funds in the early 1990s to compete with investors using index funds. ETFs are unit investment trusts or depository receipts that hold a basket of stocks designed to mimic a defined benchmark such as the S&P 500, the Nasdaq 100, or the Russell 2000. The ETFs are listed on stock exchanges and represent the assets that hold these baskets of stocks. As a result, individual investors can now trade stocks that behave exactly like index funds.

Unlike most index funds, which are only open to money inflows or outflows once a day, ETFs trade very actively throughout the day. They're like stocks in almost every way: ETFs trade on exchanges, they can be sold short—some even without the need for an uptick—they can be purchased on margin, and they're bought and sold through brokers. Due to their popularity, ETFs representing specific sectors and countries have been designed to give investors exposure to very precise asset classes.

Day of Week and Day of Month Effects

Early research on day of week effects was conducted in the early 1980s to determine if Monday was more volatile than other days of the week. If information drives prices, and the amount of information is disseminated equally everyday, then, the reasoning goes, Monday should be three times as volatile as Tuesday through Friday due to the news buildup over weekends. In fact, researchers discovered that, on average, Monday was equally volatile as every other day of the week. What was *not* equal were the average returns that each day of the week generated. Monday had significantly worse returns than Friday.

Over the years, it appears that the day of week effect has become muted. Well, how about the day of month and its effect on market returns?

Examining daily returns of the S&P 500 since 1990, we average returns by each day of the month. Note that we're talking specifically about calendar days. Although March 3 may be the first trading day of the month, it would be recorded as Day three in our study. Figure 10.4 details the market ups and downs by day of the month.

I first noticed the day of month pattern in my days at Salomon Brothers in 1997 while part of the equity derivatives research group. I found that stock market returns had a bias based on where they occurred within the month. Distinct periods of outperformance and underperformance emerged.

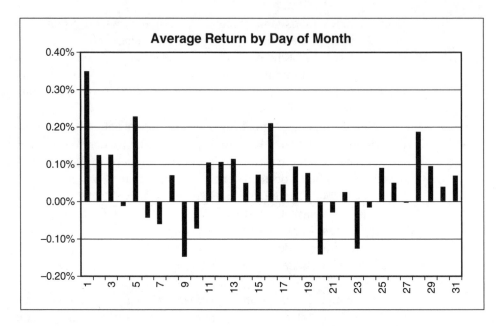

FIGURE 10.4

Average Return by Day of Month. Returns at the beginning, middle, and end of the month are higher than average.

Looking at the above graph, you'll see three intervals of above average returns and two intervals of below average returns. If we divide the month into five periods, there's a visible tendency. The beginning (Days 1 through 5) and end of the month (Days 27 through 31) have the strongest returns. The second (Days 6 through 11) and fourth (Days 19 through 26) parts of the month have less than average returns. A small positive hump exists in the middle of the month between Days 12 and 18. We look at two strategies that capitalize on this day of month effect:

1. We are long the market during Days one through five and Days 27 through 31. Assets are invested in cash for the remainder of the month.
2. We are long the market during Days one through five, 12 through 18, and 27 through 31. Assets are invested in cash the remainder of the month.

In Figure 10.5 we see the importance of the day of the month in the two strategies we outlined. Despite being invested less than 30 percent of the time for Strategy 1 and only 54 percent of the time for Strategy 2, both strategies outperform a buy and hold methodology. A $100 investment beginning in January 1990 yields $454 for Strategy 1 and $758 for Strategy 2, compared with $419 for buy and hold.

There are some possible explanations as to why the day of the month effect exists. Much of the American workforce now receives defined contribution retire-

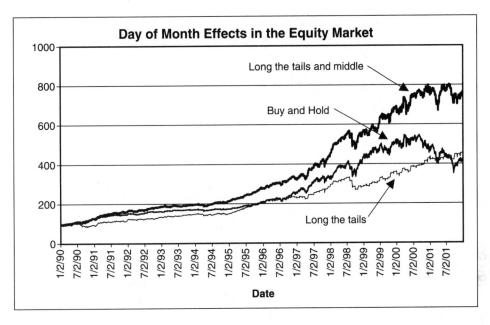

FIGURE 10.5

Day of Month Effects in the Equity Market. Our day-of-month strategy outperforms a buy and hold strategy.

ment benefits. In contrast to 30 years ago, when retirement pay was based on a percentage of ending salary—so-called defined benefit plans—most current retirement savings plans allow the individual flexibility in their savings options. These new plans, called defined contribution, usually involve a matching of funds by the employer. If I contribute $100 each pay period to my 401(k), my company might contribute $50 as part of a benefits program. The catch here is that I am responsible for making investment decisions with this pool of money.

Typically, 10 to 15 options are offered, including discounted company stock, equity mutual funds, corporate bond mutual funds, and government bond mutual funds. With each pay date, money flows from my paycheck into the mutual fund managers. Given that most are paid biweekly, a large amount of 401(k) funds flow into these mutual funds around the beginning, middle, and end of the month. When these funds are invested in stocks and bonds, the buying pressure could move prices higher and result in the day of the month bias we see above.

Using the Volatility Index to Trade the S&P 500

The price of volatility is determined by market forces, just like the price of a stock or future. Investors, nervous that a stock will fall, will rush to buy put options in order to protect against a precipitous decline in a stock. Investors who are convinced that the market will rally sharply will buy call options to partici-pate in violent rallies. This option buying pressure, which pushes up the price of volatility, increases the value of both calls and puts.

When complacency arises, investors typically sell options. Overwriters will sell call options against their long stock position in order to generate extra income in exchange for less upside in a stock. Other investors will sell put options as a method to get long a stock at a lower price. When these sellers of options enter the marketplace, volatility declines. The resulting struggle between option buyers and sellers can be seen in the CBOE Volatility Index, commonly referred to as the VIX.

The VIX is calculated from real-time option prices. As this index rises, it indicates that option buyers are outweighing option sellers and are pushing the price of volatility higher. As the VIX falls, it indicates that option sellers are out-weighing option buyers and pushing the price of volatility lower.

The VIX is a measure of implied volatility using S&P 100 options. Volatility is the main driver fueling option prices. Typically, high levels of implied volatil-ity signal that the market is nervous and pessimistic in its outlook of future returns. Conversely, low levels of implied volatility signals complacency and optimism. We can use the VIX to measure this fear or complacency and trade the S&P 500 accordingly. We want to be long the market in times of fear, and invested in cash when complacency is prevalent. In the graph in Figure 10.6, we see that periods of high VIX values usually coincide with market bottoms, while low val-ues of the VIX are prevalent near market tops.

I know of two popular methods of using the Volatility Index to trade the S&P 500. One of them is discussed in *Big Trends in Trading*, in which author Price Headley utilizes Bollinger bands in conjunction with the VIX. Bollinger bands, popularized by market technician John Bollinger, plot price channels that adjust based on market volatility. The middle band is drawn using a simple moving aver-age, while the upper and lower bands are displaced by a multiplier of recent stan-dard deviation of prices. Headley's strategy utilizes a 21-day moving average with Bollinger bands two standard deviations above and below the 21-day moving aver-age. Long positions are entered when today's S&P 100 close is above its 10-day moving average and the VIX crossed below its upper Bollinger band five days ago. This strategy requires that an oversold condition presents itself before a long signal is generated. This oversold condition is signaled by the VIX rising above its upper Bollinger band. An easing of this fear is set up by the VIX declining and falling below its upper Bollinger band. A trade occurs five days after the VIX falls below its upper Bollinger Band if the S&P 100 close is above its 10-day moving average.

The other proponent of using the Volatility Index to trade the S&P 500 is Leon Gross, managing director of the Equity Derivatives Research group at Salomon Smith Barney. Gross suggests fixed levels to enter and exit positions. Currently, he advocates entering long positions in the S&P 500 on VIX crosses above 30, and exiting into cash on drops below 20.

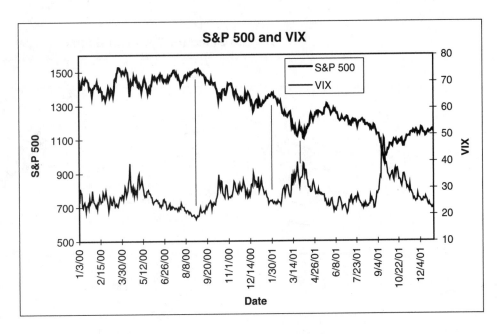

FIGURE   10.6

S&P 500 and VIX. High values of the VIX usually signal market bottoms, while low values of the VIX signal market tops.

Both these methodologies use extreme highs in the VIX to enter long the S&P 500, and use low VIX readings to exit long positions. As we see in Figure 10.6, bottoms are typically made during periods of high VIX readings, while tops are generally made during periods of low VIX readings.

If we're to create our own VIX trading strategy for the S&P 500 (since neither above method is ideal, in my opinion), we must first set out to identify periods of extremes in the Volatility Index. We start by taking a 120-day average of the VIX to develop a "mean" volatility. VIX readings above this mean signify higher than average volatility, while readings below the 120-day average signify lower than average volatility. Next, we quantify the deviation from normal volatility by comparing today's VIX reading to the 120-day average reading and then dividing by the standard deviation of changes in the VIX over the past 120 days. Here's the operative equation:

$$\text{VIX score} = \frac{VIX_{Today} - VIX_{Average}}{\sigma VIX_{Today} - VIX_{Yesterday}}$$

Positive VIX scores denote that the VIX is higher than average and suggest equity market fear and pessimism. Negative scores denote that the VIX is lower than average and suggest equity market complacency.

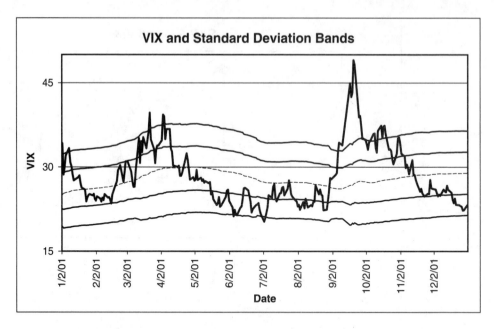

FIGURE 10.7

VIX and Standard Deviation Bands. By plotting bands around a 120-day average, we quantify periods of high and low VIX readings.

Figure 10.7 graphs levels of the VIX, its 120-day average, and the average plus two standard deviations, plus four standard deviations, minus two standard deviations, and minus four standard deviations. These bands appear to highlight relative extremes in the VIX readings quite well. Even more interesting is the way in which the market behaves depending on the current Volatility Index score. Figure 10.8 calculates the average return of the S&P 500 based on yesterday's VIX score using daily returns from 1990 through 2001.

VIX scores of +4 or greater lead to above average returns the following day, while scores of −2 or less generally lead to negative returns the next day. We can use this tendency to create a new more robust VIX strategy to market time the S&P 500.

Our new VIX strategy buys the market when today's VIX score is greater than +2. We stay long until the current day's score falls below −2. Figure 10.9 graphs the portfolio value of following our new VIX strategy compared to a buy and hold strategy. Note that not only does our strategy outperform the buy and hold, but does so by being in the market only 53 percent of the time.

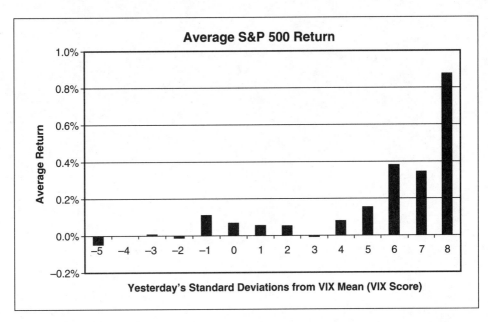

FIGURE 10.8

Average S&P 500 Return. Returns are highest following days where the VIX was far above its 120-day average. Returns are lowest following days where the VIX was far below its 120-day average.

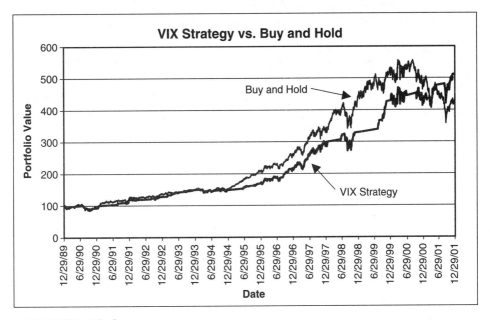

FIGURE 10.9

VIX Strategy vs. Buy and Hold. Our VIX strategy outperforms a buy and hold strategy.

CHAPTER 11

New Techniques in Money Management

Optimizing the Results of Our Strategies

Money management deals with the amount of leverage we employ in our quantitative trading programs. With leverage of up to 20:1 obtainable in today's financial markets, the money management question becomes very important. In this chapter we'll explore some of the popular methods for determining optimal leverage.

THE IMPORTANCE OF MONEY MANAGEMENT

"Money management is the most important part of a trading strategy."

You will often see this quote in books about trading, but I disagree with the premise of the statement. In reference to this, let's introduce two important tenets of money management:

1. No money management technique can turn an unprofitable trading strategy into a profitable trading strategy.
2. Poor money management technique can turn a profitable trading strategy into an unprofitable trading strategy.

According to the first tenet, we need a winning idea in order to trade profitably. Because of this, I believe that designing a profitable strategy is the first and foremost key to a successful trading program. The previous 10 chapters have been designed to teach readers to design, create, and evaluate trading strategies. I could easily end the book here and send readers out into the real world to trade. My guess is that if you follow the concepts we've highlighted, your trading would more than likely be profitable. But even with a profitable trading strategy, many would suffer losses or wipe out their trading accounts. Why? The second tenet of money management says it all: Poor money management can transform a profitable strategy into a losing strategy.

To understand the importance of money management, imagine a commodity that you've studied over the past 10 years. It typically trades between $12 and $18, and studies have shown that selling highs near $18 and buying lows near $12 has been quite profitable.

Now, let's say the market makes a new high at $20, and you decide to implement your strategy using your $45 bankroll by selling one contract. Despite the research that suggests lower prices, the market pushes higher after your first sale and trades up to $25. With a $5 mark-to-market loss, you decide to sell another contract at $25, knowing that your system has excellent historical performance. The market continues to trade higher—rallying up to $30. At first you become disappointed because you have a $10 loss on the first sale and a $5 loss on the second sale. Your account has lost $15 of the original $45. At the same time, you cannot believe your good fortune. Able to make sales at $30, you feel that you are sure to win big when the mean reversion occurs. You sell one more contract at $30. As soon as the sale hits the tape, buying pressure fuels the market to $35. At this point your account is down $30; that is, $15 on the first sale, $10 on the second sale, and $5 on the last sale.

You would love to sell more, but because of the leverage and margin you're using on the trade, you can't. In fact, you'll be forced to close your positions if the market trades much higher, due to a lack of funds. Of course, that is exactly what happens. The market rallies to a never before seen value of $40. Your broker calls to tell you that he is buying your three contracts at $40 and that your account has now lost $45. Your capital is wiped out at a time when the best sales in the history of the market are possible.

In the weeks after closing your position, slowly but surely the market trades back down. Not too long after you were forced to cover at the high of $40, prices fall to $25. Eventually, levels of $15 are seen—just as your model predicted.

This story may sound farfetched to some. Trust me, this type of poor money management occurs every day. Most frequently, this type of trading occurs with small undercapitalized traders taking positions that are too large. Other times it can happen on a much larger scale and even shake world financial markets.

THE RELATIONSHIP BETWEEN LEVERAGE AND RETURNS

We've been focusing throughout the book on maximizing the performance of trading strategies through the use of reward-to-risk measurements such as the Sharpe ratio and K-ratio. It's important to remember that our goal as traders is to maximize reward for a given unit of risk and then leverage up our risk to achieve the desired returns. Leverage involves borrowing money and using that money to fund trading decisions.

These days, leverage is often easy to come by. In futures trading, it is obtained by placing a performance bond, called *margin,* as collateral for the notional value of the trades. For example, in order to trade the 10-year Treasury note on the Chicago Board of Trade, I need only deposit $2700 to gain long or short exposure to $100,000 face value of Treasury notes. In the stock market, 100 percent leverage is obtainable in margin accounts. For every $1 that an investor has in cash, he or she can purchase $2 of stocks. The $1 that creates this leverage is borrowed from the broker in the form of a margin loan.

Expected returns scale proportionally to risk. If I expect a 10 percent return using no leverage, then by borrowing $1 for every dollar I have (ignoring interest costs for now) and applying the $2 to trading, I now have an expected return of 20 percent. Using 3:1 leverage—borrowing $2 for every $1 in capital and subsequently using the $3 for trading—my expected return increases to 30 percent. This tactic is used by many hedge fund managers to scale unleveraged returns to achieve a desired return. For example, if ABC Hedge Fund's unleveraged expected return is 10 percent and the manager wishes to make 30 percent per year, then that manager would use 200 percent leverage. He or she would borrow $2 for every dollar invested in the fund, using that total amount for trading.

But something happened on the way to leverage. When we invest over multiple periods, each single period return affects the starting capital of the next period. If returns are risky, leverage leads to an often bumpy road and creates a wide variation in the resultant possibilities, which we'll call "ending wealth"—the amount of money in possession at the end of some length of time. If a trader begins with $100 and ends with $500 after five years of trading, his profit would be $400—ending capital minus beginning capital—and his ending wealth would be $500. Although two strategies with identical average returns will yield an equivalent average ending wealth, the distribution of ending wealth varies dramatically when the volatility in returns differs.

To see how volatility can affect the distribution of ending wealth, consider the example of two strategies. Strategy #1 returns 5 percent per year with annual volatility of 20 percent. Strategy #2 returns 15 percent per year with annual volatility of 60 percent. Both have the same reward-to risk characteristics, but Strategy #2 is leveraged 3:1. Both yield equal measurement of reward divided by risk: 5%/20% = 0.25, 15%/60% = 0.25. The only difference between strategies is the amount of leverage employed in each style of trading. Strategy #2 has much higher returns, but also higher volatility.

After 10 years, $100 invested in the lower return/lower risk Strategy #1 will have an average ending wealth of $100 $\cdot$ $(1 + 5\%)^{10}$ = $162. One hundred dollars invested in the higher return/higher risk Strategy #2 will have an average ending wealth of $100 $\cdot$ $(1 + 15\%)^{10}$ = $404 (Figure 11.1).

| | Ending Wealth | |
	Average	Median
Strategy #1	$162	$136
Strategy #2	404	74

FIGURE 11.1

Ending Wealth for Strategy #1 and Strategy #2. The average and median ending wealth paints a different picture for each strategy.

We simulate 5000 random outcomes each with 120 monthly returns using the previously mentioned assumptions for Strategy #1 and Strategy #2 to analyze the range of outcomes in a 10-year investment period. While it's true that the average ending wealth of Strategy #2 is much higher than that of Strategy #1 ($404 vs. $162), we find that the median ending wealth for Strategy #1 is actually higher than that of Strategy #2. In fact, approximately 60 percent of the time the higher return/higher risk Strategy #2 produces ending wealth less than the starting amount of $100. This decrease in wealth occurs despite annual average returns of 15 percent. Obviously, it is important to control the risk of trading strategy returns.

We have two statistics telling us very different stories. Strategy #1's mean ending wealth is much lower than the mean ending wealth of Strategy #2, but its median wealth is much higher. The median of a series is the middle value when values are arranged in numerical order. For example, in the series 23 … 32 … 35 … 47 … 57, the average is $(23 + 32 + 35 + 47 + 57)/5 = 38.8$. The median is the middle of the five values when they are sorted from high to low; in this case it's 35.

The mean and median can be very different values. In the case of comparing ending wealth, we should focus on median wealth. While the mean is the average of all ending wealth possibilities, the median is the middle of a distribution where half the scores are below and the other half are above. The median is less sensitive to extreme scores, which makes it a better measure for skewed distributions.

As we see in Figures 11.2 and 11.3, the leverage we employ in our trading can affect our outcome dramatically. While leverage might increase average returns, there's a point we cross where adding extra volatility hurts the likelihood of future profits. Despite Strategy #1's returns of only 5 percent compared to Strategy #2's returns of 15 percent, Strategy #1 makes money after the 10-year period roughly 67 percent of the time, while Strategy #2 only makes money 43 percent of the time. While the chances of doubling or tripling our money is higher with Strategy #2, it's probably not worth the risk, considering how often we lose money at the end of the 10-year period.

The reason the excess leverage in Strategy #2 harms ending wealth is because of the asymmetrical property of leverage. If I start with $100 and lose 10 percent, I require an 11 percent return on my remaining $90 investment to break even. If I start with $100 and lose 25 percent, I need a 33 percent return on my

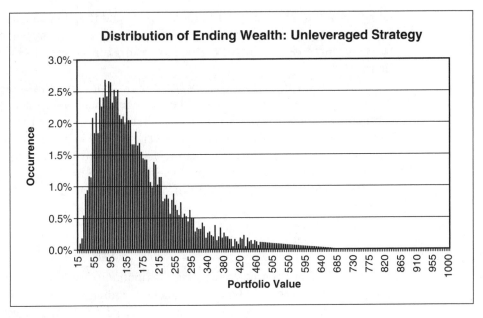

FIGURE 11.2

Distribution of Ending Wealth: Unleveraged Strategy. The bulk of ending wealth values fall between 50 and 300.

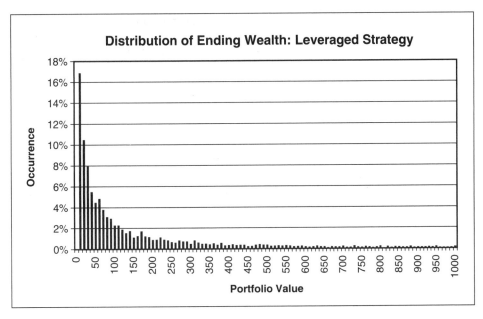

FIGURE 11.3

Distribution of Ending Wealth: Leveraged Strategy. The bulk of ending wealth values fall between zero and 600.

remaining $75 to break even. If I'm really risky and lose 50 percent, it would take a 100 percent gain on my remaining $50 just to return to my starting capital point. The larger my loss, the larger the proportional gain required to break even (see Figure 11.4).

Strategies with very high reward-to-risk characteristics are able to take larger risks, since large losses can be overcome due to superior profitability. Strategies with lower reward-to-risk characteristics are unable to overcome large losses. Here lies the mantra of optimal leverage: Higher reward to risk strategies can be traded at higher leverage than lower reward-to-risk strategies due to the ability to recover from large losses. Determining the optimal leverage becomes very important, since the volatility of our strategy will affect our median ending wealth.

$$\text{Required gain to regain loss} = \frac{1}{1 - \%Loss} - 1$$

The fact that volatility affects the distribution of ending wealth explains the concept of risk aversion in human judgment. If individuals were risk neutral, then we would play any game with positive expected value, regardless of the risk involved. In any positive expectancy trading strategy, we would leverage returns as

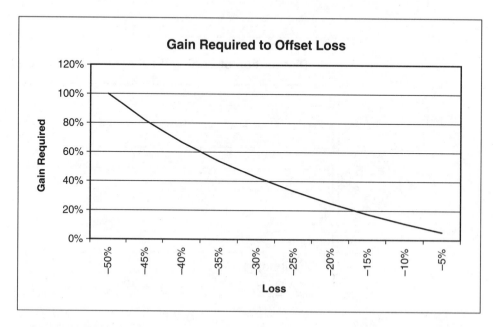

FIGURE 11.4

Gain Required to Offset Loss. A 10 percent loss requires an 11 percent gain to break even. A 50 percent loss requires a 100 percent gain to break even.

far as possible because it would maximize our expected profit. For example, a risk neutral individual would view both bets below as equally good:

Bet 1:   50 percent chance of winning $2

50 percent chance of losing $1

Bet 2:   50 percent chance of winning $10,002

50 percent chance of losing $10,001

While both bets have an expected value of + $0.50, very few people would view these two options as equally good. We do care about the risks we take with our money. Larger risks command higher returns. If we assume that individuals are risk averse, it would make sense to adjust profits by the risk taken to achieve them. By maximizing the median ending wealth instead of mean ending wealth, we penalize risk and maximize our most likely ending wealth.

THE DANGER OF LEVERAGE

Why do so many traders lose, even those who have an edge in trading the markets?

More times than not, losses can be explained by one factor: excessive leverage. The problem is most commonly found in the futures markets, where traders can utilize anywhere between 5:1 and 20:1 leverage. Two examples illustrate this hazard of excess leverage. One example involves a profitable trader employing too much leverage, while the other involves a trader with no edge employing varying degrees of leverage.

Leverage and the Trader with an Edge

Let's first consider a trader with a methodology that produces 55 percent successful trades where each winning and losing trade is of equal dollar amount and equal to the bet size. This trader begins with $1 and must decide how much capital to bet on each trade. When betting too small, the trader will not take full advantage of the mathematical advantage of his strategy. When betting too large, losing trades will wreck successive winning streaks.

Numerous studies have been conducted on the subject of optimal betting strategies. There is a unique optimal bet size to maximize the median ending wealth. As we will study later in this chapter, the optimal bet size in this case above is 10 percent of the trader's wealth on each trade. If we simulate 100 trades and assume the trader begins with $1 and uses varying bet sizes, we see why this 10 percent bet size is optimal. The median ending wealth increases consistently up to the 10 percent bet size. After this is exceeded, the median ending wealth actually decreases (Figure 11.5).

It's interesting to note that if we increase our bet size past the optimal point, we can actually decrease return while increasing risk. If we take our bet size too far past the optimal point, then we can actually lose money more times than we

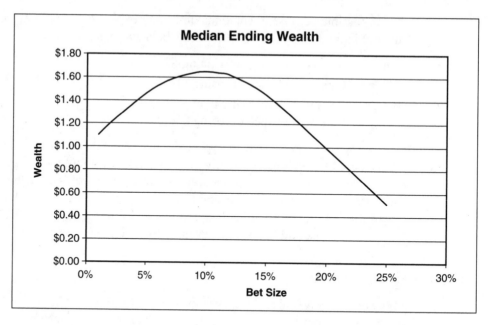

FIGURE 11.5

Median Ending Wealth. Median ending wealth is maximized by betting 10 percent of assets on each bet.

make money. In the example above, the median wealth declines below the starting wealth of $1 when we risk more than 20% of our capital on each trade. These results certainly explain why money management can be so crucial. Imagine a situation where we bet our entire capital on every bet. Even if we're extremely lucky and win 50 bets in a row, our first loss will wipe out all our capital. An understanding of this principle is of great importance to traders, and it's certainly one reason why most traders lose—even those with expected edge.

Leverage and the Trader with No Edge

In our second example of why traders lose, consider an untalented trader who has no edge in the markets. Each trade has a 50 percent chance of success, with winning and losing trades equal to the bet size. If we start with $100, make 10 trades, and always bet 20 percent of our bankroll on each trade, the ending profit and loss distribution is broken down in Figure 11.6.

Note that in this example our trader ends with negative returns roughly 62 percent of the time at the end of 10 trades. Why does the trader lose despite having a break-even trading strategy? Although the expected value of this game is still zero, the ending wealth follows a skewed distribution. In some rare instances, everything falls in our trader's favor. But in most cases, the trader finishes with

Ending Wealth	Occurrence
11	0%
16	1%
24	4%
36	12%
54	21%
82	25%
122	21%
183	12%
275	4%
413	1%
619	0%

FIGURE 11.6

Table of Ending Wealth. This table details the skew in ending wealth values.

less money than at the start of trading. How is this skewed distribution formed? If our trader has one winning trade followed by one losing trade, the ending equity is actually less than where it began. Consider the four possibilities occurring at the end of two trades where the trader begins with $100 and bets 20 percent of his assets on each trade (Figure 11.7):

Our trader loses money 75 percent of the time despite the dollar profit of the one winner equaling the dollar loss in the three losers combined. As our bet size increases, this skewed profit and loss distribution becomes more pronounced. It might explain why 95 percent of futures traders lose money while the other 5 percent are making a killing, whether due to luck or skill.

LEVERAGE IN THE REAL WORLD

As illustrated in the above examples, volatility and leverage are hazardous. These examples do not exaggerate. Just consider a real-world example of the perils of leverage, one of the most popular trends in the equity market runup of the late 1990s: indexing.

As noted earlier in the book, indexing is accomplished by structuring portfolios to mimic the performance of popular benchmarks such as the S&P 500 or Nasdaq 100. Some money managers believed that if market returns were good, then leveraging these returns would be better. During the late 1990s, leveraged index funds began to be marketed to individual investors. These funds borrowed money or used futures markets to achieve as much as 2:1 leverage.

One group of funds offered both a leveraged long and leveraged short index fund designed to track the Nasdaq 100. The "bull" fund was designed to provide

Trade 1	Trade 2	Ending Wealth	Probability
Win	Win	$100 \cdot 1.2 \cdot 1.2 = \$144$	25%
Win	Loss	$100 \cdot 1.2 \cdot 0.8 = \$96$	25%
Loss	Win	$100 \cdot 0.8 \cdot 1.2 = \$96$	25%
Loss	Loss	$100 \cdot 0.8 \cdot 0.8 = \$64$	25%

FIGURE 11.7

Example of Simple Game. Seventy-five percent of the time, our ending wealth is below our starting capital of $100.

twice the performance of the Nasdaq 100, while the "bear" fund was designed to provide twice the performance of being short the Nasdaq 100. Figure 11.8 details the performance of investing $100 on December 31, 2000, into one leveraged long Nasdaq 100 index fund and simultaneously purchasing $100 of one leveraged short Nasdaq 100 index fund. Both funds are in the same mutual fund family, and real-life net asset values (NAVs) were used to compute daily portfolio value statistics.

While the Nasdaq 100 finished down 32 percent in 2001, both the "bull" and the "bear" fund actually lost money. A $100 investment in the bull fund became roughly $31 at the end of 2001, while a $100 investment in the bear fund became $95.

How can this be if one fund is long the Nasdaq 100 and the other is short? Similar to the trade example above, the funds lose due to the leverage employed. As the market rose, both funds were required to buy assets to maintain the proper leverage ratio. When the market fell, both funds sold these assets, again to adjust to the perfect ratio. This behavior is completely consistent with each funds' mission of maintaining 2:1 leverage.

The problem is, volatile sideway price action will eat into both funds' asset values. When the market runs in one direction or another, the leveraging effect will benefit the fund's customers. But in a market that trades in a volatile sideways manner, the extra leverage seriously hampers performance.

I cannot overemphasize the importance of managing risk in a trading portfolio. It is a natural habit for traders to feel the need to push the risk envelope and take full advantage of their expected edge by leveraging assets. I know this need because I've been there.

At age 15, I developed a countertrend system to pick tops and bottoms in the Treasury bond futures market. While paper-trading the system for three full months, I correctly picked eight short-term tops and bottoms in a row. Armed with my new system, I opened a trading account and began trading the T-bond contract at the CBOT.

I could not wait for the money to come rolling in from trading. I still remember sitting in high school class calculating my projected income from pyramiding and constantly scaling up the size of the trading program. After the first year of

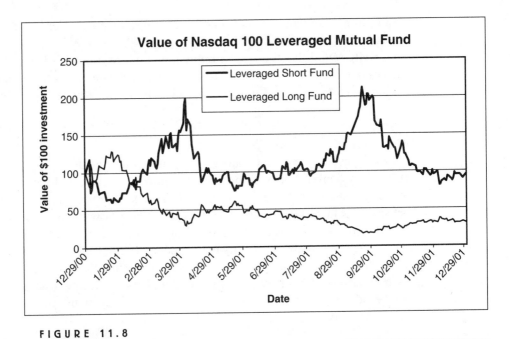

FIGURE 11.8

Value of Nasdaq 100 Leveraged Mutual Fund. Despite the Nasdaq 100's precipitous decline in 2001, both leverage long and leveraged short funds lost money.

trading, I estimated my net worth would be approximately $1 million, give or take a couple hundred thousand dollars. Ready to begin my journey, I placed the entry for my first trade. But something strange happened shortly after the trade was filled—the market went against me. Because the possibility of losing money never entered my mind, I had no contingency plan to adjust my trading. The market went against me further, and I became paralyzed by fear. Fifteen hundred of my $5000 was gone. I was confused, frightened, and unprepared. Eventually I closed the position with a $1500 loss.

Did the strategy eventually make money? I have no idea. I was so shell-shocked from the first trade that I never traded that strategy again.

THE KELLY CRITERIA

The first major work in the area of optimal leverage was researched by J. L. Kelly, Jr., of Bell Labs in 1956. Kelly studied the rate of transmission over noisy communication channels. Although his work was not particularly useful for telecommunications, Kelly noted that it would be very relevant to the gambling profession. In essence, Kelly discovered that gamblers should determine their bet size such that the logarithm of capital is maximized. Maximizing the logarithm of wealth is similar to maximizing the median of ending wealth if sufficient time periods are present.

Kelly found that there is an optimal amount of a bettor's bankroll to bet on each trial in order to maximize the median ending wealth. For simple games where a winning payout is equal to losing payouts, the formula is very simple:

$$\text{Optimal bet size as a percent of capital} = 2p - 1$$

where p is the probability of winning

If I have a 55 percent change of winning, then I should bet $(2 \cdot 55\%) - 1 =$ 10% of my bankroll on each bet. For games where I have a 70 percent chance of winning, I should bet $(2 \cdot 70\%) - 1 = 40\%$ on each bet. Logically, the maximum bet size is obtained if there is a 100 percent chance of winning. At that point I bet $(2 \cdot 100\%) - 1 = 100\%$ of my bankroll on each bet. If I can never lose, it makes sense that I would always bet my entire stake on each trial.

The above formula works for bets where winning payouts are equal to losing payouts; that is, if I collect \$1 during wins and lose \$1 during losses. The formula can be adjusted for games that do not have this fixed win/loss payout. Here's a more general version of the Kelly formula:

$$\text{Optimal bet size as a percent of capital} = p - (1 - p)/r$$

where p is the probability of winning and r is the ratio of the winning payout to the losing payout

VINCE'S OPTIMAL F

Ralph Vince was the first to apply Kelly's work to trading (1990). Vince calculates the optimal leverage point using trade-by-trade returns. His version of *optimal f* is solved by maximizing the ending wealth of a series of trades by betting a fixed percentage of the largest losing trade. The idea is that the largest losing trade will occur at some point, so we risk some fraction of the largest loss, which maximizes our ending wealth.

Although Vince's method should yield beneficial results, using daily return data from a strategy will provide a tighter, better measure of optimal leverage due to the increased number of data points. Vince's method suffers if the number of trades is small enough that the ending wealth curve becomes jagged. When the ending wealth curve is not smooth, it becomes difficult to determine the true optimal leverage point.

AN IMPROVED METHOD FOR CALCULATING OPTIMAL LEVERAGE

I believe the best method for determining optimal leverage involves maximizing the median ending wealth. Harry Markowitz (1959) showed that maximizing median wealth is equivalent to maximizing the mean logarithmic return, and he developed a good approximation for calculating the mean logarithmic return based on the arithmetic mean and variance of returns:

Expected log return = expected return – ½ variance of returns

Using an amount of leverage, M, the log return equation becomes:

Expected leveraged log return = $M \cdot$ expected return – ½ M^2 variance of returns

In order to maximize expected log return, we take the derivative of the expected leveraged log return with respect to M. Setting the derivative to zero, we solve for M. It happens that the optimal leverage—the optimal value of M—for use in a trading strategy is calculated by:

$$\text{Optimal leverage} = \text{return / variance} = \frac{\mu}{\sigma^2}$$

Using the optimal leverage calculated from the above formula, we will be maximizing our median ending wealth, the benefits of which were seen earlier in this chapter. If our strategy is expected to return 5 percent per year over the risk-free rate, with annual standard deviation of 20 percent, then our optimal leverage is $(0.05)/(0.20)^2 = 125\%$. We would actually borrow 25 percent of our capital to plow back into our trading strategy.

Let's suppose we begin with $100 and the optimal leverage of our strategy is 200 percent. We borrow $100 from our broker and invest a total of $200 into our trading strategy by buying two shares of ABC stock, trading at $100. Our strategy is correct and ABC rallies from $100 to $150. At this point, we are worth $200: $300 from our two shares minus the $100 we owe our broker.

Even with $200 in capital, we still need 200% leverage. This means that we should have $400 invested in the strategy, more than the $300 currently being used. To rebalance, we borrow another $100 from our broker, and invest this new money into our strategy by buying two-thirds of a share of ABC. This rebalance creates the optimal 200% leverage we desire as our $200 in capital is controlling $400 in trading positions.

If ABC declines from $150 back to its original $100, we again need to reevaluate our leverage. Our net worth is now $67: $267 from our 2.67 shares minus the $200 total we owe our broker. With $67 in capital and 200% optimal leverage, we need to control $134 of stock—more than the $267 currently held. To rebalance, we sell $133 of stock and repay this money to reduce our loan to the broker. Our remaining position is $134 held in stock minus the remaining $67 we owe to our broker—leaving $67 in net worth.

Our capital and leverage will change over time as profits and losses accrue. As seen above when our optimal leverage is greater than one, we will need to trade larger and borrow more as our capital grows from trading gains. As capital declines from trading losses, we will trade smaller and borrow less in order to maintain optimal leverage.

This is arguably where the principals at Long Term Capital Management made a strategic flaw. In their strategy, they employed large amounts of leverage as they believed their optimal leverage was well over 100%. Instead of decreasing leverage by closing positions as their capital began to evaporate, the partners either attempted to maintain their position size or in some cases increased position size—effectively increasing their leverage. This mistake eventually led to their demise and the corresponding shock to world financial markets in October 1998.

On the other hand, if our return and risk numbers yield an optimal leverage less than one—meaning we use less than 100 percent of our capital for trading—then a different pattern emerges. In this case, we subtract from positions as we win and add to positions as we lose—precisely opposite the situation studied above.

THE ROLE OF DOLLAR AND PERCENTAGE RETURNS

Readers may notice that with most strategies in this book, return and risk have been calculated in dollar terms, not in the percentage terms used in this chapter to calculate optimal leverage. We can use the optimal leverage formula above to determine how large we should trade when using a set amount of capital.

Assume that we start trading with $10,000. Suppose we create a profitable trading method which averages profits of $500 per day and has a daily standard deviation of $5000 per day. Note that it is imperative to measure average return and volatility in the same unit of time, whether daily, weekly, monthly, or annual measures. Using a little algebra, we find that the optimal dollar volatility is a function of capital, average return, and volatility of return.

Optimal dollar volatility = (capital) (average dollar return) / (dollar volatility)

The resulting optimal volatility is expressed in the same time frame as the average return and volatility measurements. Returning to our example, we find that the optimal dollar volatility of our $10,000 capital is ($10,000)($500)/($5000) = $1000 per day. Thus, we should scale our trading down to have a daily standard deviation of $1000. Essentially, we need to trade one-fifth as large as the size of the back-test that produced a daily standard deviation of $5000 per day.

Readers should note that even small positions yield such volatility. For example, the current daily dollar volatility of one S&P 500 contract is over $3000. Despite the fact that this strategy is very profitable, our $10,000 capital base may not be enough to trade a well-diversified portfolio of products. If we trade higher than the optimal leverage, chances are it will harm results in the long run—not improve them. Traders can see from this example why trading with small accounts is an almost certain way to end up with no money at all.

As time passes, markets and strategies may become more or less volatile. In addition, our capital will increase with gains and decrease with losses. As a result, when calculating optimal volatility for our trading strategy, we must continually recalculate and adjust the optimal dollar volatility statistic. While drastic changes are unlikely on a day-to-day basis, the optimal dollar volatility number is likely to shift considerably over months and years of trading.

THE PARADOX OF OPTIMAL LEVERAGE

Understanding the benefits and perils of leverage can help investors and traders alike. Investors can structure their stock and bond allocations more efficiently. Traders can determine their optimal risk tolerance.

While the mathematics of this chapter may sound like we've created the perfect tool, unfortunately Vince's optimal f, the Kelly criteria, and the optimal leverage concept we visited above are all tremendously flawed when applied to trading. For optimal leverage to be useful, the return and volatility of trading strategies must be known. If we know our expected return and risk with absolute certainty, then we can leverage our capital effectively.

The problem arises from the fact that optimal leverage is calculated from specific assumptions of expected return and risk. If we use even $1 more leverage than optimal on a portfolio, then we will actually be decreasing our median ending wealth while simultaneously taking more risk. If we use even $1 less leverage than optimal, we will not achieve maximum ending wealth.

For games with known expected return and risk such as blackjack, we know the edge and volatility of our bets. In such static games, optimal leverage calculations can be very helpful. But in a dynamic game such as the financial markets, we can never be certain of future expected returns and volatility despite knowing how our strategies performed in the past. As a result, we can never be sure if we're utilizing leverage effectively.

This is why money management techniques such as the Kelly criteria or optimal f are actually a paradox. While we know optimal values of the past, we have no certainty what will be optimal in the future. That is not to say these tools are useless. In fact, they are very useful. Their most important use is to determine if traders are trading larger than optimal leverage, in which case they should reduce their trading size immediately. And if trading under optimal leverage, traders must ask themselves what the true average return and volatility of their strategy will be in the future. These questions are the true difficulties when crafting an effective money management plan.

Another problem is that the optimal leverage calculation assumes that every investor and trader is attempting to maximize median wealth. But many academic researchers have found that, on average, investors are more risk averse. The typical investor picks reward-to-risk trade-offs that would be created by trading at only one-half or one-third of the optimal leverage that would yield the highest median ending wealth. As it turns out, what is optimal for one person is excessive for another.

CHAPTER 12

Solving the Trading Puzzle

Creating, Testing, and Evaluating a New Trading Strategy

Now that we have the tools to create, test, and trade profitable trading strategies on stocks, futures, and relative value markets, let's create a trading theory and then follow the process until we have a polished trading strategy.

CREATING THE STRATEGY

From my experience in trading, it appears that large moves are often followed by three to five days of follow-through. Buying the market after a big rise seems to lead to profits, as does selling after large drops. But how should we measure these moves?

The traditional volatility breakout method attempts to exploit this tendency by buying markets after a large one day price gain and selling markets after a large one day price loss. Is one day really enough data to define a trend, or do we need to look at three to five days of market returns? Our new system will broaden the scope of the typical volatility breakout strategy by analyzing multiple period returns for generating buy and sell signals.

I decided to look at volatility breakouts in a different light. In a typical volatility breakout system, longs are taken if today's close is greater than:

$$\text{Price reference} + num \cdot \text{volatility measure}$$

where *price reference* is usually yesterday's close or today's open, *num* is a positive number, *volatility measure* is either the standard deviation of closes, standard deviation of returns, or average true range. But I believe it's shortsighted to analyze one day returns for short term breakouts.

What if the market makes two consecutive above-average price moves in the same direction? Are those moves important?

I believe they are. As a result, I search for all breakouts over multiple days' price movement to generate trading signals.

Each day, evaluate for all values of x from 5 to 20:

New volatility breakout logic:
Buy if close – close of x days ago $> num \cdot$ SQRT(x) $\cdot$ standard deviation of price changes over the past 100 days
Sell if close – close of x days ago $< -1 \cdot num \cdot$ SQRT(x) $\cdot$ standard deviation of price changes over the past 100 days

Each trading day, I search for buy and sell signals by calculating signals from the rules above for all values of x from 5 to 20. We start by comparing the five-day price change with the standard deviation of price changes over the past 100 days. If the price change is greater than num times the standard deviation, we have a potential buy signal. If the price change is less than negative num times the standard deviation, we have a potential sell signal. After running the five-day price change through our model, we compare the six-day price change. After evaluating the six-day price change, we examine the seven-day price change, then the eight-day price change, the nine-day price change, and so forth until we have compared the 20-day price change.

In each case, we compare the price change to the product of multiplying three values: a constant num, the square root of the number of days in the price change, and the 100-day standard deviation of price changes. The num parameter will determine the sensitivity of price moves that generate trading signals. Smaller values will generate more frequent buy and sell signals, while larger values will generate relatively infrequent signals. From the normal distribution, we know that roughly 95 percent of values will be contained within ±2 standard deviations. If we require moves greater than two times the standard deviation, we should expect trading signals roughly 5 percent of the time (or one out of every 20 days, approximately once a month).

We can use the standard deviation to project price changes over multiple days. To accomplish this transformation, we need to multiply the standard deviation by the square root of the number of days in our new price change interval. For example, suppose the standard deviation of daily price changes is $1. We would expect 68 percent of future one-day price changes to lie within ±$1, 95 percent to lie within ±$2, and 99 to lie within ±$3. We can make similar predictions about future two-day price changes by multiplying the standard deviation by the square root of 2. We would expect 68 percent of future two-day price changes to lie within ±$1.41, 95 percent to lie within ±$2.83, and 99 percent to lie within ± $4.24. This method can be extended to predict any number of days' price changes. The graph in Figure 12.1 depicts how our ±2 standard deviation confidence interval increases with the number of days' returns into the future.

It is possible to generate conflicting signals using this method as we look for signals when running x between 5 and 20. For example, the five-day price change might generate a long signal due to a recent rally. At the same time, a previous sharp decline might cause the 15-day price change to generate a sell signal. In these cases, the longer term signal always overrides the shorter term signal. We would take the short entry associated with the 15-day price change and ignore the long entry associated with the five-day price change.

In Figure 12.2, we can see signals of our new volatility breakout strategy applied to Eurodollar futures. The signals utilize the new entry mechanism for the parameter *num* = 1.0. A quick, sharp sell-off in mid-October triggers a short entry. After a significant decline, a rally from the market's bottom in late December causes a long entry to be initiated in early January. The strategy stays with the long position through the end of April.

Our new volatility breakout strategy can probably be improved by adding an exit rule to signal when trades have run their course. So, in addition to the entry rules, we will exit long and short positions using a trailing stop. We'll trail our best

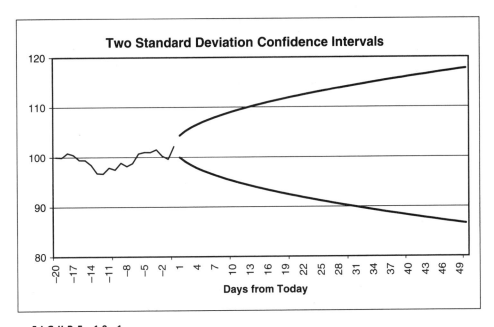

FIGURE 12.1

Two Standard Deviation Confidence Intervals. Note that the confidence intervals do not increase in a linear fashion with time. Instead, they increase at a rate proportional to the square root of time.

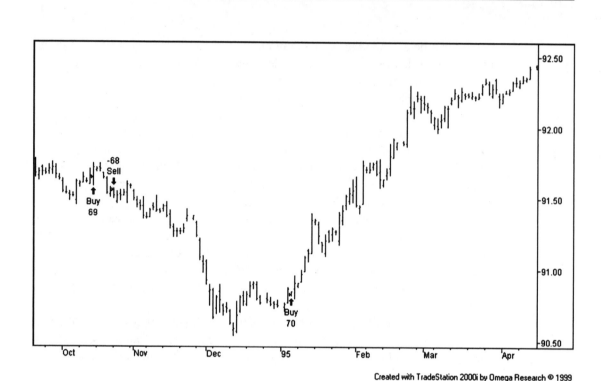

Created with TradeStation 2000i by Omega Research © 1999

FIGURE 12.2

New Trading Strategy Applied to Eurodollars. Both a short entry in mid-October and a long entry in early January produce profits.

position profit by two times the 100-day standard deviation of price changes. If we're long and prices fall from the highest high seen during the trade by twice the 100-day standard deviation of price returns, we'll exit our long position. If we're short and prices rise from the lowest low seen during the trade by twice the 100-day standard deviation of price returns, we'll exit our short position. Using this trailing exit will help ensure that we close losing trades early and that winning trades will be closed with a profit before prices turn, leading to a losing trade.

TESTING THE NEW STRATEGY

Now that the idea is quantified, we'll move to the testing phase and evaluate the performance of the strategy defined above on 19 futures markets. Our strategy is applied only on market sectors that display a natural tendency to trend: currencies, interest rates, petroleum, grains, and softs (excluding cocoa and orange juice).

Testing is performed on two versions of our new volatility breakout strategy. Version #1 includes only the entry mechanism. Version #2 adds the trailing stop to the entry mechanism. We need to tweak our system to determine if the results are

New Volatility Breakout Strategy			
Entry only	**Net profit**	**Sharpe Ratio**	**K-ratio**
Num = 1.0	$6,560,399	0.51	0.30
Num = 1.5	$7,454,859	0.57	0.23
Num = 2.0	$6,185,323	0.51	0.05
Entry plus trailing stop	**Net profit**	**Sharpe Ratio**	**K-ratio**
Num = 1.0	$8,741,153	0.74	0.42
Num = 1.5	$6,345,168	0.58	0.39
Num = 2.0	$4,390,501	0.51	0.17

FIGURE 12.3

Table of Net Profit, Sharpe Ratio, and K-ratio for New Volatility Breakout Strategies. Smaller values of the *num* parameter coupled with the trailing stop produce the highest profitability.

stable across varying parameters. To test the stability of the *num* parameter of our strategy, we run the profitability tests by varying *num* from 1 to 2, in increments of 0.5. The corresponding net profit, Sharpe ratio, and K-ratio of all versions and parameter sets are noted in Figure 12.3.

The results elucidate much about our strategy. First, by adding the trailing exit, we increase reward to risk measures such as the Sharpe ratio and K-ratio. While net profit is sacrificed for two of the three values of *num*, the benefit is less risk. Second, it appears that smaller values of *num* outperform larger values of *num*. We conclude that our strategy is robust across parameters and that performance is likely to remain profitable in the future.

Our next decision is whether we should combine multiple versions of the strategy with multiple parameter sets to achieve improved reward-to-risk from benefits of diversification. Because the signals from the two versions of this strategy are so highly correlated, we choose to skip combining multiple strategy versions together. Instead, we will trade the new volatility breakout entry with the trailing stop and *num* parameter of 1.0. Figures 12.4a and 12.4b details the performance of our new volatility breakout strategy.

DETERMINING OPTIMAL LEVERAGE

The equity curve in Figure 12.4a highlights the performance of our new strategy for selected futures markets. We earn $8,741,153 over 145 months, for an average of $60,284 per month. Our monthly volatility of returns, calculated by taking the standard deviation of monthly profit and loss numbers from the performance back-test, is $282,620. Using the optimal leverage formula from Chapter 11, we determine the optimal volatility for a hypothetical $100,000 portfolio:

Trading Strategy Evaluation (Futures)

Strategy Name: New volatility breakout strategy
Parameters: Num = 1.0, trail best position profit by 2 sigmas of 100 price changes
Description: Enter when 5 to 20 day return greater or less than Num sigmas, 2 sigma trailing exit
Run Dates: 1/1/1990 – 12/31/2001

	Market	Net Profit	K-ratio	Sharpe Ratio	Max DD	# of Trades	% Win	Avg. Contracts	Avg. Profit Per Con.	Avg. Win	Avg. Loss	Avg. Bars Win	Avg. Bars Loss
FX	AD	179,420	0.01	0.10	−618,070	257	37	21.36	32	31,301	−17,258	18	5
	BP	−124,375	−0.08	−0.06	−769,925	254	36	14.31	−36	30,380	−17,772	16	6
	CD	852,860	0.24	0.41	−265,090	244	43	35.89	98	33,814	−18,958	18	5
	JY	547,513	0.17	0.29	−276,250	252	36	10.81	163	35,047	−17,057	18	6
	SF	−599,700	−0.10	−0.31	−657,463	254	29	13.68	−165	37,866	−18,760	19	6
Rates	ED	1,858,175	0.23	0.80	−345,800	205	43	68.06	132	48,385	−21,188	21	5
	TY	337,360	0.12	0.16	−235,312	268	37	23.07	56	34,825	−18,369	18	5
	US	490,906	0.17	0.26	−225,031	240	38	17.09	121	35,472	−17,986	20	5
Stock	SP												
Metals	GC												
	HG												
	PL												
	SL												
Energy	CL	701,120	0.14	0.36	−395,470	244	39	22.40	130	36,192	−17,936	18	6
	HO	253,781	0.05	0.12	−625,216	247	38	19.33	55	33,068	−18,943	17	5
	HU	546,672	0.10	0.25	−368,189	256	37	18.03	118	35,072	−16,996	18	6
Grains	C	353,050	0.12	0.17	−379,513	251	35	61.15	22	39,030	−18,663	19	5
	S	−289,838	−0.13	−0.16	−668,063	235	36	26.19	−48	31,978	−20,082	19	6
	W	377,325	0.14	0.18	−402,050	259	37	44.23	34	34,322	−18,144	18	5
Meats	FC												
	LC												
	LH												
	PB												
Softs	CC												
	CT	189,935	0.01	0.09	−626,855	230	34	20.85	40	37,739	−18,485	19	7
	JO												
	KC	886,316	0.15	0.41	−391,144	220	39	10.86	371	39,790	−18,923	20	5
	LB	2,075,208	0.16	0.77	−272,816	273	40	22.78	337	45,806	−17,295	16	6
	SB	105,425	−0.03	0.06	−663,623	219	37	43.58	12	33,283	−18,725	18	7
	Average	460,061	0.08	0.20	−430,836	232	35	25.98	77	34,388	−17,449	17	5

Portfolio Statistics

Net Profit:	8,741,153	Sharpe ratio:	0.74
Drawdown:	−1,141,172	Correlation to breakout:	0.63
K-ratio:	0.42	Correlation to 10-40 MA:	0.54

© 2002 Lars Kestner – All Rights Reserved

FIGURES 12.4a

Performance of Final New Volatility Breakout Strategy. The new Volatility Breakout Strategy produced profits in all 12 years of our back-test.

Breakdown Statistics (Futures)

System Name: New volatility breakout strategy
Parameters: Num = 1.0, trail best position profit by 2 sigmas of 100 price changes
Description: Enter when 5 to 20 day return greater or less than Num sigmas, 2 sigma trailing exit
Run Dates: 1/1/1990 – 12/31/2001

Breakdown by Market Sector

Market Sector	Average Net Profit	Average K-ratio	Average Sharpe Ratio	Average Max DD	Average Num Trades	Average % Win	Avg. Profit Per Contract	Average Win	Average Loss	Avg. Bars Win	Avg. Bars Loss
FX	171,144	0.05	0.09	−517,360	252	36	18	33,681	−17,961	18	6
Rates	671,610	0.13	0.31	−201,536	178	29	77	29,670	−14,386	15	4
Stock	#DIV/0!	#DIV/0!	#DIV/0!	#DIV/0!	#DIV/0!	#DIV/0!	#DIV/0!	#DIV/0!	#DIV/0!	#DIV/0!	#DIV/0!
Metals	#DIV/0!	#DIV/0!	#DIV/0!	#DIV/0!	#DIV/0!	#DIV/0!	#DIV/0!	#DIV/0!	#DIV/0!	#DIV/0!	#DIV/0!
Energy	500,524	0.10	0.24	−462,958	249	38	101	34,777	−17,958	18	6
Grains	146,846	0.04	0.06	−483,208	248	36	3	35,110	−18,963	19	5
Meats	#DIV/0!	#DIV/0!	#DIV/0!	#DIV/0!	#DIV/0!	#DIV/0!	#DIV/0!	#DIV/0!	#DIV/0!	#DIV/0!	#DIV/0!
Softs	814,221	0.07	0.33	−488,609	236	37	190	39,155	−18,357	18	6

Performance Breakdown by Year

Year	Net Profit	K-ratio	Sharpe Ratio	Year	Net Profit	K-ratio	Sharpe Ratio
1990	944,797	0.41	0.99	1996	499,973	0.22	0.36
1991	795,198	0.17	0.73	1997	1,024,741	0.13	1.19
1992	139,256	0.10	0.15	1998	559,709	0.28	0.49
1993	732,121	0.07	0.85	1999	433,147	0.22	0.27
1994	144,832	−0.07	0.22	2000	2,394,993	0.62	2.01
1995	916,671	0.15	1.16	2001	143,256	0.14	0.12

Length	Number of Windows	Num. of Profitable Windows	Percent Profitable
1 Month	144	80	55.56%
3 Months	142	88	61.97%
6 Months	139	103	74.10%
12 Months	133	124	93.23%
18 Months	127	122	96.06%
24 Months	121	121	100.00%

Net Profit by Year

© 2002 Lars Kestner – All Rights Reserved

FIGURES 12.4b

Performance of Final New Volatility Breakout Strategy. The new Volatility Breakout Strategy produced profits in all 12 years of our back-test.

327

Optimal dollar volatility = capital · average dollar return/dollar volatility
Optimal dollar volatility = $100,000 · $60,284/$282,620 = $21,330

Our calculations suggest the optimal dollar volatility is $21,330 per month while our back-test above produces monthly volatility of $282,620. Based on these calculations, we need to scale down our position size by trading only 7.5 percent as much (approximately one-thirteenth) as the size that generated the profit and loss figure in our back-test. Remember, the number of contracts traded on any entry is based on dividing $10,000 by the 100-day standard deviation of dollar price changes. If using the $10,000 input results in monthly volatility of $282,620 per month for our portfolio of futures in this strategy, then to create our desired leverage when trading $100,000 we multiply $10,000(7.5%) = $750. Thus, for a $100,000 trading account, we should trade the following number of contracts each trade to maximize our median wealth:

Contracts to trade = $750/100 day standard deviation of dollar price changes

Now comes the hard part. We know that the values above are optimal using historical profit and loss performance data. What about going forward?

I will arbitrarily cut the optimal leverage in half, just as a cushion for what may lie ahead.

Adjusted new strategy contracts/shares to trade = $375/100-day standard deviation of dollar price changes

If we trade using a numerator of $375 for determining position size, we can expect ($60,284)(7.5%)/2 = $2261 return per month, with monthly volatility of ($282,620)(7.5%)/2 = $10,598 as we trade our strategy going forward. Real-time numbers that deviate far from these benchmarks should trigger caution. When trading in real time, large deviations away from results seen in historical testing would suggest that we have either made a mistake in our calculations or the strategy is deteriorating in live trading. Either situation can be disastrous for traders.

In Conclusion

Traders are the new alchemists. Our job is to predict the unpredictable. Day after day we attempt to turn lead into gold. When we fail to predict the unpredictable, we stress and we worry. After all, the near impossible task of forecasting financial markets is our job.

If readers retain one idea after reading this book, it should be that practically everything can be analyzed with numbers. Integers and digits make the world go round—not only in markets, but in every facet of life. Rarely does a situation present itself where quantitative analysis cannot help explain an event or predict an outcome. Numbers may not explain everything, but when analyzing financial data, this analysis can lead to trading success. Hopefully, the contents of this book have convinced you not to take anything at face value—certainly nothing that can be tested or solved mathematically.

We've examined trading stocks, financial futures, metals, meats, grains, petroleum products, cotton, cocoa, sugar, currencies, interest rate term structures, credit spreads, volatility, and even the relationship between stocks and commodities. If trading cheddar cheese futures becomes the next hot market, I will be there to analyze it and trade it using the exact same approaches I described in this book. Therein lies the beauty of quantitative trading: the portability of strategies and methods.

My years of experience have taught me that nothing in trading comes easy. There will always be profits, but you have to work hard to stay ahead of others. Growing up in Louisiana, I had a tennis coach who made us work on our physical conditioning, often spending over 20 minutes at the end of the day sprinting around the court. We all hated this workout and sometimes questioned its merits. I vividly recall his screams, "You know what they are doing in New Orleans right now? They are doing sprints! If you want to beat them, then you have got to outwork them!"

He was right. In every profession, sport, and academic discipline, people are working to improve themselves. They're becoming faster, stronger, and smarter as every day goes by. Heed these works of advice—if you want to beat your competitors, you need to outwork them.

I want to leave readers with one thought. In *The General Theory of Employment, Interest, and Money*, John Maynard Keynes writes:

> Worldly wisdom teaches us that it is better for reputations to fail conventionally than to succeed unconventionally.

Keynes suggests that those who succeed are more likely to do so unconventionally. However, those who choose the path of unconventional methods will have their success dismissed by others as chance and will be disparaged in their defeat. I urge anyone attempting to thrive in such an inclement endeavor as trading to follow Keynes's advice. Think for yourself and travel on paths never journeyed before. I hope that trading success will bring you personal satisfaction and that your failures will cause you to rise and try again.

Best wishes and good trading.

References

Chapter 1: Introduction to Quantitative Trading

Andreassen, Paul. 1988. Explaining the Price-Volume Relationship. *Organizational Behavior and Human Decision Processes* 41: 371–389.

Arnold, Curtis. 1995. *Curtis Arnold's PPS Trading System.* McGraw Hill.

Black, Fischer, and Myron Scholes. 1973. The Pricing of Options and Corporate Liabilities. *Journal of Political Economy* 81: 637–654.

Blume, Marshall, Jeremy Siegel, and Dan Rottenberg. 1993. *Revolution on Wall Street.* W. W. Norton & Company.

Bulkowski, Thomas. 2000. *Encyclopedia of Chart Patterns.* John Wiley & Sons.

Burke, Gibbons. 1993. Tom DeMark: Technical Guru Breaks Out to the Upside. *Futures*, Sept. 1993, 34–40.

DeBondt, Werner, and Richard Thaler. 1985. Does the Stock Market Overreact? *Journal of Finance* 40: 793–807.

DeMark, Thomas. 1994. *The New Science of Technical Analysis.* John Wiley & Sons.

DeMark, Thomas. 1998. *New Market Timing Techniques.* John Wiley & Sons.

Jobman, Darrell (1980). Richard Donchian: pioneer of trend trading. *Commodities*, Sept. 1980, 40–42.

Kahn, Phyllis. 1980. Who Was W. D. Gann? *Commodities*, Jan. 2000, 44–48.

Kestner, Lars. 1998. *Comparison of Popular Trading Systems.* Commodity Traders Consumer Reports.

Lo, A.W., Harry Mamaysky, and J.Wang. 2000. Foundations of Technical Analysis: Computational Algorithms, Statistical Inference, and Empirical Implementation. *Journal of Finance* 55: 1705–1765.

Lukac, Louis, Wade Brorsen, and Scott Irwin. 1990. *A Comparison of Twelve Technical Trading Systems.* Traders Press.

Odean, Terrence. 1998. Are Investors Reluctant to Realize Their Losses? *Journal of Finance* 53: 1775–1798.

Rosenberg, Barr, Kenneth Reid, and Ronald Lanstein. 1985. Persuasive Evidence of Market Inefficiency, *Journal of Portfolio Management* 11: 9–17.

Schwartz, Robert. 1993. *Reshaping the Equity Markets.* McGraw Hill.

Schwert, William. 1991. Review of Market Volatility by Robert J. Shiller. *Journal of Portfolio Management* 17: 74–78.

Shiller, Robert. 1981. Do Stock Prices Move Too Much to Be Justified by Subsequent Changes in Dividends? *American Economic Review* 71: 421–436.

Chapter 4: Creating Trading Strategies

Grossman, Sanford, and Joseph Stiglitz. 1980. On the Impossibility of Informationally Efficient Markets. *American Economic Review* 70, 393–408.

Chapter 5: Evaluating Trading Strategy Performance

Kestner, Lars. 1996. Getting a Handle on True Performance. *Futures*, Jan. 1996, 44–46.
Kestner, Lars. 1996. Measuring Profitability. *Technical Analysis of Stocks and Commodities*, March 1996, 46–50.
Skinner, B. F. 1948. Superstition in the Pigeon. *Journal of Experimental Psychology* 38: 168–172.
Treynor, Jack, and Kay Mazuy. 1966. Can Mutual Funds Outguess the Market? *Harvard Business Review* 43: 63–75.

Chapter 6: Optimizing Parameters and Filtering Entry Signals

Zamansky, Leo, and James Goldcamp. 2001. Walking a Fine Line. *Futures*. Oct. 2001, 48–50.

Chapter 8: New Ideas of Entries, Exits, and Filters

Cooper, Michael. 1999. Filter Rules Based on Price and Volume in Individual Security Overreaction. *Review of Financial Studies* 12: 901–935.

Chapter 9: New Ideas of Markets

Demeterfi, Kresimir, et al. 1999. More than You Ever Wanted to Know About Volatility Swaps. *Goldman Sachs Quantitative Strategies Research Notes*. March 1999.
Gross, Leon, et al. 2002. Once, Twice, Three Times: RD/SC Spread in Play Again. *Salomon Smith Barney Equity Derivatives Sales Literature*. Feb. 4, 2002.
_____. 2002. Major Change in the S&P 500, as Non-U.S. Companies Are Removed. *Salomon Smith Barney Equity Derivatives Sales Literature*. July 10, 2002.
_____. 1998. Introducing Volatility Swaps: Trading Volatility Made Easy. *Salomon Smith Barney Equity Derivatives Sales Literature*. January, 1998.
Lowenstein, Roger. 2000. *When Genius Failed: The Rise and Fall of Long-Term Capital Management*. Random House.

Chapter 10: Investing in the S&P 500

Cross, F. 1973. Behavior of Stock Prices on Fridays and Mondays. *Financial Analysts' Journal* 29: 67–69.
Gross, Leon, et al. 2001. Nasdaq Volatility Indices: Why Is the VXN 10 Points Higher? *Salomon Smith Barney Equity Derivative Sales Literature*. Feb. 26, 2001.
Headley, Price. 2002. *Big Trends in Trading*. John Wiley & Sons.

Chapter 11: New Techniques in Money Management

Kelly, J. L. 1956. A New Interpretation of Information Rate. *Bell System Technical Journal* 35: 917–26.

Markowitz, Harry. 1959. *Portfolio Selection: Efficient Diversification of Investments*. Yale University Press.

Vince, Ralph. 1990. *Portfolio Management Formulas*. John Wiley & Sons.

INDEX

Lars Kestner is currently a founding partner of Sabre II LLC, a proprietary trading firm, where he focuses on developing new trading models as well as risk management. Previously he was Vice President of Equity Derivatives Trading at Salomon Smith Barney. He also worked at Brandywine Asset Management. He has written numerous articles for industry journals as well as one book. He received his M.B.A. from Wharton.